Perspectives on Plagiarism
and Intellectual Property
in a Postmodern World

Perspectives on Plagiarism and Intellectual Property in a Postmodern World

Lise Buranen and Alice M. Roy
editors

Foreword by Andrea Lunsford

State University of New York Press

Published by
State University of New York Press

© 1999 State University of New York

For information, address the State University of New York Press, State University Plaza, Albany, NY 12246.

Marketing by Nancy Farrell
Production by Bernadine Dawes

Library of Congress Cataloging-in-Publication Data

Perspective on plagiarism and intellectual property in a postmodern
    world / Lise Buranen and Alice M. Roy, editors ; foreword by Andrea
    Lunsford.
        p.   cm.
    Includes bibliographical references and index.
    ISBN 0-7914-4079-6. — ISBN 0-7914-4080-X (pbk.)
    1. Plagiarism.   2. Intellectual property.   I. Buranen, Lise,
    1954–   Roy, Alice Myers.
PN167.P47   1999
808—dc21   99–11407
                                                                CIP

1 2 3 4 5 6 7 8 9 10

Contents

Contents

Foreword: Who Owns Language?

One of my earliest childhood memories is of being spanked at my own birthday party. A much-loved aunt, Elizabeth McKinsey, had given me a very special gift that year, a tea party set of just-the-right-size-for-dolls-and-little-girls cups, saucers, cookie plates, teapots, sugar pots, cream pots—the works. I was suitably delighted, thrilled really, at the prospect of so many parties. But I made a crucial faux pas: at the end of the party when the grownups (apparently) were not looking, I began giving tiny cups and saucers, plates and teapots, to the friends who had come to my party. Alas, my crime was discovered; the party was over—and I got my spanking. Didn't I know it was really, really bad to give my nice new doll dishes away?

I think I have been mad about that punishment ever since. And I cannot help wondering whether this long-ago event has helped spur my interest (well, okay, my fascination) with collaboration, with sharing, with giving rather than receiving, with responsibilities *to* language and its use rather than ownership *of* it. But while this memory makes for a nice kind of neat, linear narrative, such a story is only available with the aid of (long) hindsight, and is compelling *and* suspect in the way so many memories always are.

For whatever reasons, however, I have been thinking about questions of ownership for a long time now, if not since childhood at least since the early 1980s when Lisa Ede and I began writing collaboratively. We have told that story before: how we almost "by accident" decided to write a joint essay in honor of Ed Corbett; how our colleagues in British Columbia and Oregon (and indeed Ed himself) professed not just puzzlement at how we could possibly undertake such a task but a certain amount of exasperated suspicion as well (mustn't we somehow be "cheating," not really doing our own individual work?); how both our tenure reviews were affected (to say the least) by our continued collaborations; how we had difficulty getting funding for collaborative research. But you know this story—have perhaps lived it right along with Lisa and me. In retrospect, Lisa and I think almost fondly of these difficulties, however, for they certainly captured our attention, leading us to think long and hard about what it was we were doing. Moreover, these difficulties led us to investigate the kinds as well as the degrees of collaborative writing going on across a number of disciplines and workplaces, to describe differing kinds of collaborative practice, and to challenge the notion of "writing" and "writer" as singular, solitary acts and agents. The more we thought about it, the more it seemed to us that viewing a writer as a solitary and possessive owner of language works, which seemed so "natural" and "commonsensical," was anything but. We have been following up on the implications of this observation ever since.

And we have not been alone. By 1984, Martha Woodmansee had published her landmark essay, "The Genius and the Copyright: Economic and Legal Conditions of the Emergence of the 'Author,'" which led to a whole generation of ongoing work devoted to unpacking the construction of authorship in various sites, from Japan to England to the United States (Miner; Mark Rose; McGill) and across various fields (Jaszi 1991; Samuelson 1996; Boyle 1997; Williams; and Guinier in the field of law and Barthes; Foucault 1979; Jameson; Stewart 1991; and many others in literary studies, for example). Composition studies has been slow to take on the challenges articulated by the critique of the author construct and authorship, however, with only a few exceptions (Brodkey; S. Miller 1989; LeFevre; Ede and Lunsford)—and, I think, for some very good reasons. Indeed, the move from text-centered to student-centered theories and pedagogies of writing (often called the move to process theory and expressivism) served to entrench the traditional notion of a "writer" as autonomous, solitary, and possessed of individual creativity and ideas, often buried deep within. In addition, much was (and is) at stake in composition studies as well as across the liberal arts and sciences in holding onto some notion of agency, of "empowering" subjects with discourse. Moreover, these same fields, including composition studies, have a deep and abiding investment in viewing knowledge as a commodity that can be bartered in the academic marketplace—for grades, for tenure, for promotion, and so on. And finally, our nearly compulsive scholarly and teacherly attention to what I think of as hypercitation (note the many internal citations in this very brief foreword, e.g.) and mind-numbingly endless listing of sources are manifestations of the need to possess and to possess exclusively, taking our little dross of intellectual property and turning it into the gold of advancement (Lunsford and West).

For these and no doubt many other reasons, only recently have teachers and theorists of writing begun to excavate the deeply repressed and unspoken formalist, positivist, and individualist ideological assumptions underlying the seemingly simple need for exclusionary ownership of intellectual property. But that work is now underway in composition studies, in work on theory, on history, and on practice. In terms of theories of rhetoric and composition, the work of Susan West comes most immediately to mind. In a commanding dissertation study completed last year ("From Owning to Owning Up: Authorial Rights and Rhetorical Responsibilities"), West explores the construction of what she calls the "authordoxy," a term signifying "a cluster of beliefs, attitudes, and behaviors linked to modern notions of property, the Enlightenment 'self,' and the Romantic model of composition" (17), in order to critique and reshape three key terms in rhetorical theory: the subject/agent, the message, and the audience. In three fascinating case studies (one on Lani Guinier, one on Anita Hill, one on Anna Deveare Smith), West demonstrates the possibility for a transformed rhetorical theory, one she terms a "rhetoric of responsibility." This alternative rhetoric exists within an ethical framework for rhetorical practice that "respects the right to profit from intellectual labor while resisting the contemporary obsession with 'authorial' rights" (33) and focuses on Burkean "alchemic opportunities" for acting together in what West calls a "circle of response."

As an aside, let me note that one of my favorite passages in this provocative dissertation is this one: "This page in a dissertation normally is reserved for a copyright notice. I choose instead to acknowledge here the profoundly collaborative nature of all language and thus my indebtedness to the cultural commons whose resources I have borrowed to produce this work. I do so by explicitly placing the text that follows in the public domain. I hope what I have written and now freely share will spur more intellectual labor in the interest of fostering a responsible rhetoric." Though I have read many dissertations, not to mention articles and books challenging the cult of possessiveness that informs our contemporary copyright system, this is the first I have seen that, well, puts it money where its mouth is.

Within historical studies in rhetoric and composition, a great deal of exciting work is underway. In a dissertation in progress ("The Author('s) Proper(ty): Rhetoric, Literature, and Constructions of Authorship"), John Logie looks back to Gorgias, Plato, Quintilian, and Apuleius for an understanding of "rhetoric of possession." His complex analysis of what it means to try to "originate" in these cultures is followed by a leap to the twentieth century where he engages Marxist notions of property and possession, through a (very) close look at Kenneth Burke and Richard Wright; in later chapters he looks at work that seriously challenges conventional constructions of authorship and ownership—Kathy Acker and Art Spiegelman. Logie's aim, as I understand it, is to use his investigations to reshape concepts of authorship and of rights.

A related project is underway in a series of essays by Sarah Sloane, in which she concentrates on the composing processes of the Edinburgh literati in the second half of the eighteenth century. The archival and historiographical work Sloane has done leads her to posit an "ironically exclusive" form of collaborative authorship as characteristic of the time. While it sought to exclude rusticisms and other forms of "bad taste," it also relied on extensive borrowings. As Sloane describes it, "the Edinburgh literari's sharing of insight, trope, idea, and refigurings of classical rhetoric is not plagiarism in the original sense of kidnapping words; instead, it is the production of knowledge through an arrangement of sharing supported by common schooling, a familiarity with canonical texts, letters exchanged, and warm conversations about drafts" (npn).

This is precisely the kind of writing Rebecca Howard (1995) has dubbed "patchwriting," in a series of essays and a recent book *(Standing in the Shadow of Giants)*. Indeed, Howard has been insistent in calling on composition teachers and scholars to look at the implications of the theoretical and historical challenges to the romantic notion of a singular, solitary, radically individual and possessive "author." And these practical implications put the spotlight not only on our grading practices and our use of texts and commodities of exchange, but on plagiarism, what we have thought of as "false" ownership. Howard's explorations of "patchwriting," which she looks at closely in terms of student writing, is, it turns out, not so different from what advanced scholars in the field think of as good scholarly practice of weaving sources together. I was reminded of this fact forcefully one day last year when a colleague called to say he had been commissioned to write an essay on plagiarism for the *New Yorker* and had heard I was interested in the subject. I sent him a couple of essays, including one I had written with Susan West and one or two of Howard's. The next time I spoke with him he exclaimed on their usefulness to him, remarking that even as we spoke he was doing a bit of sophisticated patchwriting himself: since the *New Yorker* abjures footnotes and works cited lists, he was patching into his essay some of the material from Mark Rose's book on eighteenth-century copyright. All well and good when a senior scholar is at work; not so well and good when students are carrying out such practices.

As this brief example suggests, discursive practices may not be as easy to label as we once thought, nor have we sufficiently thought through the issues surrounding agency, action, and authoring—and the ways in which these issues frame and shape our ideas of plagiarism. As Lisa and I and scholars like Rebecca Howard and Susan West have tried to point out, contemporary concepts of plagiarism are not only fraught with contradictions but are also fairly new and, in fact, they grow up right alongside the author construct, the intricate system of copyright, and the capitalist economy in which both are deeply implicated. Hence the great need for a collection like this one, which offers a wealth of thinking about the complex and often contradictory definitions surrounding such loaded terms as "plagiarism," "intellectual property," "copyright," "imitation," even "voice." All those interested in the future of composition studies and the teaching of writing will be indebted to the editors and participants who have contributed to this timely and helpful volume.

Andrea A. Lunsford

Acknowledgments

We wish to thank Hema Chari, Virginia Crane, Lisa Ede, and Ross Winterowd for early reading and encouragement. We appreciate financial assistance from the Katherine Carter Fund of the English Department at California State University, Los Angeles. Especially we are grateful to our spouses, Michael Kerry and William Roy, for technical support, unflagging patience, and general goodwill.

Introduction

Plagiarism, as an act or a concept, is not new, but it currently commands a larger share of attention than it has done in recent years. Media reports gleefully announce the discovery of plagiarism by public figures, writers, historians, politicians: Martin Luther King, Alex Haley, Joe Biden, Bruno Bettelheim, Freud, as well as names in the sciences less known to the general public. Even Martha Stewart has been chided for publishing recipes as her own that are alleged to bear striking resemblance to some published elsewhere. Academically, a survey of presentations on plagiarism at the Conference on College Composition and Communication (CCCC) shows the growing attention to plagiarism and intellectual property in the discipline of composition studies alone: in 1983 the CCCC program lists no presentations on plagiarism; in 1993, one; in 1994, three; and in 1995, twelve. The CCCC Intellectual Property Caucus was established in 1994 and has met at the convention each year since. In a larger academic arena, in the University of California Library articles database, comprising 6,700 journals, the number of articles with plagiarism in the title nearly doubled from 1990 to 1992, and almost doubled again from 1992 to 1994.

Furthermore, questions about plagiarism and intellectual property multiply as electronic communication explodes the simpler boundaries of earlier print media. Both instructional and noninstructional issues arise: Who owns material on the Net? How shall we cite e-mail? One contributor to this volume writes of a student who lifted an entire home page and turned it in as his "own" work. On an e-mail discussion list, someone reported the case of a colleague who provided, via e-mail, a course syllabus and materials created for a distance learning course supported by his university. If other people use those materials, are they plagiarizing? Are they flouting intellectual property laws or conventions? If so, whose property, the faculty member's or the university's? Beyond the legal answer to these questions, what are the personal and ethical issues that accompany them?

Plagiarism is perceived as a problem but it is often discussed in simplistic terms: "using someone else's words without telling whose they are or

where you got them"; "stealing other people's ideas or words." This basic
view of plagiarism comes directly from the Latin source of the word, which
meant to kidnap a person, referring only to children or servants or slaves:
people who could in some sense be owned. Two recent books on plagiarism,
Thomas Mallon's *Stolen Words* and Marcel LaFollette's *Stealing into Print*
capitalize on this definition. In contrast to two earlier, more comprehensive
works on plagiarism mentioned by Mallon, Alexander Lindey's *Plagiarism
and Originality,* published in 1952, and Maurice Salzman's *Plagiarism: The
"Art" of Stealing Literary Material,* in 1931, Mallon himself chooses instead
to provide extended treatment of just a few cases. His main concern is "plagiarism's psychology and . . . punishment" (xiii). One reviewer notes that
Mallon's "chatty psychopathology" of plagiarism gives us the plagiarist as
"an oddly plaintive psychopath" (Kendrick 14). As another reviewer points
out, "Mallon's position is clear: plagiarism is an offense that admits of no degree" (Webb 71). In contrast, our position, and that of our contributors, is that
plagiarism is full of degrees, that is, replete with difference. In Mallon's own
words, he is "appalled; both at the act of plagiarism and at the lack of stern
punishment when it is discovered." Mallon says of literary plagiarism, "What
novelists are really supposed to plagiarize, of course, is reality" (21). This
view of literature, like the view of composition in current-traditional rhetoric,
assumes a given reality to borrow or steal *from,* as opposed to a "reality" constructed through language, socially acquired and negotiated.

In *Stealing into Print: Fraud, Plagiarism, and Misconduct in Scientific
Publishing,* Marcel LaFollette's interest, evident in the title, is in plagiarism
within the scientific communities. In a review by David Goodstein, from the
California Institute of Technology, LaFollette is considered to be "more concerned with listing, enumerating, and cataloging than with producing new
analysis or insight" (1,504). Another reviewer suggests that LaFollette raises
important questions but does not provide "reasonable, or at least provocative,
solutions" (Mervis 787).

We trace the intellectual genealogy of *Perspectives on Plagiarism and Intellectual Property in a Postmodern World* to Andrea Lunsford and Lisa Ede's
Singular Tests/Plural Authors and through Susan Stewart's *Crimes of Writing*
and Woodmansee and Jaszi's *Construction of Authorship.* Lunsford and Ede's
intent differs from both the moral indignation expressed by Mallon and the
search for a cure traced by LaFollette, neither of whom questions the monolithic definition and existence of plagiarism or recognizes context-dependent
features and differences. Lunsford and Ede, on the other hand, raise questions
about plagiarism as they investigate the history and process of collaborative
writing. In their third chapter they trace the history of plagiarism, showing the
changes of attitude toward authorial ownership over several centuries.

In *Crimes of Writing,* Susan Stewart looks at, as her subtitle says, "Problems in the Containment of Representation." In place of epigraph she provides

a picture, Thomas Eakins's *Nude Woman Seated Wearing a Mask.* For Stewart, this picture represents both the familiar figure of "blind justice" and, as well, the impossibility of "a seeing being seen" (vii). That is, the blindfolded model cannot see those seeing her, nor can the painters represent her seeing their seeing. Stewart uses this image to stand for, or imply, "a fundamental detachment—of writing from context, of speaking from voice" (viii). She reveals the determinants of interactions between the law and written and pictorial representations, or what she calls "a complicity in the rule of law and the system of representation" (ix).

Woodmansee and Jaszi, in *Construction of Authorship: Textual Appropriation in Law and Literature,* focus on specific authors, such as Helen Keller, Hegel, Wordsworth, Pope, and Dickens, as well as periods of authorial history and copyright theory and practices. This book is a publication of selected proceedings from a conference in the law and literature movement, sponsored by the Society for Critical Exchange, for the express purpose of reviving "interdisciplinary investigation of our ways of conceptualizing creative production" (13). The provenance of the movement traces back, as perhaps everyone considering these issues must, to Foucault's question, "What is an Author?" Woodmansee and Jaszi, and following them, the authors collected in this volume, show that laws and tribunals through which ownership of words and ideas is adjudicated "are only the final instance in a large and intricate system of institutions of authorship extending from grammatical and stylistic rules and conventions to pedagogies of literature and composition" (2). Woodmansee and Jaszi, along with Stewart and Lunsford and Ede, take us in a much different direction from that of Mallon and LaFollette, a postmodern divergence from the modern.

A search of the main electronic databases discloses a fascinating array of works on plagiarism and intellectual property, spread across history and geography, deeply embedded in the culture of the modern period. A few recent entries show words like "appropriation" and "intertextuality" in the titles, and some writers speculate about self-plagiarism, see plagiarism as a "riddle," acknowledge "conflicting views." Ron Scollon asserts the interaction of "Plagiarism and Ideology" as he looks at "Identity in Intercultural Discourse." Yet in textbooks and in university publications about academic integrity, plagiarism is often treated as a monolithic, uncomplicated concept or event, whose meaning is simply taken for granted. The assumption seems to be that we all know what we mean when we talk about it: it just *is.* In academia, in the sciences, and in writing handbooks and classroom instruction, the main emphasis is on prevention and punishment.

In this book, however, plagiarism speaks to us in many ways in many tongues, from many times and places, and the Protean shapes of intellectual property merge and diverge, remaining elusive. The goal of this book is to provide a wide range of perspectives on plagiarism and intellectual property from this postmodern position. Currently "postmodern" is a term undergoing revision from an all-purpose use as a simple alternative to "modern" and "modernism"; "Postmodern" is now itself seen to be a changeful concept, inextricably linked with the contexts to which it is applied or which it is used to describe. With this collection of essays we draw on the very fragmentation and destabilization that have characterized "postmodern" as a definition of acts and events in aesthetics, politics, education, and science, and now characterize even the concept of postmodernism itself, in order to problematize notions of plagiarism and intellectual property, to purposely bring to light the inherent fragmentation and instability of terms that are often taken for granted, "givens" in discussion of creativity, cognition, law, and pedagogy. Plagiarism is not merely the flipside of postmodern authorial uncertainty: my words, you can't have them. Although "intellectual property" is a technical term residing largely within copyright law, we use it as well in a broad sense having to do with the general possibility of ownership of ideas and language.

A postmodern perspective of plagiarism and intellectual property suggests that one cannot own ideas or words. All we can do is honor and recompense the encoding of those ideas, the use of those words, in the certainty that such honor and compensation are negotiated in contexts of time and place, class and power, within social and economic considerations. Whether ideas or words *could* be owned surely has not changed—only the contexts and with them the negotiations. Postmodern principles, concepts, and enactments foreground the problematics of such ownership.

This volume encompasses a broad base of approaches and interests, both theoretical and practical. The authors explore multiple definitions of plagiarism and intellectual property, resist traditional legalistic assumptions, look at plagiarism and intellectual property in a wide range of domains, contexts, and cultures. We offer this book to both teachers and theorists in many fields. It should be useful in teacher preparation courses and teaching-assistant development courses and workshops, in English as well as other disciplines. Because it emphasizes the discipline-specific nature of authorship and attribution, it will be appropriate for graduate courses, particularly in composition and rhetoric graduate degree programs but also in other disciplines, including legal research and writing. We hope that theorists and researchers in literary and literacy studies, law, and writing across the disciplines will find this book useful because of the variety of definitions provided, the care with which contributors establish definitions within the contexts of their research areas, the attention to historical and cultural venues, and the exploration of questions of authorship and authority in a more-or-less postmodern world.

During the question-and-answer session that followed our panel on plagiarism at the Conference on College Composition and Communication in 1994, one man commented that as he listened to our papers, he could see the issue of plagiarism becoming more and more intricate and multilayered. Like many of those who attended the presentation, he was a teacher looking for guidance and some clear answers to take back to the classroom about how to cope with this problem we label plagiarism: how to teach students to avoid it, how to deal with it when we encounter it. But as he indicated, listening to our papers he realized that there was more to the difficulties teachers face in the classroom than simply needing to learn new techniques or strategies for coping with plagiarism; in fact, we need to examine our own assumptions to lay bare the misconceptions and fuzzy definitions that derive from a dearth of inquiry into the nature of the beast we want to tame. Before we can address "it," we need to identify just what "it" is.

Although some in the audience did express frustration at our lack of directiveness—several people collared us in the corridor after our presentation and quietly asked, "But what can I *do* about it?"—we were gratified by that man's recognition that although he too had come looking for answers, we left him only with more, and more complex, questions than he came in with, and that that was acceptable to him. In this volume, we extend the problematizing and complicating of the issue that we began in our session. With a few very small and local exceptions, we have compiled this collection not to offer solutions (much less quick fixes) to the many and varied questions relative to plagiarism and intellectual property that face not only classroom teachers but writers and thinkers in many endeavors; rather, we hope to identify some of the questions that need to be formulated and contemplated before we can decide what to "do about it."

In compiling this volume, for practical purposes we have had to limit our scope somewhat, and consequently, we have not included discussions that encompass fields such as science and the arts. Although people in these fields must certainly also rely on concepts of plagiarism that they may discover are increasingly inadequate, for lack of space we were not able to represent these areas, much as we had hoped to do so. Nonetheless, the essays in this volume cover an array of issues ranging from legal and historical definitions of plagiarism and intellectual property to concerns about trademark infringements and civic responsibility in public discourse, residing in both academic and "real world" milieux.

Because of the broad scope, it was difficult to categorize the essays into discrete sections without underrepresenting the complexity of each one. There was a strong temptation merely to alphabetize them, but instead we identified two general headings, Definitions and Applications, with further subdivisions in each to reflect the main focus of each essay. Necessarily, however, our categories are arbitrary—many of the essays could as easily reside in several different sections as where they ended up.

Because many people in our litigious age erroneously assume that plagiarism is a legal term, the first chapter in the section on Definitions is "Copy

Wrong: Plagiarism and Copyright Law," by Laurie Stearns. Stearns, an attorney and former editor, discusses the difficulty inherent in applying the
metaphor of "property" to words and ideas, and offers an alternative in the law
of contracts. Also in this section, Jan Swearingen and James Zebroski trace
historical definitions of our modern notions of plagiarism: Swearingen looks
at ancient classical underpinnings and their recent translation into modern
practice in defining plagiarism in and out of the classroom, and Zebroski looks
at some sociohistorical aspects of plagiarism and intellectual property, drawing on Marxism, Christianity, and recent computer culture for comparisons.
The last chapter in this section provides a bridge from legal and historical definitions to the next section, which we have labeled Academic Definitions; in
this chapter, Sue Carter Simmons looks at historical definitions of plagiarism
in the academic world, reviewing composition handbooks, student publications, and other texts from the seventeenth through the nineteenth centuries to
uncover the roots of our modern practices and attitudes in the academy.

The next section, Academic Definitions, is the largest one in the book,
and not surprisingly so, for although questions about what constitutes plagiarism and intellectual property affect many different fields and concerns,
people in the academic world often cope with these questions daily. As many
honest and self-aware teachers have discovered, great discrepancies often
exist between what we teach our students and what we do ourselves. Further,
recent teaching practices, such as collaborative learning and writing, and the
appearance of writing centers on many campuses have exposed a number of
contradictory messages about what plagiarism and "one's own words" really
are, confusing both student and teacher alike. Alice Roy surveyed a number
of college faculty from various disciplines around the country to discover not
only how faculty members define plagiarism itself (What is it?) but also to ascertain their attitudes toward it (Why is it wrong or bad?). In her chapter, Lise
Buranen, through surveys and interviews, looks at nonmainstream American
students' definitions of plagiarism, specifically those students from cultures
whose first language is not English; she is especially concerned with the ways
in which instructors may "mythologize" students' beliefs. Similarly, drawing
on his experiences teaching in Japan, as well as on surveys and interviews
with both teachers and students there, L. M. Dryden examines Japanese systems of education and notions of the self and how they affect some Japanese
understanding of Western ideas about plagiarism and intellectual property. In
the last chapter in this section, Rebecca Moore Howard calls for a "New Abolitionism," a "decriminalizing" of what she terms "patchwriting," arguing that
much of what we reprimand students for is, among other things, a normal part
of the writing and learning process that we all go through, and that by calling
it plagiarism and punishing students for it, we unwittingly perpetuate a hierarchical and wrongheaded view of the role of composition in the academy.

Literary theory clearly has much to offer in this conversation about plagiarism and intellectual property: postmodern theory, in raising questions about the very nature of authorship and author-ity, gives us much of the impetus even to ask the questions we do in this volume. In the section we have called Literary and Theoretical Definitions, Kevin Dettmar looks at some literary enactments of overt and unapologetic "plagiarism" in the work of James Joyce and Kathy Acker; and Debora Halbert considers the role of feminism and feminist futures in understanding what we currently believe about the "ownership" of ideas and language. Gilbert Larochelle traces the philosophical and theoretical views of Kant and Foucault in trying to find "what's left of the author," and Marilyn Randall discusses notions of postcolonial conquest in her essay on "Imperial Plagiarism." Finally in this section, Robert André LaFleur examines the method of literary borrowing and compilation used in medieval Chinese historical writing and compares it to our modern notions of plagiarism and intellectual property.

The second half of the book is headed Applications—in other words, how do new ways of defining plagiarism and intellectual property translate into necessary alterations of our current practices, whether in the academic world or the "real world" (What *does* one call that part of the universe that exists outside the academy)?

The ever-increasing presence of writing centers on college campuses has been a major catalyst to questions about previously unexamined assumptions concerning the relationship between plagiarism and collaboration. Indeed, some highly skeptical faculty have gone so far as to label writing centers "plagiarism centers," but even among those with less extreme views, a decided uneasiness often lingers about the role writing center tutors really play in "authoring" student papers. In the section Applications In the Writing Center, Irene Clark presents an overview of this intersection of plagiarism and the writing center. Carol Haviland and Joan Mullin discuss the parallels and contradictions inherent in the composing practices of faculty and those of most students: what the stakes are, where ideas come from, who the writers' contacts for sources and material are, what feedback is received, and who gets acknowledged in the end. They describe startling inconsistencies between what teachers say to students and what they do themselves. Finally, Linda Shamoon and Deborah Burns argue for embracing and "owning" the collaboration between writing center tutors and students rather than trying to deny or efface it.

In the next section, Applications in Academic Administration, Terri LeClercq looks at law schools' policies, beliefs, and practices regarding plagiarism: one might expect that of all institutions, law schools would be clear about plagiarism, both in the messages to students about what it is and how to teach them to avoid it, but LeClercq's investigation suggests that law schools have no particular advantage over other academic institutions, and the same discrepancies exist that Haviland and Mullin (and others in this book) have found between the "rules" intended for students and those observed by practicing professionals in the field. In their respective essays, Henry Wilson and Edward M. White look at current administrative perspectives, suggesting what they ought to be, if not what they are. Wilson surveyed several composition programs around the country to ascertain their stated policy, if any, on plagiarism, and he analyzes these to determine how well these schools provide students with a rationale and/or instruction in avoiding plagiarism as it has been defined for them, especially where collaboration collides (officially) with plagiarism. White, speaking from his many years as a teacher of writing as well as from his experience in the study and administration of writing programs, considers the roles administration can play in supporting teachers often left to fend for themselves in coping with perceived instances of plagiarism; plagiarism, he argues, must be an educational and a curricular issue as well as a disciplinary one.

The following section looks at Applications in Instruction and Research. In her chapter, Candace Spigelman examines the intersection between collaboration and plagiarism in the context of the classroom. From case studies of students, Spigelman reveals the definitions, beliefs, and occasional misgivings and doubts that students have in trying to obey the rules of writing as they understand them. Also in this section, David Leight looks at composition and writing textbooks (from which many of the students described by Spigelman may have been taught) to see exactly what it is that these books tell and do not tell students and their instructors about plagiarism. Finally, Shirley Rose discusses citation practices as the obverse of plagiarism; in creating "disciplinary economies," citation practices operate within a discourse community as a protection against plagiarism.

The last section considers Applications in the Marketplace. Shawn Clankie takes a linguist's look at trademarks—a quite literal attempt to own and control language—to see the process by which product names make the shift from capitalized trademark to vernacular generic, and the extent to which companies will go to try to prevent that from happening. Joan Livingston-Webber explores the phenomenon and culture of "zines" and the overtly anticopyright viewpoints of the young people who write and distribute these decidedly "nonmainstream" publications.

PART I
Definitions

Legal and Historical Definitions

Copy Wrong:
Plagiarism, Process, Property, and the Law

Laurie Stearns

Several years ago, while working as an editor, I was putting the finishing touches on a forthcoming book about an event from fifty years before, which other authors had previously chronicled. The new book was nothing to get excited about, but it was well organized, competently written, comprehensive, and offered a new interpretation of the event.

One day, stranded at home because of mass-transit problems, I went to my local library to verify some historical information for the book. As I browsed through another book on the same subject, scanning the pages for names and dates, a passage caught my eye—a passage that was strangely, and disturbingly, familiar. The same passage appeared almost word for word in the manuscript I had been editing. With increasing agitation I paged through more books on the subject. In the end, I identified five passages that my author appeared to have lifted from three different sources.

The next day, back at my office, I told the senior editor about my discovery. Dismayed and clearly reluctant to take the matter up with the author, he asked me simply to rewrite the passages I had found. I declined vehemently and returned to my desk to puzzle over the questions running through my mind: How could the author have done such a thing? What would have happened if the trains had been running the day before and I had never gone to the library? Were there more copied passages I had not found? Why had I refused to rewrite the offending passages myself? And why was I so outraged at what I had discovered?

The questions I was asking that day were about literary ethics, not about the law. Later, the publisher's lawyers calmly accepted the author's assurances that the copying, which he ascribed to a flaw in his notetaking system, extended no further than the material already uncovered. Indeed, the lawyers seemed relieved that the problem was merely plagiarism rather than, say, libel.

People commonly think of plagiarism as being "against the law." But with respect to plagiarism, the law and literary ethics intersect only imperfectly.

Plagiarism is not a legal term, and though an instance of plagiarism might seem to be the quintessential act of wrongful copying, it does not necessarily constitute a violation of copyright law.

In this essay I consider the question: What is the role of copyright law in protecting creativity and scholarship? Plagiarism is the source of legal and critical disputes, an example of "creativity gone bad." Both the law and the way we define creativity can shape the way we understand plagiarism, and both the way we understand plagiarism and the way we define creativity can shape the law.

Plagiarism and the Creative Process

> The poet's eye in a fine frenzy rolling,
> Doth glance from heaven to earth, from earth to heaven,
> And, as imagination bodies forth
> The forms of things unknown, the poet's pen
> Turns them to shapes, and gives to airy nothing
> A local habitation and a name.
>
> —Shakespeare, *A Midsummer Night's Dream*

Human beings have singled out the creative process as a uniquely human characteristic, a "prerogative of man" (Arieti 4). Creativity—in literature, the visual arts, music, philosophy, or science—can inspire admiration and awe.

To claim to have created a work, one need not have made something from nothing. Mary Shelley, in her introduction to *Frankenstein,* wrote: "Invention, it must be humbly admitted, does not consist in creating out of void, but out of chaos" (xxiv). Creation is an act situated in time, taking into account what has gone before. Aristotle considered art to be an imitation of reality (1932, 57), and Longinus recommended "zealous imitation of great historians and poets of the past" (167). Sir Isaac Newton acknowledged his predecessors with the statement that his achievements were possible because he was able to stand "on ye sholders of giants" (Merton 31).

Given this interdependence of human creative efforts, the idea of plagiarism is something of a paradox. Why condemn an author for borrowing from another if such borrowing is inevitable and even fundamental to the creative process?

The answer lies in the kind of borrowing an author does. The only legitimate borrowing is that which proceeds to transform the original material by means of the borrower's creative process. The obligation of the author to make an original contribution parallels Locke's view of the origin of property: "Whatsoever then he removes out of the State that Nature hath provided, and left it in, he hath mixed his *Labour* with, and joyned to it something that is his own, and thereby makes it his *Property"* (Locke 306).

The essence of the modern understanding of plagiarism is a failure of the creative process through the author's failure either to transform the original material or to identify its source. Space constraints preclude a more complete examination of the history and contours of the concept of plagiarism, but for the purposes of this essay I will define plagiarism as intentionally taking the literary property of another without attribution and passing it off as one's own, having failed to add anything of value to the copied material and having reaped from its use an unearned benefit.[1] In a sense, plagiarism (presenting another's work as one's own) is the inverse of forgery (presenting one's own work as another's).

People despise plagiarism not because it results in inferior works— indeed, by drawing from others plagiarists may produce better works than they could by themselves—but because it is a form of cheating that allows the plagiarist an unearned benefit. This benefit could be either tangible, as when the work is of commercial value or fulfills a requirement for an academic degree or tenure, or intangible, as when it adds to the plagiarist's personal or professional reputation. The form that the plagiarist's cheating takes—claiming credit for someone else's achievements—is particularly abhorrent. Individuals who do not hesitate to photocopy copyrighted books or videotape copyrighted broadcasts for their own use would never dream of representing themselves as the authors of the books or tapes.

Plagiarism is, then, a failure of the creative process, not a flaw in its result. Although imitation is an inevitable component of creation, plagiarists pass beyond the boundaries of acceptable imitation by copying from the work of others without improving on the copied material or fully assimilating it into their own work; by failing to attribute the copied material to its actual author; and by intending to deceive others about its origin. Society's disapproval of these imperfections in the creative process seeks an outlet in the law. But the law, with its attention focused on different concerns, provides only an inexact means of addressing plagiarism.

Plagiarism and Copyright Infringement

> For poets, law makes no provision . . .
>
> —Jonathan Swift,
> *On Poetry: A Rhapsody*

Even without being able to articulate a precise definition, many people find it easy to recognize plagiarism—as with pornography, they know it when they see it.[2] People who inquired about the subject of this essay while it was being written were easily able to understand what it was going to be about, and many offered such ripostes as "Didn't someone else write about that?" or "Why don't you just copy it?"

The law, however, with its emphasis on articulating rules and standards, has had a difficult time understanding plagiarism. Although the term is sometimes used casually in judicial opinions, it has not been judicially explained or defined since 1944 (Dieckhaus 427). Hardly a single modern lawbook contains an entry for plagiarism in its index. Most courts using the term, writing about a range of subjects from patents to trademarks, employ it imprecisely as the generic equivalent of copying. One bewildered jury, uncertain exactly what the attorneys and the judge meant by "plagiarism" and other terminology used in a trial, sent the bailiff out for a dictionary during its deliberations (United States v. Steele 744).

Cases of literary plagiarism most often turn up in court as cases of copyright infringement. Copyright law aims to encourage both creativity and the dissemination of the results of the creative effort to the public. At times these aims are in opposition, as when granting authors the exclusive right to their works in order to give them the financial incentive to create has the effect of preventing others from improving or adapting those works for the benefit of society. The current Copyright Act of 1976, like its predecessors,[3] attempts to accommodate both aims by affording protection for only a limited time (Secs. 302–05) and allowing for exceptions that permit certain uses of the copyrighted work by others, such as fair use (Sec. 107), reproduction by libraries and archives (Sec. 108), compulsory license for making and distributing phonorecords (Sec. 115), public performances by means of coin-operated phonorecord players (Sec. 116), noncommercial broadcasting (Sec. 118), and secondary transmissions for private home viewing (Sec. 119).

At present, copyright law protects "original works of authorship fixed in any tangible medium of expression" (Sec. 102) by giving the copyright owner the exclusive right to reproduce the work, to prepare derivative works based on it, to distribute copies of it, and to perform or display it publicly (Sec. 106). Copyright ownership "vests initially in the author or authors of the work" and may subsequently be transferred (Sec. 201). Violation of any of the exclusive rights is termed "infringement" (Sec. 501a), and the owner of an exclusive right has standing to sue for its infringement (Sec. 501b). Remedies for infringement include injunctive relief, impoundment or destruction of the infringing articles, and a monetary award of actual damages and profits, statutory damages, and costs and attorney's fees (Secs. 502–05).

When deciding a case of copyright infringement, courts engage in a practical inquiry focusing on the result of the alleged copying. According to the method applied in Arnstein v. Porter, the court examines the allegedly infringing work to determine whether it was copied from the allegedly infringed work and not independently created; and if it was copied, whether the copying was wrongful (468). The plaintiff can prove copying by presenting evidence of similarity between the two works and evidence of the defendant's access to the plaintiff's work. The two works need not be identical, but must be substantially similar; where the degree of similarity is great enough, access can be presumed rather than proven (Arnstein 468).

Plagiarism is not necessarily copyright infringement, nor is copyright infringement necessarily plagiarism. The two concepts diverge with respect to three main aspects of the offense: copying, attribution, and intent. In some ways the concept of plagiarism is broader than infringement, in that it can include the copying of ideas, or of expression not protected by copyright, that would not constitute infringement, and it can include the copying of small amounts of material that would be disregarded under copyright law. In other ways the concept of infringement is broader, in that it can include both properly attributed copying and unintentional copying that would be excused from being called plagiarism.

The divergence between plagiarism's popular definition and copyright's statutory framework suggests an essential contradiction between what is at stake in plagiarism—the creative process—and what is at stake in copyright infringement—the creative result.

Copying

Fundamental to both plagiarism and copyright infringement is wrongful copying from a preexisting work. But the form, the amount, and the source of the copying prohibited as copyright infringement are different from those of the copying condemned as plagiarism.

Plagiarism is a broad concept that includes the copying of words and thoughts in a variety of forms. According to the Modern Language Association,

> Plagiarism may take the form of repeating another's sentences as your own, adopting a particularly apt phrase as your own, paraphrasing someone else's argument as your own or even presenting someone else's line of thinking in the development of a thesis [as] though it were your own. In short, to plagiarize is to give the impression that you have written or thought something that you have in fact borrowed from another. (St. Onge 53)

In other words, both ideas and the way in which those ideas are expressed can be plagiarized. Even facts or quotations can be plagiarized, as through the trick of citing to a quotation from a primary source rather than to the secondary source in which the plagiarist found it in order to conceal reliance on the secondary source.

The process of copying a small amount of material from an unattributed source is no less plagiarism than is the copying of a large amount. In practical terms, of course, the plagiarism in a long work of just one sentence is unlikely to be noticed or, if noticed, unlikely to be criticized. Technically, however, the taking of even a single resonant phrase would be plagiarism.

Copying from any source qualifies as plagiarism, even if the source has been in existence for centuries. Even where no harm could possibly result to the original work (which may be long out of print) or to the original author (who may be long dead), the audience is still duped, and plagiarism is still viewed as a misuse of the creative process.

In defining copyright infringement, the law has substantially narrowed all of the characteristics of illicit copying as plagiarism defines them. The Copyright Act makes a distinction between "expression," which the law protects against copying, and "ideas," which it does not (Sec. 102). Similarly, copyright law does not protect facts, only the way in which they are expressed or compiled; the facts themselves are in the public domain. Copyright law draws lines between protectible expression and unprotectible idea, and between protectible expression and unprotectible fact, in response to the fear that a grant of copyright protection that functions as a monopoly on ideas or facts will dangerously impair the free flow of ideas and information. (Of course, this distinction, commonly known as the idea/expression dichotomy, has proved difficult to apply because idea and expression are necessarily intertwined.)

Moreover, copyright law is not concerned with all expression but merely with certain statutorily defined categories of expression. If the copied work is too old to fall under the copyright statute (Sec. 302), was written by a government employee (Sec. 105), or has otherwise lost its protection, it is in the public domain and cannot be infringed. This basic difference between plagiarism and infringement demonstrates that while plagiarism is a failure of the creative process as manifested in unattributed copying from any source, copyright law examines the harm that results from copying—concluding that a work not protected by statute cannot be harmed.

Although copying even a small amount of an earlier work can be plagiarism, to be copyright infringement the copying must be substantial in either quantity or quality (Whelan 1245–46; Hoffman 379). Although "no plagiarist can excuse the wrong by showing how much of his work he did not pirate" (Sheldon 56), substantial copying is necessary to turn plagiarism in the popular sense into infringement in the legal sense. The law thus looks to the new work and its effect on the earlier work—not to the process of plagiarism but to its result.

Attribution

The connection of the author's name with the work symbolizes the relationship between the creator and the creation. This connection has monetary value in that copyright ownership, which includes the right to control publication and other uses of the work, belongs to the author (Sec. 201). There is also nonmonetary value to having one's name associated with a work. Commercial authors who sell publication rights might have little or no control over the editing, design, production, marketing, distribution, or publicity for their works—but authors who find this arrangement alienating can gain comfort from the sight of their names on the title page. In noncommercial publications, such as scholarly or scientific journals, seeing their names in print— and having their names seen by others—may be the only compensation authors receive.

Plagiarism, with its lack of attribution, severs the connection between the original author's name and the work. A plagiarist, by falsely claiming authorship of someone else's material, directly assaults the author's interest in receiving credit. In contrast, attribution is largely irrelevant to a claim of copyright infringement. The Copyright Act does not guarantee the author any right to attribution; such a right is nonexistent unless created by contract (Morton 524). Conversely, a pirated edition of a book produced by someone who does not own the publication rights is an infringement even if the work is properly attributed to its author.

Copyright law's indifference to the issue of attribution, despite attribution's central place in the definition of plagiarism, demonstrates once again the law's focus on result, not process. In the popular view, plagiarists shortchange both themselves and the original authors. In the view of copyright law, the only harm that counts is the resulting harm to the infringed work, which is independent of claims of authorship that attach to it. Attribution of authorship is the highly personal connection between author and work, but the interest that copyright protects is the impersonal connection between owner and property.

Intent

Accused plagiarists often defend themselves with the excuse of accidental copying, often through faulty notetaking in which original material was inadvertently mingled with material copied from another source. For example, a first novelist called the appearance in his book of fifty-three passages from another writer's novel "the most awful mistake, which happened because I made notes from various books as I went along and then lost the notebook telling where they came from" (Mallon 110). Observers are sometimes reluctant to accept the plagiarist's claim of lack of intent, but their reluctance is more likely due to inability to believe the excuse than to a conviction that accidental copying is equivalent to plagiarism. One suspects, for example, that the first novelist, an American, must have known that one of the passages in his notebook was not his own because it contained a reference to a British advice columnist; in his novel he substituted a reference to Ann Landers (Mallon 111).

In the language of the law, intent to deceive would be an element of the offense of plagiarism. Copyright infringement, however, is a strict liability offense: an infringer is liable no matter how the copying came about, regard-less of intent or lack of it (Buck 198).

The different views of intent reflected in plagiarism and in infringement reflect different understandings of harm. Plagiarism is a diffuse offense against society, harming many participants in the creative transaction, in-cluding the plagiarists themselves, the authors of copied works, other writers and scholars, and the public as a whole.

The law has a narrower conception of the harm caused by infringement. Only the copyright owner has standing to sue, and the law measures harm by impairment of that owner's economic interest. The law allows an infringe-ment action only where the infringer has benefited and allows recovery only where the value of the original work has been reduced. In deciding whether works are "substantially similar," courts believe that if the infringing work has not harmed the infringed work, the similarity is likely not substantial. The harm the law recognizes is not to the process but to the result alone.

Legal Metaphors: Intellectual Property and the Creative Contract

> Next, o'er his Books his eyes began to roll,
> In pleasing memory of all he stole,
> How here he sipp'd, how there he plunder'd snug
> And suck'd all o'er, like an industrious Bug.
> Here lay poor Fletcher's half-eat scenes, and here
> The Frippery of crucify'd Moliere . . .
>
> —Alexander Pope, *The Dunciad*

Modern copyright law's categorization of written material as property springs from the belief that the "law of nature" entitles human beings to reap the fruits of their labors. According to Blackstone: "When a man by the exertion of his rational powers has produced an original work, he has clearly a right to dis-pose of that identical work as he pleases, and any attempt to take it from him, or vary the disposition he has made of it, is an invasion of his right to prop-erty" (1765, xx) (1: *405–6).[4]

If words are property, they are an odd form of property. At any instant they are finite in number and yet can be freely and infinitely invented or du-plicated. They cannot be marked with the insignia of ownership. When first invented, they are subject to exclusive possession before being written or ut-tered, yet such exclusive possession leaves them incapable of fulfilling their communicative function. They can be initially withheld from others but, once transmitted, they can never be retrieved.

Nevertheless, the law has treated what it calls "intellectual property" like other forms of property: "Nothing can with greater propriety be called a man's property than the fruit of his brain" (Waring 340). Copyright law has dupli-cated the protection provided by traditional property doctrines by setting statutory boundaries similar to the physical boundaries of tangible property and by formulating exclusive rights of ownership, such as the right to exclude, to use, and to transfer.

In terms of an author's commercial interests, the notion of intellectual property is both appealing and appropriate. It provides a conceptually simple model on which to base legal and economic analysis. If a poem is property, people can buy and sell it, inherit it, or otherwise transfer it. It has a legal existence separate from its author and from which the author can benefit.

But authors also have noneconomic interests to which the notion of intellectual property corresponds less well. Ownership would give people who make a discovery, write a novel, or invent an epigram the ability to withhold their contributions from others, but what most authors want is to communicate them. Intellectual property law does not provide a useful framework to govern this communication or to ensure that creators receive full credit for their creations when the communication occurs.

The property doctrine is just one of many legal doctrines. Some, such as contracts, deal largely with planned interactions between people; others, such as torts, deal largely with interactions that are unplanned; and still others, such as property, deal largely with the objects of those interactions. Despite their differences, all legal doctrines share their identity as metaphors. They reflect various ways of seeing the world, each way incomplete by itself but overlapping with and complementary to the others. In combination, these metaphors are more effective than they are singly. For example, adding the spontaneity of torts to the deliberateness of contracts produces a more accurate picture of the spectrum of human interactions than would either alone.

Yet all too often legal metaphors are not used in combination to enlarge understanding but in isolation to constrict it. Like any metaphor, the property metaphor is capable of distorting the law's analysis of human creativity. When lawyers talk carelessly about intellectual property, they reduce a voluminous, diverse mixture of stray thoughts, dogged research efforts, fragmentary phrases, stunning insights, and blind alleys to simple commodities. Property is thought of as being subject to exclusive ownership, over and over, in sequence. But each creative act takes place within a web of contributions from a community of creators. The property metaphor is misleading for words because words are meant to be shared, not possessed. "The heart of language is not 'expression' of something antecedent, much less expression of antecedent thought. It is communication; the establishment of cooperation in an activity in which there are partners, and in which the activity of each is modified and regulated by partnership" (Dewey 179).

To improve the legal metaphor we can look beyond the idea of property to the larger legal context within which property exists: a network of relationships, constantly realigned and readjusted through transactions that the law understands as contracts. The contract metaphor adds to the intellectual property metaphor because it focuses as much on the process of the trans-action as on the result. It assumes the existence of dealings between people, unlike the property metaphor, which assumes the existence of a bundle of rights that an owner holds against others. Contract is a meeting of minds, not a placing of boundaries.

Some political philosophers, such as Hobbes, Locke, and Rousseau, have theorized that societies are based on a "social contract" in which people come together in communities to gain the benefits of safety, security, and support, and in exchange relinquish their freedom to behave however they choose. This metaphor may lack historical validity, and may make unwarranted assumptions about the contract's power to bind the members of the community, but it recognizes that society is a collection of human beings whose lives are spent in interactions with one another.

As the social contract is a metaphor for political life, perhaps another kind of contract could be a metaphor for efforts at creativity and communication: the "creative contract." By virtue of living among other people, everyone is a party to the creative contract as both a creator and a member of the audience.

Thinking of creativity in terms of this larger social relationship and viewing infractions against literary ethics, such as plagiarism, as breaches of the creative contract as well as infringements of property rights can open new avenues of legal analysis. Intellectual property is an inadequate metaphor not because the structure of property law is inadequate but because the term itself makes people think too simplistically of words as property to be owned. The contract metaphor can serve as a reminder that property can be shared, exchanged, bargained over, and used, as well as owned.

Holding to the intellectual property metaphor, the U.S. Supreme Court has doggedly rejected the suggestions by various commentators that the protection and consequent financial interest granted by copyright should be based on the labor invested—the process, not the result (Feist 1295). By looking to the contract metaphor, courts could take process into account as well as result. When an author begins to write, there is never a guarantee of what the result will be. The law's goal should be to safeguard the process by rewarding those who undertake to create a work according to the terms of the creative contract.

Alternatives

> Plagiarism? the hell with it! I thoroughly
> believe Rostand swiped my friend's play
> But Rostand made it into a beautiful
> thing, didn't he, so what's the odds?
>
> —George Jean Nathan

I left publishing and was in my second year of law school when a former publishing coworker called me. He was considering the publication of a manuscript that happened to have been written by the author whose plagiarism I had discovered a few years before. My coworker had never heard that story, but a mutual friend who had heard it had told him he ought to talk to me. Hadn't I once edited a book by this author? my coworker asked.

By then I knew enough about copyright law to understand why the publisher's lawyers had been so unconcerned. Copying five peripheral paragraphs from three books totaling some eight hundred pages altogether was substantial in neither quantity nor quality. Even if the authors of the copied passages had bothered to bring an infringement action, they would most likely have lost.

Yet, describing my experience, I felt fresh anger, not at the lawyers or the law but at the author and the publisher. By writing the book the way he had, the author had breached his duty under the creative contract—to synthesize information obtained from many sources into a fluid, coherent whole—and nevertheless received a financial reward as well as authorial credit that reinforced his professional status, a status that had helped him to earn a living in a competitive field. By silently accepting the author's excuses and publishing the book anyway, the publisher had become a conspirator in the author's scheme. Now the questions in my mind were about both literary ethics and the law. I wondered how the law should protect creativity.

In answering this question, it would be helpful to consider the social goals that the law is to implement. Perhaps we imagine a society in which creative people are free to exercise their talents without overly burdensome restrictions; in which the public can enjoy the fruits of creative labors; and in which the disappointed or untalented are not tempted to misuse the law to bring the creative process of others to a halt.

In pursuit of these goals, copyright law can open itself to a broader way of understanding words. The law need not cling to simplifications and draw endless fine distinctions between different kinds of creative achievements while forgetting that copyright law, like all law, is about people. By recognizing that books are more than products, and that words are more than property, courts can be more sophisticated in their approach to creative disputes than they are at present. For example, the law regards facts as having an objective existence distinct from the existence of the human beings who discern them. Recently the Supreme Court declared, "The distinction is one between creation and discovery: the first person to find and report a particular fact has not created the fact; he or she has merely discovered its existence" (Feist 1288). This view of objective truth has been discarded by a variety of different schools of twentieth-century legal thought, including positivism, pragmatism, postmodernism, nihilism, and Critical Legal Studies, all of which instead see the existence and content of the discovery as being dependent on the discoverer (Frank 568; Posner 1656; Schlag 173; Singer 4; Kelman 269–70). Far from subscribing to the idea/expression or fact/expression dichotomy, those who belong to these schools of thought would say that there is nothing but expression.

Applying legal rules to creative efforts is a delicate task, however, for what the law protects it also controls. The premise of intellectual property law is that creativity should be encouraged and knowledge sought. In actuality we have sometimes used the law to suppress creativity and knowledge. Along with admiration and awe, creativity can also make us feel envy or fear, prompting us to attack people such as Galileo for disputing the word of God or James Joyce for saying the unspeakable.

We cannot expect the law to be more consistent or more wise than we are. Law has its limits and cannot be relied on to provide a simple solution to every problem. A suitable forum for a discussion of plagiarism may lie outside the legal system. After all, plagiarism is just one of the creative risks that people take—of expressing themselves imperfectly, of being misquoted or misunderstood, of losing editorial control of their work—and the means of reducing these risks are not to be found in law. Hegel found "no precise principle of determination available" to decide "to what extent . . . repetition of another's material in one's book [is] a plagiarism" and concluded that the question "cannot be finally settled either in principle or by positive legislation. Hence plagiarism would have to be a matter of honour and held in check by honour" (56).

Aided by an understanding of copyright law, we can seek alternative ways to deal with plagiarism. Creators can help one another, individually or collectively. Some professional writers' groups are active in support of authors' rights and in devising accessible procedures through which writers can resolve their grievances. Some academic groups maintain sanctioning procedures. The pressure of public opinion may also be brought to bear against offenders, even in the absence of any possibility of sanction.

Aided by an understanding of plagiarism, we can continue to work toward a more just law of creativity. The law is itself a product of the human creative process, as powerful and moving as any other work of literature. As we try to facilitate and encourage the creative process through copyright law, we must continually work to accommodate process and result, creator and audience, property and contract, ownership and communication, simplicity and complexity, flexibility and consistency, metaphor and reality, and creativity and the law.

Notes

1. This definition is an amalgam of definitions from several sources. See, for example, *Black's Law Dictionary* (plagiarism is "the act of appropriating the literary composition of another, or parts or passages of his writings, or the ideas or language of the

same, and passing them off as the product of one's own mind"); *The Oxford English Dictionary* (plagiarism is "the wrongful appropriation or purloining, and publication as one's own, of the ideas, or the expression of the ideas [literary, artistic, musical, mechanical, etc.] of another"); *Webster's Third New International Dictionary of the English Language Unabridged* (to plagiarize is "to steal and pass off as one's own [the ideas or words of another]," to "use [a created production] without crediting the source," or "to commit literary theft," which is to "present as new and original an idea or product derived from an existing source"); and St. Onge 51–62 (definitions from such sources as the Modern Language Association, language textbooks, and school catalogs).

2. In his concurring opinion in Jacobellis v. Ohio, Justice Potter Stewart concluded that the motion picture at issue was not "hard-core pornography" (197). Because writing about plagiarism can make one hyperaware of the need to credit sources, I feel compelled to note that I arrived at the comparison of plagiarism to pornography before reading a similar comparison by K. R. St. Onge (51). My hyperawareness is such that I also feel compelled to cite Thomas Mallon's discussion of the need while writing about plagiarism to be especially scrupulous in citing sources (125).

3. The Copyright Act of May 31, 1790; the Copyright Act of February 3, 1831; the Copyright Act of 1870; and the Copyright Act of 1909.

4. The asterisk indicates the page in the original edition, according to legal citation convention.

Originality, Authenticity, Imitation, and Plagiarism: Augustine's Chinese Cousins

C. Jan Swearingen

Intellectual Property and Individual Identity: Cross-Cultural Conundra

Western notions of intellectual property, and the related ideas of copyright and plagiarism, are less that three hundred years old. Capitalist definitions of property drew on Enlightenment concepts of individualism, autonomy, and political rights. Earlier European notions of textual and intellectual property emerged during the powerful convergence of the Protestant Reformation and the printing press (Lunsford 1996; Woodmansee 1984). We would do well to revisit these formative scenes as we encounter increasingly multicultural student constituencies who do not share a cultural heritage that cherishes individual rights. Multiculturalism, in combination with massive changes in the media of intellectual activity that have been introduced into classroom and culture by computers, internet, and e-mail, suggest the need to review earlier rounds of debates about intellectual property, copyright, and authorship. A revised understanding of plagiarism may become a necessity in our brave new world. Comprising not only multicultural curricula, but growing numbers of multicultural students, today's colleges and universities serve students who enter the college classroom believing that truth, wisdom, and cultural artifacts such as art and literature are cultural community property, the result of years of accumulated wisdom transmitted by venerated leaders and by oral traditions, many of them religious (McLeod; Smitherman). To explain plagiarism to such students requires delicate and adroit cultural exegesis going both ways. In this context, a cultural history of Western European concepts of individualism, intellectual property, plagiarism, and copyright can provide one border of a cultural contact zone (Lu; Pratt). Our understanding of this history needs restoration before it can serve as a basis for the classroom discussions of plagiarism that promise to multiply in the new multicultural student world (Boyle 1992 & 1993; Flanagan; Hum; Lu).

The invention of the printing press sparked a number of debates concerning the ownership and restriction of texts that had long been, in effect, in the public domain. Subsequent Romantic and Enlightenment emphasis on originality and unique individual geniuses advanced the belief that great ideas and knowledge are human creations; once made they become the property of their authors. Individualist Enlightenment beliefs replaced earlier concepts of freedom of access to ideas and knowledge created by God to be used by all for the common good (Boyle; Grafton; Mark Rose 1993; Stock). Enlightenment humanism emphasized that knowledge is a product of the human mind. With the related concepts of authorship and, finally, copyright, the principle of individual ownership of thought and knowledge was locked into place (Foucault 1970). Several details in the debates that led to our contemporary notions of copyright and intellectual property are particularly relevant to understanding the classroom corollaries to these concepts—the model of authorship we use as readers and as writers, and the proscription of plagiarism.

Protestant reformer Martin Luther was among the first to utilize the capacity of the printing press to reach large numbers of people. Although he was a prolific author, he was among the earliest and staunchest opponents to the copyright and related ownership rights laws that were proposed during the first generation of Gutenberg texts. Why? Much like defenders of internet freedoms of access and speech today, Luther and others objected that copyright laws would limit the free circulation of ideas and knowledge that had been made so widely and instantly available to larger numbers of readers by the capability of the printing press. According to the sixteenth-century view of "freedom of information," knowledge is a God-given product of human reason. Alongside the vernacular translations of scripture that were among the first books to be disseminated by the printing press, any and all human learning should circulate unrestricted for the common good and betterment of mankind (Grafton, Stock). Late Renaissance humanism, in short, was breaking free from the doctrinal restraints that during the Middle Ages increasingly limited lay access not only to secular learning and literature but to scripture and sacred teachings as well.

Some of the lines of reasoning that shaped the Renaissance and Reformation encouragement of free circulation and dissemination can be traced even further back, to Augustine of Hippo. A North African from a minority sect within the Christian church of the fourth century, Augustine mounted an eloquent defense of the value of pagan classical learning in a Christian intellectual culture that was about to ban any and all reading materials other than scripture. He defined a synthesis for reconciling religious belief in the absolute authority of canonical scripture and the necessity of freedom and tolerance for interpretive latitude. Augustine held, as did Luther and other Reformation thinkers, that all human learning, even the wisdom of non-Christian literature and philosophy, should be placed alongside scripture as a gift of God freely available to all. Belief in the divine origin of human reason and its products contrasts sharply with the view that religion is a vestige of superstitious thinking and can do nothing but impede the proper pursuit of intellectual activity. The contrast between these two beliefs, I propose, has numerous counterparts among today's student cultures, and leads to important and predictable consequences in student understandings of their intellectual activities inside and outside of the classroom.

Augustine's instruction to homilists in *On Christian Doctrine* illustrates one implication of the view that human reason is of divine origin for questions of intellectual property and plagiarism. "If they [homilists] take something written by another, memorize it, and offer it to the people in the person of the author, they do not do wickedly. For those who steal take something from another, but the word of God is not another's to those who obey it; They make their own those things which they themselves could not compose" (1974, 29). Augustine's advice, like Martin Luther's arguments against copyright and property laws regarding books, assumes that knowledge is a common property created by and for human communities to edify and communicate, to advance learning and to benefit culture (Handelman, Samuelson 1993). The traditional view of learning and knowledge as a collective accumulation shared by and even constitutive of culture is far more common among many of our student constituencies than concepts of capital, individual ownership, and profit inherent in copyright laws and in their academic classroom cousins, the notion of autonomous individual authorship and its corollary: plagiarism (McLeod, Woodmansee).

We ignore the recent, local cultural history of copyright and plagiarism at our peril. "The notion of stealing ideas or words is not only modern, it is also profoundly Western. Students from Middle Eastern, Asian, and African cultures are baffled by the notion that one can 'own' ideas" (McLeod). In these cultures, as in the cultures of some indigenous American cultural groups, the notions of collaborative writing and learning do not have to be taught because they are already part of the cultural practice students bring with them to the classroom. What does have to be taught to such students, with difficulty, and often without success, are the notions of originality, authorship, autonomy as a writer and thinker, and plagiarism. Plagiarism relies on the notion of exclusionary ownership (Lunsford 1996, 264), a kind of intellectual land-rush model in which the first to stake a claim on a concept, term, title, or even idea from that moment forward must be cited as its author. Eighteenth-century Romanticism struck a brief compromise on these points by distinguishing between the idea or concept expressed in a literary or artistic work and the expression given that concept by an individual artist (Boyle; Lunsford 1996, 264). For example, "beauty," the concept, remained in the public domain; Shelley's poem "On Beauty" was his work and could be held in copyright by him. However, the delicate truce on which this distinction relies became destabilized in subsequent legal and academic definitions. The very notion of an author who creates a work is now under scrutiny within several branches of literary and cultural theory: deconstruction and post-structuralism question the autonomy and originality of any author's work. New historicist and cultural studies theorists approach authors as constructs and even victims of their social surroundings, as exponents of already written cultural tales. Within composition studies, increasing emphasis on collaborative writing and on the inevitably social construction of texts and their readers has led classroom models away from individualist paradigms of student writers and toward processes like group work and ongoing collective revision. E-mail and internet classroom models further extend this emphasis on polyvocality, multiplicity, and the plural voices that speak through most works (Lunsford 1996, 264–68; Swearingen 116–18).

Plagiarism in classroom settings has come to denote two different but overlapping crimes: the quotation of work by others without acknowledgment through quotation marks and citations, and the use of another writer's paper as one's own, including papers prepared by professional paper writing services. Apart from these blatant cases, documentation and notation conventions are much more difficult to master than most handbooks indicate. Even honors students have trouble determining when a phrase or idea—say, the global village—is well known enough to be used with quotation marks or without reference to an originator. Some teachers have chosen to focus not on plagiarism as stealing but on "misrepresenting a source" (Flanagan 6). Not only beginning or international students, but advanced native U.S. students as well are increasingly unfamiliar with the complex issues that underlie documentation conventions, and are confused about the notion of the ownership of ideas and words. "So-called intentional cases of plagiarism occur when students don't view a course as meaningful. They are given a term paper assignment that excludes any progress checks along the way and reach a 'threshold of desperation' where the likelihood that they will plagiarize increases" (Flanagan 6). To each of these contemporary meanings of plagiarism a host of historical precursors can provide engaging and instructive counterparts. While continuing to teach that plagiarism is an important academic and intellectual misdemeanor in our culture, can we not also lead students to examine fundamental concepts of identity, composition, culture, and ethics as they grapple with the difficulty of drawing on intellectual and cultural property while creating individually authored texts (Hum, Royster, Smitherman)? Despite the problematics posed by deconstructionist, poststructuralist, new historicist and cultural studies models of authorship and meaning, our classroom goal remains that of teaching individual authorship of academic prose. In this undertaking, a number of details in earlier Western models of the writer/composer, of the locus of meaning, and of the composer/author's relationship to textual meanings can be very instructive. An emphasis on the diversity of models of agency and author in earlier Western pedagogies, placed alongside counterparts from other cultures, can provide us not only with a contact zone but also with a comparative spectrum of models of author, creativity, and individual versus common knowledge.

Identity and Voice: Building Cultural Diversity into Concepts of the Writer

For Augustine, as for Plato before him, individual ownership of truth was impossible because truth and, to a certain extent, meaning, existed fully apart from any individual author. According to this view, the seeker after truth *finds* rather than *creates* meaning; the primary task of the writer is to aptly express what has been discovered. In Augustine's model, therefore, individuality of thought and expression are impossible because the world as God's creation is an already given order of things, an already existing system of signs that requires decoding, not further invention (Handelman). Paradoxically, Augustine's position resembles that of modern deconstructionist and postmodern models in that the view of the individual human author as the creator of new, original, or unique meaning, is held to be illusory. In a world of already givens where "language speaks us" all voices are conceived of as given, borrowed, inherited, imitative, not "one's own." Earlier Greek rhetorical models of invention and imitation, however, suggest the opposite: that individuals *are* authors, inventors, and composers, as when we refer to "Pericles' funeral oration," or "Lincoln's Gettysburg address." Aristotle's paradigmatic *Rhetoric,* in its multiple treatments of style, delivery, memory, invention, and imitation, is a singularly important predecessor to most subsequent Western models of the individual as the origin of truth and the construction of meaning. Aristotle's treatment of imitation in particular bears examination in the study of plagiarism because mimesis—the Greek term for imitation—meant simply "copying." If copying an exemplary author was widely practiced in the classrooms of the ancient world without a concern for plagiarism, its practice can be reviewed today as a way of teaching composition, and as a way of understanding the modern meanings of plagiarism.

Despite their innovative emphasis on human thought as the source of knowledge classical thinkers did not develop conceptions of empowering individuals or the "self" through rhetoric. They did, however, develop several related conceptions of the powers of rhetoric and of the power of voice. The nature of these powers are advanced in discussions of style (*hermeneias*), dramatic and rhetorical character (*ethos*), and impersonation/personification (*prosopopoieia*). Aristotle recurrently emphasizes how a speaker should learn to "give the appearance of" sincerity, authenticity, informality, lack of contrivance, spontaneity. "Art is cleverly concealed when the speaker chooses his words from ordinary language" (*Rhetoric* 1404). The parallel he observes between an actor's and a rhetor's character (ethos) is based on the creation of a surface style, a personality adopted as a mask, and mastered through formal practice of style and delivery. When delivery comes into its own as a course of study for rhetoric students, Aristotle predicts, "it will have the same effect as acting" (1404). Only insofar as it resembles ordinary prose speech is rhetoric successful as a means of persuasion among the educated; only the uneducated, claims Aristotle, can be moved by an emotionally intense, sensational style such as Gorgias'.

Aristotle comes close to describing successful imitation as successful impersonation in his depiction of the artifice the rhetor should use in preparing and deploying such a speech, and in his comment that the most successful rhetor, like the most successful actor, must "conceal the appearance of speaking artifically" (1404). His description of the voice of the actor Theodorus is particularly suggestive of subsequent definitions of *prosopopoieia,* for it applauds a temporary merger between the actor and the voice-mask he takes on; "his seemed to be the voice of the speaker, [those of the other actors] the voice of someone else" (1404). Aristotle does not, as we would today, contrast a self or essential identity of a speaker or actor to the voice or character that is taken on for rhetorical speech or acting. Instead, the "apparent authenticity" of the voice or character is linked to its successful replication—its imitation—of a style that most people will associate with a lack of artifice, and which they will associate with familiar trusted voices and characters. A contemporary Post-it note advises a similar strategy: "Sincerity: When You Can Fake It You've Got It Made."

The goal of imitation in Aristotle's models is emulation, and impersonation of certain well-defined roles, traits, and voices. Self-actualization was decidedly not one of his objectives; among the depictions in the *Rhetoric*— there is no reference to a true individual self apart from the array of voices that individuals adopt in different settings. Aristotle's emphasis on contrived or pretended authenticity and simplicity inaugurated a succession of models of "low" or plain styles defined in rhetoric handbooks throughout the classical and medieval periods, as well as in the recommended modesty of the "homily" or "sermon"—whose root words in Greek and Latin respectively denote "in the manner of a conversation." Aristotle's initial model of imitation of authentic and noncontrived discourse preserves the anthropological insight that even authenticity or unaffected naturalness are performances encoded by cultural conventions that change over time, that can be observed and learned.

Classical instruction in imitation emphasized the deliberate construction of character (ethos) as part of rhetorical composition. Portraying rhetorical character and style as artifice, image, and even illusion can lead to the idea that authenticity is nothing but, or can be nothing but, a performance or contrivance. This disturbing idea is not uncommon in modern critical theory, including critical theories of self and identity that are used in writing classrooms. We can and should anticipate that announcing to students that authenticity is an illusion or contrivance may be not only ethically disturbing, but particularly confusing when combined with the effort to define plagiarism. Plagiarism denotes ownership firmly tied to the original author of an original and unique idea or work. Yet the individual ownership and creative-genius models of originality have been supplanted by social constructionist and collaborative models of the writing process in many writing classrooms. Students are understandably mystified when we invoke traditional models of authorship and ownership as guides for evaluating originality and plagiarism. Is not the very idea of originality problematic within the canons of social constructionist and collaborative writing? Collective models of intellectual property and creativity align more comfortably with non-European models of thought and language than with capitalist, post-Enlightenment models based on individualism, autonomy, and ownership. Within a collaborative or team writing project, what, exactly, is plagiarism?

A second concept definitive of plagiarism, deliberate guile, also finds counterparts in older Western rhetorics. The charge that poetic invention entails deliberate duplicity is debated in Aristotle's *Poetics,* at a length that suggests that the idea was already old: that poetry—or literature more broadly—was regarded not only as fictive but also as an art of lying. The notion that what the poets produce are pretty lies parallels classical rebukes of rhetoric as an art of lying, but the concern about lying is oddly unrelated to *ethos.* The character that a speaker projects in a performance or writing—what we today call voice, or diction—was not implicated in classical notions of poetry and rhetoric as arts of lying. Instead, in the criticism of Plato and others it is the poet's or rhetor's lack of true knowledge that calls into question the truth and merit of what he has to say. He has not done his homework; he is a pretender. The most common charges leveled against today's student plagiarists are that they got someone else to write their text or that like the clever poet of antiquity, they wrote something very beautiful and beguiling, and utterly untrue. Such practices today we sometimes tolerate under the headings of poetic license or liberal embellishment. On these two points—the surface character (*ethos*) created through training in delivery, and the nature of the content of a rhetorical or literary composition—numerous subsequent refinements were developed in the schools of the later classical period and early middle ages.

Following Aristotle's treatment of ethos as apparent character, several varieties of ethos came to be defined under the subheadings of style, syntax, person, and manner. Plain style, that "spare Attic purity" preferred by the Romans of Cicero's time, recurs in many transitional rhetorics that carried Greek models into Latin Roman culture and practice. Cicero repeatedly applauds the conversational style of Socrates and the simple purity of Lysias' speeches. "Let us imitate them if we can" he advises (*de Opt. Gen Orat* 3, 8). Yet even as he uttered these pious praises of Greek rhetorical exemplarity Cicero was actually trying to alter the Roman habit of slavishly imitating earlier Greek models. He aimed to challenge the commonly held, orthodox view that speaking in the spare, simple, plain Attic fashion meant speaking well. Much as conservative pundits such as William Bennett and E. D. Hirsch today evoke a canonical classical world that never existed, Cicero's Roman contemporaries had constructed an idealized, erroneous version of spare Attic purity. It is a stylistic model that, Cicero argues, never existed and more important does not serve the political and cultural values of Roman republicanism:

> But since there was a complete misapprehension as to the nature of their style of oratory, I thought it my duty to undertake a task which will be useful to students, though not necessary for myself. . . . I translated the most famous orations of the most eloquent Attic orators, Aeschines and Demosthenes, orations which they delivered against each other. And I did not translate them as an interpreter but as an orator, keeping the same ideas and the forms, or as one might say, the "figures" of thought, *but in language which conforms to our usage.* And in so doing, I did not hold it necessary to render word for word, but I preserved the general style and force of the language. (*de Opt Gen Orat* 4, 12, my emphasis)

In sharp contrast to Aristotle, Cicero presents the suitability of style to clarity, beauty, and subject matter without reference to an orator's character. Throughout his work he requires the character of the orator, the statesman, to be of the highest caliber apart from and outside of any rhetorical training.

We might well examine our own and our students' assumptions on this point. Do student writers assume that an already-present character is the voice or presence behind what they write, and especially behind their desire to become fluent writers? Do we? Or, do they believe that through the process of becoming fluent writers their character will become improved? Similarly, do student readers assume that as they read exemplary or stimulating writers they are to model their characters and voices on those of the authors? Do we? I suggest that our answers to these questions are in need of spring cleaning, for they introduce particularly challenging questions to teachers of multicultural materials in multicultural writing and reading classrooms (Pattison). Cicero's comments on translation suggest the degree to which his cultural milieu was, in today's terms, notably multicultural. Cicero was aware of his work as creating a transitional boundary zone between Greek and Latin rhetorical classroom cultures (*de Orat.* I 1–30). There are striking differences between Greek and Roman notions of character and authenticity. In Cicero we find little reference to dissimulation or the creation of apparent character—except in the rebuke of these as Greek practices. Exemplary character is for Cicero and his contemporaries a precondition of rhetorical education, not a product of it. As a translator, Cicero makes no strict distinction as we would today between paraphrase and rewording in translation. All translation is inevitably interpre-

tive; like paraphrases, translations present several equally defensible word-
ings. In describing the quotation cited above, Cicero tells us that he did not
translate the speeches he had chosen as exemplary rhetorical models *as an in-
terpreter,* but rather *as an orator.* What does he mean by this? He claims that
he kept the same ideas or forms or figures of thought but converted them into
language which "conforms to our usage." His goal is not to render word for
word, or even to present the role of the orator as presenting word for word the
text of the model. Instead, he sets as a goal to "preserve the general style and
force of the language."

A contemporary example illustrates the relevance of Cicero's account of
the boundary zone distinguishing translation, quotation, and paraphrase to
modern questions concerning plagiarism. Imagine that a student turns in an
essay very much on the subject of recent class discussions and examples: excerpts from George Eliot's *The Mill on the Floss,* and from Emerson's essays
illustrating nineteenth-century prose styles as well as nineteenth-century social concerns. The student draws on the readings in a way that demonstrates
his or her attention to and engagement in class discussions. The style of the
essay, however, bears little resemblance to the student's conversational style
in class, and is very different from that of any essay he or she has submitted.
It is a style fitting the content of the discussion, however, for the discussion
has turned to sobering notions of declining morality in American public life.
The lofty style the student has adopted resembles that of George Eliot or
Emerson lambasting the morality of contemporary society. It is the "lofty"
that Cicero wrote into existence as he translated his Greek models into a Latin
prose style that he was the first to practice, a style that would become the exemplar of medieval Latin authors, the first vernacular essayists, French and
American Enlightenment thinkers, particularly Jefferson. Through a handbook on rhetoric and oratory, *The Columbian Orator,* Frederick Douglass
mastered this style, the style of his contemporaries, Emerson and George
Eliot. Douglass published his *Narrative* with no less than two prefaces by
white clergymen attesting to its authenticity. He anticipated that it would be
perceived as ghostwritten according to the belief that an uneducated freed
slave could never attain such powers of oral or written exposition.

Today's student, and particularly the nontraditional or multicultural student, frequently encounters similar problems of imitation and its discontents:

> During my first semester in college I was accused of plagiarism. [The
> teacher] carefully explained to me that he was proud of how hard I had la-
> bored over my response but that I needed to "use more of my own words,"
> that "copying someone else's work was considered illegal in this country,"
> and that he would not fail this first essay because he realised that I wanted
> to do well in his class. As a cautionary note, he reminded me that I would
> have to, in future, be more careful about presenting my own ideas in my own

words. Because my written English was "too good," he concluded that I
could not have written the response. This incident occurred three weeks into
the semester. (Hum 8; and see Gilyard, Royster, Smitherman)

Like Frederick Douglass and Sojourner Truth, nontraditional or multicultural students who are perceived by teachers as "different" or "unaccultur-
ated" may in effect be asked to dumb down their language on the grounds that
their authentic voice must match the mainstream culture's notion of the authentic Other (Royster). Recall Cicero's account of translation and emulation.
Has Cicero as translator and adapter of Greek rhetoric for a Latin classroom
"lied" about the content of Demosthenes by converting it into staid Latin
prose, as if one were to translate a bawdy medieval love lyric into a chaste
nursery rhyme? Has the student impersonated George Eliot without acknowledgment in writing her essay "after the fashion of?" What if neither the
teacher nor the student has been directly exposed to George Eliot, or to any
subsequent exemplar of this style apart from some dimly remembered but
nonetheless emulated patterns of "academic prose"? These questions illustrate the complexity of any and all issues of plagiarism and intellectual property, then and now, in the character of the person and in the content of the text.

Then and Now: Parallels and Paradigms

A notable change occurred in classical rhetorical tradition with the translation
of rhetoric from Greek handbooks and classroom oral traditions into Latin Roman culture. The strong association in Greek tradition between the rhetorician
and a statesman of dubious character almost entirely drops out. In sharp contrast to Aristotle, Cicero presents the suitability of style to clarity, beauty, and
subject matter without reference to an orator's character. There is no mention
of *ethos*—defined as the surface character of the person; only of style—the
surface character of the words. Throughout his work he requires the character
of the orator, the statesman, to be of the highest caliber apart from and outside
of any rhetorical training (Swearingen). Exemplary character is for Cicero a
prerequisite for rhetorical education, not a product of it. Nonetheless, in his
work on rhetorical topics, Cicero describes two topics that parallel subsequent
definitions of prosopopoieia and ethopoieia. Under the topic of similarity he
includes "the citing of examples or parallel cases," and notes, "In fact, fictitious examples of similarity have their value, but they belong to oratory rather
than to jurisprudence although even you are wont to use them, but in the following way: . . ." Here follow a list of suppositions. "Under this topic of similarity," Cicero asserts, "orators and philosophers have license to cause dumb
things to talk, to call on the dead to rise from the world below, to tell of some-

thing which could not possibly happen, in order to add force to an argument or lessen it: this they called *hyperbole*" (*Topica*10–43). The list Cicero provides suggests how different classical notions of the locus of meaning, as well as the popular understanding of oratory, are from our own. In what today would be termed a comparison essay—the topic of similarity—Cicero lists four kinds of comparison—quotation or impersonation, citation of dead authorities, citation of impossible but parallel events, and exaggeration by way of amplifying one's own point or lessening an opponent's. We do not today consider quotation of textual or deceased sources "causing the dumb to speak." We do, however, regard it as plagiarism if it goes unacknowledged.

In a different examination of the the topics proper to jurisprudence versus those reserved for the orator, Cicero describes the use of testimony: "Not every sort of person is worth consideration as a witness. To win conviction, authority is sought, but authority is given by one's nature or by circumstances" (*Topica* 20). Testimony given under stress or torture is also cited by Cicero as convincing. Emotion "lends authority and conviction" because it seems to have "the force of necessity" (*Topica* 73–74). In the *Orator* Cicero repeats these definition of *ethikon* (proof based on the topic of character) and *pathetikon* (proof based on the topic of emotion). "The former is courteous and agreeable, adapted to win goodwill; the latter is violent, hot, and impassioned" (*Orator* 36, 126). Though linked to the audience's responses and sensibility, *ethikon* is for Cicero "authority from one's nature or character" and "depends largely on virtue." Pretended authenticity is not even hinted at in his characterization. There is an actual moral character, a "nature" which in itself and because of its authenticity is an authority to be called on alongside a quotation or a witness.

Similarly, in the case of emotional proofs, it is the actual pain or passion, and not its pretence that, in Cicero's description, carries the argument to success.

Offstage, Cicero may have had precisely the insights into pretended authenticity and well-acted ingenuousness that Aristotle openly advocates. It is significant, however, that when he is onstage, Cicero's cultural milieu, including the cultural style and values he is hard at work bringing into existence, will not admit to the kind of open duplicity that Aristotle's *Rhetoric* repeatedly advocates. Cicero's account of his culture's values is a reminder that the rules we have devised for governing citation and notation were nonexistent. Quotations and allusions, as we know them, would by the time a student had completed a rhetorical education simply have been used as they were, without citation, within speeches.

What can we conclude from these classical ancestors to our modern questions of intellectual property and plagiarism, authorship, and authenticity? I have room for sketching only a few short notes and questions. How can paraphrase and imitation of styles be used without apology or questions of authenticity to prepare students to develop a diversity of voices in their repertoire? How can the proper uses of paraphrase and quotation be introduced as conventions of academic and nonacademic discourse in interesting and challenging ways, ways that encourage students to think about their own and others' boundaries of self, voice, authenticity, and indebtedness? Finally, how can the examples of our own Western, Eurocentric rhetorical traditions be placed alongside comparable intellectual and pedagogical traditions in our students' cultures so that the commonality of borrowings and voices, individualisms and collectivities, can be understood not as unbridgeable differences but as shared routes to speaking together, knowing, writing, and reading? If these are not the objectives of classroom discourses today, they should be.

Intellectual Property, Authority, and Social Formation: Sociohistoricist Perspectives on the Author Function

James Thomas Zebroski

Perhaps the reader will be wondering what all the concepts in the title have to do with the seemingly simple issue of plagiarism—the idea that we composition teachers have repeated countless times at the beginning of each of our writing classes that it is a serious offense to claim or use another's words or ideas without attribution regardless of intent. Plagiarism sounds pretty straightforward, pretty clear, and, for most of us, terribly wrong. It may seem even more strange to examine plagiarism from a sociohistoricist perspective when the primary theorist, Lev Vygotsky, seems to have said absolutely nothing about the issue, nor appears to have had the remotest interest in it. More "drive-by citations," as Peter Smagorinsky recently characterized too much of our use of Vygotsky at a recent Centennial Conference held in Vygotsky's honor? What might the sociohistoricist theory fashioned by Vygotsky possibly contribute to our understanding of plagiarism? What possibly could be the justification for dragging Vygotsky's theory into this debate?

The answer to these questions pivots on the value of theory for composition. It is my view, elaborated at some length elsewhere (Zebroski, forthcoming), that certain kinds of theory can ultimately be valuable as a heuristic, a sort of thinking device or a speculative instrument. If Vygotsky's sociohistoricist theory is of any value, then it had better be profound, developed, and robust enough to address questions not dealt with at all, or only dimly imagined by its originators. A theory that posits change as fundamental ought to be especially adaptable in its application to changing conditions. It is precisely because many researchers using Vygotsky have not understood his theory as a dialectic whole that we still have few powerful applications. It is exactly because Vygotsky has been too often confined to the process ghetto in composition studies that there still has not yet appeared, as of this writing, a single essay in a major journal of the professional apparat (*College Composition and Communication* or *College English,* for example) that is devoted entirely to Vygotsky's sociohistoricist theory and its ramifications—either theoretical, professional, curricular, or pedagogical.

In this chapter then, I will extend the sociohistoricist theory to theorize plagiarism (also see Zebroski, forthcoming). I show that our commonsensical idea of what constitutes plagiarism needs to be broken open and filled with historical, dynamic content. To approach plagiarism as a sociohistoricist means taking up developmental issues at several levels, one of which is social formation, which I will discuss in some detail. I conclude with a classroom anecdote of a recent experience with plagiarism.

Following Vygotsky's method in chapter five of *Thought and Language* and Marx's method in the first volume of *Capital,* a sociohistoricist theorizes and historicizes a concept, and then integrates the renewed concept into increasingly concrete empirical studies. A sociohistoricist then might see plagiarism as part of a notion of authorship, both conceptually and historically. Plagiarism is, in part, a negation of authorship. Both arise from claims made about authority as exercised through texts. Both seem to intensify with the rise of capitalist printing establishments. Both plagiarism and authorship are a matter of ownership of intellectual property and the policing of established boundaries between owners and their property, whether corporate or individual. Our notion of plagiarism and authorship can only have meaning that is specific to our society and economic order. A sociohistoricist sees it as significant that this book is coming out at precisely this historical moment of capitalism's development, at the very time when there is a shift in relations and forces of production from an industrial to an information economy.

We have only to consider some examples of "authorship" and "plagiarism" in other cultures and times to notice the specificity of these terms. The clearest cases are texts found in the Bible, specifically the New Testament. Over the last decade or two, great advances have been made in text and historical criticism. Although its roots go back to the Enlightenment, biblical text criticism has really only come of age as an independent discipline since the late 1950s and early 1960s when academic posts began to be created at universities that were free from church control, making possible a "wholesale shift of biblical scholarship away from its earlier academic home in the church, seminaries, and isolated theological enclaves" (Funk and Hoover). Biblical text criticism in the United States, then, emerged as a disciplinary social formation at about the same time as composition. Biblical text criticism declared its independence from church control at the same time that composition was declaring its independence from the literati of English departments.

Many provocative and erudite studies have exploded onto the scene. Although there are important applications of text and historical criticism to composition, I simply want to make the case that what we presently would label as plagiarism was the norm rather than the exception in the cultures that produced the New Testament. Burton Mack notes that, with few exceptions,

> The writings selected for inclusion in the New Testament
> were not written by those whose names are attached to them. . . .
> One helpful observation is that anonymous authorship of
> writings intended for use in social institutions such as schools, temples,
> and royal bureaucracies was the standard practice in the scribal traditions
> of the Near East. . . . in the early period of collecting lore, interpreting
> teachers, and trying out new ideas to fit the novel groupings spawned
> by the Jesus movements, many minds, voices, and hands were in on the
> drafting of written materials. No one thought to take credit for writing down
> community property even though authorial creativity is everywhere
> in evidence. (1995 6–7)

Blatant plagiarism was central to the best rhetorical instruction of the day:

> The real test, however, was to write a speech for someone else . . .
> Quintilian a teacher of rhetoric who lived during the first century
> explained that to write a good speech one needed to imagine oneself in the
> situation and character of the speaker . . . So the standards for judging
> appropriateness of a speech attributed to a particular person had little to do
> with modern notions of historical truth, but much to do with ethos, or the
> correspondence of a person's speech and character. (Mack 1993, 198)

But plagiarism is not only a cultural construct. It is also a construct of a social formation at a particular moment in its development. So in fact, we do not have to wait until the publishing houses of Venice in the 1400s and Holland in the 1600s, to find the precursors of modern notions of authorship/plagiarism. We only need to fast forward the historical process of social formation of the heirs of the Jesus movements a couple hundred years. The accepted notions of authorship/plagiarism suddenly become inapplicable to certain texts labeled Scripture even within the Roman culture when a, by then, hierarchical, authoritarian church made an alliance with Constantine the Roman Emperor, and became the official religion of the Empire. Suddenly there are lists of accepted Scriptural texts (the canon) and its necessary opposite, lists of unacceptable, unscriptural, heretical texts, and there are officially recognized authors (and readers) and the first real possibility of "plagiarizing." Mark Kiley provides us a stunning account of one Salvian, a presbyter (priest) from Marseilles who during the fourth century was hauled before his boss, the local bishop who had evidently gotten wind of the fact the Salvian had written and was circulating a work of "Timothy," the supposed reader for two New Testament letters falsely ascribed to Paul. Asked to give some account of his actions, Salvian said, "In every volume profit is sought more from reading a book than from the name of the author" (Kiley 22). No doubt, Salvian was straightened out about plagiarizing Scripture, something that by definition could not have occurred several hundred years earlier when the social formation was young and other concerns dominated. With Salvian we see the cultural notion of authorship/plagiarism clash with the concept now needed by the social formation. It is then no minor matter that, in addition to his priestly duties, Salvian was also a teacher of rhetoric.

Plagiarism cannot be disentangled from authorship; both deal with issues of authority grounded in a specific cultural and historical moment. But the last tier of analysis must be put in place for us to understand why plagiarism is presently an issue. The developmental process of small groups changing into communities, that is, social formation, is crucial. Salvian came rather late in the process of social formation; the writers of the New Testament came early in social formation. Plagiarism as we know it is a late product of a social formation process. Early in social formation, plagiarism is simply not a preeminent concern. In fact, it is because plagiarism is secondary that a social formation can develop the energy to construct and to articulate its identity. This is the moment when the operative aphorism is that "an idea is in the air." Written texts are being produced collectively as part of a larger enterprise. Energy is high; excitement rises. Hierarchies are flattened. The focus is on sharing and living the social experiment. About the last thing on partici-pants' minds is who said what and who owns what is said and written.

Relying on three very different exemplars of social formation—the emergence of composition studies, the rise of first century Jesus movements, and the postwar forming of U.S. gay communities—we can track a developing social formation through four zones.

1. *Proto-Community.* This is the long historical moment when individuals as individuals are unconsciously beginning to develop a felt sense that existing social formations are increasingly failing to address critical newly arising needs. Individuals in their own pursuits are simultaneously beginning to make contact with like-minded others. This is the moment when keywords begin to emerge and embody far more than it seems possible to fully articulate. In composition studies, one can track in many independent sources the phrase "from product to process" years before it got attached to specific authors and then institutionalized in articles, monographs, and textbooks. In the Jesus movements, this is the moment of the oral period (30–50 CE), the early letters of Paul and protogospels (50–70 CE). According to Mack (1995) there were at least seven very different Jesus movements independent of each other and producing texts. In the U.S. gay community, this is the period from World War II through the 1960s, when large numbers of people were mobilized into the armed services, saw parts of the world they never would otherwise have seen,

discovered there were other gay people, and began the great migration to tolerant urban centers of San Francisco, New York, and Los Angeles (see Zebroski, forthcoming). Items circulate in talk. Written texts specific to the formation are rare. Finding like-minded others is still a great surprise, itself generating further energy directed back into language in trying out differing names and identities. Plagiarism does not exist because the "community" does not yet exist.

2. *The Mythic First Generation.* An event occurs that serves to crystallize the process of social formation. Out of this event, itself retrojected as a mythic origin, come individuals in community, authoring texts. Later, the individuals (and their work) will themselves take on mythic status. But in the actual social formation, there still is much room for collaboration in ideas and in writing. The boundaries between author and text, between authorship and plagiarism are still weak and porous. Participants see their identity as still very amorphous and plural. They belong to numerous communities and the emerging social formation is simply beginning to take on more weight and import in their life. But they also are finding that the other communities are increasingly alienating. The comfort that individuals receive from the new social formation begins to outweigh the oppression experienced in the older formations. As participants get more energy and support from the new social formation, the old order bears down to cut its loss of power, prestige, control.

In composition studies, the mythic origin varies because as a disciplinary social formation, no one segment has yet achieved the power necessary to erase competing ideologies which tap differing events. Many have argued for the founding of Conference on College Composition and Communication (CCCC) in 1949 as origin, others for the 1963 or 1966 CCCC, while Nystrand et al. argue for a far later origin of 1980 (271). The Jesus movements were replaced by the church which retrojected the death of Jesus (ca. 30 CE), as origin, although there is ample evidence that the earliest gospel that we have that included a passion narrative occurred much later, around 70 CE when what later became known as the "church" "originated" as a reaction to the Roman destruction of Jerusalem and Temple Judaism. In the U.S. gay community, the Stonewall riots in New York City in 1969 have been constructed as the mythic origin, though close examination of the documents suggests this is very much a retrojected interpretation.

In each of these cases, there are difficulties labeling an origin because allegiances are still mixed. For example, the first generation of compositionists (Berthoff, Emig, Lauer, Young, Winterowd, Murray, Larson, Shaughnessy) saw themselves as English professors and literature teachers or English educators or rhetoricians who simply had a specialization or interest in writing.

3. *The Revolt of the Second Generation.* Every social formation reaches a crisis point by the time of the second generation. As the social formation continues to grow, a crisis of authority begins as a new generation takes over

positions and exercises its prerogatives. The second generation needs to construct its own identity, but it needs to do so in terms of the existing social formation. But that existing social formation addressed the needs of the first generation far more than those of the second. So there tends to be tension and often this breaks out into open revolt. This is the moment when establishing credentials in terms of authority is key, and this is the moment when it begins to get very important who said what and who owns what in writing. Plagiarism, as we know it, really begins here.

In the early church, this moment is marked by the rise of the idea of the twelve apostles as guarantors of the true faith (Crossan), itself produced by increased external persecution and internally, by the attractiveness of the Gnostic "heresy" (this is the moment when the very idea of heresy comes into existence). In composition studies, we are right at this point so it is difficult to speculate, but those who pit postprocess theory against the process movement may be articulating the revolt of the second generation. In the gay community, the formation of ACT-UP, Queer Nation, the very use of term "queer," signifies the revolt of the second generation. In this zone, plagiarism is narrowly construed; the social formation begins to construct "general knowledge" versus an individual's "rightful" contribution.

4. *Third Generation Consolidation and After.* By this point, the social formation has either fragmented or it has constructed new means for sustaining its identity. If it has fragmented, one fragment may predominate and erase all other traces of the social formation. If the social formation has collectively forged new means for continuing its work and growing new identities within the overall framework, this may become a period of renaissance, a return to and appreciation of the old sources, but also a semiotically rich moment of new ideas and texts, produced, however, within strictly acknowledged and now policed boundaries of ownership. Such absolute, enforced boundaries either bring to a close a certain corpus of writing or push groups to break off and compose a new social formation.

In sum, there are four kinds of plagiarism corresponding to each zone of the social formation's development. The first sort of plagiarism we would simply label as part of the "creative process" (e.g., Wallace and Darwin simultaneously come to the same conclusion). The second sort of plagiarism would be better termed "collaboration" in which distinctions can be made, but are not because they do not matter to the participants. The third sort of plagiarism is contested plagiarism in which there is some dispute among social fragments about what counts as general (public domain) knowledge versus owned knowledge, and who has the right to say which is which. The final sort of plagiarism is policed plagiarism when sanctions are in effect, authorities are in place, and the machinery of enforcement is ready.

The reader will have to make an imaginative leap from the last section to this. On the seam, imagine an extremely long and detailed section which, following the example of Vygotsky and Marx, begins to factor in empirical work on plagiarism. Given space constraints, I cannot do this, but instead shall shift to my experience with an upper-division writing course.

Elsewhere, I have described how I have tried to take the fragment constituencies who enroll into the advanced writing course and forge from them a community of writers (Zebroski 1994, 72–118). Until the term I taught two sections populated almost entirely by business majors, my approach was largely successful. However, this particular term, the two sections of about forty students were about 90 percent School of Management (SOM) students; normally the proportion of SOMs was closer to 30 or 40 percent with equal numbers of education, liberal arts, and journalism majors. I have not had a problem with plagiarism in all the courses I have taught since one run-in my first term as a TA. The way I teach, I like to think, discourages plagiarism. The term that I taught these two advanced courses, however, I was shocked by four clear-cut cases and seven additional possibles—an explosion of plagiarism, in other words.

Motive was clearly a problem. This was the third required writing course. Many students did not want to be in the course, it was at the bottom of their priorities, and they resented my demanding that they do something new and challenging beyond the writing that they had "mastered" for the second writing course.

I had come out of summer thinking that perhaps I had been too tightly structuring my undergraduate writing courses, and I was of the view that I needed to put more emphasis of student initiative. In short, I told them, "If you want to get something out of this course, you are going to have to take the initiative and put something first into the course." So for example, when I assigned ten journals entries, I did not assign topics, but rather made suggestions, leaving it up the writer to determine what to write on. In response, one frequent plagiarizer collected journal writing on computer disc that he had done in his freshman composition class and turned in these entries for his journals. I had, in fact, constructed those assignments and readings with the new graduate students three years before, and I knew quite well where this material was coming from. When I returned the journals, I stressed publicly and loudly that unless arrangements were previously negotiated with me, the writing turned in for this course had to be done for this course. He turned in a portfolio at the end of the term that included what I imagine were all the other assorted writings on his computer disc. The ethics were questionable, but this was not precisely plagiarism. He saved that for several formal papers where sources were not provided and writing that was not the author's was included as the author's.

I had also come out of summer thinking that juniors and seniors had far better things to do than to be walked like freshmen through each stage of a longer project. So I made myself very available, giving the students the responsibility for coming in and asking questions, running drafts by me, and planning the essays. As a result, I got essays that were clearly thrown together the night before and that were often copied from sources that I knew. It does not take a genius to know that a paper on AIDS that takes a historical approach and recounts the terrors of AIDS in the African rain forest in 1976 might well be drawing from Randy Shilts's book *And the Band Played On* and its video version, widely available at local video stores. One paper did exactly that. With no attribution whatsoever. Another did the same on the topic of Richard Nixon, going at great length into a detailed personal reminiscence of Nixon's daughter's wedding, from a first-person perspective, again with no sources, when these events occurred before the student had been born.

We could all share similar horror stories. But my point is to *problematize the situation* in which these acts occurred and begin the work of theorizing the situation. Part of the responsibility, I recognized immediately, was mine. I shifted immediately to more structured assignments that would preclude such activities, requiring students to turn in drafts at four points in the writing process for longer papers. Finding that I received better and unplagiarized writing from in-class essays, I added more in-class writing assignments (without the use of desktop computers unless a verified learning disability existed), making them a bigger part of the grade. I slashed the number of paper choices the next term, and four of the first five journal entries were on topics I provided. I am not sure that these changes were all pedagogically sound, but such compromises are the stuff of teaching. It turned out this was somewhat unnecessary anyhow, because the next time I taught an advanced writing class, the SOMs were down to about 20 percent and the students electing the course were up, close to half. The diversity of the population was restored and problems with motivation declined.

But from a sociohistoricist perspective, plagiarism is a social as well as an individual act. So I also began to press my faculty colleagues to consider rethinking the place and role of this course in the curriculum and especially the fact that SOMs do not have a choice about whether they can take this course or the technical writing course. Although the tech writing course does not exactly fill their needs either, if these students had a choice, I think many would select that course. Ultimately, negotiations between the SOM and the Writing Department need to be reopened. Though I have no power in effecting that, I can keep bringing these issues to the fore, insisting that plagiarism, among other things, is a curricular problem.

But plagiarism is also a product of this specific economic scene. My students feel the increasing pressure of the job market. As one aspect of this economic real world, they also are part of the evolving technological scene. The computer community is still caught up in the final moments of its second stage of social formation. Many computers-in-composition scholars and many of our students initiated into that technological brother- and sisterhood are basking in twilight of the first generation efforts to give voice to a new community and its communal experiment. That experiment began in the seventies almost as a mythic countercultural movement, crystallizing into a community in the 1980s, sometime between the utopian rhetoric of Alvin Toffler's *The Third Wave* and the famous half-time Super Bowl commercial for Apple computers in 1984. For all the bashing of so-called romantics and expressivists in the field of composition, the most romantic, utopian, and naive folk I have encountered in academe are my colleagues devoted almost religiously to the Computer. As a heretic, I keep pointing out to my technophiliac colleagues (I have been labeled a "technophobe") that technology will do nothing in and of itself. Computers will solve exactly as many problems as they create. They are not the panacea. Computers, and the reduction of the teaching of composition to the teaching of computers, are effects of social relations. Only by changing those social relations might the computer function to liberate.

It is no chance thing that my advanced writing students who plagiarized were *all* intensively into computers. They had all been initiated not only into computer writing practices, but into this utopian ideology and its user community. In other words, they too believed in the utopian promises of the user community and had internalized its excitement and its blurring of authorial boundaries. This boundary blurring is inherent not to cyberspace or advances in computer technology per se, but to the early stages of social formation. This will very soon change.

As the federal government deregulates, and, the same thing, as monopoly capitalism firmly establishes itself in cyberspace, services and information will be increasingly commodified, tabulated, owned, bought, and sold. This is already beginning to happen with services now advertised on television like America OnLine. But then too, the first generation of computer users is drawing to its close and their social formation is about to enter the crisis of the second generation. At this very moment, the huge corporations are lurking offstage. They are prepared to appropriate not simply the technology, which was funded, I have to note, years ago by all U.S. taxpayers through the Defense Department, which created the first proto-internet to maintain communications during nuclear war. Capital will also gladly take over the social networks the user community has together formed. When this takeover more fully occurs, we can expect that the collaborative sense of the early stages of social formation among users will be displaced by increasingly policed distinctions between authorship and plagiarism. Our concept of plagiarism and authorship then will be grounded, as usual, in the authority of capital.

Competing Notions of Authorship:
A Historical Look at
Students and Textbooks on Plagiarism
and Cheating

Sue Carter Simmons

Infinitely better it is to have something that is our own, though of moderate beauty, than to affect to shine in borrowed ornaments, which will, at last, betray the utter poverty of our genius.

—Hugh Blair

He knows just where he can lay his hands upon some fifty to a hundred "themes" written by the members of past classes, that have been carefully collected and preserved by enterprising students.

—Frank Norris

It may seem odd to many people today that when colleges and universities first began providing instruction in written English, students were not necessarily required to write papers. In the eighteenth and early nineteenth centuries, U.S. colleges usually provided instruction in the principles of rhetoric and required students to deliver speeches orally, to the assembled faculty and students or at commencement. During the nineteenth century, however, instruction in oral communication was replaced by instruction in writing and, increasingly, by the practice of requiring students to write papers.

With the requirement to write papers came student plagiarism. It is the purpose of this chapter is to offer a synthesis of the conceptions of authorship underlying various references to plagiarism I have uncovered in researching the history of writing instruction in U.S. colleges. My contention is that by the end of the nineteenth century, two discourses about plagiarism and cheating were emerging: the official discourse of professors and text-books, and the unofficial discourse of students, from student literary maga-zines and college novels. A comparison of these discourses reveals different models of authorship—the individual model of authorship students were taught in school, and the collaborative and collective model of authorship students practiced through plagiarism.

Fertile Ground for Plagiarism

Popular teaching conditions in nineteenth-century colleges created fertile ground for plagiarism. A primary factor contributing to plagiarism was the canned paper topics which were used. Composition textbooks often provided lists of suitable theme topics, and uniform course materials, including writing assignments, were used in large programs like Harvard's. When large num-bers of students are required to write on the same topics term after term, pa-pers can easily be "recycled" from one class to the next, often in fraternity files. In the passage used as an epigraph above, novelist Frank Norris was per-haps recalling his student years at the University of California in the 1890s. Similarly, Lawrence Veysey, in his history of higher education in the United States, reports that "the black market in themes was a major industry" (299).

Often students were directed, again through lists of appropriate topics, to write about what they read, that is, the subjects they learned about in other college classes. Yet the professional organizations that helped to formalize documentation conventions like the MLA and the APA were not founded un-til the end of the nineteenth century, and writing textbooks before about 1900 provided little to no instruction in how to cite from written sources without plagiarizing from them. Without instruction in the mechanics of quoting and paraphrasing, and with no formalized documentation systems to follow, stu-dents may have plagiarized even while following the advice of their writing teachers and textbooks.

Other constraints generally left students with little choice or control over the papers they wrote. Composition pedagogy forced students to "disown" their papers by forbidding first-person pronouns and assigning topics and par-ticular forms. Such practices left students with little ability to use personal ex-perience in their writing and few strategies to mark their texts with their own voices (Crowley 1990, 147–53). A further constraint was the sheer volume of writing required from students. At Harvard, whose writing courses were na-tionally influential, by the 1890s first-year students wrote a new paper every two weeks as well as one short paper six days a week for the entire academic year. The frequency with which students were required to write, along with requirements about first-person pronouns and topic choice, then, created a climate where students were required to write, but not really allowed to author their texts. In such a climate, I believe, students may have felt plagiarism to be a viable option. In addition, the large class sizes helped maintain distance between students and teachers and likely prevented teachers from recognizing plagiarism. According to Robert Connors, it was not unusual for an English professor to be responsible for teaching 200 writing students, to read a new paper from them every other week, and to devote six or so hours weekly to student conferences (1990, 112–13).

Aside from writing pedagogy and teaching conditions, however, the most important contributor to student plagiarism was the pervasiveness of cheating. Historians Helen Horowitz and Lawrence Veysey both conclude that cheating was rampant in U.S. colleges (Horowitz 1987, 141; Veysey 275, 299–300). A more personal report at the University of Michigan in the 1890s comes from undergraduate Delos Wilcox: "A large percentage of students cheat in the class-room at some time or other. . . . two-thirds would not be too high an estimate" (189–90).

Cheating is portrayed as a routine part of college life in the cartoon series "Manners and Customs of Ye Harvard Studente" by F. G. Atwood, originally published in the *Harvard Lampoon* in the 1870s. The panel entitled "A Recitation" shows one student reciting material he is supposed to have learned, while being prompted by a student from the row behind him. In the companion panel, "An Examination," one student hands a note back to another, almost under the eye of their instructor, while another looks on the sly at the notes he sneaked into class. A notably humorous portrayal of cheating appears in *Rollo's Journey to Cambridge,* a novel about Harvard. Naive Rollo is initiated into college life by his savvy friend Jonas, who proudly displays his "examination apparatus":

> "This," said Jonas, taking up a bundle of cigarette papers, "contains all Latin and Greek Grammar, Chinese 1, Fine Arts III, Ancient and modern Geography, Calisthenics, Andrew's Latin Lexicon, and Quackenbos's History of the United States. And this is a preparation for producing a sudden and violent nose-bleed." (Wheelwright and Stimson 72)

The detail with which cheating is portrayed in these examples, along with the fact that these texts were written by students for students, lends credence to the conclusion that cheating was commonplace. Yet another indicator is the lexicon developed to describe cheating; Horowitz reports these popular slang terms: "cribbing," "shining," "ponies," and—before the advent of word processors and photocopies—"theme-copying" (33, 141). As the slang term "theme-copying" suggests, students likely saw plagiarism as a particular type of cheating.

Student and Professional Discourses on Plagiarism

Certainly not all—and probably not most—college students cheated and plagiarized. Likewise, not all composition textbooks from the nineteenth and
early twentieth centuries discussed plagiarism. Some textbooks were organized to treat words, then sentences, and then paragraphs; with this structure,
the issues of original composition and blending one's thoughts with those of
one's sources never arise. However, in the spirit of providing a survey of un-
explored terrain, I use the terms "student" and "professional" to name the differing conceptions of plagiarism and cheating revealed in my sources, which
divide easily into those authored by college students (or former college students) and those authored by professors who taught writing. Both professional
and student discourses discussed plagiarism and cheating, and as one might
expect the discussions differed—primarily over conceptions of responsibility
and ownership.

Notions of responsibility differed among students and their writing
teachers—primarily over what responsibility entailed and to whom it was
due. Textbook writers advised avoiding plagiarism out of responsibility to
oneself, to one's readers, or to society. Echoing notions of mental discipline
that had informed educational philosophy throughout the nineteenth century,
correctly documenting sources was important for the mental value—the
"good"—to writers, who experienced the rigor of attempting difficult work,
as this quotation from Brainerd Kellogg's 1889 textbook *Rhetoric* illustrates:
"Remember that the more completely the composition is yours in thought
and in word, the greater is the good its construction does you and the higher
the value you yourself will place upon it" (74). Textbooks also argued that
writers had a responsibility to themselves to develop their own thought
and/or inventive powers. John Genung, in a section titled "The Habit of
seeking Independent Conclusions" from *The Working Principles of Rhetoric,*
discussed this habit as "the birthright of every one who thinks and writes"
(405–406). A similar sentiment is expressed in the passage from Hugh
Blair's *Lectures on Rhetoric and Belles-Lettres* used as an epigraph above.

Aside from such intrinsic value, writers had an obligation to readers to
clarify which ideas were whose. This rationale for documenting sources was
expressed in Newcomer's 1898 *Elements of Rhetoric:* "The student of composition should not . . . entertain the idea that he may freely appropriate
without change of form whatever matter he finds in encyclopedias or elsewhere. . . . Literary ethics to-day require absolute precision in quoting"
(20–21). Some attention was given to unintentional plagiarism, which might
occur in a curriculum where students write about what they have read. For
example, John Duncan Quackenbos, in *Practical Rhetoric,* recommended
that student writers read more than one source on any topic in order to avoid
simply reproducing the view of one author (65–66).

The most frequent rationale for avoiding plagiarism drew on a responsibility to society to act honestly. In this view, plagiarism is theft of the ideas or words of another person, and hence is stealing. In 1878, David J. Hill wrote in his popular textbook *Elements of Rhetoric and Composition* that "It is an important question how far one may use the writings of others without breaking a moral law" (15). Forty years later, Lomer and Ashmun's *The Study and Practice of Writing English* defined the term for students as a matter of honesty: "The use of another's ideas or words without due acknowledgment is known as *plagiarism;* it is commonly regarded as a literary theft—as inexcusable as any other kind of dishonesty" (217).

A contrasting view was expressed by students that involved responsibility to peers and to college life. Puzzled and shocked by the behavior of his students at the University of Illinois in 1910, English professor George B. Denton wrote in a letter to his mentor that "students come to college with no idea that cheating in school is dishonorable, and there is consequently no feeling against it among the student and no secrecy." Horowitz concluded that "Students approved of all cheating necessary to stay in college" (32). That is, a student might have cheated in order to avoid being expelled for failing grades, as well as in order to devote less time to studies and consequently more time to social obligations. As a result, responsibilities toward one's peers and maintaining college life superseded those discussed in textbook injunctions to refrain from plagiarism, that is, duty to one's intellectual development or to society.

A short story published in a literary magazine at the University of Michigan in 1894–95 illustrates the student view of responsibility with regard to cheating. Charlie is sure to flunk the big final and thus be expelled from college until he is rescued by his sister, who is also his classmate:

> All at once, just as she passed him, a slender white hand covered his examination book for an instant and was gone. On the book before him lay a sheet of paper closely written in a delicate text he knew at a glance. A great joy thrilled his whole body. It seemed to set something trembling inside him somewhere, he didn't know what. He fairly gasped in the ecstasy of his relief. There were the sentences written out entire. (Smith 203)

Charlie's plight portrays another aspect of student views of responsibility, blaming the teacher:

> "Dutch" [the German professor] was as unconscious of the crime against the laws of the college that was being enacted before him, as if he had been blind, it was all done so adroitly. Charlie never stopped to argue fine ethical points. He felt he was entitled to the credit and he would be willing to "do Dutch" to a much larger degree to satisfy his thirst for vengeance. (203)

Rather than acknowledging responsibility for his own behavior, Charlie cheats in retaliation for the failings of his teacher.

Blaming the teacher is a popular trope in student discussions of cheating and plagiarism. As the following examples indicate, students who blamed the teacher for their cheating re-assigned responsibility for their own behavior from themselves to their teachers. Thus the trope may have functioned to justify an action considered to be immoral by placing it in a larger moral framework where an aspect of schooling is critiqued. That is, students who cheated or plagiarized may have rationalized their own seemingly dishonest, immoral behavior by reframing it as a critique of inadequate teaching.

Critique of schooling is certainly the message in this passage from *Rollo's Journey to Cambridge*, which involves a bank note on which were written conjugations for irregular verbs:

> "But suppose they ask me the regular verbs?" said Rollo.
> "They will not," said Jonas. "They only wish you to know the exceptions, because they prove the rules."
> "But suppose they see me with the bank-note—"
> "They will only think you are endowing the proctor: and a percentage of all bribes goes to the fund for pensioning good and faithful servants."
> (Wheelwright and Stimson 72)

Instructors are critiqued both for testing the most arcane areas of knowledge and for being immoral—for "cheating"—themselves.

A more pointed argument about who is to blame for student cheating is made in the following cartoons, from the University of Michigan's humor magazine, the *Wrinkle*. The cartoons together with their title, "Our Examination System," not only expose cheating, but critique it as a result of an inequitable system for measuring students' accomplishments in college that relies on a single examination at the end of the term. "We cheat," the cartoons seem to say, "because you make us."

An even more stinging indictment of college teaching appears in R. C. Evarts's *Alice's Adventures in Cambridge*, a novel about Harvard published in 1913. The teacher, portrayed as a frog, made students write an impromptu essay in class on a nonsense topic, and the response was rampant cheating: "The Lizard, who was sitting in the front row, was the only one who wrote anything original. All the others copied from his paper, and crowded round him so closely that Alice was afraid the poor creature would be smothered" (11). After collecting the papers, the teacher began to mark them:

> He marked the first one A, the second one B, and so on down to F, when he began over again with A. All this time he kept his eyes tight shut. "So he will be sure to be impartial," the White Rabbit explained to Alice.

HOW HE WOULD PREPARE IF PASSED ON HIS RECORD.

> After the marking was finished, the frog handed the papers back to their
> owners. The White Rabbit, who had written nothing at all, had a large A on
> his paper. The Lizard, however, had an F marked on his. (11–12)

Dutiful students who perform the work as teachers expect are lampooned in
the character of the Lizard, the only student to write an original paper, and
whose effort earned him an F. The hero, of course, is the White Rabbit, who
wrote nothing and received a premium grade. And most notably, the teacher
is presented as a frog, who cannot see the students cheating because "his eyes
are in the top of his head" (10). The argument these materials make is simple:
when students cheat, it is the teacher's fault.

　　Such a view of responsibility contributed to the way some students responded to the textbook notion of ownership. While textbook discussions, as
I will show shortly, discussed plagiarism as a matter of ownership of words
and ideas, this notion was one that students rejected, due to their allegiance to
each other and to staying in school. Rather than being an activity peculiar to
writing and thus a matter involving individual ownership of ideas, plagiarism,
to students, was cheating. As such, plagiarism was one of many activities one
might engage in out of responsibility to one's peers and duty to maintain one's
position at college. In this context, the concept of ownership was irrelevant to
the larger goal of fulfilling the responsibilities of college social life.

HOW HE PREPARES TO PASS ON HIS EXAMINATIONS.

Student views of ownership were further shaped by composition pedagogy, which, as I have explained, prompted students to disown their writings. Under such constraints, students—even those who styled themselves as
writers—may have felt little ownership of their papers. Frank Norris pointedly blames teachers for their students' plagiarism in the following passage
from *The Wave,* which defends the actions of a student who gets a theme
from the fraternity file:

> He does not necessarily copy it. He rewrites it in his own language. Do you
> blame him very much? Is his method so very different from that in which he
> is encouraged by his professor; viz. the cribbing—for it is cribbing—from

text books? The "theme" which he rewrites has been cribbed in the first place. (134)

Norris critiques the process of composing students are taught: "He has learned to write 'themes' and 'papers' in the true academic style, which is to read some dozen text books and encyclopedias on the subject, and to make over the results in his own language" (134). Notably, Norris uses the student slang term "cribbing" to name the composing process taught in writing class. As Norris's argument illustrates, despite textbook injunctions to distinguish between "original" and "borrowed" ideas, students could have felt that *all* ideas expressed in their college papers were borrowed.

In contrast to student discourse, the professional discourse conceived of plagiarism as a matter of individual ownership of ideas. To return to David J. Hill's 1878 textbook,

> Literary property differs from other possessions in many ways, but it is none the less property. Facts are common to all; but, while no one may put a fence around truth and claim it as his own, forms of expression, figures of speech, and combinations of thought, belong to their author, for they are his products. (15)

In this typical passage, plagiarism is a matter of improperly "borrowing" the property of another writer through inadequate documentation. Students were responsible for developing their "own" ideas through drawing on written sources, yet they were obligated to distinguish very explicitly "their own" ideas from those they were "borrowing" from other people's writings. Wooley and Scott's very popular *College Handbook of Composition* explained the matter in this way in 1928:

> If the student is not careful to distinguish between quotes and cited passages, he may allow borrowed phrases to appear in his paper as his own; he must make perfectly clear in his paper which ideas he has borrowed and which are his own. (18)

Other textbook treatments combine the notion of ownership and the responsibility to be honest, as in Greever and Jones's *The Century Collegiate Handbook*, from 1924: "*Indicate sources.* If you borrow a passage, a sentence, or even an idea, from a book, an article, or a lecture, acknowledge your indebtedness fully. Any other course is dishonest" (81).

More revealing is whether and where writing textbooks address plagiarism. From my examination, mid- and late-nineteenth century textbooks discussed plagiarism very sporadically. When it was addressed at all, plagiarism was mentioned in an early section on the value of reading or on invention, often as part of a general admonition to engage in the nineteenth-century practice of self-culture by reading widely (e.g., John Duncan Quackenbos's *Practical*

Rhetoric [65–66]). In this context, plagiarism was a matter that potentially pertained to any sort of writing students did and was described as a sort of theft, and thus dishonest.

By the 1920s, however, research papers had become staples of composition courses and specialized handbooks were available that included sections on documentation conventions. Plagiarism was discussed most often in a chapter on using the library and discussed most often as a phenomenon peculiar to research writing. That is, discussions of plagiarism were moved, from general discussions involving selecting and developing topics to specific discussions of one type of writing, the research paper. Thus plagiarism was addressed more consistently and frequently once research papers became a fixed part of the writing course—yet it was discussed much more narrowly as simply a matter of using documentation conventions.

This move was significant, for plagiarism was portrayed not as a potential problem in all kinds of student writing—as, of course, cheating is—but instead as a problem in only one kind of writing, or one type of paper. It is important to note that this narrowed notion of plagiarism-as-learning-documentation-conventions ignored those plagiarism practices that were clearly examples of cheating, that is, "theme-copying," using fraternity files, and purchasing papers.

In this chapter I have used a small sample of primary materials and have focused on large universities—Harvard, the University of Michigan, the University of Illinois, the University of California. Common sense dictates that student and teacher experiences with plagiarism and cheating differed at institutions with different missions, and that even at the large universities studied by Veysey, Horowitz, and myself, at least some students held different values than those I have addressed. Horowitz herself concludes that the rampant cheating she describes was practiced primarily by a particular student subculture, the "College Man." As a result, the following generalizations about plagiarism and cheating I offer cautiously.

I have used the terms "student" and "professional" discourse intentionally in order to highlight the hierarchical power relations inherent in the pedagogical situations where my sources originated. These power relations, I believe, are fundamental to understanding plagiarism and authorship in academic culture at the turn of the last century.

In the classroom setting, students wrote but did not *author* their papers. That is, students were required to write in order to stay in and graduate from college, and write they did. However, students' written expression was constrained by writing pedagogy of the time. Consequently, even when students wrote their own papers, they may have felt little ownership of the texts they produced. And indeed, some students dispensed with actual authoring altogether by plagiarizing, that is, by claiming authorship of papers actually composed by someone else.

Students' plagiarism and cheating practices reveal a collective notion of authorship, wherein students draw on the variety of sources available—including human ones—to complete a writing task. This collective effort is illustrated in the scene described in *Alice's Adventures in Harvard,* where the entire class copies off the paper of one student. Moreover, the existence of "fraternity files"—and the phrase itself—indicate the collective effort that can be involved in plagiarism. Most important, embracing this collaborative model of authorship could also have functioned as a way to collectively critique inadequate pedagogy, that is, through rejecting teacher-held notions of authorship. Perhaps embracing the collaborative notion of authorship involved in plagiarism and cheating was, as well, a means for students to reject the limited, individualistic notion of authorship promoted by professors and writing textbooks.

Authorship is presented in the textbooks and writing pedagogy in different and contradictory ways. Textbooks written before 1890 tended to presume above all that students were writers, or wanted to be, and hence would want to claim ownership of their papers. From this view, plagiarism was a simple matter of acknowledging one's responsibility to learn to distinguish one's "own" ideas from those of others, and the requisite responsibility to develop ideas of one's "own." However, writing courses in practice gave students mixed messages about authorship. Students were given responsibility for developing their "own" ideas, yet they were cautioned to avoid first-person pronouns and were provided with lists of suitable theme topics drawn from their reading. Students were given the responsibility for distinguishing their ideas from others, yet were provided with little direct instruction in how to do so. Echoing Norris's critique of writing pedagogy quoted above, students may well have felt that when they were to compose a paper by reading sources and reiterating what these had said, there was little difference between locating those sources in the college library, and locating them instead in the fraternity files.

Academic Definitions

Whose Words These Are I Think I Know: Plagiarism, the Postmodern, and Faculty Attitudes

Alice M. Roy

A professor of sociology recounts an experience with plagiarism in which a student had presented, without attribution, sections that the professor could readily identify as originating with C. Wright Mills. When he confronted the student with the paper and the source, the student explained his strategy: "I figured in high school you copy from the encyclopedia. In college you copy from a real book." The title of an article in the German journal *Radiologue,* "Plagiarism—Copying for Advanced Students," suggests a similar view (Dihlmann). The sociology professor went on to teach the student how to use and document sources and asked him to rewrite the paper.

In contrast, Richard Murphy, in his 1990 *College English* article, tells how a student who persistently denied copying material that Murphy had gone to some lengths to track down was ultimately suspended. He also offers the chillingly sad story of the young woman who falsely admitted to plagiarism rather than acknowledge that her essay on anorexia was really about herself. Believing that the story had come from a magazine, Murphy had "wasted time in the library" trying to find its source. In her attempt at self-protection, the young woman confessed to a curious kind of plagiarism, pretending to have written about someone else's personal experience as if it were her own. Murphy says he did not believe that explanation and remained convinced that she had taken parts of a magazine story. Murphy's explanation of his assignment (what "I wanted her to write" [902]), his definition of the teacher-student relationship ("it has nothing whatever to do with what the job of teaching should be" [901]), and his appraisal of responsibility ("her apparent inability to see the purpose of our work together" [902]) suggest that the fault—and the responsibility—lies with the student.

As Elaine Whitaker says in "A Pedagogy to Address Plagiarism," "Plagiarism means different things to different people" (509). Whitaker focused on students' definitions of plagiarism, finding that her undergraduates at the University of Alabama at Birmingham considered "copying" and "stealing" synonymous but were unable to explain the difference between "plagiarism and legitimate forms of imitation" (509). Earlier, Barry Kroll had surveyed 150 freshmen in composition courses at Indiana University to determine "how students conceptualize the issue of plagiarism" (1988, 203) and found "fairness, individual responsibility, and ownership" to be the major ethical issues for these students. And in this volume, Buranen and Dryden consider nonnative English-speaking students' attitudes and definitions. But what about faculty, the other term in the teacher-student relationship that so troubled Murphy? How do faculty define plagiarism? What are faculty attitudes toward plagiarism and students who they believe plagiarize? Irene Clark in this volume examines current faculty attitudes toward the role of the writing center in issues of plagiarism. Clark cites Patrick Sullivan, writing in 1984, who found that faculty he surveyed generally disapproved of students' engaging in editing of final drafts and receiving writing center assistance.

When some faculty on my campus raised suspicions that the recently established writing center provided opportunities for plagiarism and the new system of portfolio assessment for writing courses encouraged it, I was struck by the connections to postmodern theories, with the emphasis on revision and collaboration destabilizing the notion of a fixed, immutable text. Although, as James Berlin has said, "*postmodernism* has come to stand for a staggering array of contemporary developments in economic, social, political, and cultural conditions" (248), we can probably agree that it has unsettled a former (apparently) tidy relationship between writer, reader, and text. The postmodern project offers us (or, some will say, burdens us with) a set of questions: Where is the text? Who's got it? Whom does it represent? Who controls it? Who is controlled by it? Within these questions lies a serious contradiction. If we must, or can, ask the whereabouts of the text, if we feel, as Gertrude Stein did about Oakland so long ago, that "there is no *there* there," then how can we ask who is or is not represented within it, who controls or is controlled by it? These questions arrange themselves around the classical rhetorical triangle of *ethos, pathos,* and *logos,* revealing issues of authorial power, readerly power, and the perceived power of the text itself. These questions and the act or issue of plagiarism are inextricably linked, since plagiarism assumes the concreteness of texts, the reality of authorship, of both words and ideas, and a well-defined role of the reader as receiver of the message. No disappearing subject here, no creative transaction between reader and writer, or reader and text, no negotiation of meaning, no indeterminacy of text.

Thus I chose to explore faculty attitudes toward plagiarism and, by extrapolation, to guess at the extent to which postmodern concepts have become part of general academic discourse. To accomplish this purpose, I interviewed randomly selected faculty by telephone. From the faculty directory I selected more or less the third name from each department in my university, alternating male and female potential respondents. From an initial panel of fifty-two names, I was able to contact by telephone twenty people. This is about 40 percent of the pool, a higher rate of return than normally produced by a mailed questionnaire, and more random, since in a mailed survey, people engage in a certain amount of self-selection in the return.

Among the background characteristics I noted for the respondents were the number of years in higher education, academic rank, native language, gender, and discipline. Two of the respondents were in their first and second year of teaching; one between ten and fifteen years; the remainder were evenly split between sixteen to twenty and twenty-five to thirty years. As a result, almost all were full professors; two were chairs of their departments; one was a dean of his school. One person was a semipermanent part-time instructor in an ethnic studies program where the faculty was very small and mostly staffed with part-time faculty. Clearly, the great majority of respondents were experienced academics and experienced college teachers. Although I had wanted to talk with a mix of native and nonnative speakers of English, as things worked out, depending on when I could reach them, only two of the interviewees were nonnative speakers, and both were Chinese. Again as a result of when I could reach people, the gender of respondents ended up about two-to-one males to females. Some departments are wholly or almost completely male. In fact, because I had tried to alternate male and female respondents, this distribution results in a higher proportion of females than the ratio over the university as a whole. Schools of Arts and Letters, Natural and Social Sciences, Engineering and Business, and Education were represented, with a few more respondents in engineering and business than in any of the other schools, a pattern which fits the population of the university. In two cases, people said things like, "Well, I'll talk with you, but the person you should really talk to is so-and-so—he's really opinionated on this subject!" But I wanted to talk to as random a sample as possible, even within the somewhat informal structure of this study.

I asked these questions: Is plagiarism a problem in your classes? Why or why not? How would you define plagiarism? Why is plagiarism wrong or bad? Now that we have been talking and thinking about this for a few minutes, is there anything else you would like to add?

The great majority of respondents said plagiarism was not a problem in their classes. A few said it was "somewhat" or a "moderate" problem; only two said it was a large problem. Of those few who said the problem was moderate, two distinguished the problem in different ways: one said he had had a few instances that he proved, and, on the other hand, "a fair number of examples that were clear but not serious enough to pursue," such as the occasional sentence and other minor transportations of text into a student's paper although he "preaches about inappropriate use." Another respondent made a different sort

of distinction: he found that the problem was fairly serious in general education courses where students write rather wide-ranging term papers which he
has no way of checking on when there are sudden parts that are much better
than others; he contrasted this with a writing course for the majors where he
works closely with the students as they develop their papers. So both the degree of seriousness or "provability" of plagiarizing and the type of course and
relationship between instructor and students appear to affect an instructor's
view of whether plagiarism is a frequent, occasional, or rare occurrence.

My question "Why or why not?" for whether plagiarism is a problem in the
interviewees' classes elicited both reasons why plagiarism occurs in student
writing and strategies for preventing plagiarism. Reasons for why plagiarism
occurs range from students' simply not understanding how to paraphrase,
quote, and document; to cultural explanations—the belief that in some cultures
it is acceptable; to a basic degeneration of values in, as one respondent said, "not
just this country, maybe the world." Strategies for preventing plagiarism focused on instruction (one person even said it was not entirely the responsibility
of the English Department); on context—for instance, in small programs or
courses for majors, the instructor is more likely to know the students and their
work; or on ensuring that paper topics are integrally connected to the course and
students' activity. These reasons and strategies fit solidly with current work on
the subject of instructional intervention to address plagiarism, as is evident in
the work of Wells, Drum, Whitaker, and McLeod.

In the interviews, I used an idiosyncratic but experienced shorthand to
write down nearly everything the respondents said, often in direct quotations.
On the responses to the questions "How would you define plagiarism?" and
"Why is plagiarism wrong or bad?" I then did a basic discourse analysis, identifying propositions, clustering like responses, and labeling them. I have col-
lapsed the data from these two questions because people were generally using
the same language and making the same judgments and interpretations in both.

The vast majority of responses fell almost equally at two poles. In one
main response, people said things like:

It is taking from someone else's work;
incorporating in one's own work writing generated by someone else;
copying other people without giving credit;
taking something that belongs to someone else;
stealing.

The words "taking" and "stealing" occurred over and over again. One person
delicately said "borrow," but clearly this indicated a borrowing that was not
lent and could not be returned. One person encapsulated explicitly a consumer
model of research and documentation: plagiarism, she said, is like "taking
someone's property and not paying for it." Citing is paying, a kind of re-

imbursement for the use of goods stamped, though not indelibly, with the maker's mark.

In the other main response, people said things like:

> It suggests making a statement representative of your own ideas;
> misrepresenting as your own research;
> making something seem like your own;
> using other people's work as your own;
> taking credit for it;
> not authentic;
> deceptive;
> a form of lying.

In this group, "misrepresenting" was the word most frequently used.

So plagiarism is wrong or bad on two main counts: stealing and deceiving. The word "unethical" was applied by respondents to both plagiarism-as-stealing and plagiarism-as-deceiving, and certainly modern usage allows this dual application. However, I suggest that the view of plagiarism-as-stealing is more particularly related to *ethos,* or the position of the speaker/writer in the classical rhetorical triangle, and the view of plagiarism-as-deception connects more specifically to *pathos,* foregrounding the reader of the text or the receiver of the message.

The ethical appeal establishes the speaker/writer as a person of good conscience, a responsible, even admirable citizen—someone to be believed. But when the writer is a thief, *ethos* is unsatisfied, undermined. To complicate matters, in plagiarism, the place of the writer in the rhetorical relationship is oddly double-layered; there is the writer now, and then there is the writer she or he got it from. The layers, of course, are deeper than two, as Bakhtin and Vygotsky and every theorist who draws on them tell us. The result of this collapse of *ethos* leads to the response of the reader as "the deceived," at the *pathos* corner of the triangle: the writer is duplicitous, and the reader cannot tell who is speaking and, moreover, did not know that it was necessary to ask, indeed should not have to ask, who is speaking. The reader is not getting "'the real goods." One respondent said, "it's an affront to me." Others voiced their distress: one said, "it makes me sad"; another said, "it makes me so mad I want to scream." These responses echo Murphy's anguish over the deception he felt at the hands of the two students he recalls so vividly.

If the writer is a thief and the reader is a dupe, the (postmodern) text does not get off easy either. The text, which we thought we could trust, has turned into intertext, and mediates the deception. None of the responses in this study foregrounded the text, or *logos.* No one invoked the authenticity of the text itself or the integrity of the message, things that might be damaged or undermined by plagiarism.

Postmodern theory is hard to pin down, but at least one of the things we must struggle with is the interrelationship of these three sets: *ethos, pathos, logos;* speaker, hearer, message; and writer, reader, text. Our sense of these relationships differs from a classical one, I suggest, in that we have added a circle around these imaginary triangular models, a circle that represents *context,* and more precisely, variable context. The classical rhetor or orator, as I see him, spoke to a fairly homogeneous audience on occasions and subjects that were more or less predictable and familiar. But in the mid-twentieth century sociolinguistics added the variables of region, class, style, age, ethnicity, and gender that operate in any communicative event. To *ethos,* the speaker-writer, we add a multiplicity of voices; in *pathos,* the hearer-reader, we acknowledge multiethnic and multilingual experience, and difference of gender and class.

Other theories and knowledge bases have informed our understanding of speaker-hearer relationships. The contextual circle includes Vygotskyan concepts of the developing speaker's internalizing language through the voices of other speakers and Bakhtin's assurance that the word is always half someone else's. The contextual circle includes, as well, social and cultural criticism, helping us understand relations of power encoded in these terms of speaker/writer, hearer/reader, and message/text. The contextual circle presses on the simple triangle, producing something more like a multidimensional blob, with speakers, hearers, and texts shifting, overlapping, incorporating, and being incorporated dialogically.

In the postmodern project, the triangles have lost their points and the circles are permeable and a bit ragged in places, as a very few respondents in this study suggested. One woman said ideas should be "unexclusive." She said she "hate[s] the trend toward reserving the right to ideas. It's anti-education." One man said, regarding the definition of plagiarism as stealing: "It wouldn't have to be that way. It could be different. It's not murder." He said when people ask him if they can use something of his, he says, "Use it any way you want." He asks, "Would you rather have something seen by ten thousand people or four who know you wrote it?" These respondents perhaps foreground the text as cut adrift from authorial control and protection. And the only other respondent to comment in this vein, echoing Vygotsky and Bakhtin, said she hears herself in others, "Others hear themselves through us, and maybe there's nothing new out there."

This study, though small, has shown faculty, with a remarkable degree of unanimity, wrestling in good faith with something that seems, or seemed when we were receiving our education, monolithic but which is in fact multifaceted at the very least and perhaps not merely multidimensional but really more than one entity, thing, concept, event. For example, although Wells and McLeod argue for both conceptual and instructional differences between intentional and unintentional plagiarism, most faculty interviewed in this survey did not distinguish between the two, and one rejected outright the possibility of unintentional plagiarism, on the part of students or anyone else. Rather, they saw acts and instances of plagiarism stemming either from a failure of *ethos,* deceiving and lying, or an attack on *pathos,* injuring someone through taking and stealing. No one, however, mentioned the practice of most faculty in all disciplines (I hazard this guess) of using materials from various sources in their lectures, sometimes directly quoted, without telling their students at each place where the facts and concepts come from.

In the past few years, Lunsford and Ede (1990), Woodmansee and Jaszi (1994), and Howard (1995) have documented the sources of modern attitudes toward plagiarism, growing out of Cartesian mentalism and individualism and the economy and culture of authorship in the Romantic period. The interviews reported here show how deeply embedded, "naturalized," are these assumptions of ownership and identity, at least among older, established academics. Those of us who grew up in New Criticism, where meaning resided in the text and the "authority" to "know" those meanings resided with an elite few, may feel liberated, "empowered" by theories such as reader-response theory, which foregrounds the transaction between writer and reader, or theories in which both writer and reader occupy subject positions constituted through language and history, foregrounding social, economic, and political contexts. But the liberation of the reader has come at the cost of the unmooring of the text, a cost that is for some too great to bear. As one of my interviewees said: "most deplorable."

Like "political correctness," "po-mo" has become a slur invoked to deprecate and perhaps fend off threatening changes in authorial relationships to text. Yet signs of the destabilization of text are all around us, from MTV-like advertisements to "GenX" dissing of textual strictures against illicit, uncited borrowing. Susan McLeod suggests that "as theories of the social construction of knowledge . . . begin to move our Western notion of individual ownership of ideas toward a more collective, collaborative model, we may need to change our Western stance on the owning and sharing of ideas" (12). Such change may evolve, however, with the arrival of new generations, more multilingual, more multicultural, less entitled, rather than through an unlikely about-face by the generation(s) educated in and currently invested in the maintenance of textual ownership, for whom the blurring of author-text-reader boundaries constitutes not liberation but unethical, immoral acts of deceit and theft.

But I *Wasn't* Cheating:
Plagiarism and Cross-Cultural Mythology

Lise Buranen

One of the few advantages in being a (so-called) part-time instructor is that it affords one the opportunity to see different student populations at work in different types of writing programs. After having taught writing at a large, extremely multicultural urban university for some years, I got a job teaching freshman composition and ESL at a local community college. At California State University, Los Angeles, I had never faced the issue of plagiarism in anything other than very insignificant ways, so I was more than a little surprised to be told, almost first thing, by the division chair at the community college, "They cheat." Naturally cheating and plagiarism are something that any teacher in any academic department is acquainted with to some degree, but never before had I seen it foregrounded so dramatically—since this was practically the first thing she told me after I was hired, its significance, at least to her, was obvious.

As I mulled this over driving home, a number of possible explanations for her seemingly premature—not to mention alarming—warning occurred to me: (1) the chair and the other instructors were unreasonably suspicious of the students; (2) they had set up a program making it easy to "cheat," requiring too many out-of-class, product-oriented writing assignments and providing too little instruction in (and emphasis on) the processes; (3) the students were put in the position of feeling that cheating or plagiarizing was the only method likely to produce success; or (4) some or all of the above, and perhaps other factors I had not yet articulated. Another question I had was, who were "they," anyway? I had the decided impression that it was not the local suburban white kids she was talking about, but this fairly conservative town's newest "they," a very large and growing Armenian community.

Much to my surprise, I discovered that "they" did, in fact, "cheat"—and suddenly I found myself having to deal with the question of plagiarism as I never had before. I was not ready, however, to believe that the students at this particular school were somehow unique in their willingness (or willfulness) to succeed through plagiarism, and I did not believe that the other university at which I taught was mysteriously attended by innocent, naive, or uniquely "moral" and "honest" students (although, astonishingly, some of my colleagues there did in fact claim to believe that this was the case).

Prior to this exchange with the division chair at the community college, my experiences with student plagiarism in basic writing and freshman composition classes were limited to very occasional instances similar to those described by Mike Rose in *Lives on the Boundary:* a student, unsure of her own knowledge or understanding of a subject, would go to an encyclopedia or textbook and copy or barely paraphrase it, interspersing the borrowed text with her own writing (179–81). The result is usually easily recognizable as "not the student's own work"; this is especially obvious in ESL students' writing, but it is often evident in the writing of native speakers of English as well. In the case described by Rose, Marita, a student at UCLA, was asked to write a paper agreeing or disagreeing with Jacob Bronowski on the subject of creativity, and what kept coming back to haunt Marita was her father's insisting, "Don't talk unless you know." Acting like the good student she was and yet heeding her father's warning, Marita went to the encyclopedia, used what she found there, and even listed it and her composition textbook as references, all of which landed her in her counselor's office, facing a serious charge of plagiarism. Clearly in this case she was approximating as best she could the actions and behaviors expected of college students and scholars, but her knowledge of the conventions of citation and documentation was incomplete. Unfortunately, as Rose points out, many instructors are quick to pin a moral judgment on the perpetrator of this academic and intellectual crime, accusing her of cheating.

Now, I am not so naive as to believe that there has never been a student with the guile to consider cheating or "plagiarizing"—in fact, a teleconference reported that cheating was more widespread among students than we would like to believe ("Academic Integrity"). But rather than being concerned solely with how "widespread" the problem is, we need also—first—to define it. At the teleconference, I was reminded that when the terms "cheating" and "plagiarism" are conflated and treated as completely synonymous, the issue becomes even more complex and hard to address. One of the major problems with the word *plagiarism* itself is its use as a kind of wastebasket, into which we toss anything we do not know what to do with: it can refer, at various times, to outright cheating (for instance, purchasing a research paper and presenting it as one's own work); to appropriating large blocks of text without attribution; to omissions or mistakes in citations; to paraphrasing an original too closely; to collaborating too closely—and then there is the question of intent. . . .

In my own experience with situations similar to Marita's, rather than seeing evidence of "cheating," which implies an intent to, well, *cheat,* I have invariably discovered from talking with the students that behind such misguided copying is a motive more like that identified by Rose: namely, when faced with an issue she cannot confidently or knowledgeably address, the student's impulse is to go to other sources of information. Granted, in Marita's case and for innumerable other students, there is a lack of proper documentation and differentiation between the (un)cited source and the student's "own" work. But as Rose points out, rather than making hasty accusations and punishing the student for her lack of experience in the conventions of academic discourse, her lack of skills in manipulating texts, or her lack of "ability to slip into Bronowski's discussion" (181), we should reward and encourage her quite proper impulse to look beyond her immediate experiences for the answers to her questions and help her refine the ability to make use of what she finds. Considering that the incident Rose describes took place in a freshman composition class, the instructor's response, accusing Marita of plagiarism, seems all the more egregious: Isn't that, after all, one of the jobs of freshman composition, to introduce emerging scholars to the rules of the game, or more precisely, to the often esoteric conventions and "secret handshakes" of academic culture?

Plagiarism is a vastly more complex issue than we as teachers may recognize and certainly far more complex than we customarily suggest to students; too often, we tell students "Don't do it," and perhaps we give them some mechanical guidelines to follow, telling them where to put the commas and quotation marks, and maybe how to introduce quotes or paraphrases with "According to . . ." (or worse, simply pointing them in the general direction of a handbook). But as we have no doubt learned from our own writing, and, if we think about it, from our teaching, it is not always easy to know where to draw the line: Do we cite our sources in the classroom, giving credit for the information we use in handouts or other course materials, or for things we might have borrowed, stolen, or adapted from colleagues, handbooks, or journal articles? *Should* we give such credit? How are these cases different from our students' collaborative efforts? Or are they? Clearly the answers to these questions depend at least in part on where we are in the academic hierarchy; whether an act is considered plagiarism is related to the amount of power we possess.

Many of the essays in this book deal with these kinds of questions (Haviland and Mullin in this volume especially compare the different rules of the game for students and professors), but, as the title of this chapter suggests, the focus of this inquiry is on plagiarism as a cross-cultural issue. Because the great majority of students at the Southern California institutions where I have taught are nonnative speakers of English or are bilingual, having come to the United States as children or having been born and raised in non-English-speaking households, virtually every issue I face in my teaching is a de facto cross-cultural one. Assumptions about what constitutes plagiarism or "ownership of text" may or may not be exclusively or even predominantly a matter of culture, but cultural difference can serve to further muddy some already murky waters.

As noted earlier (and as evidenced by the existence of this book), questions about plagiarism are intricate and convoluted enough in a monolingual, monocultural classroom, but in the multicultural settings in which increasing numbers of us teach, they become further complicated by the differences in cultural assumptions or expectations of both students and teachers.

(A parenthetical note about identification: I am acutely aware of the difficulties inherent in applying various labels to groups of students, even seemingly innocuous ones, and the dangers implicit in ascribing a monolithic quality to whole cultures or to the speakers of a particular language, engendering an "us and them" mentality; but for the sake of convenience, I will, reluctantly, use the all-too-handy "ESL" label, though it is not entirely accurate nor without its own ambiguities and imprecisions.)

Even more than other pedagogical issues and questions, plagiarism has always seemed to me to be a cross-cultural issue, because ever since I began teaching, I have heard it said by other writing and ESL instructors and by speakers at conferences and seminars that students from other cultures view plagiarism in a different way than students from Western cultures do (no great shock there; the idea makes sense and has a kind of automatic appeal). This was particularly true, so I heard, in Asian and Middle-Eastern cultures: rather than seeing copying from books or other sources as "cheating," so I was told, Asians see it as a way of acknowledging one's respect for the received wisdom of their ancestors and in fact they are taught to copy directly from other texts with no attribution; and Middle Eastern students see copying or "borrowing," whether from books or from friends, as a kind of community or family value, a way of helping someone achieve a goal. In addition, I have heard it suggested that part of our own Western insistence that copying from another source constitutes stealing stems in part from the uniquely competitive nature of our capitalist culture, and consequently in cultures that are less competitive, there is less emphasis on the need for claiming "ownership" of ideas or of text.

Having heard variations on these depictions of cultural differences, and having had occasional experiences with students turning in various kinds of "plagiarized" papers, I wanted to find out what was really going on. For one thing, I realized I had never heard any version of the stories just described directly from a student, that is, that copying was a form of respect or a cultural value; I had only heard this explanation from other instructors. I started informally to ask other instructors, colleagues with many years of experience teaching in culturally diverse classrooms, if they had ever heard such reports from students. Some said they had never encountered these particular characterizations of cultural differences from any source at all, and others were familiar with them but could not remember ever having heard such a report from a student, only from other teachers, as I had. The stories began to resemble what a friend of mine, a folklorist interested in urban legends, calls an FOAF story—friend of a friend: in other words, although no one has ever actually blown up a cat in the microwave or eaten a Big Mac made of ground worms, many people have a "friend of a friend" who has (furthermore, these urban legends often reveal some rather thinly disguised racist fears or attitudes). In this case, no one I talked to had heard directly from an Asian student that his copying from the text was a form of respect for the received wisdom of his ancestors or from a Middle-Eastern student that her family were only trying to help her graduate, but many seemed to have a "friend of a friend" who had.

To further investigate the issue, in addition to holding informal discussions with colleagues on the subject, I asked students in one ESL class to write short essays about what they had been taught by their parents and teachers in their own country about copying or using other people's words or ideas. I also asked about one hundred basic writing students at Cal State LA (where there is no separate ESL track) and fifty-five ESL students (that is, in specifically identified ESL classes) at the community college where I was teaching to fill out a questionnaire about their own definitions of plagiarism, their experiences with it, and their attitudes toward it. I did not intend this as a scientific sampling, but rather I hoped to get some anecdotal accounts from students about their attitudes and experiences with this thing called plagiarism.

Others who have written on the subject have conducted similar surveys of students' knowledge and attitudes: In 1988, Barry Kroll looked at "How College Freshmen View Plagiarism," a study in which he asked 150 students in a questionnaire to address their understanding of and attitudes toward plagiarism, with a particular emphasis on why it is wrong. Similarly, in 1993 Glenn Deckert surveyed ESL students in Hong Kong on their ability to recognize "plagiaristic writing," why it is inappropriate, and how they judge other students who plagiarize. In attempting to quantify the problem, these studies provide us with useful statistical information, but they were both operating from the assumption that "plagiarism" was (1) easily identifiable and (2) wrong (the latter especially seemed to be a version of "Have you stopped beating your wife?"). Until recently, this assumption, that plagiarism was unquestionably bad and wrong, was clearly the norm, and of course it still is for many people; but the role of "plagiarism" in learning, especially the form of it that Howard (1995) calls "patchwriting," has been overlooked. In my surveys and questionnaires, what I was looking for assumed neither that it was easily identifiable nor that it was necessarily understood to be wrong; rather, I was hoping to find out *what* students understood about the concept of plagiarism and *where* their ideas came from.

The results of my inquiries surprised me. One question students were asked was, "In your opinion, are attitudes toward plagiarism or copying different in the United States than they are in another country? If so, tell how; if not, how are they the same?" In response, I got a number of "I don't knows," but those students who did offer an opinion (a majority of the respondents) were almost unanimous in their belief that there was *no basic difference* between what they had been taught in their home country and in this country—on this issue, it seems, they are in agreement with Decker's and Kroll's (1988) assumptions that plagiarism was unequivocally bad and wrong, and that people who engage in it are to be either censured or pitied. This was true regardless of the student's country of origin, and at least twenty different countries on five continents were represented, including Iran, Armenia, Lebanon, Poland, Hungary, the former U.S.S.R., Indonesia, Vietnam, China, Korea, Taiwan, Hong Kong, Japan, Nigeria, Mexico, El Salvador, Nicaragua, Colombia, Peru, Equador, and Guatemala, among others.

The questionnaire was anonymous, and in administering both the essay and the questionnaire I took great pains to persuade the students that I was gathering information about people's attitudes and beliefs, that I wanted to hear about their own experiences and knowledge, and that there were "no right or wrong answers." However, despite these disclaimers, we cannot necessarily accept the results of such a questionnaire or essay at face value: the respondents are, after all, sitting in a college classroom and being asked by their English teacher to discuss—make that *write about*—an issue they probably know is important in American education, though they may not be sure how or why it is so important. It is rare that an instructor does not emphasize or even mention plagiarism in a given class, but students are inevitably exposed to it at some point during their time in American schools. For example, in ESL classes at one college where I taught, the students are given a brief handout, printed in five languages, describing appropriate classroom behavior, including an admonition against plagiarism. In addition, virtually all college catalogs publish a policy about plagiarism and the punishment for it; it is addressed in any handbook or writing text you care to name; and in fact most English and ESL teachers (as well as those in other disciplines) *do* raise the issue sooner or later. And clearly those students who are at all familiar with the word plagiarism have an idea of its gravity and significance, evidenced by the language many of them used to define it: a number of students said that it was "illegal," and one went so far as to say that if one were caught plagiarizing, the punishment was jail.

A further complication in interpreting the students' responses is that what they have been asked to think and write about may be deeply embedded in cultural values or assumptions of which they themselves may not be entirely cognizant. We are not always aware of the extent to which we are products of our culture, and what we purport to value and believe may not necessarily be what we *do* value and believe. In the United States, for example, while we proclaim a belief in the value of education (more or less loudly, depending on the prevailing political winds), a look at the relative amount of money spent on it or on the lack of positive media images suggests that maybe we do not value teaching and learning as highly as we tell ourselves. Cultural myths, as we know, have the power to make "facts" of many fictions, and vice versa.

In addition to the responses I got from the questionnaires and essays, I spoke at length with two individuals about the differences between American views of plagiarism and those of other cultures. One, a colleague in the English Department at Cal State LA, is originally from China, where he worked as a translator before coming to this country to complete a doctorate in English at a research university on the East Coast. I described to him what I had heard about Asians' belief that the use of other sources is a sign of respect for the received wisdom and the knowledge of others, and he agreed that that characterization made sense: being able to quote or cite the work of "the masters" is a way of demonstrating one's own learning or accomplishment. One need not formally document such references in footnotes and bibliographies, because the assumption is that any knowledgeable reader or audience *knows* the source. Thus, since the "acknowledgment" of the source is in the very use of it, listing them in a bibliography is at best redundant and at worst an insult to a reader's intelligence. My colleague sees a distinction between the Western "scientific model" of discourse often used in this country, in which the emphasis is on proving a position by giving a great deal of documented evidence, as opposed to a more subtle kind of persuasion used by the Chinese, perhaps best described as philosophical or even literary rather than scientific. But there is still a "moral issue" at stake in both cultures, despite the differences in emphasis, because, he feels, the assumptions that underlie the use of that received wisdom are not so different from ours. One still credits one's sources, but what is different is the form in which that "credit" is given, whether explicit or implied. According to my colleague, however, this tradition has been changing over the past twenty or thirty years, and the Chinese are moving to a more Westernized method of citation and bibliography, in part because of the global shrinkage taking place.

The other person I interviewed at length was a former student, an Armenian woman in her fifties who came to this country in 1988 from Iran, where she grew up and went to school. Since her arrival in the United States, both she and her children have attended schools here: her children finished high school here and were in community college and university, and she was also attending community college part time and working in the tutorial center at the college. I asked about her own experiences in elementary and high school in Iran, and specifically, what she was taught about plagiarism. In essence, what she told me could have been a description of the experiences I had in suburban public schools in the Midwest: the emphasis was on doing one's own work and putting ideas "into your own words"; one will not learn anything by copying from books or from friends. This message came not only from her teachers, but also from her parents. When I told her about the notion that helping your friend pass a test or write an essay is sometimes seen as a Middle-Eastern cultural value, a kind of pragmatism as well as a means of creating and maintaining community, she was surprised to hear such a thing. She not only thought it was untrue, but felt that it was evidence of a kind of "discrimination" or "stereotyping" (her words); clearly she was a little insulted by the suggestion.

The results of the survey and these two anecdotes are not meant to serve as the solution to the cross-cultural puzzle; in fact, in many ways I feel more confused now than when I started this project. I am confused by the fact that I have been told independently by any number of people from many different countries, cultures, and language backgrounds that in essence there is very little difference here and elsewhere between the assumptions and messages about "copying" or "plagiarizing" other people's writing, whether published or not, yet at the same time it is difficult to believe that there are *no* differences in the cultural values that must surely underlie ideas about such things as plagiarism and intellectual property, which by its very name must have capitalistic roots. If the stories I have heard really are a form of myth or "urban legend," one wonders whence they sprang: are they, as many myths are, a distortion of some grain of reality? It would seem so, judging by what my colleague told me about attribution practices in China. Or are they, as my student suggested, stereotypes that seem on the surface meant as an excuse, an apology, or an explanation for cheating by strange and unfamiliar "others" in our classrooms? Certainly we would be loath to essentialize many other groups in this fashion, to make such pronouncements about what all African-American students (or women, or Jews, or fill-in-the-blank) think or believe.

It may be that what we often identify as plagiarism is simply easier to identify in the writing of nonnative speakers of English. Anyone who has read examples of this kind of "plagiarism"—that is, passages copied or barely paraphrased from another source interspersed with the nonidiomatic usage of a second-language writer of English—is aware of the way they fairly leap off the page, and its very salience somehow incites us to invent stories to explain ESL students' apparent propensity for copying/borrowing/patchwriting/plagiarizing.

What may be a more likely explanation for these students' "plagiarizing" in the first place is *our* propensity for insisting on a rigid and often uninformed kind of grammatical correctness, our lack of tolerance for the kinds of errors native speakers simply do not make, even though such "errors" (misplaced articles and prepositions, novel syntax, misused idioms) do not necessarily interfere with our comprehension of the writer's message and meaning. At worst, there may even be an element of self-righteousness and indignation at someone's ruining "our" language. Or it may be that such myths originated with well-intentioned ESL teachers (we *are* notoriously well-intentioned) to protect their/our students from prosecution for unknowingly breaking the rules; if we can also essentialize ESL teachers, they/we are certainly goodhearted and generous enough to want to protect their/our students from such charges. It is easy to sympathize with such a protective urge, but these kinds of stories may have a less benign effect, despite the good intentions of their (supposed) originators. In fact, I have no idea what the origin of these stories is, but that is the point; there is a quality of myth evident in these "explanations": the lack of a clear origin, the use of oral tradition as a means of transmission, and the fact that they are taken without question as truth and passed on.

Because our classrooms are becoming more and more multicultural, open to students whose economic, racial, linguistic, or social backgrounds would have meant their exclusion from college forty years ago, and because of changes in pedagogy that emphasize greater collaboration among students and possibly tutors and that often employ portfolios as a means of evaluation, questions about plagiarism have become not only more numerous but more immediate and more complex. It seems that we have always oversimplified to all students, not just ESL students, what is meant by plagiarism, and thus we have misrepresented it, if unintentionally, even while we ourselves engage in perfectly legitimate writing behaviors that undertaken by students would be denounced as plagiarism. And we continue to deliver mixed messages about plagiarism: even in our "enlightened age" of writing centers and portfolios and collaboration, don't we still, for instance, implicitly acknowledge a fear of students' committing acts of plagiarism by having them sit for timed, carefully proctored impromptu written exams with no more collaboration allowed? The stakes for such exams are often extremely high, with graduation or a credential riding on the result. Why ask students to write under these conditions, which mimic and prepare them for almost nothing in the "real world," but for fear we will not know if they have produced their "own work" otherwise?

The same kind of cultural myopia alluded to earlier, that is, our frequent inability to recognize our own cultural values and biases, may also be at work in our beliefs about plagiarism: rather than stemming from our own morally impeccable, confident proclamations about the value of education, the importance of doing one's own work and not stealing the fruit of someone else's labor, and so on, many of our own attitudes as well as our indignation at perceived instances of plagiarism may instead betray a deep suspicion of students themselves, especially, perhaps, students from backgrounds and cultures very different from our own. Or our reactions may merely be anger and embarrassment masquerading as moral indignation, because we have been "had on" by our students: we may have been taken in by a student's lovely essay and the evidence of growth this demonstrates (no doubt because the student had such splendid guidance!) only to discover that it is not the student's own work after all. Such explanations as these are no doubt only partially true, but one can easily wonder when teachers protest too much; the moral indignation and

even rage that is commonly seen in response to plagiarism simply is not evident with other kinds of transgressions: no one comes quite so unglued about
late papers or mistakes in subject/verb agreement. In fact, it is not hard to
imagine that a student could quite easily receive less punishment for failing
to turn in a paper at all than for turning in one that is "plagiarized."

Despite the results of my inquiries, which on the surface suggest that
there are few or no differences in attitudes toward or definitions of plagiarism,
I believe that there *are* important differences in values and assumptions across
cultures that no doubt have an impact on the teaching of writing in general
and on the issue of plagiarism in particular; yet at the same time, from a pedagogical standpoint the immediate lessons to be derived are remarkably simple
and obvious: we must recognize, acknowledge, and continue our research and
inquiry into the complexities and nuances of what we call plagiarism, while
at the same time taking care not send overly simplistic or conflicting messages
to students, no matter who they are. We need to keep investigating, for instance, where we believe collaboration in the classroom ends and "plagiarism" begins, even if—or especially if—there are no easy answers to that
question. We need to look carefully at the relationship between what we too
easily and carelessly designate "plagiarism" and what we might better conceptualize as modeling or imitation. One of my colleagues, for example, insists that she learned to write by "plagiarizing," as she puts it; she chose a
writer whose style she admired and then consciously copied and paraphrased
his work until one could no longer see where his style left off and hers began
(see Howard's discussion of "patchwriting" in "Plagiarisms, Authorships, and
the Academic Death Penalty" for more on this phenomenon). Similarly, a
medical technician in a teaching hospital told of medical students who, at
some point in their training, suddenly looked, acted, walked, and talked like
doctors, the transformation from student to professional finally complete and
accomplished through modeling and imitation, yet we do not think of this as
"plagiarism." No doubt instances of these kinds of imitation and modeling are
true for all of us, if we were as honest as my "plagiarizing" friend is in looking at our genesis as writers.

Clearly there are *some* cross-cultural differences in the way "ownership"
of text or ideas is treated, both more and less profound than we believe we
know; the term ownership itself betrays a great deal about our own biases and
values. But getting at precisely what those differences *are* needs to be seen as
the monumental task it is, always undertaken with the recognition that one's
understanding of cultural differences is bound to be imperfect and incomplete.
I am troubled by the attitudes of those who do not anticipate or who refuse to
accommodate cultural differences at all; our world is getting smaller and has
less and less room for shortsighted, wrongheaded notions about cultural superiority. But I am equally troubled by positive pronouncements about the beliefs or values of other cultures by those who have not sufficient familiarity

with those cultures to comprehend the subtleties inherent in something so complex as a culture's system of values. When I hear confident assertions like "Asian students don't believe such and so," or "Middle-Eastern students think this or that," the hair on the back of my neck goes up, because, although these statements may be intended nobly, meant to foster greater understanding and tolerance, they are as inaccurate and misleading as any stereotype, and the effect is often condescending or patronizing, revealing an arrogance that says in essence, "Your culture is simple and transparent enough to be contained in a few pat phrases." The next logical step from there is a variation of the "simple native" theme: "I understand your culture, though I know you can't grasp mine." This kind of mythologizing of students (or of anyone), regardless of intent, is a subtle and pernicious breed of stereotype, and it works to promote the same illusory cultural and moral superiority, not to mention intellectual laziness, that we spend so much time trying to unteach. We need to take care that in looking for ways to protect or defend students from unwarranted charges of plagiarism, we are not "blinded by the light of [our] own benevolence to the imperial designs that may lurk in the midst of [our] compassion" (Knoblauch 75).

Perhaps more than anything we need to make it possible for all students, but for ESL students in particular, to approach writing without the fear of punishment for the grammatical "mistakes" they will likely produce, mistakes we should recognize as a sign of growth; we need to cultivate the habit of looking not just for surface errors but for what Mina Shaughnessy called the logic of the error, and to put such errors in their pedagogical place. Such fear of punishment for mistakes and errors that are probably inevitable (and often unimportant) and the desperation it can prompt is what provokes much of the copying and "plagiarism" that takes place in writing classes, for both ESL and "regular" students. (In fact, something very like this happened to a retired professor of my acquaintance; in her high school Latin class, the teacher literally threw the book at her for wrongly translating a passage from *The Aeneid.* While her classmates knew enough simply to copy from a translation, she was punished for trying to do the work herself and making a mistake. It is not hard to figure out what she concluded from that experience.)

When the division chair at the community college told me, "They cheat," she was absolutely right: they did. And as I learned more about their writing program, I did not blame the students for cheating. Frequently it was the only hope they had for passing the courses. Students in this program had little or no opportunity to engage in the struggle to understand and communicate complex ideas or to acquire the language adequate to convey those ideas, to consider and reflect on their experiences rather than simply presenting them as artifacts deemed correct or incorrect, or to separate the stages of the writing process (questions of invention and arrangement first, then a concern for grammatical and formal conventionality later in the process). Without having the opportunity to grapple with the real messiness of the writing process and to cope with the decisions and judgments that all writers have to face and make, no wonder the students clung to the sure thing that copying and "plagiarizing" seemed to be. Too much attention was centered on grammatical and formal "correctness," very narrowly and rigidly defined (topic sentences at the beginning of every paragraph, strict five-paragraph essays, etc.) and reinforced by "skill and drill" exercises in a computer lab, and too little attention, frequently none, was devoted to what the profession has been affirming for more than thirty years as the real work of a writing class: the generation of ideas, the recognition of audience and purpose, the communication of meaning—in short, the development of competent and confident writers.

A Distant Mirror or Through the Looking Glass? Plagiarism and Intellectual Property in Japanese Education

L. M. Dryden

"Why is it," a colleague asked, "that Westerners consider plagiarism such a big issue?" A bilingual Japanese professor of English, she confessed to being puzzled by complaints from some Western instructors that Japanese students and even some native academics copy texts without acknowledging their sources (Ujitani). It is a familiar situation in which cross-cultural misunderstanding arises: Some Western academics find copying common in Japan and invoke their own culture's injunctions against such "dishonest" and even "criminal" behavior. The Japanese, working in a very different epistemological tradition, regard such moralizing with bewilderment. Each views the other with a sense of unreality, as if "through the looking glass."

This mutual disorientation, which occurs commonly enough in Japanese-American relations, leads to at least one undeniable conclusion: plagiarism is not the culturally universal transgression that many Western academics assume it to be. According to one American scholar of sixteen years in residence in Japan, plagiarism for the Japanese is simply "no big deal" (Nord). Pursuing the sources of this state of affairs—that is, looking more closely "through the looking glass" at Japanese education and, more generally, at Confucian-based educational values—may paradoxically yield a sharper image, a distant mirror in which to reevaluate the Western view of plagiarism with refreshed insight.

Through the Looking Glass and into a Cultural House of Mirrors

My research yielded responses that were surprisingly consistent as well as unexpectedly contradictory. On the one hand, in an English-language survey of

75

approximately two hundred Japanese undergraduates at my own university in central Japan, I found, most commonly, that copying a source without attribution was considered "improper" and "not conducive to a good education." In fact, the responses were often so similar that I wondered whether the students were simply writing what they thought they were somehow "expected" to say. On the other hand, in surveys and interviews of several dozen professors— Japanese (many of them English-speaking) as well as native-English-speaking foreigners at half a dozen universities in central Japan—I frequently heard echoes that plagiarism is "no big deal." But then, many would offer remarkably similar theories and anecdotes attesting that, yes, plagiarism as we think of it in the West (particularly in the United States) *does* commonly occur in Japan among students and even among some Japanese faculty.

In contrast, however, to the customary penalties for plagiarism in the West, ranging from failure to expulsion, the policy of most professors in the survey followed a much softer line. Often faculty simply overlooked the practice, while some, generally Westerners, said that they themselves had dealt with students whose work appeared to be plagiarized by asking them to redo the assignment and identify their sources—without further penalty. A surprising number of Western and Japanese colleagues also reported—with requests of anonymity—even more serious lapses in attribution in the published writing of some Japanese scholars, in which large-scale cribbing of foreign-language texts might occur during the process of translation into Japanese. The practice persists even though the most flagrant violators are eventually accused and dismissed from their posts. Nonetheless, such scandals are fairly rare, occurring as rituals of group or national atonement only a few times each decade.

The various forms of "punishment" described above may very well fit the crime—that is, as plagiarism is no real transgression in Japan, therefore no significant penalty gets meted out with any consistency. No single Japanese word for plagiarism appears in the major unabridged Japanese/English dictionaries, though the general verb for stealing property, *nusumu,* includes "plagiarism" as one of its submeanings. That a separate word for plagiarism does not exist in Japanese may account for the initial confusion of many students and some Japanese faculty when being surveyed.

Western terms that do exist in Japanese sometimes assume unexpected meanings. "Composition" is one. The Western conventions of critical reading, argumentation, and citing sources have little place in Japanese universities, where courses called "composition" may involve nothing more than translating—that is, somehow "composing"—Japanese texts into English. (English "reading" courses sometimes amount to mere translation in the opposite direction, from English into Japanese.)

In Western academia, we often assume that students, as unfolding individuals, should be taught and encouraged to express opinions, to undertake "original" statements in writing, and also to distinguish clearly between their own words and ideas and those of authorities. It may be hard for Westerners to imagine a culture in which personal opinions, originality, and the need to distinguish one's own views from those of received wisdom might carry little value and, in fact, usually harbor the potential for social disharmony and personal stigma. But those conditions must be acknowledged if we are to understand Japanese attitudes toward the ownership of words and ideas—attitudes that differ widely from those in the West.

Japanese Primary and Secondary Education: Mastering Form and Information versus Critical Thinking

Japanese students write a good deal in elementary school (where curricular freedom is allowed), composing book reports and expressive writing in Japanese. But once students reach junior high and then senior high school (where they put on uniforms, as if mobilizing for some arduous campaign), writing and personal expression—along with other indulgences of early childhood—give way to the rigors of preparing for the relentless economic world: Students follow a curriculum that is driven by entrance examinations. These exams are written and administered locally at each school and consist mainly of discrete-point multiple-choice questions in major academic subjects, including foreign languages. Analysis and personal expression have no place here: mastery of factual information, personal discipline, and endurance are the pedagogical and social goals that entrance exams uphold.

The central purpose of Japanese middle and secondary education is to prepare students for entrance exams leading to the next academic level. To this end, as cultural anthropologist Thomas Rohlen observes in his classic study of Japanese high schools, most classes consist of teachers lecturing on certifiably bland textbooks—predigested factual summaries of history, social science, ethics, religion, grammar—that take an "encyclopedic" and ostensibly politically neutral view of knowledge. Debate and discussion are rarely undertaken. While Japanese students learn to listen patiently, pay attention to fine details, and master immense amounts of factual information, they also learn to keep their opinions to themselves and to adopt passive and utilitarian attitudes toward their education. It is generally understood that if something does not help prepare for the entrance exams it is not worth attending to. As Rohlen concludes, "By implication, Japanese high school education provides no intellectual roots, it turns out students long on information and short on intellectual understanding" (267).

Behind Rohlen's measured assessment lie certain assumptions found in contemporary Western education—that intellectual growth proceeds from arguing through and sometimes against authoritative sources. This process usually involves composing one's ideas in writing, while practicing "intellectual honesty" by acknowledging the sources to which one is indebted. Japanese education, with its emphasis on the mastery of officially approved "factual" information, rests on very different views of learning and knowledge, leaving little time in the Japanese secondary curriculum for much attention to composition in the Western sense. The general neglect of writing instruction and practice—in both Japanese and English—is one important reason why plagiarism is "no big deal" in Japan.

In Japanese education, the biases toward discrete-point testing lead to a greater concern for another kind of academic dishonesty altogether: "Cheating" on exams, rather than plagiarism in written discourse, is considered the cardinal sin, and elaborate security procedures are taken to prevent it— among them the legendary secrecy in the process of exam construction by the faculty at each school and university; and then, on the days of entrance-exam testing, the systematic seating of students in long ranks and files in vast lecture halls, with exam takers carefully identified and placed at a suitable distance from each other to forestall copying. Ironically, the English reading passages in many such entrance exams have often been lifted from sources published in the West, without attribution or compensation to their authors. Violating international copyright law causes far less concern than maintaining security throughout the process of local production and on-site administration of entrance exams—in a yearly ritual which, incidentally, is highly profitable for many Japanese universities.

The Undergraduate Interlude:
Further Friction between Eastern and Western Conventions

One might innocently assume that something like "freshman English" would bring Japanese undergraduates up to some expected "university-level" of written discourse, compensating them quickly for the lack of intellectual development in their secondary education. While understandable, this expectation misses one of the fundamental truths about Japanese university life that is largely unknown in the West: High school students may cram furiously for "exam hell," but the subsequent period between college admission and graduation amounts to a rare time in a Japanese person's life when relaxation and some measure of choice are permitted. In effect, even at the most prestigious institutions, attending a Japanese university is a four-year vacation.

The expectation that Japanese college freshmen will suddenly become infused with intellectual vigor also reveals a failure to grasp the underlying Japanese assumptions about the cognitive and psychological development of individuals. These assumptions are, in effect, the undercurrents that inform Japanese education from junior high onward; they are at least as powerful as the economic and pedagogical forces noted earlier. Students are not asked to express their opinions in writing because it is assumed that they have no right to an opinion. They are *koohai,* or subordinates, in the complex hierarchy of

Japanese society and must defer to their *sempai,* their seniors, whose authority derives largely from the fact that they are simply older. In Japan, one earns the right to an opinion slowly, literally over decades during which one is constantly reminded of his or her subordinate position (Morrone, July 1996).

As Rohlen explains, Japanese students are asked to develop no more than "diligence in the mastery of facts" because "expressive and critical skills generally emerge later and progress gradually throughout adulthood" (245). The Japanese assume that critical judgment cannot be developed in school but will only appear as one is tested by the realities of the workplace over the course of many years of hard-won experience (267–68). By extension, then, it would be absurd (or, as it were, very "un-Japanese") to ask students to express original views or to question the opinion of recognized authorities. Students are expected to internalize the views of authorities, not to distinguish their own supposedly "original" thinking from the opinions of experts.

Not surprisingly, the Japanese university curriculum does not encourage much independent writing or critical thinking. The lecture method and classes of forty or more students in most subjects, including foreign languages, remain common, and evaluation turns on the mastery of factual information. American professors in business and social science at my university have told me that they devise assignments that cannot be plagiarized—that is, ones that do not require outside documentation. When questioned, they explained that if they did not frame assignments in this way, they could expect much of the submitted writing to be reproduced unchanged from published sources.

In contrast to this pragmatic approach, teachers who try to observe such Western conventions as the authorial ownership of words and ideas find themselves at odds with an academic culture that does not value those conventions very highly. One American colleague, a Harvard-educated sociologist, said that she once tried to explain to a Japanese undergraduate why the student's copying of an article was "inappropriate and did not constitute an original idea or individual research." She reported that "the student showed shame, not because he was 'caught' but because he hadn't realized that his method of doing a research paper was 'flawed.' He acted as if he had done the directions wrong—and this could have reflected badly on me" (Morrone, February 1996). The story illustrates the dilemma Western educators face in the collision of Eastern and Western assumptions about the nature of knowledge and research methodology.

Usually the writing assignments of Japanese undergraduates do not approach Western levels of university discourse until the fourth year, when students may elect to write a "graduation thesis." At that time they receive some instruction and guidance in the conventions of developing a focused argument and supporting it with documented sources. A metaphor that two of my Japanese colleagues independently used to characterize the prescribed Japanese undergraduate writing process was that of a "patchwork." One of

these colleagues, who earned an EdD in the United States, drew on her experience as both a student and an instructor at Japanese universities to describe
the way Japanese undergraduates are asked to write: "Students are supposed
to show how well they can understand several books and digest them in a report or a paper. They aren't asked for original ideas or opinions. They are
simply asked to show a beautiful patchwork." She noted that "as long as you
mention all the books in your bibliography, you can present the ideas from
the books as if they were yours, especially if your patchwork is beautiful"
(Furuya). The acceptable blurring of distinctions between the students'
sources and their own writing suggests that knowledge exists to be appropriated, assimilated, and internalized.

The same assimilative process can be seen in the education of young
Japanese in the arts, according to Merry White, a Harvard sociologist spe-
cializing in Japanese education. Many Japanese students from elementary
school through university attain high degrees of proficiency and creativity in
the modern fine arts as well as in the older Japanese arts—traditional folk music, dance, painting, flower-arranging, and martial arts. For each, laborious effort in the "precise imitation of the master" is considered the necessary and
only way to excellence (80).

As an illustration, a Japanese colleague recalled that in her study of the
shamisen, a traditional Japanese stringed instrument, her instructor had ex-
horted the class to "steal" the teacher's technique, using the previously mentioned verb *nusumu* for "taking someone else's personal property." This kind
of "stealing" was officially endorsed as the proper way to learn. My colleague
said that she tried to "steal," but that it was difficult. All she could do was "imitate." It might require years of practice before one successfully "steals" the
technique to the point of attaining *gei* ("accomplishment in performance")
and becomes a "creative artist" with an "original way" (Kinoshita). Such unexpected reversals of Western expectations about creativity and theft—or, if
you will, plagiarism—take us once more "through the looking glass."

Japanese Graduate School and Beyond:
In-Groups and Shared Intellectual Property

In another reversal of expectations, a certain amount of plagiarism is "not only
acceptable but necessary" at the graduate level of Japanese university work.
Japanese graduate students are apprenticed to their master professors in what
is essentially a life-long relationship between *koohai* and *sempai,* juniors and
seniors. According to one colleague, "In the case of a graduate student–teacher
relationship, it is not uncommon for the graduate student to produce work for
the professor and put the professor's name on it" (Morrone, February 1996).

Westerners might easily misconstrue such a relationship as exploitive and
intellectually dishonest. Viewed from a Japanese perspective, however, it is

neither. Membership and participation in a professor's group are voluntary and depend on a process of reciprocal giving and receiving—whatever one receives, one must give back in some form. Very pragmatically, individuals choose to reciprocate as a way of keeping everyone else happy with them. The master professor, for example, imparts information and guidance—gifts that must be reciprocated—and then doles out duties to his subordinates. As a kind of gratitude, they do their work and put his name on it. But as the ideas presumably originated with the master, ascribing the entire work to him is, in a way, acknowledging the source; it is not really plagiarism on the master's part (Morrone, December 1996).

A key to understanding the dynamism of such a group is the Japanese term, *uchi.* The members of a master professor's group all belong to the same *uchi,* or "inner circle": Their relations are governed by a polar tension found in all societies and identified by the Japanese as *uchi* ("inside") and *soto* ("outside"). Takeo Doi, the renowned Japanese psychiatrist and social commentator, explains that *uchi* refers mainly "to the group to which the individual belongs" and should not be confused with the Western notion of individual privacy. "Little value is attributed to the individual's private realm as distinct from the group. . . . [T]he Western idea of freedom has been slow to take root in Japan" (42).

Nonetheless, *uchi* as represented by a master professor's inner circle is not the repressive, impersonal arrangement that Westerners might imagine. In a way that is typically Japanese, *uchi* arises out of human feeling—most particularly *amae* ("dependent love" or "indulgent love"), which, according to Doi, dominates all aspects of Japanese social life. *Amae,* an idealized sense of "oneness" that is "typically embodied in the parent-child relationship," endows members of such quasi-parental in-groups as a professor's circle with *giri,* or "socially contracted interdependence" (Doi, 37–41).There are no barriers or holding back within the in-group, though *between uchi* and *soto*— between those on the "inside" and those on the "outside"—the barriers can be great indeed. Within the secure *uchi* of a professor's group, however, intellectual property does not have individual ownership. It is shared, much as a family shares its personal property for the general good of all, through an elaborate system of reciprocity for favors bestowed and returned. In such an enclosed paternalistic circle, how can there be plagiarism when one's work is never done completely independently and when ideas effectively belong to everyone and no one?

Broader Cultural Implications of Plagiarism in Japanese Education

One of the great virtues of the Japanese, their prodigious "lust for knowledge" has historically—and paradoxically—laid the Japanese open to charges of intellectual property theft and plagiarism. For centuries, the Japanese have

freely adopted foreign words, writing systems, religions, technology, and
social institutions. At times, however, the Japanese proclivity of foreign borrowing goes too far, as in the case of some Japanese professors who effectively plagiarize foreign texts in the process of translating them into Japanese.
Despite the generally tolerant view I have taken in this discussion, one could
argue that such Japanese academics need to act more responsibly within the
global community of scholars and should pay more attention to international
copyright law. Nonetheless, even the instances of overzealous "borrowing"
hinted at by so many of my informants can be understood in the context of
centuries-old practices by which the Japanese have invariably "Japanized"
foreign products and ideas, assimilating them into the distinctively Japanese
way of doing things.

One can, for example, trace the source of the Japanese entrance examinations to the Confucian civil-service exams of imperial China, devised nearly
two thousand years ago to select candidates on the basis of merit rather than
social class. Rohlen notes that nearly four hundred years ago, the Japanese se-
lectively imported Confucian thought for the distinctly "moral" purposes of
social and educational reform. The Tokugawa rulers sought to organize all of
Japanese society in line with the Confucian metaphor of the proper family,
"correctly ordered by differences of function and authority, with filial piety the
central virtue." Similarly, they hoped to structure education "with the classics
as guides and daily conduct in the school as the mirror" (48–49).

Learning in the Confucian schools established in Edo Period Japan was
considered properly to be "the process of submitting to and mastering the wisdom of the sages." But the Japanese rejected Confucianism's tradition of theoretical dispute and endorsed instead a single correct way of understanding
the Confucian heritage. As Rohlen explains, "Thus, learning was not built on
the assumption that knowledge awaits discovery. Truth was known and was
contained in the classic tradition. Scholars still discreetly debated their interpretations, but for students there was only right or wrong in learning the meaning and significance of the classics. . . . Independence of thought was not
regularly rewarded or encouraged" (49–50).

The Confucian patterns of social and educational institutions established
nearly four hundred years ago have persisted into contemporary times. Japanese education at all levels retains not only its debt to the "conserving" tradition of Confucian thought, but also the distinctly Japanese value of deflecting
conflict. Knowledge is considered static, something to be mastered through
arduous study and preferably memorized, because of the intrinsic moral benefits such discipline imparts. Original thinking should be avoided. As Rohlen
observes of modern Japanese education, "What seems unaltered from past to
present is the emphasis on a disciplined apprenticeship. . . . The student is
trained first to be a patient, persistent worker, a good listener, one preoccu-
pied with details and correctness of form" (269).

Rohlen's review of the centuries-old currents of Japanese education helps to explain why plagiarism does not make much sense to the Japanese as a moral issue. They have been educated to think of morality in ways that are fundamentally different from the common Western view: that is, it is proper to mistrust or discount one's own opinions; it is good and virtuous to study, memorize, and imitate proper models; and it is necessary to defer one's own judgments to the consensus of the group. Given such views of learning and morality—that students should, as a matter of correctness, defer to the opinions and models provided by received wisdom—the tendency to copy freely from published sources seems only natural. When students are taught that there is a single correct answer to be obtained from an authority above and beyond their own judgment, they can be expected to seek it out.

Toward a Far-East Asian Perspective on Plagiarism

A number of native Japanese academics whom I interviewed downplayed the question of whether Japanese students plagiarize. But when it came to foreign students with whom they had worked at one time, the same academics were much quicker to pass judgment. From several, I heard almost identical remarks: "Those Chinese students, now *they* plagiarize!" One might consider the possibility of national denial and projection at work here, but there may also be, as there clearly is among some Western educators, an unreflective sense that "the way *we* do things is the single proper way. Other cultures are the ones that are out of line." As Ballard and Clanchy argue in "Assessment by Misconception," and as I have suggested earlier in this essay, "different epistemologies are the bedrock of the different cultures, yet they are so taken for granted, each so assumed to be 'universal' that neither the teachers nor the students can recognize that they are standing on different ground" (21).

Ballard and Clanchy describe the cultural conflicts between the faculty at Australian National University (ANU) (who hold Western rhetorical and epistemological expectations) and the "overseas" students, mainly from China and Southeast Asia who comprise twenty percent of the student body. The situation recalls the dilemma of Western teachers at Japanese universities. For the native English-speaking instructors at ANU who are, in effect, representatives of an "extending" rhetorical culture, "the dominant tendency is to urge students toward an ultimately speculative approach to learning, to encourage them to question, to search for new ways of looking at the world around them." By contrast, for the Asian students from a more "conserving" rhetorical culture, "the traditions of scholarship attest to knowledge as wisdom. It is the student's duty to learn this knowledge, to acquire this wisdom as it is handed on by wise and respected teachers" (Ballard and Clanchy 22–24).

The resulting stereotype of the plagiarizing Asian student arises from this conflict of cultures and leads instructors, often not fully aware of cultural differences, to punish students for doing in writing what they have been trained to do in their home countries. Ballard and Clanchy argue for greater awareness and tolerance, so as to avoid "misconceptions based on fundamentally differing cultural approaches to knowledge, education, and the whole enterprise of assessment" (34).

In a similar spirit, G. B. Deckert, a professor at Hong Kong Baptist College, reviews the research that explains Chinese students' "so-called plagiaristic tendencies" as a reflection of "established Chinese literary conventions." Deckert concludes, however, in light of his own experience of teaching Hong Kong college freshmen to write research papers, that "most Chinese students overuse source material through an innocent and ingrained habit of giving back information exactly as they find it. They are proverbial rote memorizers or recyclers" (132–33). Deckert, like Ballard and Clanchy, argues that one must consider the differences in "scholarly traditions"—the Western tradition's tendency to honor a person's "divergent thinking," as opposed to the Chinese tradition's emphasis of "close allegiance to a few acknowledged authorities with resulting convergence of perspective and greater social harmony" (Deckert 132).

The Changing Face in the Distant Mirror

Ballard and Clanchy observe that for several decades Robert Kaplan has drawn the attention of applied linguists to the ways that "different cultures" produce "different rhetorical styles." Yet, as the authors lament, "his seminal insights seldom percolate through to academic colleagues working in other disciplines" (20). Teachers, especially of composition and foreign languages, must do more to inform themselves about the cultural differences between themselves and their students—differences that left unexamined can give rise to charges of "plagiarism" and "intellectual dishonesty," when the disagreements usually arise from different theories of knowledge, patterns of discourse, and cultural values. Teachers must also acknowledge the contradictions within their own cultures that, for example, permit instructors to violate copyright laws by photocopying published material for classroom use while becoming exercised, as Deckert writes, "when ESL students, who represent different ideals and educational experiences and who lack confidence in using English, violate Western standards of scholarship" (132).

Gazing "through *and beyond* the looking glass" can help us avoid culturally insensitive labels—"plagiarism" being one. But teachers might also do well to look squarely into the distant mirror that arises during encounters with students from different cultures and discourse traditions. For in that mirror we may see, possibly for the first time, our own unexamined biases, inconsistencies, double standards, culturally determined preconceptions, misunderstandings, denials and projections—all reflected back at us with unforgiving clarity. Nevertheless, with effort and commitment, we may also see a changing face, a sign of the inner transformation that an active and growing mind is capable of—the defining quality of a good teacher in any culture.

The New Abolitionism Comes to Plagiarism

Rebecca Moore Howard

In her 1991 *Textual Carnivals* and more recently in a 1995 *Composition Forum* article, Susan Miller insists that the function of composition pedagogy is to perpetuate an intellectual class system, to maintain distinctions between those of "high" literacy (the professors and students of literature) and those of "low" literacy (the instructors and students of composition). Miller's thesis, though controversial, has gained a number of adherents, including Sharon Crowley, who would avert intellectual hierarchy by abolishing the requirement that students take composition service courses. Crowley's proposal is offered first in "A Personal Essay on Freshman English" and later in "Composition's Ethic of Service." Endorsing her proposal and noting its support among leading composition scholars, Robert Connors (1996) provides the label "the New Abolitionism."

Even the extreme measure of abolishing the requirement for composition service courses would not by itself erase the hierarchical effects of composition instruction, for those effects are evident throughout the college curriculum, not just in required freshman composition courses. They are in fact evident in composition theory, even in scholarship on collaboration that purports to undo authorial hierarchy. Much of collaborative theory presupposes a positive-negative binary of collaboration versus plagiarism, a presupposition that is inherently hierarchical, perpetuating an authorial "high" and "low." That this binary includes at the "low," transgressive pole not only the purchase of term papers but also patchwriting (rearranging and slightly altering phrases and sentences from a source text) means that the binary operates to *prevent* students from gaining access to the authorial "high." The notion of plagiarism, in other words, is an important means whereby composition studies fulfills its charge of maintaining intellectual hierarchy. As long as we criminalize patchwriting by including it in the counterauthorial category of plagiarism, it does not matter whether we are requiring composition service courses or, indeed, teaching composition in any form. "Service" courses, in their gatekeeping function, are only one symptom of the hierarchical baggage of composition studies. When patchwriting is included in its purview, the juridical installation of plagiarism can carry the hierarchical load very well all on its own. At present, composition scholarship offers very little impediment to its continued progress.

Exploring the opposition of liberal culture to composition instruction, David R. Russell describes composition service courses as part of "democratic reform" (133). But even when "democratic" composition prevails, our adherence to received notions of plagiarism amount to a liberal-culture colonization of composition studies. We can be overtly engaged in liberatory pedagogy while unwittingly perpetuating intellectual hierarchy.

Although contemporary critical theory asserts that all writing is collaborative, composition scholarship's treatments of collaboration characteristically assume the possibility of an autonomous writer and depict collaboration as an option that the autonomous subject may elect. More tellingly, almost all composition scholarship requires the student to function autonomously when interacting with written texts. Collaboration, in other words, occurs between writers or between one writer and another or between writer and reader—but it must not occur between writer and text. Thus plagiarism is represented as the perverted form of collaboration. Even in the face of critical theory that asserts published writers' plagiarism as a positive counteractive to oppressive discursive regimes,[1] students' plagiarism is defined in negative terms, characterized as the textual recourse of the intellectual Other.

Modernism has always entertained a nontransgressive possibility for plagiarism—the heroic plagiarist described by T. S. Eliot: "Immature poets imitate; mature poets steal; bad poets deface what they take, and good poets make it into something better, or at least something different" (1932). Even Thomas Mallon, who devotes his book *Stolen Words* to denouncing plagiarists as well as those who do not denounce plagiarism, acknowledges that our society condones plagiarism if the writer "makes what he takes completely his" (25). Because Mallon dislikes what he calls "Critical Theory" (69) and this "squishily relativistic, post-*in loco parentis* era of campus life" (99), it is a safe bet that he would not follow scholars like Marilyn Randall and Ellen McCracken in celebrating postmodern appropriation. Yet Mallon does seem to countenance, however wryly, Eliot's notion of heroic plagiarism. As does Dennis Baron (for whom Mallon is a significant source). Baron's light-hearted *Guide to Home Language Repair* has some fun with the subject of plagiarism. It also puzzles over the contradictions of plagiarism. While Baron concurs with Mallon that plagiarists should be brought to justice (86–87), he also asserts that the pursuit of plagiarists is a "no-win situation" (84). Pointing out the disturbing fact that it is students and not professional writers whose plagiarism is punished, he concludes, "I do not propose that we need to rethink the greatness of King or Jefferson or even

Coleridge—theirs is a Teflon greatness that mere plagiarism cannot tarnish" (87). Keith D. Miller has devoted a quantity of scholarly effort to establishing that King's plagiarism is far too complex—and valuable—to be dismissed with the neo-Aristotelian categorization of "plagiarist." Baron takes a milder stance, asserting only that some plagiarists are of too much cultural value for us to dismiss them because of their plagiarism. Miller, like Randall and McCracken, offers arguments for the positive value of what could, in traditional terms, be rejected as scurrilous plagiarism. Mallon would no doubt dismiss these arguments as "squishily relativistic." While Baron subscribes to Mallon's definitions of plagiarism, definitions that accord exactly with the representations of autonomous authorship that have prevailed since the critical work of Edward Young and William Wordsworth, he does not believe that they set up mutually exclusive categories from which ready adjudication can be enacted; nor does he believe that plagiarism functions as a default mechanism for rejecting the plagiarist.

In this mix of ideas about authorship, the perspectives of critical theory, which variously describes plagiarism as a cultural arbitrary that functions to maintain sociointellectual hierarchy, have become commonplace in intellectual circles. Certainly these perspectives prevail in the Intellectual Property Caucus of the Conference on College Composition and Communication. Yet these perspectives—which amount to beliefs—have had little effect on composition pedagogy. Composition studies has not entertained the possibility that students would number among the mature, good poets who might engage in T. S. Eliot's heroic plagiarism. Nor has composition studies represented students' plagiarism as a potential commentary upon and revision of received notions of authorship. Nor has composition studies proposed that students' written work is so valuable that their plagiarism should be overlooked. Composition students are what Susan Miller, following Stallybrass and White, describes as the "grotesque": differentiated from (and ranked below) the "classical beauty" of great authors like T. S. Eliot, Martin Luther King, Jr., and the writers described by Ellen McCracken and Marilyn Randall.

Hence composition studies has been slow to imagine that there is, in fact, a category of positive plagiarism for students, a category in which their plagiarism might not be transgressive, might not be a mark of their textual Otherness. That category would be "patchwriting"—"copying from a source text and then deleting some words, altering grammatical structures, or plugging in one-for-one synonym-substitutes" (Howard 1993, 233).

Patchwriting is customarily regarded as a subset of the category of plagiarism. Plagiarism, in turn, is a subset of the category of academic dishonesty. Hence patchwriting is, by virtue of its inclusion in the category of plagiarism, a dishonest, transgressive act. Plagiarism, when committed by students, is bad. Period. Witness Augustus M. Kolich: "[P]lagiarists deceive, they are unworthy of our shared virtue, and they are not generally teachable or, worse, have refused teaching. Once they plagiarize an essay, their problems are essentially moral and not pedagogical" (147). Edith Skom says that plagiarism is lying, because it announces the "mind's grasp" of material that the mind does not actually grasp. The teacher is outraged because it is she, individually, who has been lied to. "Discourse is at the center of the academic life and anything that seriously damages it deserves our indignation" (166–167).

Plagiarism is lying. Plagiarism is deception. And patchwriting is a subset of plagiarism. Hence copying from a source text and then deleting some words, altering grammatical structures, or plugging in one-for-one synonym substitutes is lying, is deceit. The only alternative is to regard it as a function of the writer's ignorance of citation conventions. Thus the teacher has the option of punishing the plagiarist, or of instructing him or her in the niceties of citation.

Now, let us do a little bit of soul-baring here. Who among us has not patchwritten? Who does not still do it from time to time? Lying? Deceit? Ignorance of citation conventions? Patchwriting is a textual activity that we all take part in. Do we do so in moments of moral lapse? In moments when the *MLA Handbook* (Achtert and Garibaldi) is not at hand? Or does it sound more plausible that we do it in moments of cognitive difficulty? As I think about my own excursions into patchwriting, I recognize that it almost always occurs when I do not really understand what I am reading. Hence my reading notes (I am one of those compulsives who writes abstracts of everything she reads) from my first encounter with Foucault's "What Is an Author?" are characterized by (1) patchwriting and (2) absence. What I wrote during that first reading is almost exclusively patchwriting. Moreover, there are substantial passages of "What Is an Author?" on which I took no notes at all; I was simply stumped. For me, patchwriting during that first reading of "What Is an Author?" was a way of making sense of wildly unfamiliar material. The year was 1991, and I was a fairly new reader of postmodern theory of authorship.

Rereading Foucault's essay several years later, I revised my abstract. It now contains less patchwriting and fewer absences. I know more about the field of authorship theory, and I have now read several more of Foucault's texts. Both the author and the field are less strange to me. Fortunately for me, in 1991 there were no teachers requiring me to write papers about "What Is an Author?" Hence I was not forced to patchwrite publicly; my patchwriting was confined to my private reading notes.

Or was it? Bakhtin's perspective is important here. Of the many compositionists who have embraced his representation of writing on the borders, George L. Dillon's recapitulation most resonates with my own point of view: "Finding one's language, one's voice . . . is not finding something which is out there, or in here, but is forged dialogically in response to the already written and in anticipation of the hearer's responsive word—it is forged on the borderline" (70–71). Can we, from this perspective, ever *not* patchwrite? The answer, of course, is "no." Again, Dillon: "Finding one's voice is . . . not just an emptying and purifying oneself of other's words . . . but also an admitting, an adopting, an embracing of filiations, communities, and discourses" (71). We all patchwrite, all the time. There is no "my" "own" language; there is only the shared language, in its shared combinations and possibilities. When I believe I am not patchwriting, I am simply doing it so expertly that the seams are no longer visible—or I am doing it so unwittingly that I cannot cite my sources. Indeed, as Susan Stewart points out, if we were to comprehensively cite our sources, we would be involved in what she calls "a full (and necessarily impossible) history of the writer's subjectivity" (25).

Students' puzzled questions about plagiarism are not as ignorant as we might like to believe them to be. When I am explaining plagiarism, quotation, and citation, there is always a student who looks at me in exasperation and says, "But that means I have to cite every word I write!" Right. It does. Because every word every one of us writes is patchwritten.

So we get into all sorts of crazy guidelines and rules for how to differentiate plagiarism from not-plagiarism, requiring the pretense (1) that we are not all patchwriting all the time and that (2) there is some sort of line that the initiated perceive between plagiarism and not-plagiarism. Once you are inside, you will see it. "When you're older, you'll understand." Humbug. So we try to quantify it. Not repeating "more than three words in a row," Alice Drum reminds us, is "one popular formula for how to avoid plagiarism" (242). Ridiculous.

Worse yet, we try to pretend that those who do patchwrite are either people who do not understand citation conventions or people who are unethical. This binary set of choices allows us, as teachers, to tell students that patchwriting, a means whereby everyone encounters, enters, and appropriates discourse, is transgressive—which amounts to our telling them that learning is bad—which amounts to our telling them that they must always remain on the bottom of the textual hierarchy. Learning, we tell them, will move them up the textual ladder. Yet by outlawing the learning that is patchwriting, we are obstructing rather than facilitating that movement.

The classification of patchwriting, then, affirms composition's continuing place in the Susan Miller account of the sociology of textuality. In *Rescuing the Subject* Miller declares, "Traditional literary freshman English courses are given on a model of 'failed authorship. . . .'" (12). The "authorship" that is "failed"—the measure to which the student writers of freshman English cannot attain—is one whose history Miller traces in *Rescuing the Subject*. She observes that the printing press more than the late-medieval rise of individualism is responsible for modern notions of the author.

What the printing press made possible was writers' sustaining a living without benefit of noble patrons. With wide distribution of texts and with a larger literate public, the conditions for independent authorship were nearly in place.[2] All that remained was establishing authors' rights in copy. This was not a simple task. The theology of Martin Luther, for example, would favor free access to texts; and English tradition established a firm Crown control of publication.[3] To shift right in copy to authors, who could then sell that right to publishers, required not only the technological and social conditions already sketched, but also certain ideological premises. An important component was provided by John Locke's assertion that a man owns his body and its labors. As soon as writing was defined as labor, one of those necessary ideological premises was in place.

But the one that is most significant for the place of plagiarism in intellectual hierarchy today is the premise that the writer is capable of producing an original text, one of a kind. This premise was supplied energetically by a succession of eighteenth- and nineteenth-century writers. Edward Young's is an early and influential statement:

> The mind of a man of Genius is a fertile and pleasant field, pleasant as *Elysium,* and fertile as *Tempe;* it enjoys a perpetual Spring. Of that Spring, *Originals* are the fairest Flowers: *Imitations* are of quicker growth, but fainter bloom. *Imitations* are of two kinds; one of Nature, one of Authors: The first we call *Originals,* and confine the term *Imitation* to the second. I shall not enter into the curious enquiry of what is, or is not, strictly speaking, *Original,* content with what all must allow, that some Compositions are more so than others; and the more they are so, I say, the better. *Originals* are, and ought to be, great Favourites, for they are great Benefactors; they extend the Republic of Letters, and add a new province to its dominion. . . . .(9–10)

Young's assertion of the possibility of original writing, and his privileging of it, became a tenet of nineteenth-century literary theory. That tenet, in turn, became valuable during the dark hours in which readership in the West expanded *too* much, when the plebeian tastes of the masses and their voracious appetite for newspapers and "little reading" threatened to topple the long-standing intellectual hierarchy of the privileged. No longer was intellectual hierarchy marked by one's ability to read and write; practically everyone could do that. And the newly educated masses were not kneeling at the alter of the esoteric texts written by the traditionally literate; instead, they were subscribing to dime novels. During those dark hours, it became necessary to assert a hierarchy of literacies.[4] The high-literacy writers were original; the low, imitative. Lester Faigley describes the operationalizing of this binary: A 1931 report issued by a CEEB commission declared, "true originality will be the result of discriminating and vigorous perception and thought" (118). Clearly, says Faigley, this group was dedicated to the "preservation of an asymmetry of literary taste." They sorted the "'intellectually weak' from those with the 'power of reflection'" and valorized the "spirit of competition," which is "what makes the commission's notion of self a particularly American version, one that is still with us today" (119). And during those same dark hours, it became necessary to find pedagogical ways of civilizing the newly literate masses. Composition instruction was born. Its writers were the low, the imitative. They were assigned to study not newspapers, little reading, and dime novels, but the esoteric texts of the highly literate. Attention to the correct written vernacular, Susan Miller explains in *Textual Carnivals,* made writing a useful vehicle for evaluation (56). "As in traditional Christianity, the metaphoric precedent for established literary study, a conviction of sin is necessary for sanctifying redemption to have force" (58).

Nowhere is that sin's redemption by pedagogical discipline more obvious than in composition's continuing representations of students' patchwriting. Not only is patchwriting classified as plagiarism and thus as academic dishonesty, but commentators' language consistently calls up metaphors of sin, immorality, and transgression.[5] Even when attributing patchwriting to an ignorance of citation conventions, the commentator will often allude to "academic integrity." Hence when in *Voice of Deliverance* Keith D. Miller describes Martin Luther King, Jr.'s textual strategies as "voice merging," he strives mightily to avoid the word *plagiarism.* Instead he uses words like "intertwine" (6), "borrow" (3,7), "echo" (4), "intertextual" (55,81), "replaying" (78), "overlapping" (81), and "voice merging" (4) or says that King "did not acknowledge" (3) or "failed to acknowledge" (5) sources. Only when he announces the Stanford findings concerning King's dissertation does he use the word "plagiarism" (62). The loaded word then reappears on pages 125, 128, and 191, each time with Miller's obvious reluctance. The very use of *plagiarism,* with all its attendant common premises about authorship, voids Miller's thesis; hence his onomastic gyrations are essential to his argument.

Plagiarism, in the modernist account that derives from the literary theories of Edward Young and his successors, is a social problem. But a social problem, Murray Edelman reminds us, "is not a verifiable entity but a construction that furthers ideological interests" (18):

> Problems come into discourse and therefore into existence as reinforcements of ideologies, not simply because they are there or because they are important for wellbeing. They signify who are virtuous and useful and who are dangerous or inadequate, which actions will be rewarded and which penalized. . . . .They are critical in determining who exercise authority and who accept it. (12)

Composition studies' maintenance of the notion of plagiarism would, in Edelman's framework, function not only to support the intellectual hierarchy that gave birth to composition studies but would also function to supply an ongoing rationale for the presence of composition teachers in the academy today. Imagine a composition program that treated patchwriting not as an ethical transgression subject to dismissal from college, but as a pedagogical issue on the moral plane of the comma splice. Imagine a writing program that responded to patchwriting not with punishment but with instruction in the source material. Imagine a writing program that treated the patchwriter not as an ethical transgressor nor even as a bumbler, but as a student laudably striving to learn. How much would the college's negative scrutiny of that program increase? And imagine a composition teacher who freely acknowledged that she routinely patchwrites, and who taught her students how to do it skillfully. With how much respect would her students regard her, and how easy would she find her case for promotion and retention? Would she, in Edelman's words, be regarded as "virtuous and useful," or would she, along with her plagiarizing students, be classified as "dangerous or inadequate"? The possibility that a writer collaborates with texts, appropriating and manipulating their language and ideas as a means of understanding the texts and gaining membership in the community that values those texts, substantially undermines the hierarchical discourse regime that separates error-ridden students from perfected published texts.

Revising our responses to and representations of students' patchwriting is not an easy undertaking. It requires that we acknowledge our notions of authorship as regulatory fictions rather than as transcendent signifieds. That recognition places on us the additional task of responding authentically to students' patchwriting. Instead of the easy solutions of punishing it or teaching citation conventions in response to it, teachers are plunged into the arduous engagement of students' learning processes, their understanding of source texts, their manipulation of language. And then there are the consequences of such pedagogy: decriminalizing patchwriting is a direct contradiction of the "charge" of composition instruction. Composition teachers who treat patchwriting as a normal part of even an expert writing process are opening yet another gate in the Great Standards Debate. Now we will not only be eschewing our duty to teach grammatical correctness, but we will also be Allowing Plagiarism.

Such a move, therefore, brings even more pressure to bear upon an often beleaguered profession. Robert Connors describes the cycles of reformism and abolitionism that have characterized institutional attitudes towards composition studies since the nineteenth-century inception of freshman composition at Harvard. New Abolitionism represents an interruption of these cycles, because its proponents are speaking in students' interests rather than their own. Not requiring first-year composition would, in their vision, serve liberatory rather than hierarchical purposes. But Connors surveys the causes of previous cycles of reform, in which abolition of freshman composition is eschewed in favor of reforming the course. These reformist cycles, he observes, are instigated by a new media-touted literacy crisis; a "serious or lasting war"; or protection of the freshman requirement by those who teach the courses (1996, 62).

My concern with the categorization of patchwriting as plagiarism parallels those of New Abolitionism. Can we engage in "liberatory" pedagogy when the assumptions driving our practice are hierarchical? New Abolitionism offers a way out—by refusing to serve. It functions as a sort of conscientious objector to intellectual hierarchy. Refusing to participate does not, however, diminish intellectual hierarchy; rather, it buys into the binary arguments of the dominant, in which one's choices are to succumb or secede.

While I respect and applaud the premises of New Abolitionism, its argument is inductive, not deductive. At present I am inclined to pursue different conclusions: that we *can* productively challenge and revise the dominant structure. Intellectual hierarchy is neither unitary nor stable. The challenge of composition studies is to find and honor worthy premises within the dominant structure, and to interrogate and revise others. One of those "others" is the classification of patchwriting as plagiarism, as an ethical transgression or a form of pre-authorship or failed authorship. Revising such premises requires that we not founder on the shoals of the Great Standards Debate: to offer a fresh vision of patchwriting must not lend itself to critics' arguments that we are (once again) abrogating our gatekeeping responsibilities. But surely composition scholars, with their skills in managing counterevidence and attending to audience, are up to the job.

Notes

1. Marilyn Randall's scholarship is notable in its pursuit of this thesis. See, for example, "Appropriate(d) Discourse: Plagiarism and Decolonization." *New Literary History* 22 (1991): 525–41.

2. Elizabeth Eisenstein provides a comprehensive account of the influence of the printing press on authorship, and Martha Woodmansee (1994) focuses on the complexities of an expanded reading public in the West.

3. Mark Rose offers a succinct and accessible history of English copyright.

4. John Carey describes in detail this passage of Western literacy, and Peter Stallybrass and Allon White provide its background.

5. As I have argued in "The Gendered Plagiarist," these metaphors are grounded in the maintenance of gender hierarchy as well as intellectual hierarchy. Plagiarism as a cultural notion—and especially patchwriting when culturally identified as plagiarism—affirms the superiority of the masculine intellect.

Literary and Theoretical Definitions

The Illusion of Modernist Allusion and the Politics of Postmodern Plagiarism

Kevin J. H. Dettmar

Badyr looked at his father. "The war has been over this many years—
I thought guards would no longer be necessary."
   "There are still many bandits in the mountains," his father said.
   "Bandits?"
   "Yes," his father said. "Those who slip across our borders to steal,
rape and kill.'

—Harold Robbins, *The Pirate*

Look up *modernism* in any handy literary reference source, and *allusion* will not be far behind. Though the technique of allusion dates back to the earliest days of English poetry, it was elevated to the status of a master trope in modernist fiction and verse: Weldon Thornton's *Allusions in "Ulysses"* and Don Gifford's *"Ulysses" Annotated* together dwarf Joyce's monumental text; and T. S. Eliot, with the book publication of *The Waste Land,* seems to have felt it incumbent on him to supply his own notes for his densely allusive poem.

   Eliot also provides the best-known short defense of the modernist penchant for allusion, in his review essay "The Metaphysical Poets," where he writes: "Our civilization comprehends great variety and complexity, and this variety and complexity, playing upon a refined sensibility, must produce various and complex results. The poet must become more allusive, more indirect, in order to force, to dislocate if necessary, language into his meaning" (Eliot 1975, 65). Eliot here is almost single-handedly responsible for making allusion part of the official confessional statement of modernist literary practice; in one seemingly casual stroke of the pen, he helped to institutionalize a modernist allusive method, and not coincidentally, did so just one year before the appearance of his own allusive tour de force, *The Waste Land.*

   Allusion is, as Eliot puts it in his review of *Ulysses,* "a step toward making the modern world possible for art" (Eliot 1975, 178); but the success of allusion, as Eliot must at some level have realized but seems never to have admitted, depends always on its recognition by a properly educated readership. As the venerable Harmon and Holman *Handbook to Literature* puts it, allusion "seeks, by tapping the knowledge and memory of the reader, to secure a resonant emotional effect from the associations already existing in the reader's mind" (Harmon & Holman 14). Thus an allusion that is recognized *as* an allusion by the majority of a poem's readers—nudge-nudge, wink-wink—represents the closure of the circle of Tradition; as Eliot writes in "Tradition and the Individual Talent," "not only the best, but the most individual parts of [a poet's] work may be those in which the dead poets, his ancestors, assert their immortality most vigorously" (Eliot 1975, 38).

But what happens when an allusion is not recognized as an allusion by readers? Though modernist writers and theoreticians preferred that we not talk about either a writer's intention or his or her writing's effect—Wimsatt and Beardsley's intentional and affective fallacies, respectively—allusion is pretty difficult to analyze without considering both the writer's intention and the reader's consumption. A quick look at *The Waste Land* may help make this point. Traditionally, allusion has been cordoned off from other forms of textual appropriation—from pure quotation on the one side, and from plagiarism, or even piracy, on the other. Thus *The Waste Land* opens with a self-evident quotation, in Latin and Greek, from Petronius' *Satyricon;* Eliot had considered, earlier in the poem's composition, using a quotation from Conrad's *Heart of Darkness,* a stratagem to which he returned in the epigraph for "The Hollow Men." Though lacking quotation marks, the selection from Petronius is marked out as quotation rather than allusion both by its classical languages (clearly marking it as an "import") and in its positioning as the poem's epigraph—traditionally an honorific, quotational space.

The body of the poem, however, is a vertiginous mélange of quotation, allusion, and "original" writing; surely one of the most powerful effects of *The Waste Land* for a reader is this insistently disorienting quality. For instance in Section III, "The Fire Sermon," Eliot alludes to Edmund Spenser's *Prothalamion* with the line, "Sweet Thames, run softly till I end my song." For the reader who recognizes the line as Spenser's, and remembers its original context—a poem "in honour of the double mariage of the two Honorable & vertuous *Ladies, the Ladie* Elizabeth *and the Ladie* Katherine *Somerset,* Daughters to the right Honourable the Earle of Worcester"—the allusion does very specific cultural work; most important, it throws into deeply ironic relief Eliot's twentieth-century scene on the banks of the Thames, where "love" has been confused with the sterile, nearly anonymous sex of a summer's evening.

What of those readers, however, for whom Spenser's *Epithalamion* is not familiar? The poem, never one of Spenser's most popular, is today not included in the most popular college texts of Spenser's poetry; indeed, it is now best known precisely because of Eliot's allusive use of it, rather than for its having withstood on its own "the test of time." For the reader who does not recognize the line as an allusion, two responses are possible. The first would be simply to see the line as the work of Eliot and/or his muse—the spontaneous overflow of powerful emotion, recollected in tranquillity. If, however, the source is somehow discovered—and Eliot is assumed to be trying to hide his debt to Spenser—the line is neither original, quotation, nor allusion: it would be understood as plagiarism. For this hypothetical unsuspecting reader, the contextual clues of this plagiarism would be the same that often raise red flags in student writing: the passage calls attention to itself on stylistic grounds, as somehow not quite "fitting in" with the writing in which it's imbedded. In *The Waste Land,* the limpid, delicate line of Spenser's lives in a rather rough poetic neighborhood: "The river bears no empty bottles, sandwich papers, / Silk handkerchiefs, cardboard boxes, cigarette ends / Or other testimony of summer nights. The nymphs are departed" (Eliot 1964, 58). An allusion, according to the *Oxford English Dictionary,* is a "covert, implied, or indirect reference"; as an inevitable consequence, it will sometimes, by some readers, be misconstrued. A handful of critics over the years have argued that the inevitability of allusion's misfiring was perfectly acceptable to Eliot; allusions are, in this argument, a sort of land mine with which a poet peppers his text, keeping trespassers out—or if not keeping them out entirely, at least keeping Culture's secrets safe from the *hoi polloi.* The *cognoscenti,* of course, will recognize an allusion for what it is.

Modernist practice depends absolutely on the maintenance of firm boundaries between quotation, allusion, plagiarism, and piracy. Eliot himself evidenced no small anxiety, however, about these very borders; the notes he so carefully added to *The Waste Land,* for instance, can be read as a symptom of modernism's contamination anxiety, and Eliot himself, years after the fact, gave something like this explanation for appending the notes, claiming that he had "intended only to put down all the references for my quotations, with a view to spiking the guns of critics of my earlier poems who had accused me of plagiarism" (Eliot 1957, 121). Looking through contemporary criticism of Eliot's early poetry it is difficult to see who, exactly, he thought had leveled these charges; in fact, it is hard to know how seriously to take this line of Eliot's defense. But if his real intention was to limit the scope of intertextual play—to demarcate neatly his poem from the literature that infuses it, putting up a cordon sanitaire—notes are not the thing. Notes pretend that all sources can and will be noted, and that the author is able to map the network of intertextual relations that cut across his poem. This illusion of mastery of the intertext, however, is easily shattered; for no matter how fastidious the annotator, the intertext will always overflow its intentional references. Eliot's notes are not so much a result of some sense of scholarly responsibility, as he suggests, but rather an anxious (in Harold Bloom's sense) attempt to short-circuit suggestions of "influence." By indulging in conscious echo, in other words, one runs less risk of being accused of unconscious echo. That is the dream, anyway; as John Hollander's book *The Figure of Echo* makes clear, however, through his cataloging of presumably unconscious echoes of Milton, Tennyson, and Whitman, among others, it does not work terribly well.

Elizabeth Drew, for example, was the first to point out the unacknowledged "echo" in lines 266–76 of the second paragraph of *Heart of Darkness;* Eliot himself points to *Götterdämmerung* III, I, the song of Wagner's Rhinedaughters, as the (safely distant) source. Drew's argument, however, is convincing; and given Eliot's admiration of Conrad, it is altogether likely that Eliot's verse here has been secretly colored by Conrad's prose. Since it was not identified by Eliot, must we call this allusion (conscious or unconscious) to Conrad a plagiarism? In the end, the notes come to look like Eliot's attempt to assert his mastery over the intertextual play of his poem—to claim authority over a poem woven of both conscious allusion and unconscious echo—but when Old Possum's away the poem, much to his chagrin, will play.

What precisely distinguishes allusion from quotation? Is an unmarked quotation an allusion? Is an unmarked allusion a plagiarism? Can allusions ever be considered plagiarized? Where does quotation end and allusion begin? The posing of such questions depends at least in part upon a postmodern understanding of textuality. In a famous passage, Roland Barthes writes that the Text is "woven entirely with citations, references, echoes, cultural languages . . . antecedent or contemporary, which cut across it through and through in a vast stereophony. . . . The citations which go to make up a text are anonymous, untraceable, and yet *already read;* they are quotations without inverted commas" (Barthes 160). We might recall that Emerson had said almost precisely the same thing over one hundred years earlier, in his essay "Quotation and Originality": "Our debt to tradition through reading and conversation is so massive, our protest or private addition so rare and insignificant,—and this commonly on the ground of other reading, or hearing,—that, in a large sense, one would say there is no pure originality. All minds quote. Old and new make the warp and woof of every moment. There is no thread that is not a twist of these two strands. By necessity, by proclivity and by delight, we all quote" (Emerson 178).

James Joyce is the other great allusive genius of modernist literature, and his *Ulysses* the great laboratory for the use of allusion in English-language prose. Eliot's model of textuality—at least the one he put forward publicly in his prose writings—is very similar to the understanding that Joyce's precious autobiographical poet/hero Stephen Dedalus is working from in *Ulysses* (as well as in the "prequel," *A Portrait of the Artist as a Young Man*). But also in *Ulysses,* Joyce introduces another character—one without Stephen's massive personal investment in the institution of literature, and one who thus was perhaps able to contemplate the intricacies of textuality somewhat more pragmatically and dispassionately. That character is, of course, Leopold Bloom.

Thus I want to divide "Joyce" the writing subject into two characters, the Stephen and Bloom of *Ulysses*. This is a traditional enough move that I am not going to attempt to defend it, though I am certainly aware of its short-comings. Next: Let Stephen Dedalus equal T. S. Eliot. Stephen has, as a char-acter, made a heavy investment in the notion of artistic originality; think, for instance, of the effort that the vilanelle in *A Portrait* cost him ("Are you not weary of ardent ways, / Lure of the fallen seraphim?" [Joyce, *Portrait of the Artist* 217]). I have written elsewhere about Stephen's paralysis in *Ulysses* as the result, at least in part, of his anxiety as a would-be Romantic poet in the age of mechanical reproduction.[1] To put it crudely: Stephen wants to be By-ron when he grows up, but it is starting to look like there will not be any open-ings by the time he is ready to go on the market. In a futile attempt to rope off the territory of the original from the encroachment of Tradition, Stephen, like Eliot, tries to make plain his borrowings, so that whatever is not tagged as on loan is, presumptively, Stephen's own. Now this is not always true; think, for instance, of his trying to pass off the "cracked lookingglass of a servant"— which he has lifted from Oscar Wilde—as his own to Haines and Mulligan, and their apparent acceptance of it as such—Haines wants to put it in his book, and Stephen wants to be paid for it. Stephen seems also to have stolen his vam-pire poem ("He comes, pale vampire . . .") from Douglas Hyde, and his quip (in *Portrait*) about the artist resembling the God of creation from Flaubert.

But as a general rule, I think, Stephen, like Eliot and Ezra Pound, adopts an Arnoldian, "touchstone" approach to the Tradition. As Arnold writes in "The Study of Poetry," "There can be no more useful help for discovering what poetry belongs to the class of the truly excellent, and can therefore do us most good, than to have always in one's mind lines and expressions of the great masters, and to apply them as a touchstone to other poetry. . . . Short passages, even single lines, will serve our turn quite sufficiently" (Arnold 168). Allusion, especially in the work of Eliot, Pound, and Stephen, becomes a matter of touchstones. Think, for instance, of the touchstones that Stephen draws forth from his treasury in *Portrait*, "A day of dappled seaborne clouds," and either "Brightness" or "Darkness" "falls from the air"—though Stephen cannot quite seem to remember which (suggesting, perhaps, Joyce's attitude toward the Arnoldian project).

Not surprisingly, then, Bloom is the character in *Ulysses* who most nearly embodies the postmodernist model of textuality; Kathy Acker, that piratical Riot Grrrl of contemporary American fiction, seems instinctively to have rec-ognized this. Acker's textual practice, her guerrilla textual strategies, cast a strange new light on the textual strategies of some of our canonical high mod-ernists. In her novel *My Death My Life by Pier Paolo Pasolini*, for instance, Acker strategically plagiarizes a few passages from *Ulysses* in order to com-ment obliquely on the modernists' attitude toward intellectual property and her own. In the fashion Eliot outlines in "Tradition and the Individual Talent,"

Acker's fiction—specifically, her experiments in textual appropriation—have raised fundamental questions about the origins and ownership of textual material, questions that Eliot worked hard to skirt, and that Joyce I believe foresaw without seeing clearly their answer. Acker's work forces us to reconsider that most modernist of textual strategies, allusion—a strategy which has, in postmodern fiction, been subsumed under the more spacious rubric of "appropriation." Before looking at those passages in more detail, however, we might pause here to consider more generally the outlines of Acker's plagiaristic critique.

Acker's writing is remarkable for a number of reasons; Richard Foreman says that reading her prose is "like playing hopscotch with a genius." Many of the hallmarks of Acker's prose would be immediately apparent if you were to dip at random into any one of her novels: especially their graphic depictions of violence, their unremitting obscenity (both verbal and, in the case of her novel *Blood and Guts in High School,* visual obscenity in the form of crude graffiti), and the flickering, unstable gender identities of her characters. In a 1988 interview with Ellen G. Freidman, Acker helped to explain her strange brew this way: "The first books I ever read came from my mother's collection. My mother had porn books and Agatha Christie, so when I was six years old, I'd hide the porn books between the covers of the Agatha Christie. They are my favorite models, the books I read as a kid. That's why I originally became a writer—to write Agatha Christie-type books, but my mind is fucked up" (1989, 20).

But if Acker's writing has been taken up by critics for any one feature, it is her use of what she calls "appropriation," and what her detractors are inclined to call either "plagiarism" or, in some cases, "piracy." For Acker, to write is to steal; her texts insistently pose the paired questions "When is art theft?" and "When is theft art?"[2] She steals titles—those, for instance, of her novels *Great Expectations* and *Don Quixote.* She steals characters, especially from Shakespeare, and forces them to do things and speak lines that would give the Bard the willies. She steals plots, as for instance in her rewriting of a long section of *Huckleberry Finn*—the discovery and exploration by Huck and Jim of the wreck of the Walter Scott—in her novel *Empire of the Senseless.* And most pointedly, and pertinently for our purposes, Acker steals text— sometimes nearly verbatim—whole, bleeding hunks of it.

The masterminds behind *Mondo 2000* magazine have declared that "Appropriation is the hallmark of postmodernism"; "Somehow it seems more important," Stephen Ronan writes, "to use recombined images supplied to you through the media . . . than manufacturing or drawing something wholly new" (Ronan 25). The lineage is typically traced through Andy Warhol back to John Cage and Marcel Duchamp; among the most important contemporary appropriationists would be the photographers Sherrie Levine and Richard Prince, who reframe classical photographs, or bands like Cabaret Voltaire and

Negativland, who work found music and found sounds into the texture of their compositions. In one of her interviews, Acker invokes the work of Levine as an analogue for her own texts:

> When I did *Don Quixote,* what I really wanted to do was a Sherrie Levine painting. I'm fascinated by Sherrie's work. . . . What I was interested in was what happens when you just copy something, without any reason—not that there's no theoretical justification for what Sherrie does—but it was the simple fact of copying that fascinated me. I wanted to see whether I could do something similar with prose. (Ellen Friedman 1989, 12)

Acker's most notorious act of appropriationist terrorism to date was her transferring of almost 1,500 words, nearly verbatim, from Harold Robbins's 1974 best-seller *The Pirate* into her own 1975 novel *The Adult Life of Toulouse Lautrec by Henri Toulouse Lautrec.* The only significant changes that Acker introduces into the appropriated passage itself are that she recasts it from a third-person into a first-person narrative; and the woman that Acker promotes from object to subject of the narrative, rather than Robbins's Jordanna Al Fay, bored and spoiled wife of the Arab oil baron Badyr Al Fay, is, in Acker's rendition—Jacqueline Onassis. The passage is clearly set off as an inset in Acker's text, and given a rather sensational title: "the true story of a rich woman: I Want to Be Raped Every Night!" (237). When the heist was pointed out in the press, Acker was accused of plagiarism; she, however, took the moral high ground, insisting that she had not plagiarized, but rather "pirated" (my term, not hers), *The Pirate.*

The distinction, which might at first blush seem a trivial one, in fact has profound implications. To plagiarize is to present the words or ideas of another as your own. This, Acker insists, she has never done. "I'm not guilty of plagiarism," she explained to Friedman:

> To be guilty of plagiarism, according to the law, is to represent somebody else's material as your material. I haven't done that. I have been very clear that I use other people's material. I haven't quite listed sources in my later books not to sound like an academic, but in many interviews, many theoretical texts, I said where each section came from. I've always told my publishers. There's an introduction to this publication of my early work where I talk about my method of appropriation. I've always talked about it as a literary theory and as a literary method. I haven't certainly hidden anything. (Ellen Friedman 1989, 20)[3]

In Acker's own literary "code of the West," plagiarism is a cowardly act, in which one attempts to solidify one's own position as a writing subject, to bolster one's own authority, by clothing oneself in another's prose.

Brazenly to steal text, however—to violate the laws of copyright, to pirate—is not merely to transgress those codes erected for the maintenance of civil literary society, but to brag of the fact—to publicize one's thefts. In an interview with Sylvère Lotringer, Acker put it this way: "If I had to be totally honest I would say that what I'm doing is breach of copyright—it's not, because I change words—but so what? We're always playing a game. We earn our money out of the stupid law but we hate it because we know it's jive. What else can we do? That's one of the basic contradictions of living in capitalism. I sell copyright, that's how I make my money" (Lotringer, 12). The boundaries between various of these terms—quotation, allusion, plagiarism, and piracy, as well as related terms like reference, echo, parody, and pastiche—are rather porous and ill-defined. Surprisingly enough, the identification of her technique with piracy is one Acker herself seems not to have made. She writes with some frequency about pirates, especially in her more recent work; her most recent novel (1996), for instance, is entitled *Pussy, King of the Pirates*. The third and final section of *Empire of the Senseless* is titled "Pirate Nights," and centers on Thivai, who wants to be a pirate, and his sometime-girlfriend Abhor, who does not want to play along. But while Acker never makes explicit the connection between pirates as subject and piracy as technique—and, in all fairness, it is probably just so obvious she does not feel the need—her comments on the pirate figures in her novels do suggest some important parallels. Speaking of *Empire of the Senseless*, Acker told Friedman that "The myth to me is pirates. . . . It's like the tattoo. The most positive thing in the book is the tattoo. It concerns taking over, doing your own sign- making. . . . Tattoo artists, sailors, [and] pirates . . . [are] people who are beginning to take their own sign-making into their own hands. They're conscious of their own sign-making, signifying values really" (Ellen Friedman 1989, 17–18). Acker here invokes her favorite metaphor for writing, the tattoo; as well as suggesting the notion that, as Shem in *Finnegans Wake* realizes, the author's body is at some level the author's first and primary text, the tattoo for Acker is also the mark, the stigmata almost, of the outlaw, and is written not by oneself, but is inscribed on one's body by another—it is not, as Shem's is in *Finnegans Wake,* original writing, proceeding from one's own guts, one's own bowels, but is rather the writing of another, which paradoxically comes to create the public space, the artistic façade or persona, of the writing subject. Thus the writer's body is foolscap indeed, but is "tagged" (in the sense of spray-paint graffiti) by the texts of the literary tradition. Therein lies the difference between modernism and postmodernism.

Appropriation, as Acker practices it—bold-faced piracy on the high seas of Western literary tradition—is in her hands a specifically feminist critique. As Jo Stanley writes in her history of women pirates, *Bold in Her Breaches,* "Women pirates are social outrages—and the embodiment of women's terrifying power. The woman pirate figure is sexually desirable because of her wickedness—a devil; she is bound to come to a bad end—because all *femmes fatales* do; and she offers a breath of fresh air in ideas about women and power" (6). Acker's Don Quixote, after all, is a woman; "I realized," Acker has said, "that *Don Quixote,* more than any of my other books, is about appropriating male texts and that the middle part of *Don Quixote* is very much about trying to find your voice as a woman" (Lotringer, 13). Acker's Don Quixote sets off in quest of voice, not vision, and finds that she must piece it together—cut-and-paste, bricolage—from what Eliot calls "the existing monuments" of European literature. She is Don Quixote admixed with a touch of Lord Elgin, stealing what she will from the monuments. And when those pages from Harold Robbins are grafted into *The Adult Life of Toulouse Lautrec*—Acker's Lautrec is also a woman—the narrative context does violence to Robbins's text of sexual violence. Again in her interview with Lotringer, Acker explains, "I took the Harold Robbins and represented it. I didn't copy it. I didn't say it was mine. . . . It seems to me quite a different procedure than the act of plagiarism. I had changed words, I had changed intentionality. Obviously appropriation has been some sort of postmodernist technique in the arts for a number of years, both in the visual arts and in the literary arts. . . . Robbins is really soft core porn, so I wanted to see what would happen if you changed contexts and just upped the sexuality of the language. It's a simplistic example of deconstruction" (Lotringer, 13). Acker speaks here of upping the sexuality of the language, but that remark might easily be misunderstood. For she does not introduce exaggeration into the male, racist sexual fantasies to which Robbins gives voice; how, I wonder, would one even go about exaggerating, "upping the sexuality," of a text that can state with a straight face, "You better learn to beg a little if you want some black cock in your hot little pussy," or, in the words of our narrator "Jacqueline Onassis," "Greedily I sucked at him. I wanted to swallow him alive, to choke myself to death on that giant beautiful tool" (Acker, *Adult Life of Toulouse Lautrec* 136, 137). Rather, Acker defamiliarizes, makes strange, the worldview that would allow one to write in such a manner by embedding it within a text that suggests the utter abjection of being woman within patriarchy (recall that the pirate's girlfriend in *Empire of the Senseless* is named Abhor), and shows that all attempted expressions of female desire are caught up within the masculine narrative of sexual conquest. One of the none-too-subtle ironies of the Robbins passage is that "Jacqueline Onassis" becomes the sexual slave of the unnamed black man who is conveniently enough from Georgia (their interlude takes place in Paris), and he has held forth about the evils of slavery while they were dancing back at the disco (in Robbins's world, this passes for subtle social commentary). As a black man, he predictably, stereotypically, danced well: "He moved fantastically well, his body fluid under the shirt, which was open to his waist and tied in a tight knot just over the seemingly glued-on black jeans" (Acker, *Adult Life of Toulouse Lautrec* 239; Robbins, *The Pirate* 132).

Let us conclude with a brief look at Acker's plagiarism of Joyce. For a reader familiar with *Ulysses,* and Joyce's life, the contextual clues are there; Acker suddenly switches her scene to a restaurant in Zurich, and moves into obsessively exact scenic description:

> The American and one Italian-Swiss and two German-Swiss for breakfast ate one poached egg and a slice of Swiss cheese over a piece of white bread. The bread tasted winey. Some say he is not in the grave at all. That the coffin was filled with stones. That one day he will come again.
> Hynes shook his head.
> —Parnell'll never come again, he said. He's there, all that was mortal of him. TO SEARCH IN ALL THESE THINGS (OF COURSE MENTAL) WHICH SIMPLY PRESENT THEMSELVES FOR THE ROAD OR MEANING. . . . (Acker, *My Death My Life* 200)

This first "plagiarism"—from "The bread" through "all that was mortal of him"—is lifted from the closing pages of the "Hades" episode of *Ulysses,* and belongs neither to Stephen nor Bloom, but the unnamed third-person narrator of the episode. The following passage, two pages later, is stolen from Stephen Dedalus's thoughts at *Ulysses* 3:209–10 and 211–12, and betrays the self-conscious, "literary" sort of construction that Stephen appears to be trapped in:

> Comparison: Paris rawly waking, crude sunlight over her lemon streets. Moist piths of farls of bread, the froggreen wormwood, her morning perfume, coffee coffee court the air. . . . There Belluomo rises from his wife's lover's wife's bed, the kerchiefed housewife stirs, a saucer of sunk gone oh below the cement. (Acker, *My Death My Life* 202)

There are other plagiarism-based passages in *My Death My Life,* however, that suggest another way—the way of the bricoleur. Now clearly, Acker herself is enacting Lévi-Strauss's famous description of the bricoleur, that junkman who makes what he can, what he needs, from the materials at hand; and the cut-and-paste importation into Acker's text of this depiction of Bloom certainly fits that description:

> Gross-booted draymen rolled barrels dull-thudding out of Prince's stores and bumped them up on the brewery float. On the brewery float bumped dull-thudding barrels rolled by gross-booted draymen out of Prince's stores.—There it is Red Murray said. Alexander Keyes.—Just cut it out, will you? Mr. Bloom said, and I'll take it round to the TELEGRAPH office. HOUSE OF KEY(E)S—Like that, see. Two crossed keys here. . . . (Acker, *My Death My Life* 201)

But more interesting, I think, if we pay attention to the action she has chosen to re-present here, this is an appropriation of an appropriation, for Bloom's own textual strategy here is to "create" an "original" text, his ad for Alexander Keyes, by cutting and pasting material that has appeared in another paper. Bloom's creation, like Acker's, is an unapologetic theft; but while Bloom's transgression occurs in the field of commodity culture, in which one is thought justified in moving the merchandise in whatever way one can, Acker's thefts play themselves out in the world of art, and are therefore held to answer to a higher standard. Edward Young, in his *Conjectures on Original Composition,* recognized the existence of this double standard more than two centuries ago: "An Original may be said to be of a *vegetable* nature; it rises spontaneously from the vital root of Genius; it *grows,* it is not *made:* Imitations are often a sort of *Manufacture* wrought up by those *Mechanics, Art,* and *Labour,* out of pre-existent materials not their own" (7).

But according to one of Eliot's definitions of the great poet, Bloom is greater than Stephen; for, Eliot argues in his review essay on Philip Massinger,

> Immature poets imitate; mature poets steal; bad poets deface what they take, and good poets make it into something better, or at least something different. The good poet welds his theft into a whole of feeling which is unique, utterly different from that from which it was torn; the bad poet throws it into something which has no cohesion. (1932, 153)

Eliot's prose here points the way to a postmodern poetics; and if he was not able himself to carry out the program it suggests, Joyce, to some degree, was. And Kathy Acker, coming along half a century behind, has effectively blown the cover off the modernist practice of allusion and quotation, helping us to see how unstable it always was.

Notes

1. See *The Illicit Joyce of Postmodernism: Reading Against the Grain* (Madison: U. of Wisconsin Press, 1996), pp. 104–136.

2. These are Rickey Vincent's questions, posed in regard to postmodern art in general, in the entry on "Appropriation" in Randy Rucker, R. U. Sirius and Queen Mu, *Mondo 2000: A User's Guide to the New Edge* (New York: HarperCollins, 1992), p. 29.

3. The entire episode is treated in Acker's story "Dead Doll Humility," available at the *Postmodern Culture* World Wide Web site (http://jefferson.village.virginia. edu/pmc/).

Poaching and Plagiarizing: Property, Plagiarism, and Feminist Futures

Debora Halbert

Over the past two hundred years very little has changed regarding how we view intellectual property. Plagiarism, piracy, and copyright infringement are the names given for the illegal copying of copyrighted works. Plagiarism is the logical outgrowth of the creation of intellectual property. Plagiarism as theft exists because a system of knowledge production that emphasizes creative genius, originality, and the proprietary author defines how we understand the expression of ideas. Once it becomes possible to think of literary work as property it becomes possible to "steal" that property.

Some literary critics argue that we are all plagiarists or, at the very least, engage in "textual poaching" (de Certeau 165–76). The recognition that we all embrace some form of plagiarism, even at a subconscious level, is increasingly important as intellectual property protection becomes a matter of big business. Where we draw lines between the cultural commons and private property has important implications for future creative work. The acceptable amount of appropriation becomes smaller each day as the law is utilized and expanded to reap larger profits from every aspect of a creative work. Copyright produces a tension between how texts are created (a process that relies on textual poaching, exchange, and sharing) and how texts are legally protected (a process reliant on originality and private property).

The proprietary author is indebted to a gendered understanding of authorship and ownership. The history of intellectual property is a history of masculine creation and birth. It is possible, and essential, to question the very foundations of the intellectual property system—that of the proprietary author. Even as intellectual property law grows in strength, the potential of a postmodern feminist approach makes it possible to offer a substantive critique. Uncovering the assumptions on which copyright is premised can make it possible to revise copyright in a manner appropriate for greater sharing and creativity.

111

Feminism is important in understanding intellectual property because it provides a lens through which to view the past, a theoretical understanding that can help interpret the present, and a set of principles for framing the future. Postmodern feminism is especially meaningful when thinking about the future because of its emphasis on ambiguity, appropriation, creativity, and play. This chapter makes the argument that given the gendered construction of intellectual property in the past and the overemphasis on ownership in the present, a possible alternative construction for intellectual property in the future can be discovered through a feminist framework.

I will first discuss the gendered historical construction of authorship and the envelopment of authorship within the paternity metaphor. Second, I will look at the postmodern nexus of plagiarism, property, and creativity as it plays out in a modern story of intellectual property. It is through this story that a postmodern feminist framework can best be understood. Finally, if we are to move toward any form of a feminist goal we must begin the process of envisioning an alternative to intellectual property law. I will look to the future and evaluate the possibilities for creativity if we unhinge it from intellectual property law and begin to view it through a feminist framework.

Discussing the history of intellectual property illustrates how impoverished our language is regarding creative work. There is only the language of property available to discuss creation. If we want to understand the possibilities of creativity in a feminist world we must create those possibilities ourselves. A feminist-oriented future can illustrate what an alternative to the current legal system may be and in the process dissolve the powerful assumptions of authorship and ownership so readily taken as truth.

Some Words on Intellectual Property

Copyright emerges in its modern form during the eighteenth century. By modern form, I mean that a system of property laws was created to deal with works of authorship and that authorship underwent a definitional revision through which the proprietary nature of the author over his work (and I say "his" on purpose) was emphasized (Mark Rose 1993). At a variety of levels, the emergence of intellectual property laws, specifically copyright laws, was gendered.

The philosophy of intellectual property has its roots in Locke and Hegel and hinges on the definition of intellectual work as private property (Hughes 297–358). The combination of Locke's theory of property, the patriarchal environment of the late seventeenth and early eighteenth century, and the characteristics of the book market created a discourse on copyright based on masculine creation. Both Locke and Hegel are the subject of extensive feminist critique, which I will not repeat (Butler 74–94; Benhabib, 129–145). However, the link between gender and intellectual property deserves space.

Intellectual property is about masculine creation. Ideas, expressed through the labor of an author, become possessed as property. Women, whose status as authors was problematic long before the institutionalization of intellectual property laws, were discouraged from writing and from public life. Women were discouraged from printing because it did not fit with the socially accepted feminine ideal (Wall 279–80). Additionally, early discourses on authorship masculinized publication and feminized that which was published, which impacted women's access to authorship and resulted in a masculine understanding of authorship. As Wendy Wall asks, "If women were tropes necessary to the process of writing, if they were constructed within genres as figures for male desire, with what authority could they publish? How could a woman become an author if she was the 'other' against whom 'authors' differentiated themselves?" (282). Thus, by the time booksellers institutionalized property rights in published works, women were already virtually excluded from authorship.

Excluding women from authority and authorship is only one aspect of early intellectual property. Originality through authorship was also interpreted as the domain of the masculine. In Hegel's philosophy, property becomes an expression of the will and personality (Hughes 333). Literary property was "original" because it originated from the uniqueness of a person's mind (Mark Rose 1993, 120). Many metaphors were tried in an effort to describe the act of authorship and legitimate ownership of the ideas, but the most common, according to Mark Rose, is the "author as begetter and the book as child" (38). Thus, the most common metaphor was one of paternity.

The paternity metaphor is significant for understanding copyright from a feminist perspective. Copyright invites the author to own his work. The work is not only the child of the author, but his property. Authorship was a method for establishing paternity over a text, the male creation. The paternity metaphor was replaced with the metaphor of the landed estate in the eighteenth century in part because it provided a better understanding of the proprietary nature of authorship. However, paternity metaphors continue to be part of the law to this day. In a recent law suit, the author sued for damages from the "denial of [his] paternity" when a publisher published contributions under a different byline (Morris Freedman 508). The paternity metaphor illustrates what later metaphors conceal—literary creation is masculine creation.

Despite the prejudices against them, women still became authors. Wendy Wall suggests they did so either at great expense or by appropriating specific genres of writing considered "acceptable" for women. An acceptable genre for women was the will, because it was socially appropriate for a dying woman to leave instructions to her children. Women appropriated this genre as an avenue into the public sphere as authors, creating subversive avenues into the largely male dominated public sphere (Wall 282–283).

Friedrich Kitler provides ever greater insight into the gendered production of authorship circa 1800 in *Discourse Networks: 1800/1900*. Kitler argues, much along the lines of Wendy Wall, that women in the discourse network[1] of 1800 were not authors because they played a distinctly private role in society. However, he pursues this theme further and suggests that women during this period played a much more significant symbolic role. As Kitler states, "Nature, love, and women—the terms were synonymous in the 1800 discourse network" (73). From her place within Nature women could not write, but rather became the source of ideas voiced by men: "To the author's surprise, his words have not been his at all. It is as if they had been whispered by a prompter who in turn had them from the Woman or Nature" (Kitler 73).

When woman, in the role of nature, is the origin of ideas, then all is appropriated (or plagiarized) from her: "Through their mandate to represent The Mother, women made authors write. The Mother neither speaks nor writes, but from the depths of her soul arise the unembellished accents that the author rescues by writing" (Kitler 67). Through the gendered development of authorship in the 1800s, not only were women relegated to the private sphere where they could not write or speak, but through the symbolic transformation of women into "The Mother," male authorship appropriated from and spoke for women. It could be argued that authorship itself, in the 1800 discourse network, is plagiarism. Masculine creativity is dependent on appropriation and this appropriation is not recognized as plagiarism. Such textual appropriation played out in everyday life when women allowed themselves to be plagiarized. As one woman put it:

> For ten years even our closest friends had no inkling of my part in my husband's creative work, and during these ten years even I was unaware that a portion of the praise, the honorable judgments pronounced by gladdened readers of stories my husband published, belonged to me. I was too deeply devoted to him, too immersed in my domestic duties, to call anything my own. (Kitler 126)

Such appropriation was considered a natural aspect of authorship. The very development of intellectual property, which carefully established the paternity of the text, is indebted to appropriation. By ignoring the connections between ideas and highlighting originality, intellectual property favored those who could be authors—men. Plagiarism is what happens to men, not women. Women, within the 1800 discourse network, did not have the authority or the originality necessary to make claims to their own ideas.

A Modern Story about Appropriation, or is it Plagiarism?

What choices do women have as they enter the world of authorship? This world, governed by intellectual property, is one where appropriation is called plagiarism and ideas are property. Postmodern feminism provides strategies for cultural creation, but these strategies clash at the ideological level with the law. Jeffrey Koons could be considered a poster child for the clash between postmodern appropriation and the law. His experience illustrates why it is impossible for a postmodern feminist project to operate within the already existing laws of intellectual property (where they will be called plagiarists) and perhaps move into a future absent a notion of intellectual property.

Jeffrey Koons is a modern American artist accused of plagiarizing a photographic postcard created by Art Rogers. Rogers had originally taken the photograph, *Puppies,* for the owners of a litter of German Shepherd puppies. Rogers licensed *Puppies* to Museum Graphics who turned it into a postcard. The picture depicts the owners sitting on a bench holding the puppies. Koons encountered the postcard in a museum gift shop and decided the scene would fit in his art show on banality. Koons had the photograph reproduced as a wood carving entitled "A String of Puppies."

Koons understood he was reproducing a copyrighted photograph, but argued that since he had seen similar pictures of people holding animals, the picture should be viewed "as part of the mass culture—'resting in the collective sub-consciousness of people regardless of whether the card had actually ever been seen by such people'" (Rogers 304). He instructed artisans to make the wood carving just like the photo. Because Rogers had not given permission to Koons to use his photograph he considered it an act of piracy and took Koons to court.

The court labeled Koons a plagiarist because Rogers had created an "original" work of art and held exclusive rights to its use (Rogers 307). Koons argued that his "String of Puppies" is a parody of society at large and thus a legitimate fair use (Rogers 309). As his art show suggests, he was commenting on banality in society. After all, what can be more banal than a couple holding a bunch of puppies? The Appeals court and the Supreme Court felt otherwise and argued that Jeff Koons had indeed violated Roger's copyright (Koons 365).

Appropriation, like that done by Koons, is plagiarism according to the law. It does, however, play an important role in social critique. As Martha Buskirk notes,

> The appropriation of imagery from mass media and other sources is, of course, a strategy central to postmodern art. Koons is only one of a number of artists who have responded to an increasingly image-saturated society by taking pictures directly from the media, advertising or elsewhere and repositioning them within their own work. (37)

In a commodified world, appropriation provides an avenue for awareness of our situation. The postmodern voice is important. As Rosemary Coombe notes, "Postmodernists breach rules of discourse because they believe that form has implications and conventional forms of discourse may be inadequate to express alternative visions" (1856, fn 19). Thus, a postmodern strategy is to avoid playing by the rules and attempt to expand our understanding of creation, commodification, and property law. However, when brought to court the postmodernist will (evidently) lose.[2]

Intellectual property laws restrict the flow of texts, "freezing the connotations of signs and symbols and fencing off fields of cultural meaning with 'no trespassing' signs . . . " (Coombe 1866). Appropriation like that of Koons's is an example of the fences constructed by intellectual property laws and the limits they put on cultural creation.

Postmodern appropriation has important links to feminist strategies as well. Ellen G. Friedman, in a discussion about Kathy Acker's work, makes this point:

> Acker's purpose in appropriating well-known texts is profoundly political. Through plagiarism, Acker proposes an alternative to the classical Marxist explanation of the sources of power. With Jean Baudrillard she believes that those who control the means of representation are more powerful than those who control the means of production. Plagiarism undermines the assumptions governing representation. (243–44)

According to this feminist perspective, the means of representation are governed by male texts and desires:

> In plagiarizing, Acker does not deny the masterwork itself, but she does interrogate its sources in paternal authority and male desire. By placing the search for modes of representing female desire inside male texts, Acker and others clearly delineate the constraints under which this search proceeds. (Friedman 244)

The process of appropriation (or plagiarism) has political motivations with a very specific cultural and feminist subtext. Appropriation encourages us to understand the sources of cultural production and "paternal authority," both aspects of intellectual property from which creation ought to be liberated. For the feminist and the postmodernist, appropriation or plagiarism are acts of sedition against an already established mode of knowing, a way of knowing indebted to male creation and property rights. Friedman suggests that there are "many reasons to adopt a complex attitude toward plagiarism" (174–75). Among these she lists different examples of appropriation, especially those by women who take texts and "refashion them into interrogations of the originals" (174–75). Ultimately, this radical approach to plagiarism is on a collision course with legal interpretations.

While Koons and his "String of Puppies" is not a feminist work, its example is close to a strategy that has postmodern feminist tendencies. At the very least, Koons helps problematize the concept of plagiarism, a goal which can be endorsed by feminists interested in deconstructing intellectual property. Current law, instead of recognizing the cultural dependence of all creativity, enforces ownership of original works. Appropriation within such a world is a valid social critique. To use the title of a recent article describing the trouble and cost of adhering to copyright law: "Just do it" (Stowe 32).

The law, confined as it is to statutes and precedence, cannot begin to address the cultural complexities of postmodern theory or practice. Nor can the law adequately address the problems associated with plagiarism unless there is a profit at stake.[3] Unless drastic change occurs, further ownership will provide the assumptions on which our future is based.

It is important to ask why plagiarism is so upsetting. Plagiarism is upsetting because it is personal. Keeping in mind the cultural specificity of this claim,[4] people want to be acknowledged for their contributions (M. Freedman 508). Plagiarism can be a silencing mechanism as Neal Bowers, an American poet whose work has been plagiarized for several years by the same person, points out (545–55). There is a distinction the law does not address and which any future theory of intellectual property ought to address—that plagiarism is about personal feelings, not profits. It is a personal offense when someone plagiarizes your work. Copyright, by focusing exclusively on profits and the potential loss of market share, lacks the ability to deal with the personal issues of authorship and plagiarism.

The American system of copyright very clearly asserts property ownership over every possible aspect of a creative work and is used to halt appropriation that occurs without permission. The sense of a cultural commons within the copyright framework of the United States is one constructed through profit and production. If we want the future to take into consideration the fact that creation is inherently cultural we need to begin developing a language in which to talk about the future.

The origins of intellectual property law, authorship, originality, and plagiarism are indebted to understanding creation as the domain of males who are the only ones authorized to speak and write. Additionally, our present use of intellectual property calls virtually all acts of appropriation plagiarism without giving thought to the damage done to cultural exchange and sharing. This present approach provides an avenue for subversive feminist plagiarism such as that done by Acker; however, it remains a fringe possibility with most everyone playing by the intellectual property rules. The past and present cannot provide us with a language of creativity from which to begin our future. Thus, it would be best if a future language is a feminist one. As Ellen G. Friedman notes, "As male texts look backward over their shoulders, female texts look forward, often beyond culture, beyond patriarchy, into the unknown, the outlawed" (244).

Looking into the future is one way of theorizing about what ought to be. Speculating about the future or devising the type of future one would want is not only a futurist practice but a postmodernist and feminist one. Postmodernism and feminism are normative approaches that outline what ought to exist instead of what does exist. As Frances Bartkowski writes, "Feminist fiction and feminist theory are fundamentally utopian in that they declare that which is not-yet as the basis for a feminist practice, textual, political, or otherwise" (12). In the process, many feminist theorists help us envision a future. The most important task for feminist theorists is to help envision a future that provides alternatives to the way intellectual property is conceptualized and legally protected.

Feminist Intellectual Property Futures

Feminists are especially good at developing alternative futures because nothing remotely akin to a feminist present can be found. Thus, throughout feminist theory and fiction one can find rich descriptions of alternative futures. I would like to draw on several feminist fiction writers to help begin the process of speaking a new intellectual property language—one that does not center on individual ownership of expression, but emphasizes the cultural communities we find ourselves to be members of.

The future of authorship and intellectual property is not certain. As David Lange puts it, "Authorship as an artifact of authority is indefensible; it deserves to die. But authorship in the preliminary sense of identifying, merely *entre nous,* the 'person to whom something owes its origin' is not only defensible, but inevitable as well" (qtd. in Aoki ft 108). Instead of calling for the death of the author (Foucault 1977, 113–38), we need to think more relationally about authorship. If we can emphasize a framework focused on sharing and exchange instead of personal ownership, then the concept of authorship as identifying "to whom something owes its origin" is appropriate.

A feminist future for intellectual property would differ substantially from the legalistic, commercial future we can now expect. Where the legalistic/commercial future emphasizes ownership and control of property, a possible feminist future emphasizes the relational aspect of all learning and creation. It would emphasize the intellectual debts one owes and recognize that all work is connected to the intellectual streams within which one swims.[5] A relational attitude toward creative work, while acknowledged by many actually doing such work, is mutually exclusive with the current state of intellectual property.

To put it more concretely, no concept of intellectual property should exist in a feminist future. While authorship would remain and individual contributions would continue to matter, the emphasis would be taken off the proprietary nature of the creation and placed on the communitarian aspects. Actually, emphasizing the relational aspects of creation fits well with how ideas are communicated. Ideas once verbalized can never be privately owned. Unlike a tangible item, an idea can be shared by many and ownership of expressions can be difficult to enforce. As Ursula Le Guin notes in *The Dispossessed*, "It is the nature of the idea to be communicated: written, spoken, done. The idea is like grass. It craves light, likes crowds, thrives on crossbreeding, grows better for being stepped on" (79). Thus, a feminist future would eliminate the law of intellectual property, which is too often used to halt creativity, and replace it with an understanding of the community in which one creates. Feminists writing science fiction have already begun to develop such futures.[6]

Fully fleshing out the future is beyond the scope of this chapter. However, it is necessary not only to identify how intellectual property depends on gendered assumptions to exist, but also to provide feminist visions for alternatives. The most important role feminists could play is to think about the future, to move beyond the law and the concept of private property, and develop meaningful relationships for humans and their creative work that fall outside property relationships. The law is a helpful tool as long as one wishes to stay within the pre-arranged definitions and agree to its premises. However, if new ways of thinking about what we call intellectual property are to be found, we must move outside the law and into the works of those who engage in envisioning the future. This is where the intellectual energy of feminists is most needed.

Notes

1. A Discourse Network is described in the Introduction to Kitler's book by David E. Wellbery as "A system in which knowledge was defined in terms of authority and erudition, in which the doctrine of rhetoric governed discursive production, in which patterns of communication followed the lines of social stratification, in which books circulated in a process of limitless citation, variation, and translation, in which universities were not yet state institutions and the learned constituted a special (often itinerant) class with unique privileges, and in which the concept of literature embraced virtually all of what was written." (Wellbery, qtd. in Kitler xviii).

2. Buskirk notes that other artists have been sued for copyright infringement including Andy Warhol, Robert Rauschenberg, and David Salle, but all have settled out of court.

3. Neal Bowers, a poet who has worked for several years to halt the plagiarism of his poems writes that no lawyer would touch his case because the plagiarist did not have money to sue for and Bowers would have a difficult time proving the plagiarism

had caused him to lose money. This in itself is a critique of a system that only functions to preserve commercially valuable products while leaving nearly unprotected the creative works of those who have little or no commercial stake in their intellectual property. (Bowers 545–55)

4. China, for example, did not have copyright laws until forced to embrace them by the West. For a specific account of the history of Chinese copyright see William Alford's book *To Steal a Book is an Elegant Offense: Intellectual Property Law in Chinese Civilization.*

5. I owe this language to Kathy Ferguson who helped provide clarity to these thoughts through several discussions.

6. These include Ursula Le Guin, Joan Slonczewski, and Marge Piercy.

From Kant to Foucault: What Remains of the Author in Postmodernism

Gilbert Larochelle

Unprecedented growth in communication and information technology, nowadays, makes it necessary to thoroughly review the rules that must prevail in the production and transfer of knowledge. The mechanisms regulating intellectual works were created, for the most part, at the end of the eighteenth century. The creative ingenuity of the Age of Enlightenment, from Diderot to Voltaire and Kant to Fichte, had set the foundations for juridical individualism, in terms of diffusion of ideas, thus helping shape a vocabulary that would have seemed strange in the Middle Ages. This brings to mind the interwoven relationships of this era, between the writer, hereafter known as *author;* the text, having become *literary property;* a contract with a chargé d'affaires called *publisher;* an abstract public space perceived as *readership;* the market, transforming the book into a *copy* for mass production; commercial regulation by a *bookstore;* and finally, the imposed registration of intellectual works known as *copyright.*

Introduced into the legal system, the dissemination of thought thus integrated the standardization of exchanges and a network of economic universality. The limits set by the legal framework provided an understanding of the respective possessions of the author, reader, and publisher, whose task remained, as noted by Kant, to ensure "the conclusion of a business deal in someone else's name" (120). The protection of ideas by law fits into the process of capacitation of market return. Normalization in the control of intellectual works included, on the other hand, the principles for the definition of a counterfeit (pirated edition). The practice proliferated at the end of the eighteenth century and reinforced the need for a contractual philosophy to define the borders between a legitimate publication (authorized by the author), a counterfeit (pirated edition), and plagiarism (despoliation of someone else's ideas).

The notion of plagiarism cannot exist without referring to the philosophy of modernity that gave birth to the idea. Reconfiguration of the idea of author in the postmodern discourse recently helped emphasize the ambiguity of

121

accrediting any form of writing to an individual, particularly a text. The death of the subject immediately heralds the end for the metaphysics of authorship. Determination of the origin of a discourse, and of its ownership, remains problematic, unresolved, and perhaps more obscure than ever. This reflection centres on one concern: can plagiarism still exist in an intellectual universe where it has become impossible to differentiate the representation from the referent, the copy from the original, and the copyist from the author? To answer this question, and pinpoint its stakes, it is necessary to understand how Foucault dismantles the theories of Kant and Fichte to discern the meaning of plagiarism, when the very foundations of modernity have come into disfavor.

Kant and Fichte: Modern Foundations of the Notion of Copyright

Philosophy has handed down to law and economy the normative framework for the conception of what an author should be initially, and then, of the attributes involved in writing. Now two centuries old, this time-honored heritage relies on the institutionalization of the author-reader relationship. Evidently, the institutions of production, distribution, and consumption of books needed recognition before the origins of their respective rights could be identified and defined. Kant himself did not invent the notion of author, but modernized it by emphasizing the relation of dependence between the author and his work; the latter acquiring a double determination that allows to make the distinction between ownership and author, and possession and buyer. A book always has two levels of reality that, when taken separately, determine its status. On the one hand, the material aspect makes it a "body" of which the owner can easily dispose. Consequently, it lends itself to market operations and transactions of capitalism. On the other hand, Kant (134–135) maintains that books imply an intellectual aspect that manifests at once the subjectivity of its author (individualism), and the intersubjective sharing out of the intellect (universalism).

The Kantian scheme is based on paralogical structure. Its development polarizes the intellectual and functional domains. Initially, it renders them incommensurable with each other. The process is somewhat equivalent to separating the noumenon from the phenomenon in the substance of the book. On the intellectual plane, a consubstantial link, or perfect solidarity between the author and his creation, makes them inalienable one from the other: "The ownership an author has on his ideas . . ., he retains despite reproduction" (Kant 119). From his perspective, the publisher represents, but never acquires any right on this portion of the work, because he remains stranger to its origins and can accept neither its merits nor its flaws. The statement resides, in short, in the adherence of the subject to his discourse, the ultimate causality of discourse, and establishes the criterion of *personal right* in the essence of the book. The "conducting of business in someone else's name," Kantian principle par excellence of editorial delegation, thus finds in this its raison d'être for the referral to the interiority of individuals and their qualities.

Concerning the material aspect of ideas, *real right* provides the holder of a copy with legitimacy, on the other side of paralogy. Linked to phenomenon, *real right* covers only the alienable part of the book, in other words, the part that can be bought or sold. It can be seen that the work, according to Kant, finds itself divided between nonobjectivable subjectivity and an idea that has been set down in a concrete medium that opens it up to exchange. Kant thus formulates the idea clearly: "The author of a book and the owner of a copy can both say of the same book, and with the same right: this is my book! The statement has different meanings, however. The first considers the book a piece of writing or a discourse, while the second simply regards it as a mute instrument for the diffusion of discourse to himself" (131).

Legal determination of copyright, according to Kant, unfolds in a self-contradicting logic, or so it would appear: *paralogic* initially, and finally *synthetic*. That which Kant advances as distinct in philosophy, he reconciles in law. On the one hand, the definition of categories of author, and of work, aims to discern the ontological differences present in all uses of the notion of property. What does this mean? Simply, that owner and property are not one and the same, or, in other words, that one can only own that which is outside oneself (Bernard Edelman 35). For example, the statement "this is mine" involves two nonidentical terms, one of which cannot be the other. On the other hand, intellectual property implies, in the legal sense, that the parallel between author and work, or their irreducibility, can be overcome. According to Kant, this convergence becomes possible when the person is transparent in the work (as the noumenon in the phenomenon), and when the work becomes the manifestation of the author's interiority. Such synthetic representation constitutes a determining factor in practice, for the law recognizes this as an efficient way to operate by considering the work an extension of the person.

This idealism, which relies on a principle of indivisibility of work and author, is echoed in Fichte's discourse, more "Kantian than Kant himself" (Benoist 99). Not only is moral personalism strengthened, it is also coupled with an aesthetic phenomenology that attempts to emphasize the image of the narrator in the book. He exacerbates the distinction between material and intellectual strata by reinforcing the hierarchy between them. The problem it poses is based first on a question, followed by an argument. He proposes the following question: What are the reasons for buying a book? Surely not to "show off the printed paper, or to use it as wallpaper." Instead, Fichte writes: "Through purchase one must feel to have obtained a right to its intellectual content" (Fichte 142; Lachs 1987–88). For Fichte a book is primarily the manifestation of the intellect. However, the communication of this intellect becomes inconceivable when it is separated from its source. The full meaning of intellectual property is maintained through identification of the word. The right to publish, for Fichte, is not so much "conducting business in someone else's name" (Kant), but rather the concession of *usufruct,* which aims to limit the power of the publisher to the strict economic exploitation of the book. The sovereignty of the author comes out uncompromised, more absolute than ever, since the commercialization of the book is reduced to a simple exercise that could be coined "the lending of words."

Fichte's argument toughens up on Kant's vision by introducing a new division to the intellectual aspect of a work. This consists in saying that a book does not only contain ideas, but also a *style* that unfolds within it. He begins with a premise: "This intellectual aspect must still be subjected to division" (Fichte 142). The vectors of its originality are augmented. They enrich the enunciation considerably by clearing out at once a thought and a way of thinking. Fichte also emphasizes the idea that, contrary to the usual disrespect for rhetoric, form, phrasing and artful devices of language equally belong to the particularities of subjectivity and are consequently subject to copyright. The aesthetic disposition of this reasoning supports a principle of inalienability. "However, that which absolutely no one can appropriate," wrote Fichte, "since it is physically impossible, is the form of these thoughts, the linking of ideas and of the signs within which these ideas are exposed" (145). The notion of plagiarism thus comprises a double anchor, intellectual property having henceforth two sources of legitimacy. Determination of the word through *form* and *content* multiplies the markers of individuality, and contributes, in the end, to accentuate the importance of authorship.

Kant and Fichte have in turn intellectualized the book, and placed the author's accomplishment at its origin. Indirectly, they have participated in the acknowledgment of plagiarism. The foundations they have established thus contradict the ancient system of privilege, as renewed and upheld by Diderot and Voltaire. If author subjectivity was wholly recognized in the work, it implied, in this pre-Kantian scheme, the possibility that it would be abolished: the transfer of the manuscript to the publisher stripped the writer of all rights. It was treated on the same level as any other goods for sale, and its origin was in no way proof of its inalienable character. On the contrary, the author's freedom included the right to *give herself or himself away as a person* through the materiality of the work.

At the end of the twentieth century, however, serious doubt was cast on the Kanto-Fichtian discourse by initiating a two-front attack against the philosophical structure of copyright. Without repealing the legal mechanisms and rendering inoperative the regulations that had been elaborated over two hundred years, let us bear in mind that the skepticism surrounding the notion of subject, as well as the spectacular growth in information technology, suggests that the law is being outflanked on all sides. On the one hand, experience shows daily that communication modes can defy the regulating bodies of the legal system with great efficiency since they are dispersed on a worldwide scale. On the other hand, had structuralism favored the development of an idea on the limitations of the subject, poststructuralism would have accelerated, indeed would have radicalised this tendency, and proposed, in addition, the writing off of any referential function. More clearly, the work no longer has anyone to answer for (the author), nor does it have anything to answer to (reality). The autonomy of the text vis-à-vis the author goes together with the emancipation of words toward things. Rupture of the constituent solidarity of copyrights could make admissible the idea that plagiarism can no longer exist once discourse has become a space filled with a multiplicity of interference of untraceable origin. As leader in the dismissal of author supremacy, was Foucault suggesting that the claim to paternity on intellectual production had become a thing of the past?

Foucault and Author Criticism: The Consequences of Postmodernism

Contractualist discourse by Kant and Fichte presupposed that signatories could instantly control their own destiny by experiencing their identity as a naturally appropriated space. Therefore, nothing could challenge that relation with the self that had originally been considered a given. This deliberation is at the very foundation of modern *jusnaturalism,* and favors an idea of right as a transposition of primary nature. The work was seen as an expression of self-disclosure. It personified the author, and created, as it were, a material figure of the writer. Foucault attempts to question this classic archetype of humanism. Indeed, he tries to shake its principles, and change drastically the framework on which it relies. The question he poses appears principally in a text he presented to the *Société française de philosophie* in 1969, and aims particularly at getting to the bottom of the enigma: "What is an author?" The text defends a series of arguments against Kantian fundamentalism and intellectual personalism: it can no longer be assumed that knowledge of who the speaker is in a text is obvious. The process of writing escapes the designation of its creator. No one can become entirely determinant or sole instigator of a thought (Foucault 1969, 73–74; Nehamas 685–91). In other words, the complexity of the contributions in writing makes pretension to imputability an ideological undertaking, not an empirical proceeding. In short, the work is abandoned to the uncertainty of its origin.

"Absence is the first premise of discourse" (Foucault 1969, 75). This idea is present throughout Foucault's inspiration. It marks out its course and, more particularly, it guides his criticism of authority. Consequently, it criticizes intellectual property, as constantly claimed on texts during the cultural movement of the eighteenth century. For him, the privilege of authorship is of a very precise nature. As the result of an exercise in attribution, the application of authorship opens up on a statement of extradiscursive guaranty. This is effective for creating readership a priori, generating selections, establishing limits, playing on regularities, and, in extreme circumstances, reproducing the historic ceremonials in use in a given society.

To understand Foucault, a fictitious example could prove useful. Let us suppose that a text of unknown origin, and unsigned, is in circulation. Somewhat like a popular tale, it is narrated in the style of "Once upon a time, such and such an event, or such and such a person . . ." Similarly, let us imagine that, after some research, the author has been identified, and that the discovery of authentic authorship has brought it out of anonymity. Finally, let us for a moment think that Shakespeare was, to everyone's amazement, the genuine creator of the text in question, or still, along another plot line, that a complete unknown was, in fact and to general indifference, the real author. Then, a standardization process comes into being. This process will call for at least another reading of the text, if not the search for some other coherence, depending upon whether Shakespeare or the complete unknown is the genuine author. In each case, different interpretations, perhaps divergent, would be based on the identity of the author-person by investing a coherence through this adjudication. Foucault states it succinctly: "To 'find' the author through the work, modern criticism uses a design closely related to that of the Christian exegesis, where sanctity of the author was proof of the value of a text" (1969, 86).

What does the evocation of such an imaginary circumstance denote? What pedagogy does it present for the rereading of the relation between work and creator? What conclusions does it arrive at in Foucaultian criticism? The subject has no importance in the understanding of a text. Rather, it damages its potential polyvalence. Lawrence Olivier describes the same shortcomings as recognized by Foucault: "The author is another form of limitation, of the rarefaction of discourse" (56). Once the illness has been diagnosed, the prescription for a cure follows, impregnated with poststructuralist medicine: "The text is not the voice of its creator, but an anonymous process, without subject, an action of language upon itself" (56). There is an implementation of a liberation movement that is not political, but rather epistemic, that can be traced back to *criticism* (senseless appreciation of a work by an author), and *cognition* (untraceable origin). Whether the identity of the author is known or not, Foucault believes that this knowledge will never lead to an explanatory factor. This form of reasoning clearly leads to the destitution of a literary genre: the biography, or life story. It also cripples a discipline: psychology. What are the reasons for this discredit? Both are horizons of exposition of the subject, of its precariousness and inconsistency.

Insistence on discursive practices rather than on the deferment of the "authority of the author," to use a pleonasm, does not refer to the physical disappearance of the speaker, but to the deconstruction of his efficiency in discourse. For Alexander Nehamas (685–686), adopting this position imposes nothing less than a clear *writer-author* dissociation. The first challenges all forms of imperative guardianship on the text because, in his view, it is outside himself, a separate entity. The second magnifies the writing process to make it his own production, the landing place of his profound intentions or his desire to say. To Foucault, the problem with the author is that he describes himself as the formal cause when he only constitutes its addressee after the fashion of the readers. Neither extremity can hold the other hostage by pretending to the exhaustion of meaning. That being the case, it brings to mind an observation of first approximation: intellectual property no longer exists in a postmodern context in which Foucault is an author of discourse, in a sense that would surely not suit him.

The notion of originality and that of plagiarism, its opposite, make up, strictly speaking, metaphysical categories; neither one, when taken literally, can withstand close inspection. As we have seen, originality relies on the crowning of a Monarch whose irreducibility toward statements by others serves to confirm his claim on ownership. The authors of Antiquity could not conceive of this as being advantageous, concerned as they were with actualising their loyalty to the rules of the genre: tragedy and epic. During the nineteenth-century romanticism greatly contributed to the isolation of the author from his work, and to make of him an "exceptional being." In contrast, is not plagiarism a copy that is completely devoid of singularities? Could the plagiarist simply be an authority in the retransmission of another's voice? Postmodern authors believe that the reproduction of a text can only be whole if the context is the same. Therefore, because context changes constantly, a true reproduction cannot be reduced to conformity of text, and plagiarism then becomes an idealization on the report of the ideas of others.

Despite the diversity of use, and of reading material that prevails in postmodernism, it confines the writer to constant reconstruction. Faced with the impossibility of stopping the evolution of meaning, of fixing it firmly in definite representations, plagiarism is challenged because repetition is also the displacement and reinvestment of semantic content. This point of view, philosophically pertinent but legally absurd, conveys an "idea of repetition" as foundation of writing (Giovannangeli 15). The argument follows this line of logic: any recognizable or simply communicable work goes through a network of signs, through the multiplicity of voices that proliferate within linguistic experience. So much so that nothing exists that is not already subject to a practice of intersubjective nature.

The notion of intellectual property involves, even requires knowledge that belongs to oneself, and to others. Jean-François Lyotard sees no relevance in the establishment of this distinction, nor in the analysis of incidences of copyright. Literary property, he notes, "does not really represent a big problem" (12), but simply "a case of application of the law of values" (12) in the capitalist system. This type of criticism needs to make clear all that can be considered commonly owned by refusing to acknowledge authorship as the "closure of the writing field" (12). To some extent, says Lyotard, the very exercise of speech always fits into the framework of misappropriation, and of constant dispersion from the origin. Vandendorpe quotes Roman Jacobson on this point: "Private property, in language, does not exist: everything is socialised" (7). Postmodern thinkers do not merely subscribe to this tendency, they take it one step further. According to them, the writer's activity is found only in intertextuality, where reconstruction and reorientation of borrowed material are predominant. The unfolding of discourse cannot be explained by the characteristic outline of the Baroque era: a mixture of contributions on unknown origin, from whence the end of originality.

From Foucault to Lyotard, from Derrida to Baudrillard, the gradual erosion of authorship, if not of the very existence of the author, does not only answer to the radical deconstruction of self-reference (the illusion of being the subject of one's work); it also constitutes a program, if not a new policy. Postmodern utopia is that of anonymity. It surrenders the act of writing to common ownership. Anti-humanist, it calls for a kind of effusion of the self, until final dissolution. Anti-Kantian, it demonstrates that nothing stands behind authorship, except for the imperatives behind the regulation of commercialization. Lyotard wanted to incorporate this idea into a text: "We have dreamed . . . of a book with no title or authorship" (13). He confides that such a dream was naive. It did however reveal an ambition, nourished a sublimeness that essentially consisted of investing the indeterminable and the unknown in a kind of mysticism. This ineffable notion is called "the other." Derrida constantly refers to "the other." In a broad and somewhat abstract sense, the other is that which bears no name and escapes denomination, or, in a way, imprisonment and exclusion. A strategy of *heteroreference* (referral to the other rather than the self) makes its appearance in Derrida as a replacement option for the Kantian concept of the book: "I let him sign, if he only can. The other must always sign and it is always the other who signs last. That is to say, first" (Derrida 132). This draws a picture of enchantment through the depersonalization of the book.

Dismissal of the author involves a series of repercussions on the status of the written word, and consequently, on the postmodern definition of plagiarism. The challenge becomes the need to identify a path, to pave the way on the edges of the insurmountable contradictions inherent to the reasoning in Kantian personalism, and to Foucault's no less severe disqualification of authorship. In conclusion, let us look at the implications of postmodern response to Kant, in order to provide a potential reading of the author, and of plagiarism:

1. *Separation of ontology and law.* These discourses are no longer corollaries of each another. Postmodernism serves to distance them: it forestalls all pretence to extract what is justifiable from what is plausible (Lyotard); to in-

scribe power in a mechanism of acceptance of knowledge (Kant); or, finally, to invest the law, starting with the privilege on knowledge that ontology seeks to conquer (Derrida). It surrenders the work to the wavering of intersubjectivity, and removes truth from its origin by disrupting unity with the author. In short, it disarticulates the moralism found in the connection between philosophy (what can one know), and politics (what can one do).

2. *Separation of historicity and textuality.* The work can only give testimony on its own existence; it refers only to itself. It is no longer supported by history as the principle from which stem its possibilities. The development of a text separates it not only from the historical process as a source of explanation, according to the model upheld by Marx and Hegel, but also from the *conditions* that prevail in its environment. In short, the suggestion that history gives meaning makes no sense for postmodernists who are trying to take history out of the work. This is what Derrida put forward in *Grammatology* when he remarked that there is nothing beyond the text.

3. *Dissolution of plagiarism through the author's nonresponsibility.* To plagiarize is to translate in a negative mode, because legitimacy is absent. Nontranslatability of the work by the author, for postmodern thinkers, leads to the disappearance of originality and of plagiarism by reason of a lack of responders to whom one is prejudicial. Rather, this would announce the end of usurpation of copyright, and of alienation in the intellectual universe. In this vein, Baudrillard (128–129) notes that the transparency of others becomes the universal norm, in such a way that it is no longer possible to dispossess anyone of his rights.

What remains of the author in postmodernity? Nothing, at least according to the above observations. However, in concluding, a criticism needs to be made, not to close the debate, but perhaps to demonstrate the inadequacy of contemporary attempts to overcome Kantian imperatives in this matter. First, regarding the relation between ontology and law, Foucault, Derrida, Lyotard, and others to date, have been unable to create a new form of recognition for the writer, rather than the author (following the previously mentioned distinctions by Nehamas). Moreover, it is difficult to see how the law can function concretely from the principles of postmodern philosophy.

Next, dissociation between history and text poses a certain number of problems. For, if history does not have an intrinsic meaning, it remains true that context is essential to grasp the meaning a text. For example, had *Mein Kampf* been written by Mother Teresa, rather than Adolf Hitler, the reading of the work would change radically, indeed it would command a closer look at the historical data that could help clarify its meaning. However, the fact that one author rather than another was in the immediate vicinity of the work completely upsets perception of the message, which cannot exist if sheltered from its environment. The author is a component of contextuality and cannot be abstracted from the understanding of the work. Gracia is clear on this issue:

"Texts do need historical authors, for texts without authors are texts without history, and texts without history are texts without meaning, that is, they are not texts" (252). Finally, since the relation between text, history, and meaning exists, the notion of responsibility must be reinvested, not denied on the pretence that the author may not be the creator. It is therefore necessary to reinvent a functional conception of plagiarism that, taking into account humanist criticism, is capable of escaping the traps of nihilism, and of the idealism that it implies.

Imperial Plagiarism*

Marilyn Randall

Captive Greece captured the savage victor and brought the arts into rustic
Latium.

—Horace, *Epistles*

One of the most stable aspects of the concept of plagiarism over history is the
negative connotations that accompany it. Rarely, except in the hands of cyni-
cal plagiarists—that is, great authors—has the practice been considered in a
positive light. Postmodernism, however, seems to demonstrate a heightened
tolerance for appropriative strategies which, practised by Sherrie Levine or
Kathy Acker, are scarcely distinguishable from "real" plagiarism and, indeed,
have been threatened with copyright lawsuits. Is there, in fact, a functional or
formal specificity that distinguishes postmodern plagiarism? Is something like
an aesthetics of plagiarism part of the specificity of postmodernism?

Two distinct concepts are at stake: that of plagiarism, which has existed
since the beginning of letters, and that of the legal protection of intellectual
property, which came into modern existence during the European eighteenth
century. By abstracting, perhaps artificially, from legal questions of copyright
infringement, I would like to explore the sociopolitical ramifications of the
postmodern aesthetic of plagiarism in the historical context of a critical discourse that has remained relatively stable over the centuries. In order to understand plagiarism as a discursive strategy, rather than as a legal infraction,
let us imagine a context where the "right to copy" construes no economic benefits either on author or plagiarist. What exactly, in this situation, would be
the crime of plagiarism; what the benefit; and what the loss sustained by the
victim? And in what sense is the postmodern world different from this utopian
world, which may in fact have existed in a not-so-distant past?

*This research was funded by a grant from the Social Science and Humanities Research Coun-
cil of Canada.

131

A full answer to these questions is beyond the scope of this paper. But one answer does seem to explain a sensitivity to plagiarism which transcends historical considerations of a juridical, economic, and aesthetic nature. This answer maintains that discourse is power, and that discourse powerfully wielded is a potential weapon for exerting control over one's rivals in a contest for ascendancy.

The particularity of plagiarism is that while the potential power of all discourse is an effect of its reception, the covert nature of plagiarism endows the discourse of reception with an additional role: the discovery of plagiarism is simultaneously constitutive of its creation. Plagiarism can, of course, be an intentional act perpetrated for strategic reasons; but the recognition and consequences of this strategy are effects of its reception. As a discourse of power, plagiarism is thus double-edged: construed as an authorial act, it may be seen as a symptom of illegitimate desires on the part of the plagiarist to achieve symbolic power by misappropriating to him- or herself the authority of another; construed, however, as an act of reception, plagiarism—or rather accusations of it—reveals intentions which must be ascribed to the accuser. Historically, the motives ascribed to plagiarism-hunters are seldom more noble than those ascribed to "plagiarists"; the former, usually styled as pedantic critics, are traditionally among the most reviled members of a generally reviled category of men of letters. This discourse of accusation can be seen as an attempt to exert authority over one's rivals in a contest for more than symbolic power. Although plagiarism exists in an entirely symbolic realm, its consequences and effects project it forcefully into social and political arenas where its potential as a source of power is realized.

Plagiarism and Conquest

One indication of the stability of the concept of plagiarism over the course of history resides in the terms used to describe it. Among the plethora of metaphors which have been handed down over the centuries to condemn or justify discursive repetition, none is more tenacious than that of "conquest." This rich metaphor not only expresses the power relations present in the act or perception of plagiarism as a dynamic of dominance, appropriation and possession, but is also sensitive to evolving conceptions of conquest in the sociopolitical realm. While both plagiarism and political conquest have undergone significant transformations over the millennia that constitute their history, the semantic and connotative shifts of "conquest" are more radical than those of "plagiarism." Historically, "plagiarism" has always been bad, while the value of "conquest" depends on one's historicopolitical point of view.

One measure of the specificity of the postmodern aesthetic appears to be its adoption of "plagiarism," not only as an aesthetic practice, but more significantly, as a potentially positive aesthetic descriptor (albeit securely encased in quotation marks). But this apparent discursive shift masks an underlying stability: an exploration of the metaphorical transformations of plagiarism as "conquest" will serve to uncover the functional continuity between premodern and postmodern uses of plagiarism. This exploration will take us into the territory of postcolonial critical discourse seen as an integral part of postmodernism.

Historically, it is by means of a comparison between *translation* and foreign conquest that the metaphor enters the cultural imagination: from Antiquity to the Enlightenment, the conquest and pillage of foreign (cultural) territories was a positive metaphor expressing the enriching effects of the importation of foreign cultural property. Echoing Nietzsche's aphorism that in the period of Roman antiquity, "indeed, to translate meant to conquer," Rita Copeland describes Roman theory of translation as emerging "from a disturbing political agenda" where it "can scarcely be theorized without reference to conquest as a component of rivalry, or aggressive supremacy in the challenge to Greek hegemony" (17).

This tradition becomes firmly entrenched as a principle of translation in the European Renaissance where translation and adaptation from the Ancients were deemed to be legitimate forms of imitation. The terms used by Ronsard and Du Bellay to describe their practices were freely bellicose: Ronsard pillaged Thebes (*Odes* 22: "A sa lyre") and du Bellay pillaged the Delphic temple (*La Deffence et illustration de la langue française*). As the vernacular and the use of national languages gained literary credibility, the terms of legitimate borrowing proscribed the translation from Modern national languages, such that the Ancient-Modern distinction becomes supplanted by the national-foreign one. One of the most often repeated versions of the conquest metaphor is J. B Marini's maxim: "To steal from one's compatriots is theft, but to steal from foreigners is conquest."[1] Roland Mortier describes the transition over the course of the eighteenth century from translation as a source of original to the "new" aesthetic of originality, a transition during which the distinction between legitimate translation and "servile imitation"—or outright plagiarism—becomes cloudy. Not only is translation no longer a sufficient condition for literary creation, but the conventional distinction between translation from a foreign culture, and "borrowing" from within one's own culture also becomes problematic. Already, at the end of the seventeenth century, Pierre Bayle points out that the proscription against translation from Modern and national sources was a rule rather more respected in the breach than in the observance:

> I believe that all authors agree on this maxim, that it is better to pillage the ancients than the moderns, and among these, one should spare one's compatriots, rather than foreigners. . . . All plagiarists, when they can, follow the distinction that I have claimed: but they do not so by principle of

conscience; it is rather in order not to be recognized. When one pillages a modern author, prudence requires that one hide one's loot. (Bayle, "Ephore," *Dictionnaire historique et critique,* qtd. in Nodier 5)

As a consequence of the waning of the tradition of imitation and translation as a source of original work, the metaphor of mercantile conquest, which retains a positive connotation, becomes mobilized as a discursive strategy to deflect suspicions of bad copying and to transform discursive repetition into a legitimate act of appropriation. In his defense of "innocent plagiarism," Nodier justifies borrowing from foreign "moderns" in terms of "the riches acquired by all of the conquests which it has pleased that writer to make over others" (6). He also remarks: "Genius has other ways, in truth, to battle a rival nation, but it has been considered that this one [that is, plagiarism] was not to be disdained" (6). The crux of the problem comes in the breach between borrowing from *foreign* modern authors, and borrowing from one's compatriots. The "pillage" or "piracy" metaphor describing foreign cultural conquest for the purposes of enrichment of the national culture is invalid as a defence against intranational borrowing, where "pillage" is simply "theft."

The evolution of European geopolitical practice provides a new form of the metaphor. Mercantile *conquest* as "pillage" is centripetal: the Other, or his possessions, are drawn into the sphere of the Self in the spirit of self-improvement. This model evolves over the course of the eighteenth century into *colonization,* in which a centrifugal impetus extends the boundaries of the Self over the Other and his territory which are to be recreated in the image of the conqueror. While both movements are appropriative, conquest aims at self-transformation through assimilation of the Other; colonization effects rather an extension of the Self through transformation of the Other.

It is in this context that the *pillage* metaphor of translation evolves into the *colonial* metaphor of legitimate possession through the civilizing work of improvement. Since Classical times, appropriation, transformation and improvement marked the new work with the genius of the imitating artist: the bee's making honey from pollen, or the digestive functions of the human body are ancient and recurring metaphors for describing "good" forms of imitation. The metaphor of discursive borrowing as colonization appropriates these Classical metaphors and imbues them with the colonial logic of possession by improvement, which is itself underwritten by the Lockean principles of production and work as sources of legitimate ownership. It is no longer foreign riches that are to be imported into the indigenous culture for its own benefit, but savage territories which the colonizer, Crusoe-like, makes his own by the appropriative labor of improvement and civilization. Alexander Dumas, whose prolific production was supported by methods much denounced by his detractors, among them "plagiarism," provides the most explicit example:

The man of genius does not steal, he conquers: he makes of the province that he takes an annex of his empire; he imposes on it his laws, he peoples it with his subjects, he extends his golden sceptre over it, and no one dares say, upon seeing his beautiful kingdom: This territory is not part of your rightful heritage. (qtd. in Quérard 72; Larousse, "Plagiat")

But the colonizing metaphor of "plagiarism" is, at best, a rhetorical sleight of hand which hardly serves to achieve its ends. At least, such is the judgment of J-M Quérard who, in the middle years of the nineteenth century, treats Dumas's rhetoric of self-defense with outright sarcasm:

No one plagiarizes any more, no one steals any more, one "conquers"; it's in better taste. . . . Therefore, thanks to the perfect morality of our century, it is not by examples of literary theft that we will continue our survey, but by examples of conquest. (88)

Significantly, this attack against plagiarists does not imply a criticism of conquest: on the contrary, the critic deplores Dumas's attempts to legitimize the odious practice of plagiarism by reframing it as a positive enterprise of conquest.

In the shift from the "pillage" to the "colonization" model of conquest, its positive connotations remain intact. We are, after all, in the realm of the conqueror. And in the shift from the aesthetic of imitation to the aesthetic of "originality," the negative connotations of plagiarism also remain unchanged; it is simply that different texts now fit the model:

The nineteenth century has revolutionized everything. First of all, it proscribes as plagiarism what in the preceding three centuries was considered to be simply legitimate imitation, or "happy theft" (*heureux larcin*). (Larousse, "Imitation")

In spite of this confident declaration, the nineteenth century appears to be one of the most prolific in terms of the production of plagiarists. This, notwithstanding, or more likely because of, the emphasis on originality and the authority of the individual in literary production. Both in British and French letters, celebrated, popular and, in our day, canonical authors engaged in wholesale and large-scale acts of "plagiarism" that the critical community is still debating.[2]

Counterimperial Plagiarism: Return to *Bound to Violence*

In the twentieth century, the metaphor again undergoes a discursive transformation: while neither plagiarism nor imperial conquest are positively valorized, both continue in various guises. The negative connotations of conquest, usually considered today from the point of view of the conquered, are reflected in the metaphor of plagiarism as cultural imperialism that surfaces in rhetorical attacks against those who would usurp the voice and the experience of others—significantly, dominated others—for their own ends. Defenders of the authenticity of voice maintain that the privilege of speaking from the subject-position of experience should be reserved for those who actually inhabit that position.[3] At the same time, the "appropriation" of the dominant voice by the constructed Other of colonialism is a positively valued strategy of retaliation and contestation of the oppression suffered by the colonized. This positive form of the metaphor has currency in instances of cross-cultural copying where "plagiarism" is seen as a weapon of revenge wielded by the former victims of colonization. In the postcolonial inversion of the moral positions of colonizer and colonized, "plagiarism" has undergone a symmetrical transformation. It is rarely the colonizer who plagiarizes from the colonized, presumably because of the presumption of superiority which precludes borrowing from the colonized culture. In this scenario, the colonized is the plagiarist, and in two significant stages. In the first instance, the colonized culture is inevitably a culture of mimicry as described in postcolonial theory where mimicry is a personal, institutional, and cultural response to colonialism.[4] In a second stage, the colonized passes from an unconscious condition of mimicry to a prerevolutionary or oppositional enactment of his condition on the level of cultural production. Appropriating the language of the colonizer and forcing it into the expression of the colonized linguistic and cultural identity is one strategy of the self-conscious inversion and subversion of the destiny of mimicry. Plagiarism may be another.

The paradigm example of the postcolonial uses to which the metaphor of plagiarism-as-conquest has been put is the controversy surrounding Yambo Ouologuem's *Le Devoir de violence* (*Bound to Violence*). The case is exemplary because, over the course of the years since the initial accusation of plagiarism in 1972, following its translation into English in 1971, the critical discourse about the "plagiarism" in this novel has claimed for it almost all available positions, intentions and values. Interpreted negatively at the time of their discovery as an attempted revenge by "reverse colonialism" against former colonizers, the "plagiarisms" have undergone every form of vilification and recuperation, following the progress of postcolonial theory. The story of these readings reveals not only the potential cultural power of (perceived) plagiarism but also the ways in which accusations of plagiarism can be manipulated for political and cultural ends.

Either an intentionally dishonest act of an untalented African student in Paris, or a brilliant politically committed gesture of reverse colonialism, this "first truly African novel" earned the important French *Prix Renaudot* before plunging from glory into an ignominy which ended Ouologuem's career.

Since rehabilited by contemporary criticism, the novel now stands as an exemplar of postcolonial oppositional discourse. The affair has been recounted many times, both by myself and others, and I will not rehearse the details here (Randall, and others cited in this essay). What interests me specifically, both in terms of the continuation and transformation of the conquest-metaphor of plagiarism, and in terms of the pragmatics of plagiarism as a discourse of power, is the evolution of the critical discourse which successively constructs divergent values for the novel and its plagiarisms. What is particularly revealing in this evolution is that whether the plagiarisms are negatively or positively considered, the same two elements are maintained in a constant relationship to one another: the novel embodies plagiarism, and the novel is consequently a counterimperial gesture. Both for the detractors and the defenders of the novel, plagiarism and the colonial condition are intimately linked: whereas in earlier contexts, plagiarism as reverse colonialism was a transgression, in later contexts, the same transgression is celebrated.

Early sympathetic readings of the "plagiarisms" evolved from a denial of their presence to a denial of the intention to plagiarize, arguing in favour of a new aesthetic of collage which we would come to call "intertextuality." Later arguments continue to link plagiarism and colonization, but the ground has shifted such that "plagiarism," in a postmodern context where the subversion of dominant authorities has become widely endorsed, is construed as a powerful weapon wielded for strategic reasons in a morally justified opposition to former colonizers.

The original anonymous denunciation of the novel, "Something *New* Out of Africa?" in the *Times Literary Supplement,* suggested sarcastically that perhaps Ouologuem was "on to something": "a style of literary imperialism intended as a revenge for the much-chronicled sins of territorial imperialists" (525). The controversy which ensued involved Graham Greene (*Le Dernier des justes*), one of the principal victims of Ouologuem's use of "international examples" (Watkins 7), as well as André Schwarz-Bart (*It's a Battlefield*). However, the international references cited by Ouologuem himself are limited to such innocent examples as the stylistic influence of "Afro-American writers," and "Greek and Latin references. . . intended to heighten its meaning on a human level" (Watkins 7); in the same vein, both Ouologuem and his defenders argue that "the so-called plagiarism is a stylistic technique to further the purposes of the novel" (K.W. 941).

The novel's aesthetic "internationalism" which Ouologuem defended is consonant with contemporary theories of "Negritude." In his 1963 text "La littérature d'expression française," Léopold Senghor had argued for the "integral humanism" of "Negro literature written in French" and its important contribution to "Universal Civilization" (402, my translation). Seth Wolitz contributes to this defence by pointing out the "international" composition of the contemporary African intellectual, "whose linguistic knowledge and whose knowledge of African and Occidental cultures is as vast as those of their occidental critics (134).

According to Sellin, the original denouncer of the plagiarisms, there *is* in fact an "authentic African" motivation for the plagiarisms—unfortunately, such authenticity is inappropriate in an Occidental context. First, he acknowledges that the concepts of private discursive property and of personal posterity for the artist are unknown in the traditional African context, making plagiarism irrelevant. He then imagines that Ouologuem's unacknowledged use of European intellectual property constitutes an aspect of the novel's African authenticity. The novel's tragedy is a consequence of the "European tradition of ownership and the question of private immortality that would cause Mr. Greene or Western critics to care if Ouologuem has borrowed patterns and words from the British novelist" (161). This is Sellin at his most conciliating: Ouologuem's African authenticity, his primitive lack of concern for questions of originality and intellectual property, has encountered the indomitable force of European civilization. Ouologuem should have known that he could not "get away," in the European context, with "violating accepted procedure" (162). Sellin's qualification of the unequal encounter as a "tragedy" underlines the inevitably of Ouologuem's defeat by the superior authority of the European tradition. Sellin is untroubled by the paradox he himself has constructed: Ouologuem did not plagiarize—African tradition would make plagiarism "absolutely irrelevant" (161); and Ouologuem did plagiarize—he violated accepted European procedure (162). Ouologuem is playing a European game, and he should abide by European rules: neither the prestigious "éditions Seuil," nor the *Prix Renaudot,* nor European authors, in general, tolerate plagiarists.[5]

Later critical discourse whole-heartedly adopts the notion of plagiarism as an intentional political act. For one critic, plagiarism in *Bound to Violence* is both act and sign: "an act of piracy doubled by the sign of the ironic attitude of the African writer faced with the Occidental text": plagiarism, for Ouologuem, is

> a metaphor signifying the revenge of the African on the slave-trader who has committed rape on the slaves, rape being seen as the physical trace of the oppressive subject of civilization—understood in this case as the system of thought which refuses to the Other his right to difference. (Bouygues 3)

Here, plagiarism is not only an act, for which the metaphor of conquest is the justification, but becomes itself a metaphor for revenge. Given the consequences of this act, the longevity of the controversy and its effect on the European literary institution and on the author, it seems rather understated to relegate plagiarism as an act of revenge to the purely metaphoric realm.

Christopher Miller's defence of Ouologuem's plagiarisms describes them not as a positive revolutionary response to colonialism but rather as a contestatory moment of negativity expressing respect neither for the taboos of "the African nor the European literary establishment" (218). In this reading, Miller postulates a subversionary function for the plagiarisms (and the novel) as an attempt to "exaggerate and undermine the whole tradition" (218), both European and postcolonial. His analysis is consistent with contemporary postcolonial theory in which a new form of cultural hybridity is proposed: Said maintains, for example, that "[n]o one today is purely *one* thing" (1994, 336), and that literary experiences are overlapping and interdependent, retaining their authenticity in new, more unstable maps and entities (317). Homi Bhabha, for his part, identifies, in the case of Algeria, a freedom to "negotiate and translate . . . cultural identites in a discontinuous intertextuality of cultural difference" (38). Such a "dialectical reorganization" allows the construction of a national identity and culture which integrates Western elements without the loss of its indigenous authenticity (38).

Whatever Ouologuem's goals and motivations, it is probable that being accused of plagiarism was not among them. In his case, the accusations of plagiarism wielded power: the book was reedited minus the offending passages; Ouologuem's literary career was over. But his alleged plagiarisms were eventually powerful as well, ensuring an ongoing debate in postcolonial criticism about the power of discourse in the contest of authority between the colonizer and the colonized in the Western cultural domain. The shifting status of the "plagiarisms" in *Bound to Violence,* determined by the various discourses which construct them either as negative or positive examples of counterimperialism, expresses the pragmatic nature of plagiarism and its potential as a discourse of power. Universally interpreted as derived from the author's colonial origins, the "plagiarisms" become, in postcolonial critical discourse, a legitimate act of revenge perpetrated on the colonizer: a contemporary enactment of the metaphor of plagiarism as (counter-) conquest.

In the context of postcolonial discourse, plagiarism retains its functional continuity with premodern instances of plagiarism as a form of power constructed by a discourse of reception. Although enacted in the symbolic realm, plagiarism and its accusations extend the boundaries of this realm into the "real" world, one in which fame and often fortunes are made and destroyed, and in which the contours of cultural authority are established. The motivations for plagiarism and its effects are clearly not monolithic, but as a discursive strategy for gaining dominance in a struggle for cultural power, postcolonial "plagiarism" descends from a long and stable heritage as a symbolic form of conquest; but this time, the conquered turns the tables on the conqueror and asserts, with Said, that the discursive situation is more usually like the unequal relation between colonizer and colonized, oppressor and oppressed. . . . Words and texts are so much of the world that their effectiveness, in some cases even their use, are matters having to do with ownership, authority, power and the imposition of force. (1983, 48)

Notes

1. Marini (1569–1625) is an Italian poet whose aphorism was made famous by Scudéry who quoted it in his preface to *Alaric*. This wisdom is repeated in all sources on plagiarism from Diderot's *Encyclopédie* to Nodier's *Questions de littérature légale*.

2. Coleridge is probably the most famous example of a notorious nineteenth-century cross-cultural "plagiarist" who is still generating critical debate today. See Fruman and the critical responses by Ricks and Hartmann.

3. The controversy over D. M. Thomas's appropriation of the Babi Yar story in the *White Hotel* is a case in point. Thomas was not accused of plagiarism, but rather of unethical use of source material that revealed a failed aesthetic.

4. The imitative relationship between colonized and colonizer is outlined in Fanon (1963; 1986). The idea is developed in Bhabha and Naipaul.

5. A notable exception is André Schwartz-Bart, one of the "victims" of the plagiarism, who claimed that he was happy that his book had nourished an African author: "Thus it is not Mr. Ouologuem who is in debt to me, but I to him" (129).

Literary Borrowing and Historical Compilation in Medieval China

Robert André LaFleur

Sima Guang's (1019–1086) *Zizhi tongjian* is an eleventh-century chronicle covering 1,362 years of China's past, from 403 BCE to CE 959. Its influence on Chinese historiography has been enormous, sometimes masking the reality that it was compiled from 322 different sources—ranging from official histories to fiction and anecdotal writings. Covering ten thousand pages in a recent edition, there are just over one hundred instances in which the author uses his own words—the *lun*, or commentarial passages. The rest of the text is a cutting and pasting of verbatim quotations from earlier sources, creating a mosaic of Chinese documents covering over a millennium of Chinese history.

As his *Song Dynasty History* biography notes, Sima Guang had been taught the Chinese historical classics—particularly the *Spring and Autumn Annals* and its most influential commentary, the *Zuozhuan*[1]—from an early age, and developed a lasting interest in historical study (Tuo 1977). With these works as his guide, Sima considered China's official histories to be hollow documents, and longed for the "mirror of virtue" and chronicle style of the classical works. He writes, of the book he originally titled *Tongzhi*, or *Comprehensive Records:*

> Since my youth, I have perused the various histories; it appears that in the "annal and biography" form, the text's characters are diffuse—although learned specialists read them time and again, they cannot understand them as a whole. It is still more difficult for the emperor, having myriad daily concerns but desiring to know comprehensively the gains and losses of past events. I have always desired to compile, roughly following the form of the *Zuozhuan* and *Chunqiu*, a chronological history entitled *Tongzhi*, beginning with the Warring States and continuing to the Five Dynasties. It would select from books other than the standard histories, and concern the state's flourishing and decline, with its consequences for the people's good and ill fortune. It will include those events which it is appropriate for rulers to know—good can then be emulated, evil shunned. (Li 208.2b)

This statement contains the essence of Sima Guang's historiography: a wide use of sources, an eye cocked toward problems of government, and an unswerving emphasis on traditional Confucian values—from protection of the people to the maintenance of heaven's mandate. Sima wanted his *Comprehensive Records* to furnish "models and warnings," taken from China's history, which would guide rulers toward virtuous government (Li 208.2b).

The Song dynasty (960–1279) emperor Shenzong (r. 1067–1085) took a close interest in Sima Guang's work, and confirmed the imperial interest in such an approach to history by giving it the imposing title *Zizhi tongjian—Comprehensive Mirror for Aid in Ruling.* Shenzong composed a preface to the text, and suggested that it be "presented daily for study." The preface suggests that there was a great deal more to Chinese historiography than names, dates, and events. What seems to have impressed him are the broad Confucian principles in which they are enveloped (Sima 33–34). These principles are precisely what Sima Guang sought to illuminate in the *Zizhi tongjian*, by breaking with the terse, bureaucratic forms of the official histories and connecting historical events with what he called the "underpinnings of danger and prosperity, flourishing and decline (Sima 9607).

Sima Guang *compiled and edited* the *Zizhi tongjian;* he did not write much of it. It was, moreover, not his work alone. Five different historians helped compile the drafts, first preparing the *congmu,* a chronology of the main events in the text's 1,362-year time frame. All told, Sima Guang and his associates worked on the project over a nineteen-year period, completing a long draft (*changbian*) far more voluminous than the final text. The editors of the enormously influential *Siku quanshu* have the following to say about the *Zizhi tongjian* and its researchers:

> In the year 1065 Sima Guang received the task of composing the *Tongjian,* and on January 1, 1085 the work was completed and presented to the throne. So nineteen years had therefore passed for its completion. Sima Guang said in the report with which he handed it in that he had exhausted all his intellectual strength in this work. In addition to the official historical annals he had also used three hundred twenty-two works of various historiographers for it. The long draft, which was in Luoyang, filled two rooms; by this, one can calculate what amount of material there was before he edited it. . . .
>
> [His aides] were all thoroughly-educated Confucians of the greatest knowledge, not of the kind that can only make hollow speeches about life and fate. For this reason the subject of the work is very comprehensive and of great richness. Its outer form is impressive, its thought progression sharp, the like of which has not previously existed. Concerning all questions and matters, the explanations are all-encompassing and deeply-reasoned, not in such a way that a shallow knowledge could pierce through them. (*Wenyuange siku quanshu* 304:1–2)

It is important to note that the editors give praise not only to the commentaries that Sima Guang prepared for the text, but to the richness of the text's historical narrative—almost all of which consisted of material borrowed directly from his sources, but placed in a new narrative configuration.

A letter written from Sima Guang to one of his assistants precisely spells out the method to be followed in preparing the "long draft" for the Tang dynasty (618–906). The long draft, according to Sima Guang, should "err on the side of including too much rather than too little," and should put a premium on selecting from the most authoritative texts, supplementing the resulting core of historical information with materials from miscellaneous records, anecdotes, family biographies, and even collected literary works (Beasley 161–62).

It is clear that Sima Guang sought to create a mélange of detailed statements about the Chinese past that would be framed by a rigidly chronological structure. The historian lacked a direct narrative presence in this form of historiography. With the object of concern being editing, Sima Guang and his assistants formed a new historical record from older texts, providing only transitions and occasional commentaries in their own words. Sima Guang himself referred to the method as "scissors and paste." Locations in which new material was to be added were cropped and the new portion was pasted in (Beasley 162).

The "long draft" for the Tang dynasty totaled over six-hundred chapters, more than double the size of the entire *Zizhi tongjian* when completed. Sima Guang severely reduced these to a mere eighty. The final editing process and the inclusion of scattered passages of historical commentary was the sole work of Sima Guang. The completed text—though made up almost exclusively of other historians' writings—reflects the philosophy of government and history that can be found in Sima's collected letters and memorials.

Indeed, the *Zizhi tongjian* bears a very strong resemblance to the *Zuozhuan* which Sima Guang so admired. Its anecdotal approach and wealth of diverse materials wrapped together in a strict Confucian worldview shows the powerful influence of that text on Sima's work. Rarely in either work does the author intrude on the narrative; when he does, his opinion is always prefaced by a clear introduction of his personal voice—"Your servant, Guang, observes . . ."

Some of the *Zizhi tongjian*'s commentaries are several hundred characters long, cover four or five pages of text, and often have a relatively complex rhetorical strategy. Most, such as the entry below, are brief, and comment quite directly on a preceding textual entry:

> Eighth month. Sun Quan sent an envoy to declare himself subject [to
> Wei], his memorial worded in humble language. He also returned Yu Jin and

others [who were prisoners in Wu] . . . Yu Jin's mustache and hair were white, his appearance disheveled. Before the sovereign, he wept and knocked his head against the ground. The sovereign consoled him, relating the stories of Xun Linfu and Meng Mingshi. He appointed him *anyuan jiangjun,* ordering him north to Ye, and to visit Gaoling. The sovereign then had images of Guan Yu's victory, Pang De's rage, and Yu Jin's surrender painted on the Gaoling mausoleum walls. Seeing this, Jin was ashamed, grew ill, and died.

   Your servant, Guang, observes:

   Yu Jin commanded several tens of thousands of troops. Defeated, he could not bring himself to die, surrendering alive to the enemy. For Wendi, dismissing him or executing him would have been acceptable. Yet he had paintings made on tomb walls in order to insult him. This act was not that of a [worthy] sovereign. (Sima 2192–93)

It is important to point out that the vast majority of commentaries in the text are of precisely this sort—employing the text's narrative as its "introduction" and getting to the commentarial point in an efficient manner. They are, in short, closely intertwined with the borrowed narratives that surround them.

History, Chronicle, and Commentary

In terms of organization, the chronicle form certainly made the collation of over three-hundred sources covering a period of more than a millennium more manageable. However, there is far more to Sima Guang's use of the form than mere organization. "I have compiled the work in chronicle form," he writes, "in order to show that there is a pattern for the sequences of later events, that pure and coarse are not random, and that a single dynasty has too little strength to be able to achieve perfection" (Sima 9607).

   Sima Guang wished to return to a more basic kind of history—one in which moral guidelines could be interwoven with historical events. That later histories strayed from the chronicle structure of the classical histories was a fact bemoaned by literati for many centuries. Hu Sanxing (1230–1287), in his notes to the *Zizhi tongjian,* observes with satisfaction that Sima Guang *returned* to the chronicle form and achieved widespread acclaim by combining historical narration with ethical teaching. Sima Guang's critical response to mainstream official historiography was a carefully researched and organized chronicle history intended, at its highest interpretive level, to wed classical example, historical event, and contemporary statecraft in a single, powerful conceptual scheme.

   The *Zizhi tongjian* inspired a virtual renaissance in Chinese historical writing during the Song dynasty and beyond. In addition to Zhu Xi's (1130–1200) *Zizhi tongjian gangmu* and the extremely important commentaries of Hu Sanxing and Wang Fuzhi (1619–1692), the *Zizhi tongjian* spawned a wide variety of texts that essentially borrow materials from it but rework them according to different structural principles. The most prominent of these is Yuan Shu's (1131–1205) topical arrangement in the *Tongjian jishi benmo,* which collected entries from Sima Guang's work under more than two hundred subject headings so that they could be read as separate, self-contained accounts, from the division of the state of Jin in 403 BCE to the events surrounding the last emperor of the Later Zhou dynasty in CE 959. Throughout the work, Yuan Shu makes use of the *Zizhi tongjian*'s precise, though borrowed, wording—in essence changing the original text less by rewriting than by restructuring.

The structure of the *Zizhi tongjian* is fundamentally diachronic—a river of events flowing from the fifth century BCE to the tenth century of the common era. But the bare chronicle accounts for only a relatively small portion of the text; the remaining material consists of ministerial discussions, official memorials, and the commentaries of earlier scholars, often quoted verbatim from previous sources. If the "events," as I have described them, constitute a river of time, then this supporting material can best be described as a vast flood plain, many times larger than the water itself.

For example, the core historical fact of a lengthy entry in the year CE 235 is terse: "Autumn, seventh month. In Luoyang, *Chonghua* hall burned." This concise entry states clearly what happened, where, and when—a minimum requirement for any history. What follows, however, is prolix. The discussion between ruler and minister places the event in moral perspective; it addresses the broader question *Why did this happen?*

> Autumn, seventh month. In Luoyang, *Chonghua* hall burned.
>
> The emperor asked the *shizhong* . . . Gaotang Long of Taishan, "What inauspiciousness is this? Is there a way of removing it in the rites?"
>
> Gaotang Long replied, "The *Yizhuan* states, 'When those above are not economical and those below are not frugal, fires of retribution enflame their houses.' It also states, 'When rulers build high their quarters, heavenly fires cause disaster.' This indicates the people's ruler ornaments palaces, unaware of the people's fatigue. Therefore heaven responds to it with drought, and fire rises from the lofty halls."
>
> The emperor asked Long, "I have heard that in Han Wudi's time, Boliang burned, yet he undertook great construction of palaces and halls in order to exorcise it. What is its meaning?"
>
> Long replied, "That was something done by a shaman of the Yue barbarians, not enlightened instruction of sagacity and virtue. The *Wuxing zhi* states, 'Boliang burned; afterwards there was the Jiang Chong palace poison affair.' As the *Zhi* says, the Yue shaman and [the building of] Jian Zhang palace did not exorcise anything. "At present it is appropriate to release laborers. As for palace regulations, follow frugality and economy; sweep clear

the place which burned, and dare not construct anything there—then *shapu*
and *jiahe* plants will certainly grow on that land.

"Now, as for sapping the people's strength and depleting their resources, these are *not* the means by which you will cause auspicious influences and attract distant people. (Sima 2310–11)

Although modern readers may be puzzled by some of the historical
precedents and allusions in Gaotang Long's (d. 237) memorial, his practical
advice can be summarized in one sentence: the ruler must discontinue frivo-
lous spending and redirect government resources toward more important
spheres. But Sima Guang did not summarize the minister's advice; he quoted
extensive portions of it from the minister's *Sanguo zhi* biography (Chen
708–719). He included a passage rich in cosmic imagery and allusions to an
intellectual universe that is anything but "given" in the nature of things—with
reference to heaven, antiquity, and the common people, as well as shamans,
barbarians, and exotic plants. Gaotang Long's discursive analysis frames the
raw event—a palace fire—in a moral universe. Repeated, as these images are,
throughout the history, they give shape to a quintessentially Confucian social
and political philosophy—a culturally specific outline of the world *as it ought
to be,* contrasted with the world as documented in the historical record.

Although the *Zizhi tongjian* is often spoken of as a didactic history, the
author himself only rarely interprets events in stark moral terms, as clearly
right or wrong. Sima Guang was loath to pronounce directly on most matters,
preferring to let the context of the historical work validate his worldview.
Ministerial discussions quoted in the text set this context, and later events
often confirm its validity. For example, the following set of passages from the
Zizhi tongjian narrative of CE 223 represents—entirely from borrowed
material—a rich mosaic of flashback, classical imagery, multiple voices, and
moral instruction:

Heaven sent down a great epidemic. The emperor ordered his entire
army to retreat.

Third month, the day *bingshen.* The emperor returned to Luoyang.

Before this, the emperor asked Jia Xu: "I wish to attack those who do
not follow my commands in order to unify *all under heaven.* Wu, Shu—
which should be first?"

Jia Xu replied: "One who attacks and occupies looks first to military
strength. One who establishes foundations looks first to transforming his fol-
lowers through virtue. Your Majesty responded to the historical moment, received the Han emperor's abdication, and, in a soothing manner, rule over
the land. If you approach these territories through refinement and virtue,
waiting for changes, then pacifying them will not be difficult. Although Wu
and Shu are small states, they are protected by mountains and water . . . The
Way of using military power is first to gain advantage over the enemy and
only later to fight—to measure the strength of the enemy and only later to

name commanders. Therefore, no strategy will go awry. Your servant finds that none of your many officials approaches [Wu or Shu]. Although with heavenly awe you may invade them, you will not overcome them. In antiquity, Shun danced with shields and axes, whereupon the Miao surrendered. Your servant maintains that at this time it is appropriate to promote refinement and peace and distance our thoughts from warfare.

The emperor did not accept the advice. In the end, the campaign did not succeed. (Sima 2212–13)

The entire text of the entry, except for the first and last sentences, consists of Jia Xu's memorial, quoted directly from his *Three Kingdoms History* biography. Its main theme—diplomacy before warfare—was reinforced by reference to both classical example and what might be called contemporary political insight. But the last sentence, a simple statement, taken with only slight wording changes from the biography, places the emperor's (and Jia Xu's) actions in moral perspective and validates a traditional set of values regarding diplomacy and warfare in the Middle Kingdom. Jia Xu's remonstrance frames the emperor's choices in a moral universe in such a way that later officials could apprehend lessons for future moral conduct—all without the author formally addressing the audience.

Reading the *Zizhi tongjian*

As should by now be clear, Sima Guang's willingness to let earlier documents "speak for themselves" by placing older texts into contemporary writings was a characteristic of Chinese historiography well into imperial times. The author was clearly aware of the origins of these passages—it lay at the heart of his historiography, and was part of a long tradition of "literary borrowing" in Chinese historical narrative. Yet the vast majority of passages contain no hint of their textual origins. Although many recent scholars have worked to trace Sima Guang's sources for each entry (impossible in many cases because the original texts have been lost), this was clearly of minor importance to medieval readers of Chinese historical writing.

Close examination or criticism of historical material at this time was not nearly as important as the continuity of the historical record. Chinese historians in medieval times had a marked reticence toward tampering with the work of their predecessors, even though they rarely acknowledged the original sources of textual passages. This approach to historical composition is one that echoes the words spoken to a lecture class by the French historian Fustel de Coulanges. On hearing the students' applause for a stimulating lecture on history, he said "Do not applaud me. It is the voice of history that speaks through me" (Gooch 212). Displaying a similar attitude toward authority of the past, Sima Guang let a wide array of documents "speak through him" in his lengthy

Comprehensive Mirror. He engaged these texts through his own commentary, raising in the reader evaluative skills far stronger than if the entire history had been made up of a more seasoned blend of embedded comment.

For the reader of the *Zizhi tongjian,* Roland Barthes's maxim that "reading consists of bringing texts together," that reading is "a constructive activity, a kind of writing" (Barthes 98) is particularly relevant. The *Zizhi tongjian* is a series of older texts woven into a single document that was meant to connect the myriad events of Chinese history into a comprehensible pattern. The reading of the text is significant, but so too is the inevitable interaction with the *memorized* materials from a classical education. This is the link between the written page and the larger moral universe of meaning within which a Chinese scholar-official worked. This is why, to paraphrase Confucius' *Analects,* the *Zizhi tongjian* could give one-tenth of an event's meaning (just the "facts"), leaving the literati reader to supply (or "write") the remaining nine-tenths in the context of his life (*Analects* 5:9).

To my mind, the constructive activity in reading the *Zizhi tongjian* lies in contrasting the historical materials recounted in the text with what might be called a Confucian moral universe of meaning that was very much a part of the classical training of eleventh-century readers of history. Not only is the *Zizhi tongjian* a collection of many earlier works, but, like all didactic Chinese narrative, the text inevitably called to mind the common reading in classical texts shared by every reader of the work. Such an example can be found in another memorial attributed to Gaotang Long, who again richly quotes from classical materials in making very basic political points to his sovereign:

> The day *dingsi.* The emperor returned to Luoyang.
> The emperor ordered that *Chonghua* palace be erected again, renaming it *Jiulong*—Nine Dragons. Gushui's waters were engineered to flow to the front of the Nine Dragon palace; a jade well and beautiful railing were built . . .
> Construction of *Lingxiao que* had just begun when magpies nested on it. With this on his mind, the emperor inquired of Gaotang Long. Gaotang Long replied, "The *Shi* says 'The magpie's nest, the dove's abode.' Presently you have erected palaces and raised *Lingxiao que,* yet magpies nest there. This is an omen that the palace will never be finished and that you yourself will not succeed in residing there. Heaven's opinion is: "Palaces will not be completed and one of another surname will control them." This is a warning from heaven above. Now, heaven's Way does not show favor—only good people benefit. Taiwu and Wuding observed disasters and were struck with fear. Therefore heaven showered them with fortune. If now you cease construction, build upon reverent and virtuous government—then the Three Kings can become four and the Five Emperors can become six. How could it be only the Shang ancestors who turned disaster to fortune?
> Because of this, the emperor changed color. (Sima 2311–2312)

There is a dissonance of voices in the *Zizhi tongjian* that is not resolved by the author's commentaries. The reader is expected to play an integral role in shaping the meaning of the text, in working through the multiple assertions and meanings found in the quoted materials which make up the work. The *Zizhi tongjian* is hard to read, in short, beyond the most basic relation of events in time. It assumes a broad classical education as well as a reader capable of putting the text back together in his own vision.

The core concept is that readers would digest the material in the text and use the lessons thus internalized within the (con)texts of their own lives. "Reading is always a rewriting of the text of the work within the text of our lives," writes Robert Scholes (Scholes 1). In short, literati readers of the *Zizhi tongjian* would make wiser, more incisive decisions in their own governmental practices not because they had *read* the book or garnered a few "facts" from its narrative, but precisely because they had internalized, "rewritten," the text for their own purposes.

It is instructive to turn to a comment by the Qing dynasty (1644–1911) scholar Zhang Zhupo (1670–1698) to better explain this way of reading Chinese narrative. Zhang wrote that by reading the complex novel *Jin Ping Mei* "as a description of actual events you will be deceived by it; you must read it as a work of literature not to be deceived by it." Zhang continues:

> If you read the *Chin Ping Mei* as a work of literature by the author, you will still be deceived by it. *You must read it as though it were your own work* in order not to be deceived by it.
>
> Though you should certainly read it as though it were your own work it is even better to read it as a work that is still in the early planning stages. Only if you start out with *the assumption that you will have to work out every detail for yourself* in order to avoid being deceived will you avoid being deceived. (Roy 224)

While I do not wish to argue that Sima Guang or his contemporaries would say that reading the *Zizhi tongjian* as a description of actual events would lead to *outright* deception, it is clear that the scholar who reads passively through the vast swaths of quoted material will miss the power and complexity of a work that borrows extensively from earlier documents and calls to mind a classical education that was the common property of every educated scholar-official of the time.

Although many voices can be found on any page of the text, it would be a serious misinterpretation to assert that the *Zizhi tongjian* is characterized by an array of *equally valid* voices. Sima Guang let many voices speak, and his own is far more muted than in later examples of "normative" historiography, such as Fan Zuyu's *Tangjian,* Zhu Xi's *Tongjian gangmu,* and the Tokugawa scholar Arai Hakuseki's (1657–1725) *Tokushi yoron.* Yet it is also apparent that Sima Guang felt there was a clear pattern to historical events—a "right"

way of perceiving the broad pattern and lessons of China's past. The arrangement of the *Zizhi tongjian* assumes that the intelligent reader will grasp this
without excessive help from the author.

The historian's personal voice need not be clearly heard on every page to
achieve a substantial effect, however. One must recognize that, following the
classical scholar Friedrich Meinecke, the historian's use of evaluative language, which is often highly implicit in Sima Guang's narrative, arouses in
the reader stronger evaluating skills than more clearly didactic works:

> The presentation and exposition of culturally important facts is utterly
> impossible without a lively sensitivity for the values they reveal. Although
> the historian may, in form, abstain from value-judgments of his own, they
> are there between the lines and act as such upon the reader. The effect
> then . . . is often more profound and more moving than if the evaluation
> were to appear directly in the guise of moralizing, and therefore it is even to
> be recommended as an artifice. The historian's implicit value-judgment
> arouses the reader's own evaluating activity even more strongly than one
> which is explicit. In that, seemingly, causalities alone are offered, the ele-
> ment of value, the revelation of a spiritual power in the midst of a network
> of causality, comes through more immediately and more productively.
> (Meinecke 273–274)

In short, the commentaries explicitly and the historical events implicitly
teach the reader how to read the long and complex narrative that is the *Zizhi
tongjian*. History—the details of *what happened, where, and when* in China's
past—was regarded as the communal intellectual property of the scholar-
officials who wrote and read it over the centuries. The results of their *personal*
engagement with that past—their own written commentaries—were very
much perceived as belonging to the individual writer, and became part of the
collected writings of poetry, court memorials, letters, and essays that all serious literati compiled before their deaths. From the perspective of Sima Guang,
it was in the *reader's experience* of historical narrative and authorial comment
that the full power of such historical composition was to be found.

Notes

1. The *Spring and Summar Annals* are attributed to Chunqui, traditionally edited
by Confucius (551–479 BCE). For text and translation, see James Legge, *Ch'un Tseu
with Tso Chuen, The Chinese Classics,* Vol. 5, parts 1 & 2. See also Zuo zhuan, Mr.
Zuo's Commentary on the Chunqui, compiled 4th century BCE, in the same volume.

PART II
Applications

In the Writing Center

Writing Centers and Plagiarism*

Irene L. Clark

On a visit to New Zealand in 1985, I was invited to the University of Waikato to discuss the role of writing centers in the United States*. Initially confident that my presumably "enlightened" approach to writing instruction would be greeted with approval, I was somewhat disconcerted to discover that my audience, comprised of faculty members from several departments, was less than enthusiastic about the instructional model I was presenting, because they viewed writing center assistance as a form of sanctioned plagiarism. "Your students must love your center," a professor from the English department observed. "You do all of their work for them."

At first, of course, I was appalled at this attitude. But now I recognize it as characteristic of that time, even at American institutions with their own writing centers. As the writing center literature of the seventies and eighties attests to, it was not unusual for writing center assistance to arouse suspicion from colleagues in other departments. At a university where I taught in the late seventies, I recall that a professor in the English department actually forbade her students to receive writing center assistance, because it would give them "an unfair advantage." And even now, in the presumably enlightened nineties, when writing centers have proliferated all over the United States as well as in Canada, Australia, and New Zealand and when the term "collaboration" has become a professional shibboleth, some faculty remain steadfastly suspicious. "The problem is my dean," someone in the process of establishing a new writing center told me recently. "He worries that tutoring students in a writing center will result in plagiarized papers, so he thinks we should stick to grammar instruction."

However, despite attitudes such as this, and despite a prevailing cultural concern with intellectual property rights that has been reflected with particular scrupulousness within the university community, there is some evidence

---

*Some of the background material referred to in this chapter also appears in Clark, Irene, and Dave Healy, "Are Writing Centers Ethical?" *Writing Program Administration* 20, 1/2 (Fall/Winter 1996): 32–49.

155

to suggest that attitudes are changing. At the University of Southern California (USC), a recent survey concerned with assessing faculty attitudes toward writing center assistance indicates increased faculty understanding of the importance of collaboration in writing acquisition and a correspondingly decreased anxiety about the possibility of plagiarism. This article traces the impact that concern with plagiarism has had on writing center pedagogy over the past thirty years, discusses the results of the USC survey, and speculates on the effect that a greater acceptance of collaborative learning and a lesser concern with plagiarism could have on writing center instruction.

The Evolution of Writing Centers

Writing centers' concern with defending themselves against charges of plagiarism became of particular significance in the late seventies and early eighties as writing centers evolved from "labs" that focused on skill and drill, to "centers" that worked with the whole writing process. Before that time, as Peter Carino notes in his chronicle of early writing center history, writing centers tended to consist of "labs" that were situated within writing classrooms. These labs employed an individualized approach to instruction, frequently focusing on grammar and surface correctness. "Drills were part of the methods of early centers" (113), Carino notes, and even if other forms of instruction took place (as apparently they did, at least sometimes), the university community perceived writing centers as centers of remediation for less able students. Carino cites the example of the writing center at Stephens College, which was set up for "[t]he student who finds it very difficult to spell correctly or who makes gross errors in English usage. Here causes are determined, exercises under supervision are given, and practical applications to everyday writing are made" (Wiksell 145).

For established university departments, this presumed emphasis on remedial instruction was a "safe" role for writing centers to fulfill because it posed no threat to the "ownership" of the student text, and therefore did not generate suspicions of plagiarism. However, as Composition began to redefine itself as a distinct discipline, embracing a process/collaborative, student-centered instructional approach, skill and drill in writing centers began to be supplemented and sometimes replaced by a pedagogy that addressed the shape and content of an actual text. This new pedagogy, as described by Steve North, was:

> a pedagogy of direct intervention. Whereas in the "old" center instruction tends to take place after or apart from writing, and tends to focus on the correction of textual problems, in the "new" center the teaching takes place as

much as possible during writing, during the activity being learned, and tends
to focus on the activity itself. (439)

Such a change in emphasis, however, generated a corresponding concern in
faculty members from other departments, suspicious that authorial autonomy
was being threatened and that writing center instruction was straining ethical
boundaries.

Cultural Concerns with Intellectual Property Rights and Writing Center Pedagogy

Concern with plagiarism in writing center instruction reflects a pervasive cultural concern with intellectual property rights that has gained particular
prominence in academia. Although critical theorists have raised questions
about the nature or even existence of authors and texts, instruction in Composition and Literature courses "continues to enforce the Romantic paradigm"
(Woodmansee and Jaszi 1994, 9) of the lone author creating original work, an
emphasis that is also compatible with the focus on evaluation and the maintenance of literacy "standards" over which so much academic ink has been
spilled. As has been noted by Bruffee (1984), Trimbur (1987), Clark (1988),
and Lunsford and Ede (1994), the nineteenth-century concept of the solitary
creative genius eventually manifested itself in a twentieth-century emphasis
"on writing as an individually creative act, and on 'objective testing' as a
means of evaluating the intellectual property of solitary writers" (418). But
such a perspective is least in accord with the collaborative work that characterizes writing center assistance.

As I have noted elsewhere (Clark 1988, 1990, 1996), the writing center's
need to defend itself from charges of plagiarism from other departments has
resulted in the creation of an entrenched policy of noninterventionism, self-
defensively aimed at preventing challenges to a teacher's judgment or a tutor's
appropriation of a student text. In working with students, writing center tutors
are advised to embrace a "see no evil, speak no evil" policy in regard to instructors and to refrain from suggesting ideas or specific words (my colleague,
Dave Healy, refers to this as a "sitting on its hands" approach to writing instruction). North's much cited 1984 article "The Idea of a Writing Center"
states that writing centers "never play student advocates in teacher-student
relationships . . . [and] never evaluate or second-guess any teacher's syllabus,
assignments, comments, or grades" (441), and his oft-quoted statement that
"in a writing center the object is to make sure that writers, and not necessarily
their texts, are what get changed by instruction" (438) constitutes an assurance
against the possibility of plagiarism. After all, if it is only the student, and not
the text, that improves as a result of writing center assistance, then surely no

textual property has been appropriated and no ethical principles have been violated. This idea was endorsed enthusiastically by many writing center professionals, who, without questioning either its desirability or viability, instituted policies to ensure its implementation.

The literature of the early eighties, when the *Writing Lab Newsletter* and *Writing Center Journal* became vehicles for public discussion of writing center issues, reflected the need for writing centers to reassure traditionalists in other departments that writing center instruction did not equal plagiarism and to promote a fiercely noninterventionist pedagogy. In an article appearing in 1981, Larry Rochelle refers to "enemies" of the writing center, in particular "overwrought English professors . . . who . . . think that Writing Centers are helping students too much" (7). An article by Patrick Sullivan in 1984 expresses similar concerns and emphasizes the importance of clearly articulated policies on plagiarism. The following year, Sullivan reported the result of a survey assessing faculty attitudes toward students' receiving writing center assistance. "I don't approve of them editing final drafts," one teacher responded:

> My Vietnamese student who came in to see you received much too much help with his composition—even suggestions for ideas to be incorporated into the paper. In cases where a student has serious grammatical and organizational problems, I would even prefer he or she not take a draft of the paper to the center at all, but rather get help through the use of verb exercises. (6)

Awareness of how suspiciously writing centers were viewed by faculty members from other departments thus generated a set of ingrained noninterventionist policies, referred to as a writing center "bible" (Shamoon and Burns), writing center "dogma" (Clark 1990), or writing center "mantras" (Blau), and which remain operant, even today. Do "not write any portion of the paper—not even one phrase," Suzanne Edwards wrote in June of 1983 in the *Writing Lab Newsletter*. Never "edit the paper for mechanical errors. This includes finding or labeling the spelling, punctuation, or grammar mistakes in a paper or dictating corrections" (8). In 1988, Evelyn Ashton-Jones characterized the tutoring situation as "Socratic dialogue," warning tutors not to "lapse into a 'directive' mode of tutoring," which she labels as "counterproductive" to learning (31). Even in the nineties, when the Internet is calling into question a number of ideas concerning text ownership, Jeff Brooks in his argument for minimalist tutoring maintained: "When you 'improve' a student's paper, you haven't been a tutor at all; you've been an editor. You may have been an exceedingly good editor, but you've been of little service to your student. . . . The student, not the tutor, should 'own' the paper and take full responsibility for it" (2). And in 1995, Thomas Thompson equates the nondirective approach to tutoring with the military honor code at the Citadel:

[T]utors try to avoid taking pen in hand when discussing a student paper. They may discuss content, and they may use the Socratic method to lead students to discover their own conclusions, but tutors are instructed not to tell students what a passage means or give students a particular word to complete a particular thought. (13)

Principles of nondirective tutoring, deriving from concern about accusations of plagiarism, thus took on an orthodoxy that, as Shamoon and Burns point out, "seem less the product of research or examined practice and more like articles of faith that serve to validate a tutoring approach which 'feels right,' in fact so right that it is hard for practitioners to accept possible tutoring alternatives as useful or compelling" (135).

Other Factors Justifying Noninterventionist Policies

Of course, there are other reasons one might cite in favor of a noninterventionist pedagogy in the writing center. Learning theorists, such as Jerome Bruner, point out the importance of engaging students in the learning process in order for learning to occur. A tutor, Bruner emphasizes, "must direct his instruction in a fashion that eventually makes it possible for the student to take over the corrective function himself. Otherwise, the result of instruction is to create a form of mastery that is contingent upon the perpetual presence of the tutor" (53). Attribution theory similarly emphasizes the importance of learner responsibility in the learning process, claiming that the reason or factor to which the learning is attributed has a significant impact on subsequent learning. According to Weiner, learner achievement is maximized when learners attribute success to their own efforts, not to the input of tutors or to "luck." Thus, in terms of writing center assistance, attribution theory suggests that student writing ability is most likely to improve when students attribute improvement to their own work, not to the skill of the tutor. Consequently, it is important for students to participate in the learning process as much as possible.

The Impact of Noninterventionism on Writing Center Assistance

No one questions the desirability of students involving themselves in their own learning as much as possible. However, by unquestioningly and dogmatically embracing a nondirective approach to tutoring, writing centers have overlooked a number of situations in which a more directive approach might be more appropriate. Shamoon and Burn's "critique" of pure tutoring cites a number of examples in which a directive approach was extremely effective. Burns recalls the person who supervised the writing of her master's thesis who used directive intervention, yet was the most helpful to her in her graduate studies. Violating every principle of entrenched writing center pedagogy, Burns's thesis director "substituted his own words for hers, and he stated with disciplinary appropriateness the ideas with which she had been working. Essentially he rewrote them while they watched" (Shamoon and Burns 138).

Moreover, such directive tutoring was apparently equally effective with other graduate students:

> He took their papers and rewrote them while they watched. They left feeling better able to complete their papers, and they tackled other papers with greater ease and success . . . His practices seem authoritative, intrusive, directive, and product-oriented. Yet these practices created major turning points for a variety of writers. (138)

The Shamoon and Burns article, which created quite a stir on WCENTER, the writing center Internet discussion group, also cites other examples of directive tutoring in faculty workshops:

> Over and over in the informal reports of our colleagues we find that crucial information about a discipline and about writing is transmitted in ways that are intrusive, directive, and product oriented, yet these behaviors are not perceived as an appropriation of power or voice but instead as an opening up of those aspects of practice which had remained unspoken and opaque. (139)

The type of instruction cited in the Shamoon and Burns article is consistent with other explanations for learning, in particular, Vygotsky's notion of "the zone of proximal development," which has been defined as "the distance between the actual development level as determined by the independent problem solving under adult guidance or in collaboration with more capable peers" (86). In terms of its application to writing center assistance, Vygotsky's theories suggest that tutors should address "functions that have not yet matured, but are in the process of maturation, functions that will mature tomorrow, but are currently in an embryonic state" (86). Such a goal might best be reached if a tutor assumes a more directive role until the student is able to assume the function alone, since "what children can do with the assistance of others might be in some sense even more indicative of their mental development than what they can do alone" (85). However, concern with plagiarism has made writing centers reluctant to experiment with this sort of assistance.

Results of the Survey*

Because concern about plagiarism has had such a profound impact on writing center pedagogy and policy, a survey to assess faculty concerns about plagiarism and attitudes toward writing center assistance was distributed in the spring of 1996 to faculty members from four departments at the University of Southern California: English, Political Science, Biology, and Expository Writing. The departments of English, Biology, and Political Science were selected as representatives of their respective disciplines, Expository Writing because its ninety graduate students both teach Composition classes and tutor in the writing center as part of their graduate training and hence are quite familiar with writing center pedagogy.

Since acquaintance with the writing center could not be assumed, except in the case of Expository Writing, the survey initially established the function of writing centers with the following definition:

> Students come to the Writing Center for help with the following facets of writing:
>
> * to discuss a writing assignment before beginning to write;
> * to discover and develop a thesis;
> * to create and improve the structure of a paper; and
> * to incorporate and document information from outside sources;
> * to learn revision and editing strategies.

This definition made it possible for faculty members from all four departments to respond, even those who had never sent students to the writing center.

Faculty Concern with Plagiarism

The results of the survey, tabulated in Tables 1 and 2, suggest that the majority of faculty from all four departments did not view plagiarism among undergraduates as a "very common" problem. Table 2, which includes the results of question #3 (Do you view plagiarism among undergraduate students as a common problem?) indicates that none of the respondents felt that plagiarism was very common and that 60.6 percent of all respondents felt that plagiarism was not common, although 39.4 percent of them thought that the problem was "fairly common."

---

*The tabulations for this survey were done by Jeffrey Wheeler, who was working as my assistant in the Writing Center at the University of Southern California.

Table 1

Question 3: Is plagiarism common?
Question 7: Do you feel that papers receiving writing center assistance reflect student's own writing ability?
Question 8: Are you concerned that writing center assistance is a form of plagiarism?

Responses are indicated by percentage

Discipline	Number of respondents	Is plagiarism a common problem?			After WC assistance, do papers reflect students' own writing ability?			Are you concerned that the help students receive constitutes plagiarism?		
		Very	Fairly	Not	No	Somewhat	Yes	Very	Somewhat	Not
Biology	7	0	66.6	33.3	0	57	43.0	0	0	100
English	10	0	50.0	50.0	10	10	80.0	10.0	10	80
Poli Sci	9	0	55.5	44.4	0	33	66.6	0	10	90
Expo	48	0	30.4	60.6	2	35	63.0	4.3	23.4	71.3
TOTAL	**74**	**0**	**39.4**	**60.6**	**2.7**	**33.8**	**63.5**	**4.1**	**17.8**	**78.1**

(by percent [%] of all respondents)

Table 2

Question 5: Will papers improve through Writing Center assistance?
Question 6: Will writing ability improve through Writing Center assistance?

Discipline	Number of respondents	Do you think that when students receive Writing Center assistance: *papers* are likely to improve?			*writing ability* is likely to improve?		
		Will Not	Might	Will	Will Not	Might	Will
Biology	7	0	57	43	0	57.0	4.0
English	10	10	20	70	10.0	70.0	20.0
Poli Sci	10	0	50	50	0	33.3	66.6
Expo	48	0	50	50	0	62.5	37.5
TOTAL	**74**	**1**	**46.6**	**52.1**	**1**	**59.5**	**39.2**

(by percent [%] of all respondents)

A high percentage of respondents (83.8%) indicated that they addressed the issue of plagiarism in their classes, as opposed to 16.2 percent who did not. The means of addressing the issue varied from defining plagiarism carefully, reading university or department policy, or explaining its seriousness in terms of ethics and personal consequences ("F" for the paper and possibly for the entire course; in some cases, expulsion from the university). As one respondent wrote, "I have a written definition, explanation and policy, which is essentially 'plagiarize and die.'"

In breaking down the responses by department, it is interesting to note that the departments of Biology (66.6%) and Political Science (55.5%) and English (50%) felt more strongly than did Expository Writing (30.4%) that plagiarism was "fairly common," which raises the question of the source of these perceptions. Had these other departments encountered specific cases of plagiarism on a regular basis? Or was their response based simply on a general impression of undergraduate students' lack of ethics in regard to papers and grades? If so, why didn't instructors in the Expository Writing Program feel the same way?

One explanation for the lower percentage of "fairly common" responses in Expository Writing might be linked to the fact that the instructors in that program are all graduate students, and, for the most part, younger and perhaps more idealistic than professors in the other departments. It is conceivable that after a few years of teaching (and encountering cases of plagiarism), more instructors in Expository Writing will feel that plagiarism among undergraduates is "fairly common." Another explanation might be that the process pedagogy adhered to in the Expository Writing Program, which includes small classes, multiple drafts and frequent student conferences, enables instructors in the program to become quite familiar with their students' writing, making it difficult for students to submit work that is not their own. In contrast, many courses in Biology, Political Science, and English utilize a large lecture model, supported by small discussion groups led by teaching assistants who focus on content mastery, rather than on writing acquisition. Thus, because professors in these departments have less familiarity with their students' writing and often do not work with multiple drafts, opportunities for plagiarism or at least the suspicion of it might be greater.

Students' Writing Ability as Reflected in Papers Receiving Writing Center Assistance

The results of question #7 (Table 1) also suggest that the majority of respondents are not concerned that papers receiving writing center assistance will present an unrealistic picture of the student's writing ability. Of the total respondents, 63.5 percent indicated that when students receive writing center assistance, they are not concerned that the resulting papers will reflect students' own ability rather than the ability of their tutors, while 33.8 percent indicated that they are only somewhat concerned. This perception is supported by the results of question #8 (Are you concerned that the help students receive in the writing center constitutes a form of plagiarism?), which indicates that 78.1 percent of all respondents are not concerned that the help students receive in the Writing Center constitutes a form of plagiarism.

In assessing concern about plagiarism in the writing center, it is significant to note that no faculty member in the department of Biology and only 10 percent of faculty members in Political Science expressed concern about writing center assistance being a form of plagiarism, whereas 20 percent of respondents from the English Department and 27.7 percent of respondents from Expository Writing indicated that they were very or somewhat concerned. In regard to the English Department, this response can be partly explained by the fact that one respondent expressed extremely negative views about the concept of the writing center in general, creating a disproportionate impact on what was a relatively small sample (10). This professor, who proudly included his name, also indicated that he *never* recommended that his students visit the writing center, did *not* think that when students receive writing center assistance that either their papers or their writing ability are likely to improve, did *not* think that papers revised in the writing center would reflect students' own writing ability, and was *very* concerned that the help students receive in the writing center constitutes a form of plagiarism. Fortunately, however, this was the only response of this type.

In terms of the Expository Writing Program, the 27.7 percent who expressed at least some concern that writing center assistance constituted a form of plagiarism may reflect the fact that some students do, indeed, use the writing center to such an extent that their work becomes a composite, rather than an individual, effort. All writing centers have at least a few of such "writing center junkies"; frequently these students are anxious nonnative speakers, concerned about their inability to write "error-free" papers. As a result, they spend a great deal of time in the writing center, particularly when they revise their papers for portfolio evaluation, patiently waiting until an appointment is available in order to gain as much tutor input as possible. Instructors from the Expository Writing Program, working with students such as these in the writing center, may thus be at least somewhat concerned that a paper receiving so much writing center assistance may not accurately reflect the student's own writing ability.

The Impact of Writing Center Assistance:
Paper Improvement versus Improvement in Writing Ability

In response to questions 5 and 6 (Do you think that when students receive Writing Center assistance that their papers are likely to improve? Do you think that when students receive Writing Center assistance that their writing ability is likely to improve?), 52.1 percent of respondents felt that the papers *will* improve and 46.6 percent felt that the papers *might* improve. In regard to writing ability, however, only 39.2 percent stated definitively that writing ability *will* improve, although 59.5 percent felt that writing ability *might* improve as a result of writing center assistance.

These responses suggest that there is still considerable uncertainty in all departments (and, indeed, in the profession) about what sort of instruction is likely to cause improvement in student writing ability. In fact, the overall response indicated that although most respondents predicted that writing center assistance is likely to result in an improved student paper, they were less certain that such assistance would affect the student's ability to write. Particularly when responses are broken down by department, it is significant to note that the English Department faculty, with the exclusion of the one respondent who was negative about everything, was much less confident that student writing ability would improve as a result of writing center assistance than they were about improvement in the papers. Only 20 percent felt that writing center assistance would facilitate improvement in student writing ability, whereas 70 percent percent expressed confidence in the improvement in the papers. Expository Writing gave a similar response in regard to student writing ability (37.5% responded "will"; 62.5% responded "might").

Changing Attitudes Toward Plagiarism: Implications for Writing Center Pedagogy

Despite some reservations about the extent to which writing center assistance contributes directly to improved student writing ability, the responses indicated that the faculty at USC have a generally positive attitude toward the writing center and do not associate writing center assistance with plagiarism. In fact, two unsolicited written comments from professors in the English Department, cited below, suggest that attitudes toward intellectual property rights, at least in terms of writing center assistance, may be changing:

Comment #1

Writing need not be a wholly private activity, and in any case, we cannot function well as generous, dexterous educators if we're always policing. The idea is to improve writing—to give students access to more varied and functional expressive and argumentative possibilities. Notions of writing as private property to be patrolled and secured are pernicious.

Comment #2

When it inevitably does happen that a student merely transposes what the instructor says into the paper, I would hope the effect would still be heuristic. To say that help of this sort is a form of plagiarism per se seems absurd.

If these responses are at all typical of faculty at other institutions, they indicate that writing center instruction is viewed with less suspicion than it was in the past, an attitude that has profound implications for writing center pedagogy.

The Social Construction of Ideas

Changing attitudes toward plagiarism will enable writing centers to acknowledge the limitations of individualistic concepts of text ownership and correspondingly to recognize the role of collaboration in the production of all knowledge. As Lisa Ede, Andrea Lunsford, and Marilyn Cooper, among others, have emphasized, the notion that writing is essentially a solitary act relegates the writing center to the role of "pedagogical fix-it shops to help those who, for whatever reason, are unable to think and write on their own" (Ede 7). Cooper points out that writing centers would better serve their clients not by helping students find an authentic voice or "fix" flawed papers, but rather by "helping them understand how and the extent to which they are *not* owners of their texts and *not* responsible for the shape of their texts (101, emphasis in original). As Lunsford states, to "enable a student body and citizenry to meet the demands of the twenty-first century . . . we need to embrace the idea of writing centers as Burkean Parlors, as centers for collaboration" (9).

A writing center that is less focused on text ownership would be less concerned about the often inadvertent appropriation of ideas that sometimes occurs, recognizing that it is difficult, if not impossible to determine with any certainty the source of any of our ideas. Helen Keller, for example, characterizes her own writing as a mixture of assimilation and imitation:

> It is certain that I cannot always distinguish my own thoughts from those I read, because what I read becomes the very substance and text of my mind. Consequently, in nearly all that I write, I produce something which very much resembles the crazy patchwork I used to make when I first learned to sew. (67–68)

As De Grazia points out, the view that knowledge is socially constructed "does away with origins . . . Thus, writing can be nothing more than a tissue of quotations, a pastiche of passages possessing no authorial affiliation and therefore belonging to no one" (301).

A Flexible Approach to Tutoring

Enhanced understanding of a poststructural perspective on knowledge would thus release the writing center from its absolutist adherence to a nondirective pedagogy, enabling it to recognize that for some students, a directive approach might be more effective. In working with learning disabled students at the University of Puget Sound, Julie Neff notes the ineffectiveness of orthodox tutoring practices. Such students, she maintains, require considerably more concrete and even directive assistance, before they can internalize the suggestions of a tutor. A more directive approach is also likely to be helpful to students from nonwestern cultures, who may be unfamiliar with western conventions of academic discourse or with the genre of essay they are expected to produce. As Shamoon and Burns point out, "one tutoring approach does not fit all" (139).

One possible new approach might involve the incorporation of imitation into writing center pedagogy, which, as, Anne Gere points out, was once considered an important learning tool. Gere cites Isocrates' concept of the teacher who "must in himself set such an example that the students who are molded by him and are able to imitate him will, from the outset, show in their speaking a degree of grace and charm greater than that of others" (8). Discussing the history of plagiarism, St. Onge notes that mimicry is used throughout the animal kingdom. "The mocking bird plagiarizes the call of any one of its peers and has been known to tease human whistlers" (17). Along the same lines, Muriel Harris points out the usefulness of imitation in teaching composing skills and writing behaviors such as invention and editing, even to novice writers. In the case study she cites, Harris worked through the writing process herself as the student observed, helping him learn not only what writing behaviors to engage in, but also make decisions about the topics and supporting information.

Finally, if writing centers were freed from concerns about plagiarism, they could be more honest in their pedagogy, no longer requiring students to maintain a standard that they themselves do not observe. All of us who write and publish habitually receive commentary from colleagues and editors that frequently result in extensive changes in a text. Yet, hypocritically, our concern about plagiarism forbids us to make similar suggestions to our students. The change in attitude suggested by the survey at USC should thus encourage all of us who direct or work in writing centers to embrace a more flexible "rhetorically situated view of plagiarism, one that acknowledges that all writing is in an important sense collaborative and that 'common knowledge' varies from community to community and is collaboratively shared" (Lunsford and Ede 437).

Writing Centers and Intellectual Property: Are Faculty Members and Students Differently Entitled?

Carol Peterson Haviland and Joan Mullin

Carol Shields's novel *Small Ceremonies* offers several scenes that illuminate the issues of our chapter: the dance around "resources" spun by a writer, his student, and the student's plot sources. Judith Gill (the student) uses a plot she discovers in the journals of John Spalding (another aspiring novelist) in the novel she begins for Furlong Eberhardt's (the writer/professor) creative writing seminar. Judith feels moderately guilty both about reading John's journals and about using his plot, even though she has supplied her own characters and language. Later, because she finds her emerging draft unsatisfying, she asks that her professor burn the copy she has given him. However, when she discovers that Furlong has used the story for his own successful novel, for which he has recently sold the film rights and is profiting professionally and financially, she is "chilled with disbelief and dull accumulated rage" (106). Even though she recognizes that her own inability to make the plot work was her principal deterrent to publishing her own novel, she sees his using the plot in his novel as a "nefarious, barefaced theft" (108). She feels wounded and betrayed both personally and for her source, John. Shields's novel ends full circle as Judith discovers that John, too, has written a novel that he worries she will think that he "plagiarized from real life" (166), a novel he has based on Judith's son's correspondence with John's daughter.

Judith Gill, John Spalding, and Furlong Everhardt characterize contrasting views of using sources. Novice Judith feels guilt, and novice John acknowledges his debt to the Gill family: "I did want you to know. I mean, in case you had any objections" (167). Professor and professional Furlong, however, argues, "Writers don't steal ideas. They abstract them from wherever they can. I never stole your idea. . . . One takes an idea and brings to it his own individual touch" (133), which makes it his own property.

169

While we may tease out many readings of the Spalding/Gill/Everhardt novel and its sources, of greatest interest for this chapter is the relationship between ownership of ideas and locations of power. Both Spalding and Gill are unpublished writers who see themselves as novices aspiring to recognition. Everhardt has published several novels and is recognized as a leading Canadian novelist. Spalding and Gill feel beholden to their sources; they "know" that they should ask permission to use them. In contrast, even though he demurs when an interviewer asks directly about his inspiration, Everhardt believes that he is entitled to use others' work and that once he has written himself into it, it is his; he seems to think he needs neither to ask permission nor to acknowledge, for he assumes authority over ideas.

Shields's narrative unfolds a fundamental question about intellectual property that writing centers face daily: Who owns what text and why? For example, why do faculty members who regularly revise their own manuscripts in response to journal editors' comments quiz their students vigorously about whether anyone has helped them write the assignments they turn in? Drawing on some of the current research that addresses the ways experienced academics learn how to incorporate disciplinary ways of thinking and constructing knowledge into their work (i.e., Berkenkotter and Huckin's *Genre Knowledge in Disciplinary Communication* and Bazerman's *Constructing Knowledge*) and on our own academic writing experiences, this chapter plays the writing that faculty members ask their students to produce against the writing that they produce themselves, looking for the similarities and differences that may result from power positions—or lack thereof. It examines the stakes writers have in their writing, the sources they use for their ideas, the consultations they use as they compose, and the acknowledgment practices they follow. Finally, it proposes another reading of collaboration and intellectual property that accounts for the writing practices of differently situated writers.

To examine these questions, we offer two cases. The first places faculty members who write journal articles alongside students who write freshman composition essays. The second pairs faculty members writing grant proposals with students writing graduate school and job applications.

CASE I
Faculty Writers' Journal Articles and
Student Writers' First-Year Composition Essays

Faculty Writers

Stakes

Stakes for faculty writers are high. Journal articles allow faculty members to enter professional conversations, to speak with authority, to shape the questions and answers their disciplines pose, and to enjoy the pleasures of creating. In addition, they are the *sine qua non* of professional advancement. Particularly in research-intensive institutions, faculty members cannot receive promotion or tenure without meeting research and publication requirements. Finally, appearing in refereed and recognized journals creates part of faculty members' stature, the regard with which their students and colleagues hold them, and, in some cases results in considerable economic gain. "Institutional gatekeeping is ubiquitous in modern societies" (Erickson and Schultz 1982, xi, qtd. in Berkenkotter and Huckin 97), and the publication gates are some of the most significant and inflexible.

Ideas

Berkenkotter and Huckin's detailed description of cell biologist June Davis's publication route begins with a reference to her decision to study *Candida albicans,* a decision that appears to emerge naturally and unremarkably from her (and others') scientific curiosity. Likewise, our writing commonly begins in response to something we have read or heard: sometimes we see a recurring contradiction we want to explore, other times we see theory/practice conflicts we want to understand, and still other times we see specific calls for articles or chapters on topics that interest us. In almost all cases, however, we write from within a familiar world in which we already are considered members; we write from the work in which we engage full time.

Contacts

As Berkenkotter and Huckin describe Davis's moves through experimentation and initial report, we see familiar interaction with research assistants and colleagues, interactions that parallel our own and those of our colleagues. We move, commonly, from idea or stimulus to consultation in some form—with collaborators, with journals, books, electronic texts, and on-line lists to which we have comfortable access. We have learned who and where to ask, and we know that we are entitled to ask. We attend conferences and present papers that generate specific ideas as well as arenas for further discussions. We can write or telephone experts using first names, and we know how to talk with them. As Bazerman observes, when we write, we "seek out either consciously or spontaneously the help of others. . . . The participations of others both extend the range of resources and skills entering into the construction of the texts and anticipate the outcomes of the presentation of the text" (14). Even at the economic level, our professional status offers us opportunity: our departments pay the postage, e-mail charges, and telephone bills. We can deduct the cost of journals as business expense, and we can borrow library journals for extended periods of time. While developing this network of contacts requires considerable energy, assertiveness, and even risk for new faculty members, clearly the resources available to them are far greater than those to students.

Writing

Although Berkenkotter and Huckin do not detail Davis's early drafting practices, we suspect that they are much like ours and those of our biology colleagues. When we have exhausted our limits of procrastination, we begin to write, tentatively, often worried about what will (or will not) emerge, even though we have participated in and taught composing processes many times. Throughout this drafting, we return to journals, books, conference notes, and peers, looking for challenges and extensions of our thinking. We ask on-campus colleagues to read what we have written, and we e-mail questions or manuscript chunks to friends for review. This kind of informal consultation/ collaboration continues until we submit manuscripts to an editor.

     What the editor returns has been reviewed by several readers who may recommend acceptance with numerous revisions, some substantive, some niggling. Alternately exhilarated with the conditional acceptance and weary with the additional work, we move through several revisions spurred by reviewer/editor requests until the editor pronounces it publication-ready. Again, we rely extensively on our own as well as our editors' networks of collaborators. Tracing Davis's correspondence with editors during revision and publication, Berkenkotter and Huckin report that "the reviewers aided Davis in the construction of knowledge" (59), and they offer specific examples of the ways Davis's draft changes in response to her reviewers' demands and her editor's suggestions.

Acknowledgments

Our collaborations, like Davis's, are expected and extensive, and like Davis, who neither knows her reviewers' names nor expects to credit them with the revision suggestions they contribute, our acknowledgments are thin and discretionary. We formally share bylines with coauthors, we cite clearly borrowed ideas or texts because we know we must, and we thank a general assortment of contributors—from colleague-reviewers to mentors to sponsoring foundations. However, we rarely name (or know) all of the stimuli for the manuscript: the readers in the hall, the graduate students or writing center tutors, the conference presentations long forgotten, the conversations on hotel shuttles, or the persistent e-mail threat on a now-discontinued listserv, even though they have shaped the manuscript in ways we never could have alone.

Student Writers

Stakes

Students' stakes are similarly high, whether or not they recognize the stakes or buy into them. The papers they write in first-year composition determine their grades in those specific courses, and the writing experiences they acquire accelerate or limit their progress in other courses. Those grades and those abilities to write figure substantively in their opportunities for scholarships, awards, and postbaccalaureate study and employment. In addition, their freshman composition experiences shape students' and others' beliefs about them as writers and scholars, as successes or failures.

Ideas

Students' ideas are much more likely to be externally than internally motivated; they write because freshman composition instructors require them to write. Their writing grows out of class assignments, usually supported by reading and class discussion. Generally the parameters are fairly narrow because the instructors designate topics, modes, processes, sources, and time frames. Within these narrow bands, students may draw on peers, much as faculty writers do; however, their resources rarely are insiders. Rather, students draw on outsiders like themselves for ideas they must submit to insiders. In addition, composition is rarely a student's "primary world." It is a minute part of lives that center in accounting, biology, engineering, or education majors, and are complicated by the urgencies of jobs, families, and social engagements. For students, keeping a composition issue in active gestation is far more difficult than it is for composition faculty writers who "eat, drink, and sleep" intellectual property, journal articles, or grant proposals.

Contacts

Most students have few expert contacts. They are unfamiliar with libraries, journals, and other print sources, and, in fact have been warned against using them in order to avoid plagiarizing. They have limited access to electronic sources, although they may be more adept users than their instructors. Freshmen generally are wary of talking with faculty experts. They worry about whom to "bother," how to ask, and which questions are "stupid." They do not yet know much academic or disciplinary language, and universities generally expect students to acquire these skills through osmosis rather than direct instruction. The expert contacts students do have they must conceal: the files of papers housed in residence halls, fraternity/sorority files, and friends' desks, the downloaded electronic files, even the writing center tutors. Thus, students are neither aware of nor facile at using the contacts Bazerman describes faculty members as both possessing and using (14); they struggle to become the disciplinary scholars their professors exhort them to become.

Writing

When students write, they follow an abridged form of faculty writers' practices. Sometimes they write collaboratively, but more often they single-author their work. Class workshops structure peer reviews, but students also ask writing center tutors, roommates, spouses, and friends to read their work before they turn it in for an instructor. Most often, they revise only once for a final grade. Perhaps the most difficult puzzle for students is the one Berkenkotter and Huckin describe as reading the ways knowledge and its construction changes within disciplines. While faculty members understand that "[f]orms by themselves have little meaning; it is only when they are seen as serving certain functions that they become meaningful" (43), students most often lurch blindly from form to form, trying to apply rules that lack meaning or consistency. Because professors infrequently situate assignments within disciplinary or pedagogical frameworks and because students neither see nor understand those frameworks, they rely on sources that lead them into blatant plagiarizing and cheating.

Acknowledgments

Like most faculty members, students rarely acknowledge all of their resources, other than providing the MLA or APA citations for quotations and specific references to sources. Instructors are aware of some of their consultations such as with writing center tutors, but about most others they have no knowledge unless they can trace them through the supporting draft materials students turn in with their completed packets. Instructors and students have a tacit understanding that no one will "do" students' writing for them, and in some assignments the volume of in-class invention, drafting, and revision makes ghostwriting cumbersome and difficult. However, even though the class culture encourages free collaboration on both ideas and language, students are slow to become comfortable conferring publicly. They resist admitting that their roommates suggested the other half of the argument, and for good reason. If on most of the syllabi they receive, they find sharp but vague warnings about plagiarizing, they are careful not to reveal others' influences on their work. Certainly, if they are required to sign that their work is "their own and no one else's," they will not cite or thank their spouses, fraternity brothers, or writing tutors for their arguments' coherence.

While some composition instructors may expect their students to engage others much as they do, many of their colleagues expect something quite different, something that contests this model in substantive ways. Indeed, many instructors often require students to do much of their writing in class so that they can be sure it is "their own" work, markedly constraining their opportunities for revision. Writing tutors report that many students do not want their visits reported to instructors because they fear that "getting help" will reduce the credit they receive for their writing. Indeed, one of us was warned by a colleague not to record the names of professors whose students used the writing center, for "overuse" would suggest that the professors were "not doing their jobs in class." As writing center directors, we regularly are asked to assure our colleagues that our tutors do not "write students' papers for them," and we are specifically asked about how some ESL students manage to write "intelligibly" when "I can hardly understand them when they speak in class." We are urged not to "give away commas or articles." Berkenkotter and Huckin echo our colleagues' concerns when they observe that "the tacit expectation of graduate programs is (still) to produce a relatively autonomous scholar" (147).

CASE II
Faculty Members Writing Grant Applications and
Students Writing Graduate School and Job Applications

Faculty Writers

Stakes

Grants have become an academic's necessity. Whether as a way to start a project for which there is no internal funding, an opportunity for scholarly travel and research, or simply one of the discipline's expectations (NSF or NEH funding), faculty members know that grants are "academic currency." Our abilities to secure external funding are a significant marker of professional maturity and desirability and thus are important as we work toward tenure, merit pay, or new positions. Like journal articles, successful grant proposals involve a great deal of collaboration, which is why getting grants remains a mystery to most new academics, why workshops on grant writing remain on the continuing education circuit, and why institutions have grants officers who help faculty find appropriate funding organizations, contact foundations members, and use computerized programs to determine budget lines. Indeed, this collaboration is so significant that our careers may be made or broken over accusations of "stealing ideas" or "coopting grant funds for individual purposes" or by collaborating on a project that makes a scientific breakthrough.

Ideas

The line between collaboration and intellectual piracy slips elusively through the ownership of grant ideas. For example, one graduate student described her dismay at discovering that she would be spending an entire semester studying an obscure female scholar in a small seminar taught by a well-known Renaissance scholar. Rather than working on "hot" intellectual issues or preparing for the looming oral exam, she and her peers were required to search through difficult and vague Latin and Italian texts, translating and retranslating to find single references to what seemed to be insignificant and boring literature by the featured author. However, the project's significance became clearer as she became privy to departmental tales about a prestigious book contract, a Renaissance conference, and an NEH grant application—all connected to the same not-so-famous author and now infamous professor. This collaboration netted the professor significant academic and financial gain and the students, who were recognized in a "thanks to my class" note, began to understand the "rules" of intellectual property. Certainly the professor had initiated the project by selecting the author to be studied, but the class members' research and discussion equally generated many of the subsequent developments and intersections that moved the project beyond an idea. Although the professor's research tactics nettled some of his students, his practices secured him the desired advancements and were not faulted, in fact, were not fully understood, by his peers.

Contacts

In this same example, the project moved forward on the professor's initiative, but again with significant collaboration, this time with on- and off-campus connections to NEH. Most faculty members discover that simply having good ideas does not result in receiving grants. We learn to use campus grant office files to study previous successful applications. We connect with campus grant officers who introduce us to spin searches via key words, contacting other grant officers, sending for sample completed grants, and writing appealing cover letters. We begin with modest internal grants, create links with collaborators to write larger grants, and then become experienced and bold enough to stretch for Pew, Spencer, or NEH funds. As we stretch, we watch our grant-successful colleagues relate to grant officers, read grant proposals, and make site visits to review others' proposals, and we follow their models or even ask them to mentor our own efforts. From them we learn what different funding sources want to support, what makes an idea "unique," and how to negotiate profitable and useful funding arrangements. Eventually, we too have face-to-face access to those who award grant funds.

Writing

Grants are their own genre. Although as faculty members, most of us are experienced writers who know our own disciplinary genres well, we depend on collaborators to teach us grant discourse—to write it for us or with us. The concise logical claims and elegant philosophical progressions of journal articles rarely net grants. Rather, we become successful with NEH or NSF when we use the very different voice and tone and the seemingly repetitious and unwarranted promises that mark successful grant applications. We acquire this discourse, not in graduate school or at conferences or from our journals, but from colleagues and grants officers who collaborate with us, who help us transform our ideas into fundable requests.

Acknowledgments

Even less than journal articles, grants overtly acknowledge the multiple collaborators in their success. We consider campus grants officers "support staff," technicians whose job is supporting academic ideas. While faculty members often are enormously grateful, they generally accept the hierarchy that allows them to bask in the glory of their particular awards and the grants officers to take credit for the total dollars brought into the university. Likewise, we acknowledge colleagues only verbally and informally, and no one faults us for this lack of disclosure. Indeed, receiving grants certifies us as faculty members who can think of fundable ideas and projects, locate appropriate funding sources, make the right contacts, and "get the grant written."

Student Writers

Stakes

Graduate school and job applications are one student parallel with faculty members' grant applications. In both cases, scholarly standing and money are at stake. Graduate degrees from particular schools and first faculty appointments are central to scholarly careers. Jobs provide both the experience and the funding that students need to underwrite their professional careers. Like grants, applications lead to larger projects, greater opportunities, and recognition on career ladders. For students, therefore, the stakes are high.

Ideas

For students writing graduate school and job applications, collaboration is only subtly discouraged. They rarely encounter direct prohibitions; however, the lack of faculty or other mentor attention to these needs makes the processes feel lonely and at times furtive. For example, professors whose eyes light up in discussions of the newest research paradigms or philosophical turns, often glaze when students ask about the job market or about the graduate school prospects. Researchers who court students to join in their investigations may begin to zip their bookbags when students ask for three more letters of reference. So, while "Thou shalt not collaborate" is not chipped in the library facade, faculty members' clear preference for scholarly rather than "vocational" ideas shapes students' willingness to solicit their ideas about graduate school and certainly job applications.

Contacts

Students' connections with powerful contacts is similarly lacking. While many faculty members sprinkle their lectures liberally with references to luminaries in their fields, they may do little to connect their students with these resources. Even when they do include students in their conference presentations, they slip off after sessions to pursue their own agendas with their colleagues and those to whose coattails they wish to attach themselves, leaving students to fend for themselves with other novices. While some faculty actively use contacts to promote their students who apply for jobs, many who write the letters take the position that students must earn the job on their own merits. If the students deserve the jobs, they reason, their letters of recommendation will have played their proper roles, but they often fail to mentor their students' letter writing to ensure success on that end or to connect students with others who could help them.

Writing

While students can receive help writing letters of application, most of this help is informal, and it comes more frequently from career services rather than departmental faculty members. Often, in fact, faculty members who themselves draw on multiple resources to write grant proposals are reluctant to be "too helpful" to students writing graduate school or job applications, arguing that part of what readers want to know is "what students can produce themselves, not what they know how to get someone else to produce."

Acknowledgments

Students often are forced to admit the gaps between their "own" writing and their collaborative work. For example, admissions committees and employers frequently use some kind of noncollaborative writing such as the GRE, MCAT, GMAT timed essays to cross-check writing, to control for the collaborative writing that may "misrepresent" students in the personal essays they write for their applications.

Analysis

We return, then, to our question: Why do faculty writers "collaborate" while students "plagiarize"? Our best analysis is that this difference revolves around a certifying rite of passage along with a naive, if not cruel, amnesia. Faculty members' editors, for example, assume that having received the required academic degrees and faculty appointments, they both know the unstated rules of collaboration and could do the work on their own. They expect that, like playwright Edward Albee, who saw the title for his play *Who's Afraid of Virginia Woolf?* "scrawled in soap on a mirror in a saloon ten years before I wrote the play, and I remembered it all that time" (Deutsche Presse-Agentur), faculty members know how to see, hear, remember, and use resources according to the rules.

The first assumption, that we know the rules, probably is true, even though it may not safeguard intellectual property. Faculty members who violate these rules do so with great care, hoping not to be unmasked and discredited, and when they are discovered, the community is collectively embarrassed and punishes the offenders.

The second assumption, that faculty members could write "on their own," however, is flawed. Indeed, though we may be able to fix our own there/their and it/it's errors, most of the substantive collaboration we could *not* do on our own, which is why we ask for, and are asked to use, others' help. Clearly, had Davis not begun with significant knowledge of her biology discourse community as she designed her study and introduced her initial draft and then received and incorporated her reviewers' and editor's responses, it is unlikely that her manuscript would have been initially accepted for publication

Likewise, we all turn to our colleagues because we cannot account for contradictory findings, because we cannot determine whether the arguments we are immersed in will make sense to our readers, because we cannot theorize or contextualize to our own satisfaction. We respond to reviewers' requests because for the most part they do improve our work, because they do stretch our scholarship in ways we could not by ourselves. We turn to grant-savvy colleagues, campus grants officers, and NEH contacts to write competitive proposals. And, this is precisely what our students are doing, albeit at a less sophisticated and lengthy level. They ask siblings, roommates, significant others, and writing tutors to help them to figure out what their freshman composition instructors "want," to come up with essay ideas, to develop arguments, and to proofread. They turn to the same sources for help with graduate school and job applications.

Berkenkotter and Huckin assert that "Certification of new knowledge thus depends on a collaborative effort of author, reviewers, and editor" and that these processes involve an "uneven distribution of power" (76). We draw on their work, as well as our own descriptions of the very full collaborative knowledge-creating practices faculty members regularly enjoy, to advocate a reimagining of students' intellectual property generally and of their interactions within university writing centers specifically. Rather than charging students to "work on their own" and thus conceal their collaborative moves, we suggest opening to our students what we know about the processes of writing and collaborating. Because composition research consistently points to the importance of exchange in the creation of knowledge, we suggest that rather than constraining students' exchanges, we teach them how to open their consultative processes to their own and to others' views, to foreground their creating of knowledge rather than to conceal it. Rather than indulge in fond but flawed memories of ourselves moving smoothly from nervous, secretive student collaborators to resourceful, assured professionals, we suggest showing students how we work when we write. By acknowledging our own collaborative processes, we can teach our students to use and acknowledge the resources that can enrich their scholarship and can encourage rather than penalize their experiments with determining, assigning, and assuming intellectual property.

These moves, we suggest, represent knowledge-constructing processes more complexly and usefully, for they lead students more smoothly from student roles to professional roles, they merge teacher/researcher and student/professional roles, and they allow all writers to understand and clearly acknowledge their own and others' mutual rights to have and use ideas.

Plagiarism, Rhetorical Theory, and the Writing Center: New Approaches, New Locations

Linda Shamoon and Deborah H. Burns

The problem of plagiarism and the writing center appears in writing center literature as a quiet, recurring, unsettled, troubling specter. Even though as recently as February 1995, Michael Pemberton surmised that charges of plagiarism involving the writing center "may be on the decline" ("Ignorance . . ." 13), his portrayals and scenarios of the problem are strikingly similar to those published for the past fifteen years in *Writing Center Journal* and *Writing Lab Newsletter.* In most of these portrayals a faculty member comes to the writing center to raise charges of plagiarism and ethical misconduct because students' interactions with writing center tutors have prompted deep changes in students' papers. These renditions show that in the face of such charges we writing center practitioners inevitably feel disrupted and doubtful of our practices. Sometimes we dismiss the accuser as "somewhat aberrant," or as rooted in "simple ignorance" (Pemberton, "Ignorance . . ." 13). Typically, however, we use the occasion to look closely at our underlying philosophy, where we usually find a justification of our methods, and we declare ourselves thoroughly ethical (Behm).

This history of rationalization, however, has not dispelled the specter of plagiarism from the writing center. In fact, Irene Lurkis Clark (1989) states that for writing centers, concerns about plagiarism have always been central to its short history as a contemporary academic facility: "Certainly, one of the prime concerns of writing centers is to avoid charges of plagiarism at all costs" (Clark 4). Cynthia Haynes-Burton not only echoes Clark but sharpens the portrayal of the problem when she writes that "tutor and students traffic uneasily in the stealth landscape between collaboration and appropriation . . . writing centers, technology, and intellectual property are bounded together in a network of narratives (i.e., copyrights, plagiarism, authorship, scholarship, research papers, digital libraries)" (85). Clark's and Haynes-Burton's portrayals, among many others, of our writing center experiences convince us that the writing center is inevitably tied to charges of plagiarism by the very nature of its situation and endeavors.

Thus, when a concept like plagiarism is being revisited, reconsidered, and, perhaps, redefined in the academic world, writing center researchers and practitioners have an urgent need to enter the discussion. Indeed, writing center researchers and practitioners must play a central role in this important cross-disciplinary conversation, for if the concept of plagiarism is recontextualized so as to recognize the dialogic nature of writing and to make room for a social-rhetorical approach to writing, the writing center will have an opportunity not only to exorcise the specter of plagiarism but also to reposition itself away from its precarious position on the margins and toward the center of the academy.

Writing Center Responses to Charges of Plagiarism

When writing center practitioners face charges of plagiarism, our disciplinary literature shows that we have developed several stock responses: we recount the nature of the writing process, we explain the importance of feedback for all writers, and we offer pointers about how peer tutors can negotiate the border between the "legitimate" practice of giving advice and the "illegitimate" practice of writing too much on the paper. In addition, during the last several years, a deepening discussion of the implications of social theories on the role of tutors has been added to these standard responses. But a brief review of these responses indicates to us that none really exorcises plagiarism because the problem emerges from the contradictions between our philosophies of writing and our lived practices while tutoring writing.

For example, Pemberton, in response to charges of unethical practices, more than once recounts the recursive nature of the writing process and the interactive nature of the revising process, ultimately resting on the certitude that the description of the process is "true to life," that this is the way writers really write:

> Let me point out quite bluntly what we have all learned through the last twenty years of writing research and scholarship (and what we need to convey quite forcefully to those who think otherwise): Writing is a recursive process with many stages and it is not—and never has been—a completely solitary activity. Writers draw on their personal experiences, interactions with others, imagined audiences, and knowledge of other texts to supply both the content and structure of their own writing. ("Ignorance . . ." 13)
>
> Writing centers provide clear, observable cognitive benefits to students through the assistance they provide . . . If we accept the fundamental prin-

ciples of a cognitive framework for writing processes—that writers draw
from previous experiences to help them shape plans and goals for current
writing tasks; that they utilize content information and rhetorical strategies
stored in their long term memories to solve writing problems; that their ability to address increasingly complicated tasks with success is at least partially
dependent upon their ability to draw from a diverse and complex repertoire
of stored writing plans—then writing centers seem ideally suited to enhance
these processes. ("Teaching . . ." 16)

In these versions of his argument, Pemberton reiterates core concepts of
process research with echoes from the work of Linda Flower and John Hayes,
Sondra Perl, Nancy Sommers, and others, and with direct reference to cognitive psychology and to a spiral, multistep version of a writer's personal
processes to justify writing center activities as thoroughly ethical interven-
tions in students' production of papers. Interestingly, reminding readers of the
psychology of writing—even with a social dimension—does nothing directly
to offset the charges of unethical behavior. In fact, with its emphasis on how
a single author is the originator of original ideas, this version of the typical
writing center answer has the potential to further implicate the writing center
in such charges. Writing center intervention quite obviously disrupts the psychology of sole authorship.

Writing center literature attempts to work around such contradictions
by stating that the tutor's role is to help students "discover" their own ideas.
The emphasis on "discovery" of ideas emerges directly from the writing-
as-process movement and its elaborations. In a typical explanation, Donald
Murray writes, "We start drafting, not knowing what we are going to say, and
find we are collecting material, and the order in which it begins to arrange itself on the page makes our focus clear" (7–8). Writing center advice on tutoring echoes these sentiments in the expectation that it is the writing center's
role to help students discover their own material—or create new knowledge.
For example, Pemberton suggests that what writing centers *really* do is have
"tutors model process, [and] help students to generate new content" ("Teaching . . ." 16). Furthermore, a survey of tutor training manuals written between
1982–1994 (Harris 1986; Clark 1989; Meyer and Smith; Ashton-Jones; Ryan)
illustrates to us that tutors must allow writers to discover and create meaning
for themselves. Unfortunately, what really happens in writing center practice
is that tutors participate in the generative activities of producing a text, but
their presence is effaced. In fact, much of the research produced by writing
centers rationalizes and dramatizes the boundaries between helping students
write and letting them write for themselves. Such boundary negotiation dominates writing center literature, explaining the nature of acceptable collaboration, tacitly or overtly stating rules under which this tutor-student collaboration should occur, and restricting what tutors may and may not do. Ironically,

then, writing center research promotes tutoring and, at the same time, discounts it in terms of publicly identified authorship and ownership. The effacing of the tutor's presence has the effect of leaving the concept of sole authorship in place, surely in the instructor's mind but probably also in the student's mind, too.

Finally, to rationalize any incursions over the boundary of effaced tutoring, writing center literature draws heavily on the work of early social constructionists. Kenneth Bruffee's "Collaboration and the Conversation of Mankind" is cited over and over again to show that seeking feedback is a routine activity of successful, real-world authors. Evelyn Ashton-Jones's comments are typical of many others: "Bruffee's theoretical rationale for peer tutoring, and for collaborative learning in general, emphasizes that conversation is essential to learning" (31). By drawing on Bruffee's work in this way, writing center researchers seem to embrace a social approach to writing, but Lisa Ede (1989) points out that this is not the case. She argues, "Although this early research emphasized the importance of the social and cultural contexts of teaching and learning, it still tended to view both writing and thinking—the creation of knowledge—as inherently individual activities" (6).

In the same article, Ede exhorts writing center practitioners to go beyond the theories of collaborative learning "as articulated by Bruffee, Hawkins, and others, [and build] on the work of those who have recently challenged us to view writing as a social rather than a solitary and individual process" (4). In "Collaboration, Control and the Idea of a Writing Center," Ede's colleague Andrea Lunsford pushes this critique even further to contest the extremely narrow form of collaboration that is typically used in the writing center:

> We must also recognize that collaboration is hardly a monolith. Instead it comes in a dizzying variety of modes about which we know almost nothing. In our books, Lisa and I identify and describe two such modes, the hierarchical and the dialogic, both of which our centers need to be well versed at using. But it stands to reason that these two modes perch only at the tip of the collaborative iceberg. (7)
>
> The idea of a center informed by a theory of knowledge as socially constructed, of power and control as constantly negotiated and shared, and of collaboration as its first principle presents quite a challenge. It challenges our ways of organizing centers, of training our staff and tutors, of working with teachers. (9)

Lunsford's reference to the many types of collaboration that occur in lived practice among writers is an expression of her critique of the restricted collaborative practice of most writing centers. This severely limited practice draws an imaginary line between tutoring activities and the responsibility for changes in a student's text. From our perspective, when writing centers draw this line, they remain trapped in contradictions between practices that are clearly social and philosophies about writing that are based in sole authorship and ownership.

Changing Concepts of Sole Authorship and the Writing Center

It is striking to us that the writing center continues to hold on to process-based, effaced tutoring that privileges sole authorship while other areas of composition studies and literary studies have acknowledged that sole authorship is a cultural and historical construct. As Ede and Lunsford point out, the concept of the sole authorship has been under close scrutiny in literary and theoretical circles at least since 1968 with Roland Barthes's essay on "The Death of the Author" (87). In fact, in their 1990 study of the many types of collaborative practices that constitute real-world writing, Ede and Lunsford show that sole authorship is a problematic concept for most academic disciplines including the sciences, the humanities, and the social sciences (87 ff.). Similarly, Rebecca Moore Howard's (1995) historical overview of concepts of plagiarism demonstrates that modern definitions of authorship and plagiarism are social constructs that have taken shape in the West during the last 300 years:

> The individual author defines the post-Gutenberg playing field, and that author is credited with the attributes of proprietorship, autonomy, original-ity, and morality. Although three centuries after the inception of the modern author these attributes have come to be regarded as "facts" about author-ship, their historical emergence demonstrates them to be cultural arbi-traries, textual corollaries to the technological and economic conditions of the society that instated them. (791)

According to Howard, each element in this characterization of authorship may be deconstructed to reveal its cultural and historical situatedness, and each element of modern authorship has a kind of cultural transparency. For example, that one author is the sole discoverer of original ideas, Howard and other researchers attribute to specific historic and material developments, in-cluding the rise of Romanticism (791); that authors have proprietorship over the ideas in their writing, Woodmansee attributes in large part to the outcome of "legal-economic arguments in the debate in eighteenth-century Germany" (in Ede and Lunsford 82); and the notion that the unattributed use of another's ideas is a moral trespass is often located, as Howard explains, as the result of "overdetermined definitions of and legislation against plagiarism" (795). Fur-thermore, it is almost a cliché these days to say that the advent of electronic technologies in all fields of artistic endeavor, as well as in composition stud-ies, renders the possibilities for sole ownership practically impossible

(Haynes-Burton 90; Faigley 191–92). In addition, poststructuralists' representation of the author and intertextuality put the notion of sole authorship under erasure.

Thus, a range of scholarly studies, historic and cultural comparisons, and
technological developments lay bare and situate the core concepts that ani-
mate our attitudes about plagiarism, namely sole authorship, the individual
ownership of ideas, originality, and legal protection. These concepts, rather
than having foundational status, are products of social, political, and material
arrangements that use the force of law to be held in place. Once we recognize
the conditional nature of these concepts, we may be able to look at them again,
asking specifically with regard to writing, tutoring practices, and the writing
center, if we may not loosen the ties that seem to bind the writing center to
charges of plagiarism.

We argue that the writing center could successfully strike at the Gordian
knot of plagiarism only if it ceases to draw primarily from the expressivist and
process approaches to writing, approaches that inevitably privilege sole authorship and the ownership of ideas. In other words, as long as writing center
practitioners limit their theoretical bases to expressivism and writing-as-a-
process, they will not have a satisfactory disciplinary response to the
quandary of tutoring and plagiarism. The writing center, however, can diver-
sify its practices in ways that provide alternatives to purely expressivist and
process approaches to writing. These alternatives conceive of writing not primarily as an individualistic expression of original ideas but as social and cultural communication that is inevitably dialogic and rhetorical.

Social Approaches to Writing in the Writing Center

Some writing center practitioners, drawing heavily on the work of Mikhail
Bakhtin, are already integrating postmodern, poststructuralist, and social
theory into their writing center practices. These researchers draw on Bakhtin's
concept of heteroglossia to broaden their approaches to tutoring. Alice Gillam
and Michael Joyner are two writing center researchers who have deliberately
moved away from effaced tutoring, based on their reading of Bakhtin and
other postmodern theorists. Michael Joyner summarizes what's at stake this
way: "'Minimal-input tutoring' [does not] allow students to place their texts
in a larger process of deliberation, to partake in the play of *intertextuality*, [in-
stead it offers] them a narrow and fettered conception of the text as a self-
generated autonomous piece of work which has its genesis in the central,
individual consciousness of a determined self that functions outside the dominant ideology of the scene of writing" (81). Obviously, Joyner, and Gillam,
too, find in poststructuralist perspectives an argument to loosen the writing
center from theories that sustain sole authorship and effaced tutor practices.

Their intent is to create the kinds of conversations between tutor and client that encourage a critical or political perspective.

From our perspective, however, a shift to a fully social perspective would acknowledge not only broad political and ideological values surrounding any discourse but would also address the preexisting discursive and rhetorical contexts in which writers participate. The techniques developed by Joyner, Gillam, and others still depend on a "master" script applicable to every paper and to expressivist-leaning moments of discovery, akin to the universalisms that inform the process approach to writing and tutoring. A universal mode of generating and processing text is, by its nature, a-topical and a-disciplinary, and discovery-based. Instead of being a true shift into a fully social perspective of writing, these approaches are a modification of current writing center practices.

A full shift to a social, rhetorical approach would recognize how the preexisting discursive context constitutes the writer and the process of writing. The social-rhetorical perspective turns attention, therefore, away from the individual composer and toward context, away from the personal toward the public, away from expressions of the self toward performance and communication, away from originality toward production and reception, and away from the private toward the communal and civic.

A Social-Rhetorical Approach to Writing

In our effort to understand the implications of social theory for writing center practices, particularly with respect to authorship and plagiarism, we have found Robert Schwegler's "Dichotomies: Composition vs. Rhetoric" to be an extremely helpful explanation of the social, rhetorical nature of writing. His analysis has important implications with respect to the issue of originality in texts and with respect to students' insertion into preexisting discursive fields. We have used Schwegler's ideas as a basis for broadening our own writing center practices.

Schwegler, drawing on Bakhtin, explains that the rhetorician is less interested in the individual's composing of an individual text than in "a discursive field and . . . the various articulations of production and reception, of major texts and minor texts, and the social or cultural exigencies of discourse" (12). In other words, when viewed rhetorically, writing is not a singular activity of one person's composing of one piece of writing. Instead, the composer and her text are part of an already existing discussion that already has a good deal of figuration and expectation:

> Rhetoric focuses on chains of substantive texts . . . The dynamic relationships among texts and other performances are the subjects of analysis and

evaluation. No single text or other performance is fully complete or sufficient in itself . . . Note-taking, informal talk, reports, summaries, apprenticeship tasks—all constitute the field in its various dimensions. The image
that emerges is of a dynamic network of performances whose configuration
is altered by each successive performance . . . The goal of entering into the
conversational field is action through realignment of the symbolic or the
material. (12)

In Schwegler's articulation of the social, rhetorical perspective, no single
text is understood as apart from other texts, and all kinds of "texts" create a
flow of discourse. Furthermore, Schwegler's list of texts and performances
includes—legitimizes and values—all kinds of writing and language that all
authors, but particularly student authors, usually produce if they are to master enough of the ongoing conversation to write papers that are valued by their
instructor-readers.

Importantly, Schwegler's articulation of the rhetorical perspective holds
implications for questions of originality in texts. If a text is to fit into a conversation, it must partake of the language, subject matter, issues, and authorities recognized by those holding the conversation. In fact, we argue that long
stretches of any text are probably dedicated to anchoring the given text among
earlier texts, and long stretches of any text are probably dedicated to indicat-
ing how any analysis or new expression fits into existing conversation. Therefore, in any text there must be a lot of imitation, repetition, and rehearsal of
existing conversation. There must be, too, within the structural features of
form and style, a good deal of restraint on conceptual or expressive leaps to
the implausible or to the improbable or to the conversationally inappropriate.
Thus, from a social, rhetorical perspective, originality is probably an extremely small element of most texts, and originality may be less important in
most student texts than imitation, repetition, application, and rehearsal.

Along this line, Schwegler draws on ideas from Louis Althusser and
Pierre Bordieu to explain that the rhetorical perspective does not emphasize
the small element of originality in texts, but, instead, turns our attention to insertion, inclusion, and participation of text in conversation:

Rhetoric starts with the assumption that the field predates the composer. The
field itself, therefore, generates most (say 95%) of the information, strategies, usage, and perspectives in a text or other performance . . . the reproduction of existing discursive practices and relationships is the primary goal,
one that still leaves some space for contestation or for reconfiguring the
field. Rhetoric helps students recognize that they are being inserted—or
interpolated—into an ongoing arrangement of knowledge, power, and practice. The distinguishing act of rhetoric is interpolation, a consciousness of
entering into and being constituted by a discursive field and also being alert
to sites that allow a composer to choose between simply reproducing existing relationships or rearticulating them. (13)

Schwegler's argument emphasizes that for all writers, and probably more so for student writers, context exists before authoring. In fact, discovering a topic, taking control of writing and topics, and even "originality" do not happen outside of a discourse area. Discovery, empowerment, and originality happen when both writer *and* reader (i.e., student *and* instructor) recognize a piece of writing as fitting into the conversational field. We speculate that achieving this fit is what happens when most disciplinary instructors say that students have improved in their writing, including when and how to fittingly cite sources, or when and how to sound "original."

We are particularly interested in the links between interpolation, rhetoric, and authoring, three domains that we consider so overlapping that they may not be pulled apart. When a student authors a "good" paper—a paper that is on topic, immersed in an analysis of material that is of interest to the discipline, and that addresses an area of disciplinary debate—she may feel she is, indeed, being original. Rhetorically, however, her text probably imitates, elaborates, and applies ideas and forms from the various sources that are hers to use legitimately (including what she thinks the teacher wants). While this student is, thus, engaged in imitation, elaboration, rehearsal and application, she is also absorbing both content and the ways to insert herself into the conversation, or ways to interpellate herself into the field. Her text represents to herself and to her instructor-reader one "performance" of her learning, her expressive abilities, and her interpellation into the discipline.

The intriguing aspect of Schwegler's argument is that an *awareness* of interpolation is gained by attention to the social-rhetorical aspects of writing. Without such awareness, the student's absorption of content and her absorption into the disciplinary culture may occur unconsciously and uncritically. Such unconscious learning may not prevent the authoring of texts, but it may lead to the illusion on the part of the author that she has "discovered" new knowledge or that she has become "empowered" or that she has been "original." The social-rhetorical perspective would make interpellation more conscious because it articulates the constructed nature of subject matter, of disciplinary thinking and questioning, of the related features of the discourse (including paper features), and of the values and expectations of a specific reader or audience.

A Glimpse of a Social-Rhetorical Approach to Writing in the Writing Center

Shifting to a fully developed social-rhetorical approach of the type articulated by Schwegler has important implications for the writing center. The immediate consequence of such a shift in philosophy would be to give the writing center a sound disciplinary answer to charges of plagiarism. In the long

run, such a shift would probably entail significant changes in material practices that would surely help move the writing center from the margins and
toward the middle of intellectual inquiry and conversation found at the heart
of the academy.

A writing center that is driven by the social-rhetorical approach does not
frame questions of plagiarism as either ethical problems or as groundless
charges from the uninformed. Instead, such a writing center views the issue
of plagiarism as a social and rhetorical construct, and rather than side step the
issue of plagiarism by claiming to build a fence around collaboration and tutoring, such a writing center inserts itself into a conversation about the rhetorical and social nature of the disciplines. Practitioners in such a writing center
are ready to engage other instructors in elaborate conversations about context,
about disciplinary expectations, about topical frameworks and, especially, to
engage them in conversations about difference—the differing and special expectations instructors have for their specific writing assignments and for what
is valued by them in student writing, including wiriting that is imitative and
elaborative of ideas and forms of disciplinary discourse. It is the kind of conversation that may start by being about plagiarism but will end up being about
authorship, about the sources of ideas, about disciplinary life (and lives).
From such conversations come the potential to move the writing center off the
margins of the university and into the center of academic life.

In Academic Administration

Confusion and Conflict about Plagiarism in Law Schools and Law Practice

Terri LeClercq

You probably suppose that, at least in law schools and law firms, legal writers know the rules of proper attribution so that they can avoid plagiarism. Suppose again. Survey results from over one hundred of the 177 accredited law schools reveal an alarming institutional indifference to and a disgraceful disparity in definitions of and punishments for plagiarism. It is not as if plagiarism is not a problem in law schools, either: One eastern law school had fourteen plagiarism cases pending in the spring of 1995. After students graduate and become practicing attorneys, they are required to ignore those academic rules for proper attribution because the practice of law depends heavily on mass use of unattributed sources. It's tradition.

Recently the legal writing faculties organized through the national Legal Writing Institute at the University of Seattle, set up a committee[1] and investigated how the various law schools educated their students about plagiarism. Of 177 accredited law schools, 152 responded. The results of the survey were staggering: twelve schools have no definition or policy, and many of the rest contain either self-contradictions or policies and punishments that contrast to other law schools. The majority of the law schools use the general bulletin to disseminate the academic definitions and punishments. Few law schools take the time to explain the difference between academic plagiarism and the reality of law practice, which has developed its own tolerances for professional use of others' printed work.

Law professors apparently believe graduate students already understand academic plagiarism and how undergraduate rules might differ from law schools' use of case precedent. More than one hundred law schools tuck any mention of plagiarism into an Honor Code or within a blanket generalization of "don'ts." Apparently the law school administrators have not read the recent study of over six thousand undergraduate students, which revealed that 60 percent of the future lawyers in the group admitted cheating once; 12 percent even characterized themselves as "regular" cheaters (Crowley 1992, C5).

Maybe plagiarism is not cheating, to these students. Some follow an old "rule" they mis-remember and announce that changing every third (or fifth or tenth) word from the original keeps their dependence on a source from being true plagiarism.

Faculty in higher education institutions are not much more confident of their understanding of plagiarism than are the students. When the National Council of Teachers of English asked about the consequences of plagiarism, professors argued that words, as popular vernacular, cannot be stolen; that plagiarism is "incredibly poor scholarship"[2] and "bad research methodology" (*Plagiarism in the Classroom* 14). That range of opinions is as wide as the variety of reported law school plagiarism policies.

Educating Law Students

For a community that is charged with teaching rules and laws, whose graduates go out to uphold those rules and laws, the issue of law school plagiarism is surprisingly hazy. A few schools (11) have a definition of plagiarism that includes positive examples of attribution; some schools (41) admonish against plagiarism but never define it. The largest number (85) provide a policy and definition, but usually in the general bulletin (120).

Legal institutions have new reasons to be more specific now. Plagiarism cases, once confidential and under cloak of secrecy within an institution, are moving into the courts and alerting all administrations to the problems of policy and punishment (Mawdsley 65). Law schools know more about the court system and expectations than any segment of our educational population; they should have the clearest and most coherent policies of all educational institutions. They don't.

Did the Law Student Intend to Cheat?

An obvious question in any purported plagiarism case is whether the student intended to misuse the literary property of someone else. The answer, unfortunately, is not obvious. A Princeton student used the source book loaned to her by her professor and acknowledged the source correctly six times, but did not footnote it in other places. The university charged her with plagiarism and dismissed her. She took her case to court, where the 1992 New Jersey court, in *Napolitano v. Princeton University Trustees,* agreed that the student was technically guilty of plagiarism because the university's handbook did not mention intent in its policy. Misuse was misuse, even though she had not intended the reader to assume the words or ideas were her own (Mawdsley, 68).

How educational institutions go about defining plagiarism should be studied. A complication for graduate schools is that the undergraduate institution may have an existing policy, or it might not. The graduate school policy may need to be distinguished from the undergraduate, or perhaps mirror it. It is reasonable to hold students entering the study of law to a higher standard than undergraduates. They should be expected to be honest; certainly the admissions materials stress honesty and integrity, and the state bar examiners insist on a clean record for applicants.

Most law schools can define plagiarism within their own honor code. Within that code, they have the option of requiring intent: if the law school *does not require* intent as a factor, then any student who uses another's words, phrases, format without attribution is automatically guilty, as was the Princeton student. That absolute standard has to be followed by sanctions, so that students who mistakenly plagiarize can be judged differently from those who deliberately do so. Law schools can take the option *to require* intent as a factor. Then, however, those professors and schools have the burden of proving that a student deliberately, with forethought, set out to cheat.

Law schools are divided about the necessity of proving intent—ninety-one schools make no mention of intent, forty-two require proven intent, and seven focus on intent only in the sanctions stage. To make the policies concerning plagiarism more consistent, all law schools should announce that if any writer at this stage and with these goals commits plagiarism, then he or she is guilty of plagiarism. It makes sense, though, that law schools should remove intent as a factor in their definitions and place it in the sanctions section of the crime/infraction; a law student would automatically be guilty of plagiarism if he or she submitted a paper that had portions (words, phrases, unique ideas, statistics) copied or misquoted from an unacknowledged source. The law school sanctions committee would then decide *how* guilty. Intent would be a major factor at that stage. This decision is not for the weak of heart because it would require administrators and professors to create a strong policy and to stand strongly behind it.

Problems with Paraphrasing Legal Material

Few law students enter law school understanding that unacknowledged paraphrasing frequently leads to academic plagiarism. Their first assignment is a memorandum that depends on what courts have said previously in published opinions. Students are expected to learn to explain the authority behind a judicial opinion and to know which authority carries more weight than another.[3] Thus, in legal writing, quoting legal precedent is a requirement. Many students revert to their undergraduate paraphrasing: changing words eliminates the need for footnotes. Law professors must therefore introduce the new concepts of legal attribution and its weight in the law.[4] If students can understand that direct reference to a source makes their arguments stronger, not weaker, then surely law students will have little trouble footnoting not only direct takings but also any paraphrase.

Fears about Reporting Plagiarism

Many law schools we surveyed refused to discuss either the number of, or specific instances of, plagiarism. The institutions claim that students need this veil over their misconduct and that to openly discuss cases would sacrifice the students' privacy. Many law schools would not commit recent episodes to paper, fearing that the exposure, even anonymous, could land them in court on charges of invasion of privacy or slander. Several law school representatives did call, off the record, and explain the details of specific cases that pushed the boundaries of the school's published definitions. A few law school plagiarism cases have been made public through local newspaper coverage (Berreby 2), but there are no reported law school cases that went through the court system. Yet.

An underlying fear of those responding to the survey was that any publicity about plagiarism could hurt the law school's reputation. Faculty members do not want to see headlines about cheating within their institution or worry that entering students may use that publicity to help determine which law school they will attend. These natural concerns are sharpened by the downturn in the number of students who want to attend law school. National 1997 law school admissions are down sharply for the second year (approximately 92,000 applications nationwide in 1994; 76,000 in 1996).[5] Negative publicity at this point could harm the institution more than the issue is worth to the individual professors who bring charges.

Notice Requirements

How students learn, or are supposed to learn, about their institution's plagiarism policy is another gray area. Courts require some sort of unambiguous notice (Mawdsley 5). Many schools (120) report that they publish their policy in their general bulletins sent to each student who is accepted, or to each who shows up for orientation (46 schools). Each legal institution needs to ask itself if it wants to face the court defending "notice" requirements with a general bulletin that students are presumed to read in their spare time. If not, then the institution needs to concentrate on fair notice and find a more reliable method. A dean may refer to it during orientation. A legal writing instructor may hand out a booklet on plagiarism with examples. An instructor may go over the examples in class. But someone needs to educate entering law students. A definition shared after the incident is a too-late definition (Bills 111).

School Rankings and Definitions

One odd statistic emerged from the survey that we did not expect: higher-ranked law schools generally have the weakest or most ambiguous plagiarism policy. Perhaps this trend follows the theory that institutions and professors assume their students know the rules. Students entering the higher-ranked institutions therefore are assumed to know more than students who are admitted to the lower-ranked schools, and so there is less need for those elite institutions to spend time repeating what their student body must already know. Some examples: at Yale, plagiarism is among a list of offenses "against the academic community." At the University of Chicago, plagiarism is an "e.g." example of "violations of University regulations and other breaches of the standards of behavior" with disciplinary probation and expulsion as the sanctions. At Quinnipiac, under "Standards for Professionalism," faculty explain the difference between plagiarism, work product, and writing assignment instructions, plus they present a full definition with paraphrasing, plus nine sanctions and a handout of examples (from Missouri-Kansas). Missouri-Kansas City devotes considerable attention to plagiarism, giving each student a supplementary handout containing examples and five methods for avoiding plagiarism.

Punishment

Sanctions for plagiarism can be academic or disciplinary, or both. Law schools currently decide the issue so differently that, for instance, collaboration required at one school would get a student expelled at another. Students who deliberately plagiarize at one institution will have letters placed in their files until they graduate—and then they will be removed if they commit no other offenses. At another institution, though, students who do not use quotation marks that signal a quotation's close are guilty of plagiarism and automatically suspended, with an obligatory letter of explanation to the state bar. The range should be more consistent. What if some student chose to sue the law school about a sanction that contradicted the sanction imposed for the same act in another law school? Would it matter? Both ends of the punishment scale are worrisome: a student who doesn't know how to properly footnote a paraphrase may be expelled; a student who copies paragraphs of a law review from LEXIS®■NEXIS® into a seminar paper is given a failing grade but no other sanction; a student who uses a classmate's notes is given a private reprimand with no official notice. Because many readers find that plagiarism is rarely charged if the student has misquoted or undocumented only once, some thought needs to be given to the pattern of error that signals plagiarism (Marvin 17).

If the institution has only one sanction, expulsion, then few professors are likely to make the charge. If the institution does not have a consistent honor counsel or dean handling the charges, then the definition and its sanctions can be applied unevenly even within that one institution. If the policy requires intent, or worse, a "reasonable doubt" standard, the sanction committee will have difficulty "proving" plagiarism.

Collaboration

Only thirty schools articulated some difference between plagiarism and collaboration. Nevertheless, collaboration is a national trend in rhetoric and writing classes,[6] is encouraged in more and more schools, and is a part of the real practice of law. Some law schools insist on students working totally alone on written projects, some encourage collaboration up to the writing stage, and others offer assignments that they expect to be done in collaboration with a team or partner. In any setting, the line between collaboration and cheating needs to be clearly drawn when the assignment is made, but that is not always as easy as it sounds, especially in the competitive atmosphere of law school.

Electronics

Law libraries and law students depend on computers, on databases, on on-line updates to find court opinions and law review articles. "Technology has made it easier than ever to grab text and ideas from other sources without attribution, but the definitions of plagiarism have never been in so much flux" (Flint 1). Only four schools from the survey mention the intrusions electronics make into their traditional definition, even though educators know that the increased use of computers has made unintentional copying more likely. So few law schools mention electronics in their discussion of plagiarism that readers might think law schools had no technology available.

In contrast, practicing attorneys are expected to use electronic aids that law schools discourage or restrict for educational purposes. Law schools should point out the difference between the goals of these two types of research.

Today's Rule, Tomorrow's ...

Law firms commonly use the forms provided by the state bar and scholars to short-cut having to reinvent the wheel for each assignment (Sorkin 487). Attorneys can change another's filed (public) brief into their own responses, and they are encouraged to copy commonly used materials from state-bar "form books." According to one practicing attorney, to expect the legal profession to change standards back to those of college is unrealistic:

> Intrafirm sharing is cost-effective and therefore understandable. . . . There seems to be a common belief that court documents are public records. [However] [i]t is considered inappropriate to borrow without permission from another law firm's documents that are not pleadings filed in a court file (such as wills, contracts, and leases). (*Legal Practice* 8)

The legal workplace creates its own rules. Attorneys are judged on the final product and outcome; authorship is rarely important (Sorkin 480).

New court clerks and associates are apparently expected to shift instinctively: only seven law schools explain the difference between academic plagiarism and the workplace's anonymous reliance on the work of others. A law school plagiarism policy should note this difference: "The critical distinction is that court cases and other legal matters are not decided primarily on the amount of original work contributed, while determinations of academic grades, course credits, and degrees are" (Papay-Carder 246). Once students understand this bifurcation, they will have little trouble adjusting to the different expectations.

The standard of collaborative authorship in the workplace is being questioned by both scholars and the courts, and the bar may need to brace for a formal change: An *Illinois Bar Journal* writer warns, "Plagiarism is something lawyers must take seriously. Passing off others' words or ideas as one's own work is unethical and potentially dangerous, even if it's merely the result of carelessness" (Sorkin 480).

Who Is Really Guilty?

If a law school does not disseminate a concrete definition of plagiarism, then a student cannot be any more "guilty" of the act of plagiarism than the institution is guilty of neglecting its responsibility for educating. The definition should be uniform:

> Plagiarism means taking the literary property of another without attribution and passing it off as one's own and having reaped from its use the unearned benefit from an academic institution.

202 Terri LeClercq

Each school should create a policy that clearly defines its understanding of paraphrasing (including examples), collaboration, databases, academic versus professional attribution, and sanctions—including whether intent will be a factor.

No one wants to see a graduate student expelled or unable to take the state bar examinations because he or she did not know how to paraphrase properly or did not know how to acknowledge downloaded Internet material. No one wants plagiarists to graduate and enter the bar, either. It is the duty of the law school to educate, and educating the basics of law-school documentation should be no more onerous or embarrassing than offering tax courses described as "for those with no background." Of course, once the schools decide how to get that information to the students, then they also need to provide faculty with the same education.

Law schools also need to examine their definitions and sanctions, concentrating on the variety of sanctions given throughout the country because today's diversity of opinion is bound to lead into the courts. Each policy needs consistency between the "intent" factor and the sanctions available. Some schools' policies are internally contradictory, and some are too harsh or too lax. Once the school has decided on acceptable sanctions, those sanctions need to be explained to students and faculty through the Honor Code—and class discussion, everywhere possible. After law students have been taught what is expected of them, their product can be judged accordingly.

Notes

1. Plagiarism Committee of the Institute of Legal Writing and their law schools: Terri LeClercq, Texas; Lou Sirico, Villanova; Julie Cheslik, Missouri-Kansas; Kate O'Neill, U. Washington; Alice Silky, Hamline; Judith Ann Rosenbaum, Northwestern U; Cynthia Hinman, John Marshall; Ann Gibs, T. C. Williams; Terrill Pollman, Stetson U; Pam Lysaght, U Detroit Mercy; Edward Gerdes, U Oregon; Joyce Klouda, DePaul; Susan Dunham, American University, Washington College of Law; Nancy Spyke, Duquesne U; Karen Mika, Cleveland Marshall; and Thomas Seymour, Suffolk U.

2. Letter from Paula Sullivan to Editor, in *3 Council Chronicle,* No. 5, June 1994 at 14. Sullivan concludes "What is plagiarism if not 'incredibly poor scholarship'? When doctors and lawyers practice poor medicine and law, they are subject to malpractice suits. Scholarship should be subject to the same kind of ethical standards."

3. Legal writers do not depend on MLA style sheets. Instead, they must refer to the *Harvard Manual of Style* (the *Bluebook*). The *Bluebook* is difficult to master. First-year plagiarism can easily result from fear of ever finding the correct citation form and documentation.

4. Louis J. Sirico, Jr., in *A Primer on Plagiarism*: "Paraphrasing? If you take another's sentence and change a few words, you still must give a citation. If you paraphrase, do not use quotations, but use a signal, usually *see*. There is a gray area be-

tween paraphrasing and putting something in your own words. You must decide whether or not a citation is necessary. Err on the side of caution. Usually you will want to include a citation, because a citation to authority increases the persuasiveness of what you are saying."

5. The American Association of Law Schools and the American Bar Association float these numbers at conferences for recruiters and deans. No official representative of law schools claims to have an accurate account, in part because legal education institutions are reluctant to admit individual statistics. The 20 to 30 percent drop has been reported unofficially by both upper-tier and bottom-tier schools. In the summer of 1995, a few law school recruiters even called other schools asking for a list of 1995 rejects, so that they could get their applicant pool numbers up.

6. See, for instance, Janis Forman, *New Visions of Collaborative Writing* (1992); Geoffrey Cross, *Collaboration and Conflict* (1994); Mike Sharples, *Computer-Supported Collaborative Writing* (1993).

Student Plagiarism as an Institutional and Social Issue

Edward M. White

"Research Assistance" was the headline on the crudely printed flyer on my windshield in the university parking lot*. "Thousands of papers in stock, available for any course," it continued, making clear its purpose. Students see these ads and flyers everywhere, in such magazines as *Rolling Stone* or even lurking in the back pages of their own student newspaper. Many of us faculty know not to put graded student papers outside our offices for students to pick up, since all papers are now valuable commodities and will disappear, to surface later for sale. Every experienced teacher must be aware that at least half of American students confess to cheating of one sort or another, and that copied or purchased papers are among the easiest and least detectable forms of cheating. While recent discussions of intellectual property have certainly thickened and made problematic the line between such cheating and the collaborative nature of all writing, there is no question that at one end of the spectrum we need to confront an unethical and damaging dishonesty that requires both personal and institutional condemnation. The problem now is to locate that line and to help our students understand where it is and what it means— and what it does not mean.

The lore of plagiarism at all levels is rich, including presidential campaigns and learned journals, reflecting a society that values competitive ownership more highly than integrity or scholarship. No wonder that many students claim academic credit for others' thoughts and words, both intentionally and through inadvertence. One colleague tells me of a composition class with the entire first-string freshman basketball team in it; all five turn in the same paper, word-for-word from that month's *Reader's Digest,* and stoutly maintain that it must be some sort of bizarre coincidence. Another colleague receives from a student a paper that he himself had written a generation ago, an

---

*This chapter is a revised and expanded version of an "Opinion" article in the *Chronicle of Higher Education,* Feb. 24, 1993, p. A44.

early entry from the long-ago missing stack outside the professor's door. When I ask a student, with genuine wonder, why her plagiarized paper began on page 312 of a book I had repeatedly mentioned in class, with a neat "Page 312" typed in the upper-right corner of page one, she explodes with outrage—not at me or herself but at the fellow student she had paid to write the paper for her, the cheater cheated.

As my examples show, I am concerned about blatant plagiarism, the dishonest use of others' work pretending to be one's own, writing that is well on the immoral side of the fine line between the romanticized author, the radical self, and the inevitably collaborating self we have come to see in almost all writing. Only nonwriters see that line as easy to draw. I was stunned this year to discover a metaphor I was proud to have created printed word-for-word in an essay by Hulme I have used for years in my literary theory class. It stuck in my head and came out when I needed it—and I thought it was my own. I am no plagiarism hunter and am ready to grant my students all kinds of borrowed benefit from their reading, their families, the writing center, writing groups in class, and, of course, my own suggestions, as they revise. Borrowing is not stealing, though the results are often the same, and most of what we know must come from outside sources, often from we know not where.

But there is a blatant plagiarism that we cannot ignore because it subverts the very nature of education and reflects some aspects of what is worst in American society. Like date rape, fraternity drunkenness, and hate speech, it must be attended to institutionally, though most institutions prefer to pretend it is not going on. To be sure, even at its most blatant, plagiarism is not a simple matter and a simplistic moral approach is not adequate. But blatant plagiarism is nonetheless a moral issue and one that finally asks us to take a moral position. Theft seems so much a part of human nature in our society that we must learn to live with it in all aspects of our lives. But even though we must defend ourselves against burglars and muggers, however much we may sympathize with whatever caused their behavior, we are not really called on to excuse away their depredations. Despite all of our theorizing about the disappearing author and the problematic commercial metaphor of intellectual property, we must recognize that the pretense that others' words and ideas are one's own is indeed a moral problem that elicits a moral response. If we argue otherwise we become ridiculous.

But we do need to be sensitive to the fact that even the most blatant plagiarism, like the other matters I have mentioned, is an educational and curricular issue as well as a disciplinary one. That is, universities need to deal with it on two fronts: prevention through education as well as punishment for violations. Too many students stumble into plagiarism unawares, not only because they have never learned how to use sources, but sometimes because they have been taught that research *means* plagiarism. Many high school students have learned to get good grades by putting their own name on material copied from an encyclopedia or other reference books, with a teacher's approval. Many college students will quote, or fail to cite, the words of a printed source as the substance of their papers because they have not learned that sources should support, not substitute for, their own ideas. Indeed, one way to define the line between collaboration and plagiarism is to look at the degree of ownership of ideas. We get to own others' ideas by understanding and thinking about them, by *making* them our own through reflection and integration into our own thinking processes. But blatant plagiarism remains an outsider to the ideas that are copied and sometimes fails even to repaginate the source, as my "page 312" example showed. Like altering the title to someone else's house, plagiarism seeks to claim ownership of intellectual property never visited or lived in. This is theft, not community property, and for this reason requires a moral stand by an outraged community.

The response to theft cannot be merely individual. I get weary of self-righteous professors and administrators fulminating against immoral student plagiarists, when the institutions they represent and whose policies they shape have not taken the trouble to provide the information and guidance students need to avoid plagiarism. Indeed, we should all expect that much plagiarism will naturally occur unless we help students understand what all the fuss is about; many students simply are clueless about the issue and many faculty think the issue is simpler than it is. Taking high moral ground is important and necessary, but, as with other moral issues, too many of the statements from that ground are hypocritical and not cognizant of the complex motives behind student actions.

Since most American colleges and universities require a course or two in freshman composition, this is the natural place for instruction in the avoidance of plagiarism. Some, but by no means all, freshman composition courses do attend to this matter. But even when the composition course does a careful job, that instruction must be reinforced by other courses, before students will really understand the issue and take the message to heart. Different fields of study tend to use sources in different ways and it must be the responsibility of advanced instruction in every field to teach the responsible use of sources as it is done in the discipline. Very few departments bother to see to it that such instruction and reinforcement occur, though there are some notable exceptions. When there is little attempt to help students understand the meaning and importance of plagiarism, the slippery ethical values of our commercial culture rest unopposed and too many students will take the easy way out to achieve grades.

In fact, most American colleges and universities ignore the issue of plagiarism altogether, pretending that only a tiny minority of scoundrels are guilty of this widespread offense. Every school will have a strong statement about the subject in the catalog, but it is a rare campus indeed that actively attempts to define and help students avoid plagiarism. Sometimes it almost seems as if the campus policy is designed to sweep the whole business under the rug.

Individual faculty members can on their own take steps to reduce plagiarism, even if the campus turns a blind eye to the problem. The overriding issue is to help students claim legitimate ownership over the ideas they, inevitably, largely receive from others. When a writing assignment attends to the writing process, instead of only the end product, plagiarism becomes almost impossible. For example, if a statement of purpose, an organizational plan, and an early draft are required, or if the assignment is precisely tailored to new course material, students must do their own work and all source materials must necessarily pass through the writer's mind. But such assignments ask faculty to take their written assignments and their students' progress much more seriously than is now usually the case. If teachers reconceive their function as coaches as well as judges of student written work, they will involve themselves with their students' writing process. But if the teacher sees student writing as a necessary nuisance, deserving little effort, the students are likely to share that attitude. The usual term paper assignment has few safeguards against plagiarism and, without campuswide concern, all but the most glaring cases escape attention.

Unless professors make the distinction clearly and forcibly between using sources to *substitute for* ideas as opposed to using sources to help *demonstrate* ideas, and then insist that students develop their own ideas about the sources (even if the students agree with the sources, they should say so), honest students are likely to plagiarize by mistake. If the goal of a paper is merely to show that the student has done work and read sources ("retelling knowledge"), there is not much for the writer to do but summarize, paraphrase, quote—and plagiarize. Unfortunately, many college assignments in fact ask only for retelling of knowledge, and few faculty bother to teach their students about the proper use of sources; it is someone else's responsibility.

Because most of what we know and learn inevitably comes from sources, and because our own individuality is a problematic concept (how many of us are or can be truly unique?), plagiarism is a thorny and difficult concept for students to understand. Students need to be taught how common ideas or ideas identified with particular writers can be made one's own through reflection on them. And assignments should stress that mere summary of the ideas of others is insufficient. Instead of asking for a summary of one scholar's thought, a paper could ask for comparison and contrast of two different positions, with the student evaluating them according to the course criteria. Instead of asking for the causes of the Civil War or of evolution or of postmodernism, an assignment could require the student to consider several proposed causes and show the strengths and weaknesses of each argument. Instead of loose oral assignments on this or that book, or on more or less general topics, assignments could be carefully written and be specific to the issues of the course. Perhaps most important of all, the professor needs to discuss the assignment and to show why the retelling of knowledge is insufficient for success. Careful, precise, and written assignments, along with early requirements for outlines, statements of purpose, and drafts, make academic honesty not only the best but the only possible policy.

But it is an institutional moral lapse to pretend that plagiarism is only a personal matter between teacher and student. Plagiarism is important because it violates the moral code of learning, not because it offends (or does not offend) a particular professor. Thus colleges and universities should not only insist that plagiarism receive the curricular attention it deserves in freshman composition and elsewhere, but also that violations receive institutional attention as well. Instead of placing the entire burden of instruction, detection, and punishment on individual faculty members (often the TAs and other graduate students who actually read student writing), institutional seriousness demands institutional activity. Otherwise, we wind up with the present situation, one in which most faculty members simply do not find it worth the effort to deal with the issue.

Certainly, the job of education is primarily a faculty activity. And detection of plagiarism, after the education has taken place, must also be a faculty responsibility. But the institution needs to mount a faculty development effort to sensitize teachers to plagiarism and to ways of helping students avoid it. Sometimes a Writing Across the Curriculum (WAC) program undertakes this task, but only a few campuses can boast a WAC program of sufficient scope to change campus mores. And it is idle to imagine that most faculty will routinely accept this responsibility without some institutional effort.

For these reasons, punishment for plagiarism, for active, aware, dishonest, and repeated use of others' words and ideas as if they were one's own, should not be a matter for an individual faculty member to handle alone. A collegewide committee, composed of students as well as faculty and administrators, should render the community judgment that punishes plagiarism. A few institutions, generally those with publicized honor systems, have such committees and they can work well. After teaching for five years at such an institution, I am not convinced that an honor system in itself deters plagiarism, which depends so much on an understanding of how we come to use and credit the ideas of others. But such institutions do take their moral responsibilities seriously as a community and they do see dishonesty as affecting the entire community. Thus their use of campus committees to deal with plagiarism is a model that should be widely followed, even, perhaps particularly, in large public institutions.

When we notice how few colleges and universities really take plagiarism seriously—insisting on instruction in freshman composition, reinforcement in other courses, and campus committees to receive and to deal with infractions—we must wonder why. Surely the offense is not one to be taken lightly.

Plagiarism is outrageous because it reverses education itself: instead of becoming more of an independent thinker and hence developing increased integrity as an individual, the plagiarist denies such integrity and hence the possibility of learning. Someone who will not, or cannot, distinguish his or her ideas from those of others, or trace the origins of those ideas, offends the most basic principles of learning.

My favorite plagiarist, as I look back on a long career of teaching, is a freshman in my class at a highly selective eastern women's college, which boasted a strict honor code. She was clever in her thefts, but eventually handed in an obscure piece by John Updike that I happened to know. When I went back over the year's work, I discovered that every paper had also been plagiarized. She knew it was wrong, she said, with no embarrassment, but she had no choice. Every weekend, when she should have been writing her papers, she was obliged, as national winner of the American Legion "Americanism" award, to give talks on American values at high schools all over the country. So she had no time to do her own work or to reflect on the meaning of the work she was copying and handing in as her own.

This may be the reality behind the dirty secret of pervasive plagiarism on campus—plagiarism fits nicely into the gamesmanship of learning, the passive adoption of others' ideas, the mindless repetition of slogans as if they were thoughts, the use of education as a commodity. The dark side of American values shows up in this catalog, as my student so clearly demonstrated. Where learning has been turned into the mere accumulation of facts and units, we find plagiarism naturally substituting for education. This dark side ought not to be ignored, since it is fully embedded in the American dream of success. But most of our students will respond well to instruction that shows them the cost of devaluing their education and their own minds, and that urges them toward responsible writing and learning.

When Collaboration Becomes Plagiarism: The Administrative Perspective

Henry L. Wilson

Efforts to redefine the terms "plagiarism" and "collaboration" are currently underway in the field of composition studies. Both terms describe writing processes involving more than one author, yet the former is regarded as disreputable or unethical while the latter is increasingly advocated as an effective pedagogical technique. The blurring of boundaries between these two terms is not restricted to the individual classroom, however; academic policy statements on plagiarism—which are intended to clarify issues of intellectual property—can also add to the conflict and confusion.

Most general attempts to distinguish between plagiarism and collaboration imply that plagiarism can be best understood as a method of text production involving an element of deception, exploitation, or outright theft, while "collaboration" produces texts by relying on a more balanced, open, and equitable relationship between authors. *The Oxford English Dictionary (OED),* for example, defines "collaboration" as "United labor, co-operation; esp. in literary, artistic, or scientific work." But a secondary definition presented is "Traitorous cooperation with the enemy" (vol. 3: 469). In "Collaborative Learning and Composition: Boon or Bane?" Donald Stewart points out that these subversive connotations can be quite serious for scholars "of a certain age and historical background: In the occupied countries, [a collaborator] was a person who assisted the Nazis, even . . . betraying his or her countrymen" (66).

The presence of such negative definitions within composition studies shows that "collaboration" is not uniformly regarded as a respectable technique for producing writing. In many contexts, it is portrayed as an unethical short cut that is inherently inferior to the more established and "honorable" route to text production: individual authorship. In *Singular Texts/Plural Authors,* Lisa Ede and Andrea Lunsford present a troubling picture of the professional and scholarly barriers that have been erected against collaborative authorship—including a tendency to devalue group-authored publications as

211

criteria for granting tenure. Ede and Lunsford point out that these barriers continue to exist in spite of the fact that such collaborative authorship has become very common in many disciplines.

Contrasted with the brief history of collaborative writing in composition studies, "plagiarism" is a term of ancient lineage; *The Oxford English Dictionary* defines it as "the wrongful appropriation or purloining, and publication as one's own, of the ideas, or the expression of the ideas (literary, artistic, musical, mechanical, etc.) of another" (vol. 11: 947). The OED's list of citations of the term extends back to the early seventeenth century, and includes usages by Hazlitt, Tennyson, and Samuel Johnson. The common denominator of the *OED's* plagiarism citations is an element of deception and exploitation.

Alexander Lindey's 1951 *Plagiarism and Originality* presents a typical, frequently cited—though now somewhat dated—definition of "plagiarism." Lindey's definition strongly emphasizes the same element of deception: "Plagiarism is literary—or artistic or musical—theft. It is the false assumption of authorship: the wrongful act of taking the product of another person's mind, and presenting it as one's own" (2).

Although such confidently stated definitions seem to brook no debate, the boundaries between an open, balanced exchange of authorial influence on the one hand and deceptive "literary theft" on the other may remain indistinct in practice—particularly in the specialized rhetorical realm of the composition classroom. As students make greater use of such uncited sources as peer editors, writing center tutors, and teacher commentary on evolving drafts, such a lack of clarity becomes increasingly apparent. Ready access to socially charged collaborative influences during the process of writing is effectively redefining the concept of authorship within the classroom. Unfortunately, official rules and guidelines on what constitutes ethical authorship do not seem to be evolving at the same rate as classroom practice.

The lack of clarity between policy and practice within the composition classroom is underscored by the results of a recent survey of selected colleges and universities that I conducted. Of the ninety-five inquiry letters requesting official policy statements on "plagiarism" and "collaboration" mailed to a cross-section of colleges and universities during the 1992–1993 academic year, forty-six produced a response. These responses describe a diversity of approaches and attitudes toward collaboration and plagiarism.

Many of the statements I received do not distinguish clearly between intentional and unintentional plagiarism. On the one hand, the University of Illinois's *Statement on Plagiarism* includes the useful declaration that "Intentional plagiarism extends from submitting a paper actually written by someone else to deliberately using an idea or fact or phrase without giving credit to its source" (1). But the possibility that such borrowing can also occur *without intent* is not acknowledged in this statement, nor is the crucial modifier "intentional" defined clearly enough to help student writers recognize this intent when it is present.

On the other hand, Central Piedmont Community College's *Plagiarism Statement Three* defines plagiarism as "Intentionally or knowingly presenting the work of another as one's own (i.e., without proper acknowledgment of the source)," and warns against "collaborating on academic work knowing that the collaboration will not be reported." But this statement also adds the explanatory note that "Collaboration and sharing information are characteristics of academic communities. These become violations when they involve dishonesty" (4–5). Thus, the crucial role played by deception in cases of plagiarism is acknowledged.

Another point of divergence lies in the measures designed to help students avoid plagiarism that are included in several statements. One common measure is represented by the University of Alabama at Birmingham's *Plagiarism Policy,* which advises that "All members of the educational community must carefully avoid plagiarism by fully acknowledging the source of all statements, studies, projects, and ideas which have been produced by another person" (1). In a similar vein, Temple University's *University Statement on Academic Policies and Regulations* asserts that "Normally, all work done for courses—papers, examinations, homework exercises, laboratory reports, oral presentations—is expected to be the individual effort of the student presenting the work." This statement concludes by warning students that "Everything used from other sources must be cited" (61). Clearly, such injunctions cannot be rigorously observed by inexperienced student writers; trying to attribute "everything" derived from "other sources" would require a prohibitive investment of time and energy in a freshman composition course.

At the other end of the spectrum, statements such as those presented in the University of North Carolina's (UNC) *Staff Manual* offer specific, realistic advice to both instructors and students on how to avoid plagiarizing. Under "Some Notes on Plagiarism," this manual informs faculty that "Our goal is to give students an understanding of what plagiarism is about so they will avoid it in their work in your class and in the others that they take" (15). This university also notifies its students in *The Source: The Resource Handbook for the University of North Carolina at Chapel Hill* that students have a responsibility "To consult with faculty and other sources to clarify the meaning of plagiarism: to learn the recognized techniques of proper attribution of sources . . . ; and to identify allowable resource material or aids to be used in the preparation of written work" (31). Thus, the responsibility for avoiding plagiarism seems to be equally distributed to both faculty and students in UNC-Chapel Hill's policy statements.

Overall, the statements I examined can be classified into three major groups:

1. Colleges with no written, in-house policy (N = 7 or 15%).
2. Colleges with written plagiarism policies, but with no discussion of collaboration (N = 29 or 63%).

3. Colleges that not only discuss plagiarism, but also address—either implicitly or explicitly—collaboration (N = 10 or 22%).

The first group—those with no explicit, written policy on plagiarism or collaboration—comprises a relatively minor category. The University of Wyoming, for example, reported that no "official pronouncement" was currently in place for dealing with plagiarism cases; instead, each individual instance is apparently dealt with by instructors on a case-by-case basis. According to the chair of the department at the time of the survey, Mark Booth, teachers are also urged to refer to the plagiarism statement in the McGraw-Hill handbook, *Prose Style: A Handbook for Writers,* and he "carefully review[s] the issue with new teachers." The University of Michigan reported a similarly flexible approach. In both cases, at least two explanations are possible for the absence of an official policy on plagiarism: either the need for such an explicit policy has not yet become apparent at these particular schools, or such a position is a realistic acknowledgment of the fluid state of affairs existing along the boundaries between collaboration and plagiarism.

The second major group of responses to the survey—policies that discuss plagiarism, but not collaboration—is both more numerous and diverse. One major subcategory within this group was offered by English departments that have no official policy of their own toward plagiarism, but that rely instead on statements provided by the university as a whole. While offering the advantages of homogeneity and a consistent structure, this type of statement also poses problems. In most cases, these statements are so sweeping, generic, and all-inclusive that their real-world effectiveness seems limited; they are often restricted to brief discussions of general academic policies subsumed under such terms as "Academic Honesty" and "Honor Codes." Frequently combined with discussions of related concerns such as "cheating," "copying," and "cribbing notes," these statements rarely discuss in any detail the practical difficulties of distinguishing between ethical collaboration and unethical plagiarism. Such general statements seem inadequate for assisting writing teachers in the day-to-day task of dealing with plagiarism.

A somewhat larger subcategory of responses from group two comprises schools which manage to address issues of plagiarism while omitting discussion of collaboration. In many cases, this subcategory's discussion of what does and does not constitute plagiarism can be extensive, often including an explicit yet somewhat sketchy discussion of "plagiarism." In many cases, these statements are directly derived from Alexander Lindey's 1952 standard definition of the term: "The wrongful act of taking the product of another person's mind and presenting it as one's own" (2). This rather minimal plagiarism statement is often supplemented by the more extensive Modern Language Association discussion of the concept, which states that "to plagiarize is to give the impression that you have written or thought something that you have in fact borrowed from another" (Achtert and Gibaldi 4). In several cases, such dictionary definitions represent the entirety of official policy, while in others, further elaboration of these definitions is also included. Often, this elaboration combines a brief discussion of hypothetical cases of plagiarism with an outline of possible penalties for transgressors. On the whole, this type of statement leaves the impression that plagiarism has been a long-standing, recurring problem, one which can be regulated but never entirely prevented.

Responses from schools with a more extensive yet still somewhat ambiguous plagiarism policy comprise a more pragmatic and effective sub-category within group two of responses. This type appears to make a serious attempt to grapple with the shifting boundaries in the zone of overlap between collaboration and plagiarism without entirely succeeding in establishing clear distinctions. Often, these attempts to clarify plagiarism begin with definitions similar to those offered in the previous group, and then move to further discussion and elaboration. For example, the University of Illinois's statement defines plagiarism as "the unacknowledged use of someone else's ideas and/or words (including key words or phrases, as well as longer units like sentences and paragraphs)," and, more succinctly, "using the ideas or words of another person without giving proper credit." These brief definitions are supplemented in the statement with several examples of correct and incorrect paraphrasing and quoting.

While these statements offer adequate coverage of issues associated with plagiarism and text ownership, their definition of terms and discussion of procedures could be improved. Considerable discussion of plagiarism, possible prevention strategies, penalties for transgressions, and helpful models and examples may be present, but these statements often stop at a superficial level. For example, the University of Alabama at Birmingham's statement defines plagiarism as "using the words or thoughts of another without proper citation," but does not discuss how writers—in practical terms—can distinguish their thoughts from those of "others."

One unfortunate side-effect of this type of statement is to complicate attempts to distinguish between plagiarism and collaboration in the actual writing classroom. When students engage in such composition strategies as peer editing and tutoring—which are increasingly presented as essential collaborative writing strategies—blanket prohibitions against "using the words or thoughts of others" can plant unwarranted suspicion in the minds of both teachers and students that something untoward may be occurring in their writing activities, even if these activities consist of the entirely ethical application of collaborative writing techniques.

Those policy statements that detail in a consistent and helpful manner the difference between acceptable imitation or collaboration and unacceptable plagiarism are probably more effective. This third major group of policies can be distinguished from less effective statements not only by length and extensiveness of coverage, but also by a different perspective and focus. The primary feature of this perspective is a demonstrated awareness of the precise forms and manifestations plagiarism cases can take; rather than being limited to a purely speculative discussion, these policies present context-specific scenarios. For example, the departmental statements of both Northern Michigan and Northwestern University include very helpful discussions of both the theoretical foundations of plagiarism and several detailed classroom examples. Northwestern's pamphlet, *Some Notes on Plagiarism and How to Avoid It*, begins with a definition credited to "Harold C. Martin in his essay 'A Definition of Plagiarism'": "The academic counterpart of . . . the manufacturer who mislabels his product is the plagiarist, the student or scholar who leads his reader to believe that what he is reading is the original work of the writer when it is not" (1). The Northwestern statement then discusses in considerable detail how to distinguish between "direct plagiarism," the "mosaic," and the "paraphrase." Specific, realistic examples of each category are presented.

Such statements which address both plagiarism and collaboration are often quite lengthy and detailed and reflect considerable thought on the nature of the processes involved in plagiarism and collaboration, as well as their relationship to each other. Aside from being extensive and detailed, statements like these also tend to work from a specific theoretical viewpoint, one that explicitly acknowledges that writing is inevitably a socially based process.

The University of North Carolina at Chapel Hill's written policy on plagiarism and collaboration is perhaps the most comprehensive illustration of this final group of statements. At least five different sources are in place for UNC–Chapel Hill students and teachers to find information related to plagiarism, ownership of text, and collaboration. UNC starts from a base of statements contained in University-wide honor codes, and then expands and explicates these comments to apply them more specifically to the programs and classes offered at this university. Formulations and clarifications of plagiarism policies are contained in a wide variety of sources, ranging from publications targeted toward incoming freshmen to guides for composition teachers working in the program.

From each perspective, these formulations offer specific, practical advice on how to distinguish between permissible and unacceptable collaboration. For example, the 1992–1993 *Staff Manual* admits that "there is a fine line between plagiarism and the kind of collaboration that defines writing." Recognizing the reality of this "fine line," the manual proceeds to advise teachers to "encourage students to seek feedback from people outside of class to help them revise their papers," but to "guard against appropriation [of language] by others and ourselves." This manual also includes a lengthy list of practical ways to carry out this safeguarding, including urging instructors to "Discuss plagiarism early, openly, and with some fervor" (20). UNC–Chapel Hill also provides students with a *Guide to Freshman Composition*, which refers to the Official University Honor Code. This code warns against academic cheating, "including (but not limited to) unauthorized copying, collaboration, or use of notes or books . . . and plagiarism—defined as the intentional representation of another person's words, thoughts, or ideas as one's own" (11).

In several policies of this type, although the term "collaboration" itself is not mentioned explicitly, the concept is implied in references to such collaborative strategies as "peer editing"—a technique that allows students to receive unacknowledged critiques and advice from their fellow student writers. Several policies contained substantial sections on the practical utility offered by the kind of collaborative assistance available in the writing center through individual tutoring. Policies of this sort demonstrate even greater efforts to accommodate collaborative learning strategies into the process of writing, since they have apparently moved beyond mere slogans toward incorporating the theoretical basis behind these slogans into actual classroom practice. For example, the *101 Course Information Sheet* of the English Department at the Citadel begins its discussion of plagiarism by defining the term as "the act of using someone else's words or ideas as your own without giving proper credit to the source," but then states that "peer editing is not plagiarism," and "judicious peer editing is not only permitted, but encouraged" (2).

The plagiarism policies reviewed seem guided by five primary goals and rhetorical purposes. These goals were not always expressed explicitly in the policies themselves; the following list is based largely on my own efforts to reconstruct the inferred motives driving the drafting and wording of these policies:

1. To promote the upholding of the principles of honor and academic honesty at the most general level.
2. To give students a clear idea of the distinctions between plagiarism and collaboration, and also to warn them against confusing one with the other.
3. To make it possible for teachers and administrators to punish transgressions of official policies.
4. To demonstrate to the general public that the college publishing the policies is a respectable institution.
5. To improve the teaching of writing by foregrounding issues associated with collaboration and peer editing, as well as how to use these strategies successfully.

A clear line of demarcation is apparent between items 1–4 in the above list and item 5: the first four are largely pragmatic and punitive, while the final item is both more theoretical and future-directed. Given the essential constraints on time and methods faced by composition programs, most institutions seem compelled to focus more on the former, rather than the latter. Perhaps, however, the existence of policies such as those offered by UNC–Chapel Hill indicates that plagiarism statements and "honor codes" have potential for not only warning students against plagiarism and unacceptable collaboration, but also guiding them as they develop the latent power of ethical collaborative writing for improving audience awareness and lending a stronger sense of context to their work.

Overall, the plagiarism policies examined represent earnest attempts to deal with a complex, persistent problem within the academic community. Most departmental policies start from a base of collegewide honor codes, and then refine these general guidelines in order to make them more context-specific. This process of working from the general to the specific often produces convoluted "plagiarism policy statements" that may become buried in the general school catalog, lost in a maze of punishments for students who copy math equations during quizzes or buy essays from a fraternity file.

A wide range of definitions of plagiarism and collaboration is present in these college policy statements. Although such definitions are offered to meet a real need to draw boundaries and establish helpful guidelines, the phrasing of these definitions often reflects an outdated ideology and approach to composition. If one assumes that individual authorship is "better" than collaborative authorship, one's definitions of crucial terms will tend to imply that plagiarism is simply collaboration gone awry, or more to the point, collaboration without ethics. If, on the other hand, one wishes to promote collaborative writing, plagiarism may be presented as a distinctive, unethical breach of academic honesty, utterly different from collaboration in both its forms and motivation. From this perspective, plagiarism becomes a clearly definable lapse in ethics that can be avoided with the right teacher training—and attendant student enlightenment—in collaborative writing. Such conflicting perspectives need to be reconciled.

The current lack of clarity in college plagiarism policies is symptomatic of the vagueness and contradiction generally present along the boundaries between ethical collaboration and unethical plagiarism. Fully appreciating the role played by imitation, audience, and other social forces in the production of texts is crucial to eventual clarification of these boundaries. An expanded historical approach will shed additional light on how these forces interact and conflict with the self, originality, and "expressiveness" in the gray areas between collaboration and plagiarism. Such perspectives will offer an enhanced backdrop for redefining the basic terms that comprise writing teachers' understandings of issues associated with intellectual property, collaboration, and plagiarism. Once fully developed, these perspectives should enable teachers to fully realize the power of collaborative writing in the composition classroom without being needlessly hobbled by fear of plagiarism.

In Instruction and Research

Plagiarism as Metaphor

David Leight

A few years ago, a professor from another department visited my office look-ing for a writing teacher. He had given an essay test a few days before, and on reading his students' responses, he found that two of them were nearly iden-tical. Not only were the answers similar in substance and in organization, in some ways the wording was almost the same. These students had not copied from each other, however, and were not even sitting near each other during the exam. After talking to the students, the professor found that they had taken several of his study questions and *prepared answers together* several days be-fore the exam. Although he knew the college's policy on plagiarism, he had come to our department to ask a writing teacher if what they had done con-stituted plagiarism.

What is the definition of plagiarism? For most aspects of writing in-struction, the teacher can find a reliable, authoritative source: word meanings in a dictionary, mechanics and usage in a grammar handbook, citation format in a stylebook, and so on. Yet no single, standard definition of plagiarism ex-ists across textbooks, where we would most expect it to appear.

To analyze definitions of plagiarism, I have looked at nearly seventy writ-ing instruction textbooks, almost all from the 1980s and 1990s and from ma-jor publishers. Most of these textbooks are targeted at first-year writing classes, but some are more specific, such as for writing research papers and technical writing. In analyzing these texts, I have looked for evidence of pat-terns and then seen how these patterns compare over the years. Although I will make no claim that these are the only ways people talk about plagiarism, I will show that these are clearly the most widely used descriptions.

The definition of plagiarism can be represented by four dominant metaphors: plagiarism constitutes stealing and is therefore morally wrong; plagiarism is an ethical problem in which the plagiarist violates an unwritten code of conduct for students; plagiarism is a "borrowing" in which "credit" is left undelivered; and plagiarism is a failure to intellectualize like a member of the academy. After showing examples of each of these metaphors—and the ways in which they play out in descriptions of plagiarism—I will suggest how these metaphors may be changing over time.

Plagiarism as Stealing

As pointed out in many definitions and in *The Oxford English Dictionary,* plagiarism comes from the Latin word *plagiarius,* which means "a kidnapper." It is not surprising, then, that many definitions talk about plagiarism as a form of stealing or "kidnaping" of another's words. For example, Hall and Birkerts say in *Writing Well,* "Plagiarism is stealing the words or ideas of others and presenting them as your own" (7). Similarly, Dornan and Dawe, in *The Brief English Handbook,* comment that "Done consciously or not, plagiarism in any form is the same as stealing, punishable in most colleges by immediate failure or even dismissal from the school" (333). By defining plagiarism in this sense, words become metaphorically "owned" by someone else, a kind of property in which the worst form of dishonesty and immorality is in the taking of them.

With words as property, the act of plagiarism is in every case the equivalent of taking a paper out of a roommate's desk, copying it, and submitting it as one's own. In *Twenty Questions for the Writer: A Rhetoric with Readings,* Berke states, "Plagiarism is literally a crime, a form of theft in which one person steals the words of another—in ignorance, perhaps, of the fact that 'phraseology, like land and money, can be individual personal property, protected by law'" (the latter of which is a reference to a 1963 research manual) (417). By comparing words to land and money, then, words become worth something, a possession. Frisbie et al. in *The Active Writer* similarly consider plagiarism the taking of words from another:

> Accurate notes will help you to avoid the problem of plagiarism, the use of the words or ideas of another person as if they were your own. . . . So be scrupulous about putting an author's exact words in quotation marks, even if you're only copying a phrase from a sentence. Otherwise you may pick up a card two weeks and ten articles later with an uncomfortable feeling that some of what you've written down is someone else's wording, and you won't know how much you have to alter it to make it your own. (452)

By saying "the use of words or ideas of another person" and "someone else's wording," Frisbie et al. suggest that a certain way of wording something can belong to an author. In order to "make it your own," the words must be changed and not to do so constitutes thievery.

Reinking and Hart in *Strategies for Successful Writing: A Rhetoric, Reader, and Handbook* also consider a way of wording or phrasing a possession. "Any piece of information not set off with quotation marks must be in your own words. Otherwise, even though you name your source, you plagiarize by stealing the original phrasing" (344). To phrase something in the same way as in the source "robs the original writer of recognition" (345). Lauer et al. also consider plagiarism as stealing of the way an author first put words together. Their list of forms of plagiarism includes *"Stealing key phrases, without quoting them"* and *"Stealing an entire sentence or section,* without quoting it" (221). In this way, these writers consider plagiarism a theft of the words—and the careful use of words—of another.

Some textbook authors go so far as to tell why plagiarism as stealing is wrong: it is immoral. Packer and Timpane in *Writing Worth Reading: A Practical Guide and Handbook* advance a moral rhetoric of plagiarism: "In college and university writing, as in most other walks of life, people put a great value of knowing what is yours and what belongs to someone else. Therefore, plagiarism is a serious moral issue" (368). While Packer and Timpane go on to suggest that "carelessness or ignorance" might also cause plagiarism, they continue that "Sometimes, however, people in full awareness submit as their own the ideas or work of someone else" (368). And, they add, "If the writer did this knowingly and deliberately concealed the source, it is a kind of theft" (369).

Watt in *An American Rhetoric* describes this metaphor even more fully: *Plagiarism* is a formal word for literary stealing or, to use the campus equivalent, cribbing. It is as immoral to steal from other people's writing as from their wardrobes or their wallets (7). Words, for Watt, are like cash or clothing: the plagiarist sneaks into the writer's room and takes what clearly belongs to someone else. Even "occasional alterations" are not enough for Watt, whose depiction of plagiarism as "literary larceny" best sums up the literalness of the metaphor (218).

Plagiarism as Ethical Violation

A second metaphor used to describe plagiarism is that of the violation of ethical standards. In this case, the "profession" is that of student, and the ethical violation is the shirking of one's responsibilities as a learner by using the work of another. In many ways, this definition of plagiarism seems well fitted for the first-year writer—even more so than the moral definition does. The college student is ostensibly spending money to attend classes and learn as much as possible. The metaphor suggests that the first-year writer, who may have other distractions, needs to take care to do first and foremost the work assigned. But even more so, the metaphor suggests the entrance of the student into the "profession" of studying, and the descriptions of plagiarism that use this metaphor go so far as to suggest that to be unethical is to be illegal.

As is the case in the stealing metaphor, in which either the word "stealing" or "theft" often occurs, the frequent use of the term "ethics" clearly points to this metaphor. For example, Lannon in *The Writing Process: A Concise Rhetoric* writes, "Documentation is a matter of *ethics* in that the originator of an idea deserves to be acknowledged whenever that idea is mentioned" (323). Crews and Schor in *The Borzoi Handbook for Writers* call plagiarism "the serious ethical violation of presenting other people's words or ideas as your own" (472). And in *Writing Research Papers: A Complete Guide,* Lester says, "Plagiarism (purposely using another person's writing as your own) is a serious breach of ethics. Knowledgeable, ethical behavior is necessary whenever you handle sources and cite the words of other people. . . . Above all, avoid any deliberate effort to deceive instructors and other readers of the research paper" (128). Lester's use of the wording "serious breach" along with Crews and Schor's "serious ethical violation" suggest the way in which this description of plagiarism seems especially heinous: while one might not go to hell (for the immorality of stealing), at least one might go to jail.

And the use of the terms "illegal" and "unethical" are often paired in describing plagiarism in this way. Pearsall and Cunningham in *The Fundamentals of Good Writing* say, *"You plagiarize if you use the exact words and sentence structures of other people as your own or even if you use too close paraphrases.* Plagiarism in school can result in a failed paper, a failed course, or worse. In life beyond school, it can result in law suits. Plagiarism is both unethical and illegal" (31). While the threat of legal action for the plagiarist seems "beyond school," Pearsall and Cunningham's suggestion "or worse" provides a threat to the would be student violator. Schiffhorst and Schell in *The Short Handbook for Writers* call plagiarism "both unethical and illegal" and say that "When you put your name on a piece of writing, the reader assumes that you are responsible for the information, wording, and organization and that you will acknowledge the source of any fact or idea that is not your own" (348). By placing one's name on the document, one in effect signs a contract with an instructor, Schiffhorst and Schell suggest. And, similarly, Brusaw, Alred, and Olin in *Handbook of Technical Writing* write, "In publishing, plagiarism is illegal; in other circumstances, plagiarism is at the least unethical" (362).

Moody in *Writing Today: A Rhetoric and Handbook* takes the metaphor one step further. She says that plagiarism

> means presenting as your own work the labor and creativity of someone else. Plagiarism is unethical and is against the law. Needless to say, it is a completely unacceptable practice in college work. For your own self-respect, then, if for no other reason, be sure that any work you put your name to is really your own and not that of another. (249)

By calling plagiarism unethical and illegal, Moody offers the standard threat of this metaphor, which is possible legal action taken against the violator of college ethics. But Moody also notes the real way this metaphor binds: it suggests the student is not doing his or her own work of learning and for the sake of "self-respect" should understand the importance of education. Similarly, in *The Random House Handbook* Crews argues that

> systematic dishonesty is only part of the problem. For every student who buys a term paper or copies a whole article without acknowledgment, there are dozens who indulge in "little" ethical lapses through thoughtlessness, haste, or a momentary sense of opportunity. Though perhaps ninety percent of their work is original, they too are plagiarists—just as someone who robs a bank of $2.39 is a bank robber. (405)

While Crews suggests that such plagiarism might be caused by sloppy note taking, he returns to his "bank robber" image. "Unlike the robber, however," he writes, "some plagiarists fail to realize what they have done wrong" (405). In this sense, students who "blunder into plagiarism" (405) are actually worse than thieves because they think they are doing the right thing. At least the bank robber understands the ethics of his or her chosen profession.

Plagiarism as Borrowing

A third metaphor used in defining plagiarism is that of the plagiarist as a "borrower" who fails to return the item received. Since the plagiarist cannot in any sense "put the item back"—one cannot return words to their original source—the good writer should give "credit" to the source. Perhaps because this metaphor does not seem as caustic as the first two, the many references to borrowing and then not giving credit all speak in very similar terms. The difference, though, lies in how textbook writers describe what is being borrowed and from whom. In other words, definitions describe the plagiarist as taking credit belonging to an original writer, taking credit for the words and ideas of another (credit which in this case is returned as the "acknowledgment"), or taking credit for the work of another.

In *The Writing Process: A Concise Rhetoric,* Lannon gives a good example of the first of these three types of borrowing. In suggesting care in quoting, he points out that "Otherwise, you could forget to give proper credit to the author, and thereby face a charge of plagiarism (borrowing someone else's words without giving credit, intentionally *or* unintentionally)" (319–20). For Lannon it is the author who deserves this credit, as it is for Trimmer and McCrimmon in *Writing with a Purpose,* who call plagiarism "the use of someone else's writing without giving proper credit—or perhaps any credit at all—to the writer of the original" (337). And Lunsford and Connors in *The St. Martin's Handbook* write, "Plagiarism is the use of someone else's words as your own without crediting the original writer for those words" (566).

A second form of the borrowing metaphor is the failure to credit the words and ideas of another person. For example, in *Academic Writing: Working with Sources across the Curriculum,* Kennedy and Smith write, *"Plagiarism* is the act of benefiting directly from someone else's writing or ideas without giving proper credit" (190). Similarly, Dornan and Dawe in *The Brief English Handbook* say, "Any failure to give credit for words or ideas you have borrowed from others is *plagiarism"* (333). Tibbetts and Tibbetts in *Strategies of Rhetoric with Handbook* comment that "The plagiarist usually intends to pass off his paper as being an original creation when it is not. Borrowing other people's ideas and their wording without giving due credit will create problems for you as a student because teachers can take severe action against the writer of a plagiarized paper" (376). And Adams in *The HarperCollins Concise Handbook for Writers* says, "One of your goals in taking notes is to distinguish between personal ideas and borrowed material. The direct or indirect use of someone else's ideas or language without giving proper credit is *plagiarism"* (466). Often in this metaphor, the credit for borrowed words and ideas is returned in the form of an acknowledgment to the source or the writer. For instance, Diana Hacker in *A Writer's Reference* says that "To borrow another writer's words and ideas without proper acknowledgment is a form of dishonesty known as plagiarism" (214).

Moreover, in a particularly indicting form of this metaphor, Guth in *The Writer's Agenda: The Wadsworth Writer's Guide and Handbook* writes that "Writers who plagiarize lift material from their sources without acknowledgment. They reap where others have sown; they appropriate the fruits of someone else's research without giving credit where due" (461). Guth's use of this metaphor moves interestingly into a third form of the borrowing metaphor: the plagiarist takes credit for the work of another. When Guth says "they appropriate the fruits of someone else's research," he is suggesting that scholars do a particular kind of work that they deserve credit for. McCuen and Winkler in *Rewriting Writing: A Rhetoric* write,

> The idea behind documentation is simple. If you borrow from another's ideas or work, you must document the loan and give due credit to the source from which it came. If you don't, you create the false impression that the goods are your own when they were taken from someone else. This kind of theft is known among scholarly circles as *plagiarism.* Since the currency of scholarship is ideas, it is not farfetched to say that stealing a scholar's idea is the moral equivalent of stealing money from a bank. (341–42)

Again echoing the stealing metaphor, McCuen and Winkler also refer to "work" that is borrowed from another, and this particular kind of work—or "currency"—is ideas.

For Bazerman in *The Informed Writer: Using Sources in the Disciplines,* "intellectual borrowing without giving credit is a form of theft called *plagia-*

rism. Plagiarism is passing off someone else's work—whether in the exact words or in paraphrase—as your own" (470). In other words, for Bazerman, plagiarism is borrowing intellectual work without giving credit. And in Heffernan and Lincoln's *Writing: A College Handbook,* again work is the material taken: "When you submit a paper that is wholly or partly plagiarized, you are taking credit—or asking your teacher to give you credit—for work done by someone else. . . . You commit plagiarism whenever you use a source in any way without precisely acknowledging that you have taken from it" (535).

Plagiarism as Intellectual Laziness

The third use of the borrowing metaphor, to take credit for work by others, moves closely toward the fourth and final metaphor used to describe plagiarism: plagiarism as intellectual laziness or sloppiness. Guth and Bazerman both suggest that the people doing the work are scholars and that their intellectual endeavors should get rewarded with acknowledgments. But many of these descriptions of plagiarism go even further than noting credit: they suggest that the plagiarist avoids doing valuable intellectual work that would help not only him or her but the entire academy as well.

In *Prentice Hall Handbook for Writers,* Leggett, Mead, and Kramer say that "Plagiarism consists of passing off the ideas, opinions, conclusions, facts, words—in short, the intellectual work—of another as your own" (486). And in *The Prentice Hall Guide to Research Writing,* Memering writes that "Plagiarism suggests intellectual dishonesty; practically speaking, it undermines research by confusing or obscuring the sources of information" (147). While Memering's example suggests the problems for research as a whole, Lester argues in *Writing Research Papers: A Complete Guide* that "If you plagiarize, you will abandon critical thinking of your own and become an intellectual cripple. You will never have original ideas because you lean on others—their ideas and their words" (129).

But in *The Shape of Reason: Argumentative Writing in College,* Gage may offer the most eloquent description of the intellectual reasons why one should not plagiarize:

> Having raised the specter of plagiarism, I'll discuss it briefly. Textbooks about writing always discuss it; it is one of the customary topics of anyone speaking to students about research writing. Although I would not want to ignore an issue so many think is essential, I would like to believe that if you are using this book, and have gotten this far, you are not the kind of student who would be tempted to plagiarize. To have read this far in a book that stresses the responsibilities of a writer and in a chapter that treats research

> as honest inquiry, you have already demonstrated your interest in using your writing to improve and express your thinking, for the sake of your education. You know that the definition of plagiarism is the fraudulent use of the words and ideas of others as if they were one's own. You know that plagiarism is academic dishonesty and punishable as such. You don't need to be told not to do it. It is enough to say that plagiarism is self-imposed bondage of the intellect—an unavoidable first step toward slavery of the mind. (212)

Gage's description includes the ethical metaphor when he says not to plagiarize "for the sake of your education." But his use of terms like "self-imposed bondage of the intellect" and "slavery of the mind" suggests that the real problem of plagiarism is that it takes the place of intellectualizing, which should not only be the work of the student but anyone involved in academic pursuits. But by presenting his argument as a necessary evil to "briefly" touch on, Gage further suggests that the true intellectual would not even consider plagiarizing because it is antithetical to scholarship.

Yet other textbook writers use the idea of intellectual activity to note unintentional or accidental forms of plagiarism. The true intellectual knows the rules for citing information and knows not to be sloppy about it. Clark's *Taking a Stand: A Guide to the Researched Paper with Readings* notes that "Some plagiarism is actually unintentional—students do not acknowledge their sources simply because they are unaware of the importance of doing so and are unacquainted with scholarly methods" (608). Cooley in *The Norton Guide to Writing* states, "Presenting another person's ideas as your own is plagiarism, whether you intend to do so or not. The best way to avoid unintentional plagiarism is to take notes properly and to be overscrupulous in citing your sources" (458). And Marius and Wiener in *The McGraw-Hill College Handbook* write that one form of plagiarism "may result when a well-meaning, uninformed writer takes bad notes or when a dishonest one deliberately attempts to deceive" (464).

Besides these unintentional kinds of plagiarism, Hairston et al. in *The Scott, Foresman Handbook for Writers* say that "Many students do not realize that taking notes carelessly or documenting sources inadequately may also raise doubts about the integrity of a paper" (602). Such an accidental or careless plagiarism is as bad as the worst kind of dishonesty because it breaks down the system of the academy. As Walker writes in *Writing Research Papers: A Norton Guide,* "You should also avoid plagiarizing accidentally. Some students think that they are paraphrasing correctly when in fact they have retained the sentence structure of the original source or even a phrase or an unusual use of a word. At times, people plagiarize accidentally when they sincerely forget what was their own idea and what they learned from other people" (92).

Mixing Multiple Metaphors

As many of the above examples have shown, these metaphors sometimes mix in the same paragraph and even in the same sentence. Given the widespread availability of a diverse group of writing textbooks, it would not be surprising for textbook authors to see and then include snippets of multiple metaphors (which is not to say that they are plagiarizing each other!). Also, the wide variety of theories about composition, authorship, and textuality have likely muddled the metaphors as well as shifted them. Whether or not these metaphors tie directly to specific composition theories is the subject of another study, perhaps correlating authors of textbooks to their positions in articles. In addition, the question of whether or not metaphors change over time cannot be clearly answered from this study, which sought to distinguish types of metaphors in the 1980s and 1990s, and a longer chronology may find such a change.

Since intellectual property seems more and more a focus of discussion in the academy, it is perhaps not surprising that definitions of plagiarism would start to consider its impact. But the diverse metaphors of plagiarism show that defining it as any one thing may cause problems for students and their teachers alike. Local communities need to come to a consensus and talk about how they decide to define it. And most important, teachers need to talk to students about how definitions can be socially constructed yet still carry the weight of "law."

The Ethics of Appropriation in Peer Writing Groups

Candace Spigelman

Traditionally, collaboration is considered irresponsible; in the extreme, collaboration is the worst academic sin, plagiarism.

—Kenneth Bruffee

In his 1973 article, "Collaborative Learning: Some Practical Models," Kenneth Bruffee anticipated problems that continue to perplex both instructors and students who are involved in classroom writing groups: how to negotiate the demands for legitimate appropriation and attribution, which are part and parcel of ethical scholarship, while engaging in the wholly collaborative and intertextual enterprise of peer group response and collective revision. Today, as cooperative practices pervade business, industry and daily life, many students remain skeptical and cautious about group activities, and significant numbers of college-level faculty and administrators continue to suspect the integrity of collaborative work.

While I do not deny the very real problems associated with illegitimate appropriation and representation, I believe that students are often confused, not about what plagiarism is, but about how it applies to the writing group situation. Further, I suspect that the message we send to students when we oppose plagiarism to the creation of an "original" work tends to deny the intertextual and communal nature of writing. This chapter addresses the "problem" of plagiarism in writing groups and explores the ways in which four students attempted to balance traditional demands for academic integrity and originality while actively collaborating in their freshman writing group.

231

Plagiarism in Schools: Traditional Definitions

Because students in writing groups not only share ideas and suggestions but often cowrite parts of their peers' papers, their activities do not conform to traditional definitions of academic honesty, which are always linked in some way to the private production of an original text. Most educators and students associate plagiarism with stealing or, at least, with taking and using the words or ideas of another writer or speaker and claiming them as one's own in order to gain an advantage (i.e., to get a higher grade, to be published, to get a promotion, and so on). Students generally classify as "cheating" the theft of all or part of a peer's paper, the use of a ghostwriter, or word-for-word copying from a published source. (The fact that they may have engaged in any or all of these activities at one time or another does not abridge their conception of how such cheating is defined.) In academic settings, the term *plagiarism* is used to designate not only the full-scale appropriation of a section of written text but also the failure to attend to the formal conventions of quotation and attribution. Undergraduates, for example, frequently copy words or parts of sentences from sources or combine phrases from various sources without using quotation marks to indicate the "borrowed" terms, although they may (or may not) provide the name of the original writer. Such texts are usually considered to be plagiarized. Finally, in the present educational climate, certain kinds of writing assistance may be labeled as forms of plagiarism.

American schools have made valiant attempts to teach student writers conventional methods of attribution in order to prevent their committing inadvertent plagiarism. By high school, most students have been introduced to some formal procedure for documenting sources and cautioned about the sins of "copying." Undergraduate college students seem to attend to these injunctions in a variety of ways: some are scrupulous in applying the rules; some apply them haphazardly; and some simply ignore them. But the fact that students are introduced, repeatedly, to these rules suggests the extreme difficulty of actually enforcing the procedures or prosecuting their infringement.

In the professional sphere, literary theft reflects on the integrity of the plagiarized text as well as on the plagiarizer. However, in the case of undergraduate students, whose written texts are rarely published, it is the student, rather than his or her paper, that becomes the subject of plagiaristic representation. On the one hand, for some instructors, an act of plagiarism indicates a defect in a student's moral character, although the vigor of this pronouncement is usually dependent on the circumstances surrounding the act as well as the degree of plagiarism involved. On the other hand, students are oftentimes seen as victims of inadequate instruction and preparation. In contrast, Rebecca Moore Howard (1995) contends that many of the "errors" students make in handling academic citation conventions are indicative of their efforts to approximate academic discourse and, as such, should be tapped as pedagogic strategies.

The concept of plagiarism is a fairly modern construct. Prior to the emergence of the author as an autonomous figure of literary production, there appears to have been less anxiety about the appropriation of what is now termed "intellectual property." At the same time that authors attained economic independence and legal protection for their work, the value of literary property came to be linked to its originality, the unique expression of a particular writer (Woodmansee 1984; Jaszi 1991; Mark Rose). In this environment, plagiarism naturally became a more serious consideration. But it is important to stress that "originality" is not the antithesis of "plagiarism." Plagiarism's opposite is, in fact, attribution, the willing acknowledgment of one's sources, and its attendant values are honesty and integrity, not creative genius. Nevertheless, the concept of plagiarism is linked inextricably to the pejorative sense of "copy," and the disgrace of the perpetrator is not just that she passes off someone else's words and labor as her own, but that she is an imitator, and there fore clearly incapable of original thought.

While postmodern authors and critics have demonstrated that writing, and indeed the construction of knowledge in all spheres, is inherently social and intertextual, traditional schooling reinforces private and individual student activity with a goal toward autonomous originality (Lunsford and Ede 1994; Bruffee 1993). As a result, writing activity that involves several writers may be defined as plagiarism, since the resultant text can not be the original product of a single-mind-at-work. Thus, in addition to textual theft or inaccurate documentation, some teachers hold that various kinds of supportive assistance to writers are also forms of plagiarism. In such cases, the appropriation of ideas, including those generated through verbal exchange, may be suspect. Writing center tutors, for example, frequently find themselves under attack as accessories to plagiarism, and, at some colleges, writing center tutors are forbidden to offer editorial assistance; at others, tutors may not provide examples or specific phrases for incorporation in a student's paper or even hold a pencil during a tutoring session.

Writing groups pose a particular problem for established academic attribution conventions, which affirm the text as private property and the writer as autonomous creator. In writing groups, students generate ideas, provide examples, and even furnish language for individual papers, and those ideas and words often appear in the revised essays of various group members. Although their papers will be graded as single-author documents, students in peer groups are expected to be responsive, to give and receive advice, to discuss and argue issues, and sometimes to cowrite each other's work. Researchers have found that in successful writing groups, at least during the course of the groups' engagement, all compositions are viewed as community property, open to modification and appropriation in the interests of the text's, as well as the writer's, improvement (Bruffee 1993; Gere; Holt; Nystrand and Brandt; Spear). Writing groups that have been established without these assumptions fail (Gere and Stevens).

But if, in some educational contexts (including some writing classes), students are held accountable, and even suspect, when they submit work that has been developed with the help or feedback of tutors, parents, or room-mates, they may be perplexed by the apparent freedom to engage in these ac-tivities in writing groups. They may wonder whether they truly have the "right" to unself-consciously appropriate their peers' suggestions; likewise, they may be threatened or offended by their peers' attempts to intrude on their own writing.

Writing Group "Plagiarism" and Student Values: A Case Study

Recently, I conducted a qualitative research project, using videotapes, participant-observation, interviews, and written documents, to examine the effects of students' attitudes and concerns about plagiarism on the exchange of ideas and information in the peer group setting. The central participants, Lori, Edward, Andrew, and Julie, were students in a freshman composition class at a branch campus of a large university where I taught English. Lori, Edward, and Julie were white, traditional freshman. Edward had been born in Russia but spoke English fluently. Andrew, the group's strongest writer, was an African-American junior transfer student from another university.

The students in the study liked cooperative practices and expected to use the writing group session to exchange ideas and solicit suggestions for their papers. At their peer group meeting, they assisted each other in the develop-ment of their essays by brainstorming for examples and details, explaining and clarifying material in the assigned readings, and generally talking through complicated issues raised by their topics. In addition, they actually wrote or reformulated sentences for each other. At the same time, each student brought to the discussion his or her own privately generated essay, and once the peer group was concluded, each student revised that text alone.

Participants' Definitions of Plagiarism

For the students in the study, plagiarism always involves some form of personal misrepresentation. As Lori explains, "When you copy something out of a book or don't, like, give a person credit when you're supposed to write their name and page or whatever, and you don't quote . . . , *that* makes it look like you wrote it." The problem with this misrepresentation, as the students see it, is that the evaluator (here, the writing instructor) will assume that the work is the student's own, and thus give the student writer credit he or she has not earned.

But the students' values are shaped by practical considerations at least as much as by ethical ones. In part, the impetus not to plagiarize comes from concerns about getting caught. For example, Julie asserts,

> Let's say I took it [an idea] from a book. I didn't write that. And you can tell the difference in my writing and that writing. . . . I think that anyone would probably know that it wasn't my work . . . [and] I wouldn't feel *it's mine.* I probably wouldn't do it because, I don't know, I probably wouldn't write a good paper because *it's not mine,* you know, *it's not mine.* (emphasis added)

Julie's code of ethics derives from her anxiety about external judgment and her internal moral code, which understands the production of the text as an individual enterprise. In her perception, proprietorship affects the quality of the work: when the writer appropriates another's ideas, he or she both risks discovery and produces an inferior product.

Criteria for Appropriating Peers' Written and Spoken Texts

Notably, for these students plagiarism includes the unacknowledged appropriation of student texts as well as professional writing. In place of the citation rituals they use to acknowledge professional sources, the students express a set of criteria for honest use of their peers' written documents and spoken ideas as these are disseminated during the writing group session.

Lori and Julie insist that a student writer may only use an idea that is offered directly to him or her in the form of a peer's written or oral suggestion or by asking permission of the original writer. Lori states that she would not feel comfortable using an argument she had gleaned from reading a peer's paper. Although she acknowledges that the goal of writing groups is the exchange of ideas, she makes an ethical distinction about the manner in which the ideas are obtained, explaining that "it seems different when they're giving you ideas about . . . your paper, mak[ing] suggestions to put in your paper. [It's] not like reading someone else's and taking their idea."

Both Lori and Julie distinguish between using a peer's *suggestion* and using a peer's *idea.* With a *suggestion,* Lori says, the reader indicates his or her intention to provide the writer with helpful advice: "Someone writing down, 'I advise you to, you know, add some more to this part.'" In contrast, an *idea* may be procured without the writer's knowledge, by reading a peer's essay or by listening to a peer discuss his or her work. At any given moment, the writing group may be focused on providing suggestions for a particular writer, who is free to accept them within this clearly demarcated "offering" context.

However, other peer members, who, in the act of reading or discussion, encounter ideas that would be useful for their own work are, according to Julie and Lori, ethically constrained from appropriating this material.

Andrew shares the view that student texts are sacrosanct in the context of reading: "When I'm reading Edward's paper, I'm here to help him. And during a peer group, we're here to help everybody. . . . I would feel kind of funny using an idea strictly from . . . his paper." However, he believes that ideas introduced in group discussion are freely appropriable, even if the peer group member who benefits is not the writer of the text:

> When you're in a peer group, you know, a lot of things get tossed around. . . .
> You tend to grab . . . an idea out of the air . . ., cause during a peer group, a
> lot of things are said . . . and they may not particularly pertain to . . . your
> paper. You can be doing someone else's paper, and during the discussion,
> somebody could say something on their paper, and you go, "Ah, that's an in-
> teresting thought, you know. Maybe I can run with it also."

Andrew understands ideas as free-floating objects, which become communal property if they are introduced in discussion.

In contrast with his peers, Edward declares that it is perfectly acceptable to use a peer writer's ideas, as long as they are transformed in some way:

> If I was reading a student's paper . . . and I liked something they said, if I
> used that idea and then tied something in of my experience with that idea,
> then it would be mine . . . [But] if I just take it exactly, it would be plagia-
> rizing. . . . You know, just taking and just putting it in.

According to Edward, plagiarizing a peer's text means copying word-for-word while legitimate appropriation always involves an active reshaping or personalizing of the ideas in the original.

Because writers tend to be quite possessive about their ideas, the students say, an ethics of appropriation must be governed, in part, by consideration of one's peers' feelings. Andrew asserts that he would not appropriate ideas from a private reading of a peer's paper because "it may seem like I'm stealing somebody else's work. . . . Some people are, you know, funny like that." As a result, if the writer had full knowledge and gave him permission, Andrew would feel comfortable about using the writer's ideas. He explains that although he believes that "ideas in general are not ownable . . . someone may feel his ideas are ownable." In order to avoid danger of confrontation, the writer's approval must be obtained.

Lori disagrees with Andrew's view that asking permission from the primary writer will solve the problem:

> I mean, personally, I don't think the person would really, even if they said,
> "Okay, you can do that," I don't think they'd really like that, taking [their]

idea [because h]e thought of it on his own and that's *his* paper and that will be his grade. By me taking it, I'm taking, like, his grade or something.

Methods of Dealing with Appropriated Material

The students in this group adhere to a set of criteria for legitimately appropriating their peers' ideas in order to avoid charges of plagiarism. Foremost, they all believe that a student writer must always reinterpret or personalize any appropriated material that is not already communal property. On the one hand, Lori seems to represent the groups' position when she says that even if a fellow writer agreed to share the ideas that were to appear in his or her paper, she would have to modify them "in a way that was different from the way he did it." On the other hand, the students differ in their assessments of what might constitute private or public textual property. For some, it is the writer's words; for others, the writer's ideas.

Andrew believes that writers demonstrate their skill when they reshape an idea (a public entity) into their own words (a private product). The writer's creativity is reflected in his or her word choice. As a result, Andrew feels that using another student's words, either spoken and written, "would make me feel like I didn't put the work or effort in myself. . . . [Y]ou can use the idea to make it relate to your paper. But his words are his words. I mean that's—, [you] might as well just cut and paste."

Lori, too, believes that plagiarism involves the appropriation of a writer's or reader's words, and as a result, she has devised a ritual for dealing ethically with her peers' suggestions: "When they tell me something, I'll write it down—just like a note, just so I know, and then I'll go home and, like, write it out more in, like, sentence form and then try and fit it in where it will fit." Lori conceives of her group's suggestions as a way to add to the existing text. But her use of the word *just* appears to be an attempt to minimize the role of her peers' comments in the shaping of her essay. The group's idea, reduced to a mere note, may be ethically appropriated by writing it out as a sentence and changing the words.

In contrast to his peers, Edward's criteria for honest appropriation rests on his belief in the autonomy of ideas as opposed to words, which he considers community property. In order to protect the originality of the work, the writer must preserve his or her own central argument and the general dimensions of the original draft. However, tutors, peers, and teachers may function in an editorial capacity to reconfigure syntax, vocabulary, or grammar. This kind of assistance, he insists, is not plagiarizing because the writer is appropriating only words, but not ideas.

Finally, for Julie neither ideas nor words may be appropriated directly from either writers or readers. In writing groups, she explains, "people are giving you some, they're giving you suggestions and from there you can draw your own . . . way of interpreting that [information]." In fact, during the peer group session, Julie had an opportunity to test her theory. Julie had chosen as her topic a discussion of the role of parents in shaping their children's values. When she met in the writing group, her draft was still a loose collection of statements whose thesis hinted at a child's inability to escape her parents' conditioning. During the peer group meeting, she not only read Lori's paper on the same topic but with a very different slant, but she also discussed with her peers an essay by Toni Morrison, which provided a more nuanced response to the central question. As a result, Julie's revised paper incorporates many of the issues that emerged in the discussions of both her paper and Lori's draft.

True to her code, Julie's essay steers clear of Lori's use of an instructional anecdote about a friend, and she positions her argument in terms of her relationship with her own parents. In this way, she feels, she has ensured the integrity of her text and performed ethically as a writer. Initially, Julie had openly acknowledged the intertextual dynamics that led to her revision. However, later in the interview, when I suggested that she might have "used Lori's ideas," she became defensive, saying, "I *just* read over—just looking at her paper, you know, helped me realize [where] I was going."

It seems to me that Julie, more than any of the students, made productive use of her peers' suggestions and that she chose an approach quite consistent with current writing group theory. On the one hand, for her, writing groups serve as catalysts for writer's thoughts, while the writer is charged with modifying and personalizing the group's suggestions in order to achieve for him- or herself a satisfying and meaningful composition. On the other hand, I am troubled by the fact that for Julie there is something vaguely incriminating about admitting to the use of her peers' ideas.

Crediting Peers as Sources

Although all the students feel that it is essential to credit professional sources in order to protect themselves from charges of plagiarism, when it comes to deciding whether it is equally necessary to give credit to their peers' suggestions and ideas, they respond somewhat inconsistently.

For Andrew, who believes that peer ideas, in texts and in writing groups, are community property, there is no conceivable reason to document a peer's efforts. Andrew explains, "It's like learning to ride a bike. It's like I'm on the bike and they're helping me along, and once they let me go, I'm riding. So it's like, do I give them credit for every time I ride a bike?" In Andrew's analogy, group members are assistants, helping the writer learn a new skill, at times offering suggestions that will result in greater finesse or ability. But this assistance is incidental. The rider/writer has no need to acknowledge this help since he is actually completing the task on his own.

In addition to the "offering context," the notion that in peer groups ideas are *intended* from the start for the writer's consumption also denies the need to credit suggestions and ideas. With a peer's ideas, Lori says, "It's just your friend saying something to you." Yet, Lori herself engaged very specific procedures in order to appropriate her "friends'" texts and suggestions in what she considered an ethical manner, and, in the following passage, she expresses her confusion and ambivalence about attribution in peer groups:

> I guess you should give credit, cause they're saying it, and you're putting it in your paper like you said it, . . . [but] you're probably not going to write exactly what they wrote down . . . they don't usually give you the exact words to write, but they're giving you the idea, so that's still, like, plagiarism so, I don't know—It's a hard question.

In writing groups, what constitutes plagiarism is indeed a difficult question. For in truth, institutional imperatives for originality, for doing one's "own" work, seem to oppose the social construction of knowledge that is the central feature of the writing group process. In this writing group, students eagerly shared their texts, ideas, and suggestions and clearly benefited from the group's engagement in clarifying the writing and thinking in their own drafts. At the same time, in order to assure themselves that their behavior was ethical, they constructed a complex set of criteria and an equally complex set of methods for the use of this material in revising their papers, which served to inhibit true collaborative engagement. Their rules and rituals derive, in part, from their interpretations of methods for using scholarly sources and in part from the privilege that they, as university citizens, have learned to award to "original" work and autonomous scholarship. These prior convictions may make it difficult for them to negotiate the competing demands imposed by the writing group context.

Appropriation and Attribution in the Classroom: Some Suggestions

How can we help students to negotiate writing group appropriation effectively? First, we can teach scholarly methods for citation and paraphrase, on the one hand, and the social construction of knowledge in writing groups, on the other, by introducing these concepts simultaneously and asking students to examine their competing tensions. During instruction in research conventions, students would be asked to explain their own codes and systems for scholarly appropriation and attribution and then to consider how these apply, at times, to their writing group activities. In addition, we could to point out that, outside of the writing classroom, in both academic and nonacademic settings, the collaboration of primary writers with colleagues, editors, and other helpful readers usually appears in the formal acknowledgments. Elaine Maimon suggests teaching students to write acknowledgments or prefatory notes to indicate peer assistance in the composition of their essays, and such encouragement might go a long way to alleviate some of the anxiety students obviously feel. Moreover, we might address the problematic of the student writer as individual, as primary author, and as active group member, by raising questions about autonomous originality and cooperative textual production and about public and private intellectual property. Finally, by examining together the parallel issues of appropriation and attribution for both professional and peer texts, we can help students to see that genuine scholarship always includes both private and public elements of textual production.

The Role of Scholarly Citations in Disciplinary Economies

Shirley K. Rose

In academic discourse, plagiarism and conventional citation practice exist in a reciprocal relationship: successful avoidance of one depends on strategic employment of the other. Because unconventional citation practices expose a would-be scholarly writer to censure and even expulsion from an academic community, explaining the rules and reasons for making references to other texts is a priority for those who initiate newcomers to the community. To provide these explanations, we often rely on metaphor.

In previous work I have explored the possibilities of viewing scholarly citation practices from a religious perspective, metaphorically comparing the scholarly citation to *an act of faith,* a ritual whereby a writer affirms community membership and testifies to his or her acceptance of the shared beliefs of the discourse community ("Citation Rituals in Academic Cultures"). In another essay, I have used the metaphor of the *courtship ritual* to explore the role of citations in building identification among members of a scholarly discourse community ("What's Love Got to Do With It?"). There I argued for adopting a Burkean rhetoric of identification for explaining citation practices, viewing scholarly citation as a courtship ritual designed to enhance a writer's standing in a scholarly discourse community.

The terms of this rhetoric challenge, without completely displacing, the capitalistic economic terms that currently prevail in writing handbook discussions of quotation, paraphrase, and other means of incorporating ideas from one or more texts into another. Economic metaphors are most common in these handbook explanations and in other explanations provided ostensibly for novices (such as plagiarism policies for a college campus or university system) and these metaphors are also frequently used in explanations of regulatory specifications for institutional discursive practices (the *MLA Style Manual,* e.g.).

Though these economic and erotic/religious metaphors might at first glance seem quite disparate, in fact, the etymological connections between "credit" and "creed" are quite close. In this chapter, I will explore the possibilities of extending the economic metaphor for scholarly citation practice. Using economic metaphors as a lens through which to examine the roles of citation practice in scholarly discourse, I will view citations as contributions to creating and maintaining disciplinary economies of knowledge production and distribution. Many economic metaphors for citation practices are already quite common and familiar. We need look no further than any one of the many available handbooks for student writers to find references to *giving credit* to sources and *acknowledging intellectual indebtedness,* for example. The metaphor of *intellectual property* is an especially pervasive one that takes on a special significance if we view the exchange of ideas as a major function in a disciplinary economy (see Price). If a particular scholar's work is considered to be the "product" of her intellectual labor, and therefore her intellectual property, citations of that work might be viewed as contributions to that scholar's intellectual property. Since "property" has historically referred to real property—land or "real" estate—it is not surprising that the collective knowledge of a discipline is often referred to as a "field" and that other land-related metaphors such as "groundbreaking" and "pioneering" are used to describe scholarly discourse that has significantly increased the size of a discipline's collective property.

An academic discipline's collective effort to lay claim to and work productively in a "field" of inquiry can be read in the way each new text proscribes, circumscribes, or inscribes earlier texts. However, the metaphor of *intellectual capital* may serve us even better than *intellectual property* for an exploration of the ways in which citations of scholarly discourse contribute to the disciplinary economy—both for the individual scholar/investor and for the collective whole. Whereas *intellectual property* is a metaphor suggesting a material reality, the idea embodied in the physical text or product, *intellectual capital* is a metaphor that allows us to explore characteristics of the symbolic action by which that work is valued. The term *intellectual capital* emphasizes the exchange value or symbolic aspects of knowledge rather than its concrete or material instantiations. One way to think about this shift in emphasis might be to consider the difference between the image of the medieval bard's "word hoard" and the late-twentieth-century scholar's "home page." The value of the word hoard was defined in terms of size. The value of the home page is more likely to be defined in terms of its capacity for creating relationships or "links." (That the term "home page" and other terms for electronic discourse still employ spatial, territorial, and geographical metaphors may be an indication of the persistence of the view of knowledge as property.)

Scholarly citations, then, the means by which scholars establish their "credibility" and "give credit," play an important role in the production and circulation of intellectual capital in their disciplinary economies. In the section that follows, I will outline an approach to citation analysis that will allow for a close examination of the knowledge-making and knowledge-circulating processes of a disciplinary economy.

It is not within the scope of this essay to provide more than the sketchiest of summaries of other citation analysis research. Various disciplines use citation analysis for different reasons. In the library sciences, citation analysis is carried out for the purpose of improving the usefulness of citations and citation indexes as bibliographic research tools.[1] Sociologists of knowledge use citation analysis to evaluate the contribution of cited texts and to understand relations among texts in a given body of literature. In rhetoric and composition studies, citation analysis is used to understand why scholars cite other work and how readers interpret citations.

Only recently has scholarship in citation studies addressed developing a rhetoric of citation practice.[2] In *Shaping Written Knowledge,* the work most likely to be familiar to readers outside library and information sciences, Charles Bazerman examines the ways citations in scientific articles refer to, invoke, or respond to the context of the already existing literature of a field in order to establish a relationship with that literature. For Bazerman, citation practices are clues to the "cognitive structure" of knowledge in a discipline (166–67).

In "Community Discourse and Discourse Communities: A Grammar, a Rhetoric, and a Symbolic of Scholarly Citations," my coauthors and I view citations as attempts to create a coherence among texts that would otherwise remain isolated and distinct, attempts to negotiate a role in the community discourse, attempts to organize a turn in the disciplinary conversation. I argue here that citations are also a means by which scholarly writers transform their discourse from the "dialectical" conversation among members within a disciplinary community into "ultimate discourse" that represents the discipline as a whole. In *A Rhetoric of Motives,* Kenneth Burke explains that the dialectical leaves competing voices in "jangling relation to one another" whereas the ultimate places competing voices in a "hierarchy, sequence, or evaluative series," fixing a progression or developmental relationship, offering a guiding idea or "unitary principle" behind the diversity of voices (187). Citations establish relations among texts, relationships that organize a field of inquiry, create order, and allow for accountability. Borrowing Kenneth Burke's terminology for examining human motives, I will outline three analytical stages for examining citations of a particular scholarly work: a "grammar of citations," which looks at the *types* of relationships citing texts construct with cited texts; a "rhetoric of citations," which identifies the arguments these constructions of relationship implicitly make for incorporating a particular text into the collective knowledge making and knowledge-circulating processes of a discipline; and a "symbolic of citations," which explores the values assigned to a particular text as part of the collective intellectual capital of a discipline.

First, I will describe a grammar of citations, demonstrating that citations are an obvious means by which writers name relationships between texts and thereby identify and legitimate contributions to a discipline's economy. Briefly, these relationships can be identified by the use or logical appropriateness of particular words we recognize as "transitions": "and" is implicit in the *coordinate* relationship, "but" in the *opposite* relationship, "for" in the *generative*, "so" in the *consequential*, "or" in the *apposite*, "for example" in the *exemplary*, and temporal order ("first," "second," etc.) in the *sequential relationship*.[3] The *iterative* relationship is invoked by the repetition of words or ideas in the form of summary, paraphrase, or direct quotation.[4] These relationships are created among texts when writers cite other texts within their own texts. The following sampling of citations of Mina Shaughnessy's *Errors and Expectations (E&E)* will exemplify how this is done. Each of these eight types of coherence relationships is illustrated in a separate example; but in fact, most citing authors[5] create a web of connections between their own texts and the texts they cite by asserting a variety of relationships.

Example 1: Sarah Warshauer Freedman creates a *coordinate* relationship between Shaughnessy's text and others in "Outside-In and Inside-Out: Peer Response Groups in Two Ninth-Grade Classes" when she lists them together: (**Bold type** highlights relevant passages.)

> [Students] made up and rigidly overapplied rules in ways reminiscent of Rose's (1980, 1984) descriptions of blocked writers and **Shaughnessy's (1977), Bartholomae's (1980), and Perl's (1979)** of basic writers. (101)

By placing *E&E* in a group of texts, Freedman has done more than give evidence of a recognition of some relevant similarity between it and the other texts named; she has established that similarity by creating a category or class to which all listed texts belong (descriptions of basic writers).

Example 2: David Bartholomae creates an *opposite* relationship between citing text and cited text, between his own text and Shaughnessy's text, when, in "The Study of Error," he claims:

> This distinction between individual and general systems [of error] is an important one for both teaching and research. **It is not one that Shaughnessy makes.** We don't know whether the categories of error in *Errors and Expectations* hold across a group, and, if so, with what frequency and across a group of what size. (255)

By stating a difference between his own work—in which he does make a distinction between individuals' errors and common errors among groups of individuals—and Shaughnessy's work, Bartholomae has established a relationship between the cited text and the citing text that constructs a role for both in the collective knowledge-making activity of the discipline.

Example 3: A *generative* relationship, Shaughnessy's text as cause and other texts as effects, is suggested by Glynda Hull in "The Editing Process in Writing: A Performance Study of More Skilled and Less Skilled College Writers." Hull lists Shaughnessy with other researcher who identified patterns of error, then goes on to say,

> **[Error analysis research] gave researchers a new agenda:** using errors to understand the development of and constraints on writing ability.
> **Some scholarship on error in the writing of young adults has followed Shaughnessy's lead,** taking as its aim to trace errors to their sources, with oral language being a predominant candidate. (9)

Here Hull credits Shaughnessy's work as a cause of later research. Such assertions about cause and effect relations between texts make strong claims for the texts' role in the discipline's economy of knowledge production and circulation.

The other cause-effect relationship, the consequential relationship, is created when the cited text is asserted to be an effect of or result of another text. In the case of *Errors and Expectations,* I have not found any text that constructs Shaughnessy's text as a consequence of an earlier work, though a number of citing texts point to the advent of open admissions at City College of New York as the exigence from which Shaughnessy's study arose,[6] and, of course Shaughnessy's own footnotes identified others' work on which she built.

Example 4: An *apposite* relationship, the OR relationship between *E&E* and other cited texts, is asserted by Stephen P. Witte in "Topical Structure and Writing Quality: Some Possible Text-Based Explanations of Readers' Judgments of Student Writing":

> **Apart from studies that examine such features as handwriting,** two approaches have been taken to help explain qualitative differences in student writing, one focusing on intrasentence features and one focusing on intersentence features. (177)

In this passage, Witte identifies four types of research on features of student texts—examinations of handwriting, of error, of intrasentence features, and of intersentence features—establishing *Errors and Expectations'* place within one of these categories before proceeding to elaborate on the category in which he will place his own work (intersentence features) without discounting the value of research in the other categories.

Example 5: The *exemplary* relationship between texts is created when the cited text is posited as an example of a type named by the citing text. This relationship is illustrated in the following passage from Linda Flower's essay "Cognition, Context, and Theory Building":

We need what ethnographers describe as "grounded theory" (Spradley)—a vision that is grounded in specific knowledge about real people writing in significant personal, social, or political situations. This grounding can come from many sources: **from the comparative analysis of student texts (Bartholomae, Shaughnessy)** or of talk at home and in school (Heath), from detailed discourse studies of the reading process, plans, and drafts of writers within specific communities (Bazerman, Myers), or from historical reconstructions of early rhetors in action (Enos). (283)

Here, the connection Flower creates between theory grounded in comparative analyses and Shaughnessy's *E&E* can be made explicit by inserting "FOR EXAMPLE." Assigning the status of "exemplar" to a work makes the strongest of claims for the value of its contribution to the disciplinary economy.

Example 6: A citer's assertion of a *sequential* relationship can be especially significant. Maxine Hairston suggests a particular narrative for the discipline of composition studies in "The Winds of Change: Thomas Kuhn and the Revolution in the Teaching of Writing" when she writes the following:

[Shaughnessy] was the first to undertake a large-scale research project whose goal was to teach the new students of the seventies to write. Her example, her book, and her repeated calls for new research in composition have undoubtedly been important stimuli in spurring the profession's search for a new paradigm. (22)

Ordering texts chronologically makes very specific claims about their significance to the orderly development of a discipline.

The *iterative* relationship is established when a citing text repeats a unit of the cited text, whether by repeating a term, quoting or paraphrasing a passage, or by summarizing the whole or a part of the cited text. For example, Robert J. Connors and Andrea A. Lunsford quote what several others have also acknowledged as a key insight from *E&E:*

As Mina Shaughnessy put it, errors are "unintentional and unprofitable intrusions upon the consciousness of the reader. . . . They demand energy without giving back any return in meaning" (12). (Connors and Lunsford, 396)

I have illustrated each of these eight types of coherence relationships in separate examples; but in fact, as several of these examples demonstrate, most citing texts create a web of connections between their own texts and the texts they cite by asserting a variety of relationships. This "grammar of coherence" provides a set of possible relationships that members of a scholarly community can posit between texts (their own or others) they wish to introduce into the disciplinary economy. Each of these types of relationships can be examined in terms of the claims they present for a discipline's contribution to knowledge-production and distribution and for particular texts' participation in those processes.

Coordinative ("and") citations are claims for knowledge-making as an accumulative process. Use of coordinative citations establishes the replicability of knowledge products in a discipline, serving to verify the reliability of the knowledge. Credit accrues to both the citing text and the cited text(s) when they can be linked in the process of accumulation. Oppositional citations value the knowledge-making activities of a disciplinary discourse community as a whole by making a claim for the discipline's capacity for self-critique. A critical practice of evaluating previously produced knowledge effects a kind of quality control at the same time it warrants further knowledge-making work in the field. These oppositional citations accrue credit to the citing text by arguing for valuing new knowledge and revaluing of old.

Generative and consequential citations argue for cause-effect relationships. These citations value the knowledge-making activities of a disciplinary discourse community as a whole by making arguments that the production of the old knowledge has led to further production—the production of new knowledge. Thus it is especially important for scholars in a discipline to identify work that has had a capacity for generating further production of knowledge.

Appositional citations posit particular ways of categorizing the knowledge-making processes or knowledge products of a discipline. By naming categories and placing texts within those categories, appositional citations establish that the field is not chaotic. If order can be imposed on these processes and products, a degree of uniformity and reliability can be assumed. Likewise, exemplary citations implicitly argue that within an area of study or category of texts, one text can stand for all, which can also be understood as a claim to uniformity and reliability.

Sequential citations call attention to the chronological order of appearance of particular texts, thus making an argument for a particular narrative for a line of inquiry. By specifying the sequence of the production of knowledge, naming who is first and constructing a historical ordering makes possible a discipline's claim for ongoing development of knowledge. In addition, sequential citations establish the role of each contributor in the development of collective knowledge.

Iterative citations make arguments that the knowledge products of a discipline are re-producible. Though these citations can never merely repeat the original texts, but rather re-present them, iterative citations effectively recirculate knowledge products within the disciplinary economy.

Seen from this perspective, plagiarism is intolerable in academic discourse communities not only because it is equivalent to theft of the knowledge product or because it constitutes unauthorized circulation of knowledge, but also because such an inaccuracy threatens to undermine a discipline's claims to orderly, reliable production and distribution of useful, verifiable knowledge.

Comparative analyses of citation practices in different disciplines or within multidisciplinary areas of study can help in understanding the differences in their citation practices and in identifying the knowledge-making values of these scholarly communities. This method of citation analysis, when used to study the citation practice of an individual citing author in a particular text, can aid in understanding the ways in which that text first enters the disciplinary economy. This analytical approach can also be used to understand and evaluate a particular cited text's contribution to a discipline's processes of making and circulating knowledge.

Viewing scholarly citation practice in the metaphorical terms of disciplinary economies of knowledge production and distribution offers some insights with pedagogical implications across the curriculum. As novice members of a disciplinary community, students must learn to be critical in both their writing and reading of citations in scholarly discourse. It might help them to view knowledge as not only something that is made but as something that develops an exchange value within a particular disciplinary economy.

On the one hand, viewing scholarly citation practice in terms of its role in disciplinary economies of knowledge production and distribution also puts the classroom itself in a new light. If the classroom is viewed as an initiation into a knowledge-making discipline, and classroom exercises are seen as initial contributions to the knowledge-making enterprise, it would seem especially important to impose on students the disciplinary standards for accuracy and reliability. If plagiarism and other inaccuracies in published work threaten the whole discipline's claims to reliable production of valuable, usable, worthy knowledge, then plagiarism in the context of the classroom threatens the classroom's claims to be preparing students to participate in reliable, orderly production, distribution, and application of knowledge.

On the other hand, this view of scholarly citation practice as an important element in the processes of knowledge production and distribution may help explain why textbooks and other teaching materials for general education and introductory courses often do not provide conventional scholarly citations. That is, they do not attribute knowledge production to particular scholars or researchers, but present it as the accumulated wealth of the discipline. It may be that at this level, students are deliberately being kept out of the actual processes of knowledge production and allowed to participate in its distribution or circulation in only very constrained ways, thus limiting participation in the disciplinary economy to those who have acquired the necessary expertise.

Using economic metaphors as a lens through which to examine the role of scholarly citation practice prompts some interesting questions about the processes of knowledge-making and knowledge-distribution in academic disciplines. Do citation practices help to control access to these processes by making arguments for the necessity of specialized knowledge or expertise? Do citation practices inhibit nonexperts' attempts to participate in decision making or policy making regarding the uses to which disciplinary knowledge is put? Do scholarly citations serve the economic interests of the disciplinary communities by legitimating their claims to cognitive monopolies? Perhaps conventions for citing, rather than being rules for "giving credit" for "borrowed ideas," are devices for limiting access to and use of those ideas by unauthorized writers and thinkers.

Notes

1. For a recent review of bibliometric approaches to citation studies, see White and McCain.

2. See Gilbert; Latour; Cozzens, 1998; Small; Swales; and Berkenkotter and Huckin.

3. In his essay "The Grammar of Coherence," W. Ross Winterowd identified seven "structural relationships" that contributed to creating a coherence between parts of a text. Winterowd demonstrated that these relationships exist between sentences in a text, and claimed that they existed between larger units of a text, such as paragraphs or even chapters of a book, as well. I have extended this grammar of coherence to identify the relationships created between discrete texts through the use of citations. I have substituted my own, slightly less jargonistic, terms for Winterowd's original seven: co-ordinativity (coordinate), obversativity (opposite), causativity (generative), conclusivity (consequential), alternativity (apposite), inclusivity (exemplary), and sequentiality (sequential).

4. *Iterative* is my own term for describing relationships based on repetition (quotation, summary, and paraphrase). Winterowd may have considered iteration an element of lexical coherence or semantic rather than syntactic relationship.

5. For the sake of stylistic simplicity, I refer to "citing authors," although I acknowledge that these authors have not acted autonomously when their texts have been significantly mediated by editors and reviewers by the time they reach published form.

6. Patricia Harkin makes a case for Shaughnessy's work as a resulting from the social situation, arguing that because the situation at CCNY was unique, there were no precedents in the scholarship of the composition, so Shaughnessy synthesized what was available from other fields to make "lore."

In the Marketplace

Brand Name Use in Creative Writing: Genericide or Language Right?

Shawn M. Clankie

The inclusion of a chapter questioning trademark use, or misuse, within the scope of plagiarism broadly conceived assumes that the two are inherently related. Trademarks are described as "proper terms that identify the products and services of a business and distinguish them from products and services of others. Trademarks can be a word, symbol, logo, or design—or any combination of these" (International Trademark Association [INTA]). As Patton clarifies, however, "Legally, a trademark is supposed to identify the source, rather than the particular goods themselves" (2). One form of trademark is the brand name, which, because it can be appropriated, can lead to accusations of plagiarism or misuse.

With the massive proliferation of advertising, the frequency of brand name usage as a generic referent (e.g., to make a xerox) is increasing dramatically. Friedman, in consecutive studies of best-selling novels and hit plays, found significant increases in brand name use as generic over roughly a thirty-year period (1946–1975 and 1946–1980 in the respective studies). What is meant by a brand name being used as generic is straightforward: using "kleenex" to refer to any tissue, or "coke" for any cola flavored soft drink, with no regard for the company that created the name. One may ask why writers would choose to use a brand name in place of another word. Simply stated, brand names provide a descriptive element, and often an emotive state not found in a class term, for example, "The day-glo socks of the innumerable little girls" (*Oxford English Dictionary [OED]*, 4: 276). Here "day-glo" is being used to allude to the color of the socks in a way that alternative words (fluorescent, bright) simply cannot. Yet "Day-Glo" is a registered trademark.

Companies, the creators of trademarks, value their brand names highly, registering them with the government through the Patent and Trademark Office and policing for perceived misuse and infringement. All of this is done in the hope that their brand name will gain the maximum public recognition and sales, yet not to the extent of the name becoming a generic term. Such success

253

is a fine line. If the brand name becomes generic, companies risk losing their trademark, as other companies will quickly snatch up the name, applying it as a generic to their own product, at a major loss to the creator of the name.

This chapter originates out of a conflict created between my professional interests as a linguist, and my secondary pursuit as a creative writer. It centers primarily on a long-standing policy of many companies and the International Trademark Association (a trademark watchdog and lobbying group) to protect company brand names from falling into generic use. In the area of creative writing, such companies regularly attack creative writers and editors through "trademark education" advertising in trade publications such as *Writer's Digest* and *Editor and Publisher* and through aggressive letter writing to those they see as misusers of their trademark. In more extreme cases, typically involving corporate infringement, legal action is taken.

This chapter will address the creative use of language and whether language can be considered property. To this end, it will question the nature and validity of the company and INTA interpretations of how language is or can be used.

To address this problem fully, it will be important to tend to other questions regarding trademark use in creative writing, and in the language as a whole, such as when a brand name jumps from being solely representative of one company's product and thus protectable under current trademark law to its becoming a generic term for the class of products as a whole, outside of the jurisdiction that that law affords. Moreover, what criteria, if any, should exist to determine when a brand name should be deemed generic and therefore fair play for others to use? I will address both sides of the argument, presenting first the legal side and corporate view of the problem, followed by a linguistic perspective, a side that is rarely taken into account by such utilitarian organizations and the legal counsels representing them. In the linguistic section, the "trademark education campaign" will be systematically disassembled on linguistic grounds, to show why, in the end, corporate attempts to change language use are futile.

The Corporate and Legal Views

The corporate view is a clear and deliberately protectionist one. The law regarding trademarks is known as the Trademark Act of 1946, or more commonly as the Lanham Act. Oathout states that the intent of trademark laws worldwide is to "protect a business from unfair competition and the public from imitations by means of a sign—the trademark (or colloquially, the 'brand')—that is unique to the particular business as the origin of the goods" (6). Trademarks also (in principle) protect consumers from being misled into buying something other than what they had expected. Yet this protectionist attitude has extended to deliberate attempts to protect the brand name from shifting from a specific referent, namely a proper adjective, capitalized, referring to that one original product, to the generic, a representative lexeme for the entire class of products. This is done in a variety of ways. The following advertisements are typical of those placed in *Writer's Digest* and *Editor and Publisher.*

Please Help Us Protect Our Trademark.

▼

is a registered tradename for a unique "brand" of self-defense spray. When using the Mace name in text it is important that you remember to "capitalize" the M, follow with a registration mark ® and the word "brand", because protecting our name is important to us. That's why we placed this ad in <u>Editor & Publisher</u>...

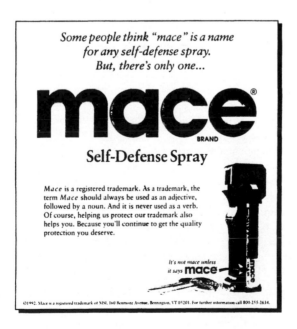

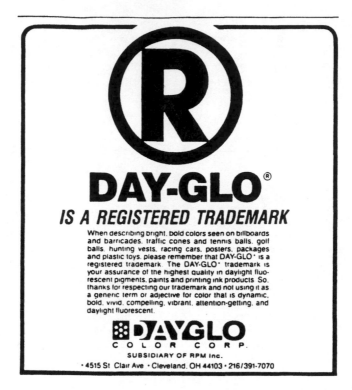

A third advertisement by Xerox was to be included in this discussion. The Xerox Corporation originally gave permission to reprint one of their trademark education ads, yet subsequently revoked that privilege upon finding out that this essay would not defend their brand name. Regardless of whether we have the actual ad or not, one may still discuss its content, particularly when the validity of that content is questionable.

It is apparent in all of these advertisements that the explicit aim is that any use of the brand name should refer only to that product and should be capitalized. Any deviation in the name from its original grammatical category, that of a proper adjective followed by a common noun, as in "Jell-O gelatin," is considered by these companies to be misuse of the trademark. The International Trademark Association, in a brochure directly aimed at writers and editors who misuse trademarks, lists five guidelines for the correct use of trademarks:

- Trademarks are proper adjectives, capitalized, and should be followed by generic terms.
- Trademarks should never be pluralized.

- Trademarks should not be used in the possessive form unless the trademark itself is possessive.
- Trademarks are never verbs.
- Tradenames and trademarks are not the same.

A's a major lobbying organization, the INTA heavily lobbies not only trade publications, editors, and writers, but also the lexicographers who compile dictionaries. In the case of a creative writer (and I am using the term to represent anyone who writes for publication) breaking one of these sacred rules, such as by using Xerox as a verb in publication (e.g., "I xeroxed several copies of the memo"), will likely result in the writer's being spotted by one of the companies hired to clip misuses from publications. The end result is a letter from the company pointing out the error and asking that the same mistake not be made again. These companies consider this "trademark education." Companies such as Day-Glo even go so far as to provide a brochure to writers clarifying how to "correctly" use the trademark. The explicit purpose of all of this is to allow the company to create a paper trail of their attempts to halt the semantic shift of the term in question from specific to generic. Such attempts are useful in court to represent the company's efforts to protect its name from becoming generic and thus falling into the public domain and into competitors' hands. When such a term does become generic, to the point of becoming the class term, then the courts may strip the copyright protection from the company, throwing the term into play, at a potentially significant economic loss. The paper trail helps to avoid that from occurring. Companies have learned from the mistakes of others whose products, for example, *cellophane, aspirin,* and *thermos,* to name just a few, have lost their trademarks and whose once-private names have come to represent the category of item rather than the product of one company. The International Trademark Association even has a term for such loss, *genericide.*

As for the direct impact on creative writers, Terez notes, "And who writes those trademark ads and letters . . . ? Writers do. As a result, they are responsible for ensuring that corporate America's trademarks are used correctly" (26). What Terez is suggesting is that it is the writer's responsibility to protect company trademarks because writers are employed by many of these companies. Yet as we shall see this is a double-edged sword.

Linguistics and Trademark Misuse

In this section, I will examine when a term becomes generic and the potential criteria for determining genericy. This will in turn lead us into a dismantling of the "trademark education campaign" presented above. First, however, it is important to establish some basic terminology. Throughout this article I have been using the word "term" to refer to the trademark. To use more suitable linguistic terminology, extrapolating away any biased connotation a trademark name may have to the company who chose the name, these are essentially *lexical items*. By lexical item, or *lexeme*, I refer to the abstract notion of word in its uninflected base form, which would typically appear as a part of the *lexicon*, or vocabulary, as represented in a dictionary (Matthews 26). When referring to a lexeme, or dictionary form, I shall use the linguistic notational convention of using SMALL CAPITALS.

To begin, it is crucial that a clear representation of the meaning of the lexeme GENERIC, as it relates to the loss of the trademark, be established. When does a trademark shift from being simply the brand name of one company's product to become a generic referent for the entire class? Finn mentions several criteria by which a lexeme might be deemed generic (and as a consequence may lose its protection). These include listing in one or more dictionaries as a noun or without specifically noting that it is a trademark, or when, as discovered through a survey, large percentages of people cannot identify a brand as a trademark (67). However, Finn fails to define "large percentages of people." Such surveys at best provide little in the way of linguistic evidence. The questioning techniques are easily manipulated and, rather than surveying a sample from a vast array of ethnic backgrounds, social classes, and dialects, may simply be aimed at one group, particularly those who may be less likely to have modified their language to such a change. These may include, for example, the elderly, whose language is less receptive to innovation. Yet the reference to the use of a dictionary is a clear step in the right direction towards establishing a definition for GENERIC.

One may ascertain that the purpose of a dictionary is to accurately reflect the language as it is used at a synchronic point in time and to provide etymological data. As such, dictionaries are a key in determining whether a trademark is being used only as a trademark or whether, as a lexeme, part of the lexicon of the language, it has begun to acquire new forms or uses. The first criterion for evidence of a trademark becoming generic is when the proper adjective begins to jump grammatical categories (typically to a noun or a verb). Yet how is such a distinction determined? This is a key question. If we simply refer to a dictionary, we must recognize that dictionaries, though attempting to reflect synchronically the spoken language as it exists, are imperfect and always outdated. Lexicographers are frequently caught up in making judgment calls for the inclusion of a lexeme or variant of a lexeme in a dictionary.

An alternative to this is simply accepting language as innovative, unmanageable as property, and understanding that the trademark becomes generic at the point where one speaker or, as is pertinent to this discussion, one creative writer uses the term innovatively, whether via a new grammatical category or through the application of a new sense to the trademark, known as *semantic neologism*. As Friedman notes, "Indeed, many students of linguistic change have adopted a functional perspective toward their subject matter, viewing new words and expressions as natural concomitants of social change that remain as long as people find them useful" (1985, 936).

In spoken discourse, it is the hearer who ultimately will determine whether the new use of the lexeme is acceptable, grammatically correct, and comprehensible. Similarly, in creative writing, it is the reader and editor who will determine whether the sense applied to the lexical item is in accordance with the grammaticality and pragmatics of the language and whether the use of a particular word in context represents accurately the emotive quality appropriate for that situation, not whether it is acceptable to the legal team of a particular company. Applying this analysis answers both of the peripheral questions posed earlier. However, the legal teams at companies such as Xerox are not going to let us off that easily. For the sake of clarification, let us refer to the withdrawn Xerox trademark education advertisement again.

In the Xerox ad, we find in bold print the statement "You can't Xerox a Xerox on a Xerox." In small print in the left corner of the ad Xerox says, "As a trademark, the term Xerox should always be used as an adjective, followed by a noun. And it is never used as a verb. Of course, helping us protect our trademark also helps you." A Xerox spokesman calls this their trademark education ad. It is apparent that what Xerox is preaching here is nothing more than mandated language use. There have been many attempts to mandate language use, most notably the attempts of the Academie Française to block loanwords from English, or *franglais,* in the French language. As most linguists would agree, language is constantly in the process of change, and it is the users of the language who ultimately determine the lexicon at a given time. Xerox in its ad maintains that the trademark Xerox is to be used as an adjective, and not as a verb or noun. The question that immediately arises is, why not? Is the sentence, *You can't Xerox a Xerox on a Xerox* ungrammatical? Clearly it is not. Is this an acceptable utterance to a native speaker of English? Yes, it is. As a matter of fact, the Xerox Corporation, through the use of this sentence, has proven that *Xerox* can, and is, used both as a noun and as a verb. Setting aside the overuse of capital letters for *Xerox,* it would be perfectly natural to write the sentence as, *You can't xerox a xerox on a Xerox.* The lexical item XEROX is more often than not written without a capital (xerox), thus providing further evidence that the term is generic. The dropping of the capital letter of the trademark is one piece of certain evidence that the trademark has indeed become generic. The question that now arises is whether or not the lexeme XEROX is generic. Perhaps the best place to turn is the second edition of *The Oxford English Dictionary (OED).*

The *OED* lists "XEROX" both as capitalized, and in lower case, as well as a trademark and generic term: "a proprietary name for photocopiers . . . also used loosely to denote any photocopy" (20: 676). This definition points out clearly that "xerox," either capitalized or in lower case, is used throughout the population, as both a proper adjective and as a noun. The noun use in OED, incidentally, dates back at least as far as 1966 when it was used in the following way: "In most American offices executives instruct subordinates to 'make me a Xerox of this report' rather than 'make me a copy of it.'" More intriguing is that there is a second lexical entry of xerox, that as a verb. The definition given of the verb form is "to reproduce by xerography; to photocopy." Not surprisingly, the earliest reported use of xerox as a verb is also from 1966: "Anything you want copies of, why we'll Xerox it out." Thus a second condition by which one might determine a generic term is the listing of a second lexeme in the dictionary. Such a listing disproves one of the Xerox Corporation's claims, namely, that xerox is never used as a verb. Of course, native speakers are well aware that nothing is further from the truth. Such attempts as that by Xerox amount to little more than mandated language use, the treatment of language as property. Attempting to limit the number of senses a lexical item may contain and lobbying lexicographers to respect the trademark amount to nothing more than governing language.

As the Xerox Corporation continues proclaiming that its name is being misused, and maintaining that the name has not become generic, we can see that, through the inclusion of two separate lexical items in the dictionary, the trademark has long since done so. Perhaps, the simple fact that the name *is* being "misused," to use the company's own term, is the most important factor governing whether a brand name has become generic.

If we refer to the Mace ad we find the statement "Some people think "mace" is a name for any self-defense spray. But, there's only one . . . MACE® Self-Defense Spray." While that statement is true (there are no other companies producing MACE® Self-Defense Spray), the ad itself makes the same general claim as Xerox, that MACE (the trademark) is never used as a verb. Yet, "MACE" the lexeme most certainly is. To give one example, I once had a college roommate who entered our room late one night after having received a face full of MACE Brand Self-Defense Spray by the local police department. He complained angrily, "I can't believe the cops *maced* me!" I wonder now if perhaps I should have asked him if he had distinctly seen MACE written on the canister in the moment immediately prior to his becoming so painfully incapacitated. Given that there is no common acceptable verb for being "maced," it seems perfectly natural that the primary brand of self-defense spray would become the prime verb for describing the act of administering or receiving that very potent dose of incapacitating spray. Referring to the *OED* (9: 152) Mace is listed as a trademark: "The proprietary name of a chemical preparation used as a disabling weapon by being sprayed at a person's face." Yet again, we also find it listed in a secondary usage: "Hence (usu. with small initial) as *v. trans.,* to attack with this liquid." Again, we see acceptable use as a verb, in small capitals. The first use as a verb, according to the *OED,* was in 1968: "Scores of innocent adult bystanders . . . were clubbed, maced, and arrested."

One can find the same faults with the Day-Glo advertisement. A full discussion would be redundant; therefore, it is sufficient to note that contrary to Day-Glo claims regarding usage, the *OED* lists Day-Glo in both its proprietary sense and a secondary sense: "an adjective, chiefly of garments: made with a material which incorporates Day-Glo colouring . . . hence loosely, fluorescent."

Alternatives

Innovation within language is a natural and necessary part of language development. The semantic shift in meaning from specific to generic, if anything, should be viewed as the ultimate accolade a company can receive. Their name is thus known by most consumers in a population. Yet companies, focused only on the money to be made from a brand name, do not want to lose their trademarks. Criticizing the policies of these companies alone, without in turn offering alternative suggestions for companies which produce trademarks, would be to set a poor precedent. Therefore, a couple of suggestions are in order that might assist companies in creating brand names to overcome this problem. One point that companies must comprehend is that if their brand name is more convenient, that is, shorter or easier to pronounce than the existing class term, they risk its becoming generic very quickly. Case in point, *xerox* (the noun) is shorter than the alternative *photocopy, xerox* containing two syllables as opposed to four in *photocopy*. Similarly, *jello,* the generic term, is shorter than gelatin. Such an observation should come as no surprise to native speakers. The proliferation of acronyms, such as *NASA, ASAP,* and of clipped forms, such as *copy* from *photocopy* or *photo* from *photograph,* clearly demonstrate the point. Companies may wish to consider the class name and to create a longer trademark for their product.

Alternatively, companies could potentially name their products in a way that violates the phonotactics of the language, thereby making them more difficult to pronounce than the existing class name. For example, one measure of this is using unacceptable consonant clusters or common clusters in positions not normally used in English. While difficult to say, there is no reason that, if the product was of a superior quality, it still could not become well known. To offer one possibility, imagine that a cola company chooses to name their new line *Ng Cola.* While it may be next to impossible for most native speakers of English to pronounce Ng outside of the coda position of a syllable (the most likely scenario would be speakers simply spelling it out as "N-G" as in *One N-G cola please,* or by adding a vowel making it *ing*), there is little reason it could not become a hit. There is little chance, however, that such a term could or would become the generic.

I noted earlier Terez's remark that because writers are employed by these companies, writers have a responsibility to protect trademarks (24). As a writer, the question I must ask is, at what cost? Sacrificing one's linguistic freedom to write what one pleases in a unique and innovative manner is tantamount to promoting language censorship. It is easy to see a financial motivation behind publications such as *Writer's Digest* doing little in protest against the trademark education campaign. Yet it is reprehensible that such publications should promote censorship of this nature, limiting the expressive ability of their writers.

While the major corporations, the counsels representing them, and the INTA diligently police for misuse to protect their brand names from going generic, the long-term battle may already be lost. As Bollinger points out, in terms of people using trademarks generically, "in the long run, the courts condone this, for they do not encourage private ownership of words of the English Language" (65). Language change and innovation are natural, and in general, unmanageable. Attempts such as those of Xerox indicate an attempt to mandate language as property, moving us ever closer to broader censorship of our writers.

If we accept language as innovative, then we must acknowledge that lexical items are created and discarded by the population using the language. The need, then, to determine when a brand name becomes generic would be irrelevant. The lexical item would simply become generic once someone chooses to use it in an innovative way, governed only by the internal structure of the language itself. Of course this is what normally happens in language. Yet this is something that many nonlinguists (politicians, businesspeople, and lawyers) fail to grasp. The answer to the question invoked by the title of this chapter, trademark misuse or language rights, overwhelmingly points to language rights. To the representative for Xerox, who, on revoking permission to reproduce the Xerox ad covered earlier, claimed that linguists do not understand the law, I must respond, that perhaps it is the law that fails to understand language.

GenX Occupies the Cultural Commons: Ethical Practices and Perceptions of Fair Use

Joan Livingston-Webber

When you're surrounded by sheep, it pays to be a coyote.

—Craig Womack

The cultural commons is that area of the culture that everyone holds in common, with rights of access and use. The public domain, whose promotion and development is the Constitutional intention of copyright,* is a large tract of the cultural commons. "Fair use" is also located in this commons. The word "occupy" in my title is intended to raise associations with armies and battles, this cultural commons an area under siege, currently and most vigorously by corporate holders of copyright who work to transform the function of copyright law from enlarging the public domain to guaranteeing private profit. Those who have taken the term "GenX" to name themselves and their cohorts are another group active in the skirmish, seeing themselves in direct engagement through practices that they believe are ethical—though they also believe these practices run contrary to laws governing fair use.

I will argue in this chapter that postmodern discourse practices of GenX culture creators put them into conflict with those who want to limit copyright practices traditionally held in the cultural commons as fair use. What is at stake are active and inventive discourse practices of GenX that are native to the postmodern world. I will focus on one genre, the collage-rant of the photocopied zine, to use in following this argument through.

---

*Congress is to enact legislation which "Promote[s] the Progress of Science and useful Arts" (U.S. Constitution, article 1, paragraph 8, clause 8). This clause is the basis for copyright.

Douglas Rushkoff, in his introduction to *The GenX Reader,* characterizes GenX as

> a life philosophy . . . based on a commitment to reject the traditional values and linear reasoning of the dominant culture and instead embrace the postmodern swirl. (6)

One genre Rushkoff anthologizes is the rant. The rant is the anathema of traditional academic argument, "I have a right to my own opinion" raised to art. Rushkoff describes rants, saying: "These long-winded GenX tirades have elevated the simple temper tantrum to free-form text-jazz" (206). He also compares a rant to a slam dunk, requiring "flourish and gusto" (206). Rants constructed with cut-and-paste components of text and image (what I am calling collage rants) are frequently included in zines (pronounced like the last syllable of "magazines"), perhaps GenX's prototypically postmodern form, since everyone can play. Zine production requires minimal technology (paper, a pen, and access to a photocopier) and minimal money (enough for initial photocopying and postage). Anyone can play this game, and that inclusivity of access is a hallmark of the postmodern. Postmodernism in art includes by collapsing (or at least claiming to collapse) the barriers between high and popular cultures. Zines include by their ease of production, by their defense of everyone's having an absolute right to an opinion of his or her own, and by their do-it-yourself philosophy. Zines provide a truly accessible playing field, since "you only have to be semi-literate to read most zines [and the collage, rubber stamp and poetry zines let the illiterate play, too]" (Pore, "Notes" 6, brackets in the original).

Postmodernism in literature elevates the reader's role both in its theoretical discourse and by way of nonlinear literary artifacts. Zine culture elevates the reader's role directly, as in this partial rant from *FactSheet5,* a newsstand periodical that reviews zines:

> The first rule of zine publishing is that you aren't going to make any money. So if you think you are, just give it up and leave us readers alone. We don't want to hear your whining. The truth is, nobody cares about your problems. In fact, nobody is going to pay jack shit to hear your opinions on anything. (O'Keefe 115)

Zine readers also talk back by producing their own zines. In fact, the distinction between production and consumption blurs in zine culture. *FactSheet5* is a unifying publication, read by both zine writers and readers, reviewing zines produced by its readers. Since many zines can be got by trade, zine culture includes incentives for readers to become writers and distributors.

Postmodernism in art also collapses the distinction between past and present, talking about the fragmentation and reconfiguration of prior texts, reconstituting the past within a different and contemporary context alongside pieces of the present. Many zines and parts of zines are constructed of "snippets," images and texts literally snipped from elsewhere and pasted together, rather like ransom notes on black-and-white tv. This practice is a literal realization of what postmodernism calls a realignment of elements in transformative recombination.

The zine blend of irony and sentimentality seems particularly at home in a postmodern world, though some theorists see them more as characteristic of two different kinds of postmodernism. Rushkoff introduces a selection of excerpts from zines:

> We are the ideological love children of Jan Brady and Bart Simpson or Kate Jackson with William Burroughs. We have inherited both the simplistic innocence of our mass-mediated social engineering and the postmodern, psychedelic ability to reframe reality as if from the outside. These two genetic threads - the joy of unselfconscious participation and the irony of metaparticipation - are the GenX birthright. (56)

This "joy of unselfconscious participation" and the "irony of metaparticipation" have been discussed in scholarly work as a "postmodernism of reaction" and a "postmodernism of resistance." John Trimbur relies on the work of David Harvey for these concepts of resistance and reaction to characterize two kinds of postmodernism or, perhaps, as separate responses to a postmodern world. A postmodernism of resistance is expressed in Rushkoff's notion of the "irony of metaparticipation," the "ability to reframe reality as if from the outside." Such postmodern resistance "begins," says Trimbur, "with a radical critique of . . . historical narrativity" (122). A postmodernism of reaction is expressed in Rushkoff's "joy of unselfconscious participation." Such reaction "depends on . . . a return to narrative, to the figure, to decorative effects, to history" (122). In zines, it is misleading to try to tease apart the sentimental and the ironic, the reaction and the resistance. The sentimental and the ironic meld into camp and kitsch, high values in zine culture.

I have, so far, linked zines with several characteristics of texts at home in a postmodern world: inclusivity, reader participation, the fragmentation and reconfiguration of the past, and the high value of sentimentality and irony as kitsch and camp. Woven in with all of these characteristics are the zine writers' strongly held beliefs and feelings about intertextuality, beliefs that, also, are at home in a postmodern world. The past is a remnant, a kind of flotsam in the stream of the present, to be prevented from toxicity and made useful by breaking it down into component elements and recycling them so that each element may continue a productive life. When this past is textual, then recycling is performed through a high degree of self-conscious intertextuality. This intertextuality, recycling and reconfiguring elements of a past, is the milieu in which sentiment and irony consolidate as camp. The textualized past must be available for cultural and artistic play in order to extend itself into a post-modern world, an extension accomplished not as narrative history but as camp. The ethics of these postmodern intertextual practices play out in the cultural commons, the space to whose contest we now turn.

Feelings and beliefs about postmodern intertextuality are evidenced both in textual practices and in clear statements of "@nti-copyright." *Aim Your Dick,* a zine from Berkeley, has an "@nticopyright" that states: "Go ahead & reprint & copy stuff if you want cuz ideas & information are free and price-less." The ethical principle here is explicit; information and ideas are price-less and belong to everyone. *Kablooie,* a zine from Merion Station, PA, is more defensive, saying on its inside front cover:

> FUCK COPYRIGHTS. Phlegm-Phlan and Beaver Storm deeply feel it is their obligation to convey important information to you. Whether this important information comes from a published author or your pet goldfish doesn't matter a bit. If bureaucracy did not exist and people could actually get things done, maybe these two editors would meticulously contact each and every one of their sources. But probably not. If anyone uses stuff from this particular zine, that's fine. Just don't say you wrote it. That's dumb.

The ethical principle is even more clear here, but so is the writers' anxiety about the possible illegality of their practices and their misunderstanding of what would make them legal. For these two pseudonymous writers, the issue is that they should have "contacted" copyright holders. They do not appear aware that they might not be granted permissions or that they might be charged money for permissions. They believe they have violated a canon of legal etiquette or professional courtesy, not an economic one.

Let us look more closely at *Kablooie.* Its contents include most of the kinds of things found in other zines. It has twenty four pages, counting both the front and back covers. Ten pages are signed by one of the two writers (or "editors"), including an introductory letter from each, two poems, band reviews, a page of numbered and titled lists, and a highly literate rant against *Sassy* magazine, a commercial, teen-age girl magazine with aspirations of appealing to girls in alternative cultures. There is one page called "This is My Defiance," a rant reprinted (i.e., photocopied) from the zine *Sacrificial Lamb.*

The author of "This Is My Defiance" is "Markerhead." Markerhead's rant includes one original paragraph against establishment explanations for attitudes of GenX. This paragraph has been thickly outlined and pasted onto a photograph of a building under construction, with girder assemblages going off to the upper left and the top center and a crane angling toward the upper right. Over the photograph and under overlapping parts of the paragraph are three very short paragraphs cut from unidentified sources and pasted in. Each

paragraph represents something about the explanations of an older generation: one attributing bad attitude to individual pathologies, one to a "larger
class logic." The third snippet is mostly covered by Markerhead's own paragraph, though the words "changes," "class," and "the lads" are visible. Each
of these snippets has been photocopied and clipped from a published work,
the typefaces of print a significant part of the effect of including them. And it
is likely that the photograph is also from a copyrighted source, since it, too, is
cut-and-paste.

Unlike Markerhead's, the original paragraph of Beaver Storm's rant
against *Sassy* takes up most of its page. This rant mostly concerns *Sassy*'s col-
lusion in commodifying alternative culture:

> It used to be that, if a girl rejected the boy-crazy, make-up and hairspray
> mainstream world represented by magazines like *Seventeen,* she found ac-
> ceptance in alternative culture . . . Then came *Sassy,* which, while claiming
> to give a voice to girls who didn't fit the popular standard, actually just
> clothed those same old standards in all the trappings that alternative girls had
> been using to identify themselves. Now the models sport noserings, the
> trendy clothes are $60 flannels, and we should still spend hours grooming
> ourselves, as long as it's with politically correct, outrageously-priced Body
> Shop products.

Along the right side and the bottom of the page are clippings from *Sassy,* evidence for the textual argument, easily recognizable by the style of the photographs and typefaces. The column head for *Sassy*'s monthly "Cute Band
Alert" is pasted at the bottom. Along the side and partially obscured by Beaver
Storm's text is the clipped heading, "Common Trends We Started/Revived,"
a frequent *Sassy* feature. Altogether twelve bits of text and photographs are
incorporated into the rant, all either column heads for *Sassy* features or obviously typical *Sassy* advertising copy. The cut-and-paste text and photographs
are inextricable elements of the two rants, Markerhead's and Beaver Storm's.
These are not illustrations accompanying a text; both text and image are the
evidence and support of the rants' arguments. Beaver Storm's and Markerhead's paragraphs are but one constitutive element in each collage and should
not stand alone.

The understanding of copyright implied by zine creators' statements and
practices is that the purpose of copyright is to erect barriers around knowledge
and information, reserving them to corporate owners of copyright and to people who will help them make a profit from them. The zine creators see themselves as asserting and enacting an ethic of fair use at odds with copyright law.
Indeed, there are strong elements in the larger culture supporting this understanding, elements I now turn to consider.

The general litigiousness of North Americans and the status of corporate entities certainly plays its role in zine writers' understanding of copyright law. One only needs to know (1) that there is a law of copyright, (2) that this is the United States, and (3) that one is not a corporate body—only a person—not rich and, often enough, not even an adult. Knowing only that much could alone account for the defensiveness of *Kablooie*'s @nti-copyright.

Zine culture keeps itself informed of events that justify the anxiety of @nti-copyright. *FactSheet5*, a periodical that reviews zines, reported the following:

> After flogging everyone's favorite girlie doll for four issues of *HTBG* [*Hey There, Barbie Girl!*], editor Barbara received an official "cease and desist" order from the Legal Department at Mattel. . . . Needless to say, upper management failed to see the humor in *HTBG*'s satirical deconstruction of Mattel's little plastic cash cow. Smart enough to know when she was legally beat, Barbara closed up shop. (Koyen 10)

A Mattel, Inc., employee had picked up an issue of *Hey There, Barbie Girl!* displayed at a Tower Books and turned it in. Editor Barbara gained some consolation by mailing out copies of the "'cease and desist' order" to anyone providing an SASE. It is, in fact, a letter from in-house counsel, threatening legal action unless Barbara provides "written compliance of our demands." One of the demands is to "*immediately cease* the publication of this newsletter" (emphasis in original). The demand does not have to be a judicial order. Without corporate resources or *pro bono* counsel, Editor Barbara, and the zine community, know she is already "legally beat."

For these GenX writers of texts at home in a postmodern world, copyright becomes more and more a clone of the Napoleonic tax code: a source of anxiety, a venue where one is guilty unless she can prove herself innocent, a bureaucracy whose tangled rules and regulations require at least a staff of lawyers to defend any practice beyond the prototypical. As many have documented, the canonical author constructed in copyright law is the Romantic Author creating original texts with no intertextuality, no influence, and no prior acquaintance with anything written. As Woodmansee and Jaszi (1995) put it:

> In Romantic ideology the collective and collaborative element in composition—including cutting and pasting—is denied. An author is not thought to create by selecting and arranging inherited ideas but to be the very source, or origin, of new ideas. (775)

Since few, if any, writers have ever held this canonical position, all writers would seem to write at the sufferance of megaholders of copyright. As long as Beaver Storm's rant remains very local and very unimportant, she is probably safe. If she should be subject to threat of legal action, she will not have the money or the supportive outrage of *pro bono* counsel to do anything but "close up shop." In order to survive, popular genres at home in a post-modern world—genres like the collage rant—must not matter very much to anyone of importance.

What the zine community already knows, the larger community is only beginning to sense: copyright law and megaholder practices are, together, diminishing the public domain and capsizing the principles of fair use. They are doing so, in part, through statements that misrepresent copyright, some of which are "intentionally misleading or, in legal terms, fraudulent" (Patterson and Lindberg 8). To press the territorial metaphor yet a bit further, such statements are equivalent to posting "no trespassing" signs at strategic places in the cultural commons—at all locations of fair use.

Patterson and Lindberg cite a statement from the Copyright Clearance Center's promotional materials: "Copyright law in the United States requires that users of copyrighted materials obtain authorization from copyright owners" (qtd. on 7). Because this sentence is stated as an absolute, it is misleading, since both personal use and fair use require no authorization. Not all use is infringement of copyright, though statements like the Copyright Clearance Center's would make it so. Such statements from those with vested economic interests in reducing the public domain and the cultural commons (where fair use and personal use may be said to reside) can crystallize into customary practice, in later turn becoming informal guidelines to application of the law.

Copyright statements on published materials also claim an increasing scope, misleading readers and writers about fair use and personal use. An example, taken at random from the shelf, is this notice from *Virtual Light* by William Gibson:

> No part of this book may be reproduced or transmitted in any form or by any means, electronic or mechanical, including photocopying, recording, or by any information storage and retrieval system, without permission in writing from the publisher.

This notice limits use in absolute terms, implying clearly that not only fair use but personal use as well is illegal. Since cyberpunk, the genre of *Virtual Light,* is especially popular among GenX readers, we can assume that zine culture is well aware of notices of this type. The same notice protects William Strong's *The Copyright Book,* a reference book for writers, a particularly grievous location for a misleading copyright statement. Anyone's bookshelf will produce several instances of this same notice.

Patterson and Lindberg cite another copyright notice that goes even further than the previous two by explicitly claiming the right to prohibit without written permission *any* use, including scholarly, personal, or fair use. They quote a copyright notice from the periodical *Granta* (Autumn 1989) for a short (seventeen-line) poem by Salman Rushdie. The notice differs from the conventional copyright statement by this addition:

> *No part of this poem may be reproduced, whether for private research, study, criticism, review or the reporting of current events,* without written permission of the publishers, Granta Publications Limited. Any unauthorized reproduction of any part of the poem may result in civil liability and criminal prosecution. (qtd in Patterson and Lindberg, 183. Emphasis is mine.)

This notice restricts use absolutely by reserving rights absolutely, making claims that cannot be supported by law, including threats of criminal prosecution. Though scholars might not include Rushdie's poem in reviews and criticisms of contemporary literature, Contemporary Literature, as a scholarly area, will survive this singular loss. Much more damaging is that such an unchallenged notice relocates the extreme of copyright misrepresentation, making appear "reasonable" the equally misleading, though less explicit, notice used in *Virtual Light* and *The Copyright Book*. Contemporary literature, as an arena of postmodern literacy activity, cannot survive such wholesale appropriations of personal and fair use. Such incursions amount to *de facto* censorship, not because of content, but because of the alleged, absolute, proprietary rights of copyright holders, accomplished by the "*in terrorem* effect" identified by Patterson and Lindberg (10) and, more prosaically, by Woodmansee and Jaszi, as "the 'chilling effect' of the law's uncertainty" (1995, 777).

This *in terrorem* effect chills, in particular, the culturally rich and economically poor GenX culture. Since GenX's cultural capital is much greater than its economic capital, a function partly of the youth of many of its members and partly of the expanding service economy (aka "McJobs") that they are hired into, zine writers must either take a defiant attitude against copyright (since all cultural signs indicate that normal zine practices infringe on copyright) or they must produce only the kind of zine that gets classified in *Fact-Sheet5* as a "Personal Zine." Even personal zines, though, often include rants, with the image-text collages that ought to be fair use but which are suspect in a climate of "cease and desist" letters from Mattel, Inc.

Zine writers often choose to defy the corporate practice and legal pressure of copyright in order to perform the community services they feel called to: to circulate information, to celebrate the past as camp, to criticize the commodity culture, to juxtapose texts to display different and innovative orders of knowledge and insight. Academic writers bow to the same pressure by adopting ever more exotic methods of citation and by becoming self-righteous about compliance with them. Indeed, academics' obsession with the potential for plagiarism among student writers is yet another context for zine writer's defensiveness. (See Rebecca Moore Howard [1995] for a consideration of this obsession.)

Zine writers are neither plagiarists nor paranoiacs. They are not plagiarists because they do not claim others' works as their own, though they rarely give the full citation an academic writer would. They are not paranoiacs, as this whole essay has attempted to make clear. There are very strong and dedicated forces at work staking out the cultural commons as their own in order to sell it back at a profit or, perhaps, just to possess it all.

Zine writers are not the first to invert the cultural expectations of copyright in order to resist the ongoing commodification of knowledge, ideas, and truth. Sometime around 1968, for example, an author favored by GenX, Richard Brautigan, published *Plant This Book,* distributed free on the streets of San Francisco. It was basically a pocket folder, with a sepia-tinted photograph of a toddler on the front cover. Inside were eight packets of seeds, four of vegetables and four of flowers. On each packet was printed a poem by Brautigan. On the outside back cover was a notice to this effect: "This book may be reproduced as long as it is not sold." This tradition of writing and publishing for other than economic compensation, a tradition promoted by fair use considerations of the free circulation of ideas and of commonplaces and even of quotations (snippets), is profoundly respected by zine culture.

A great part of zine writers' response to the increasing encroachment on intertextuality by copyright law and the corporate extensions of it is based in the perception that copyright serves only big business: conglomerates, multinationals, and other megaholders of copyrights. It is hard to see in the cultural signs any suggestion that copyright is meant as an incentive to authors for the final purpose of enlarging the public domain, as a right instrumental to achieving the public good rather than as a right inherent to private property.

Extending the scope and term of copyright may be seen as necessary for megaholders to earn profits from reprinting, their publishing and distributing technologies less and less a necessity in the world of easy photocopying and the Internet. Many writers however—as opposed to copyright holders—simply want to be read and circulated, responded to and referred to and quoted, to enter into a cultural dialogue or, more accurately, into the active literacy scenes the postmodern world affords them, scenes in which producer and consumer can hardly be distinguished. Copyright megaholders with capital in expensive reproduction technologies and distribution networks should not be permitted to intimidate writers from publishing and circulating texts that are at home in a postmodern world. The zine creators believe their own fair use practice and ethic violate the law of the land—and it is not at all clear if they are right or wrong, though the cultural signs point to their practice being wrong: guidebooks to copyright, copyright notices on publications, teachers in schools, and, of course, the "'cease and desist' order" from Mattel, Inc.

Misleading absolutist proclamations of copyright that would forbid fair use lead to a public fearful of personal and fair use, with a small group anxiously disregarding paralyzing limitations on its textual practice, even when those limitations are of questionable legality. This public anxiety, in turn, re-inforces a view that the law must be as it is perceived by allowing false pro-tection notices to stand without direct legal challenge. Such challenge is likely to come only from those with profit motives and a team of lawyers, from cor-porate holders of copyright, who will challenge only creations sufficiently popular to be profitable or sufficiently incisive to be embarrassing. Since prof-itability is incorporated into the criteria for determining fair use, such chal-lenges are more likely to be decided in favor of megaholders, creating prece-dent for arguing subsequent cases involving fair use—and, eventually personal use. Intertextual innovations like the collage rant become increas-ingly risky.

We have already prepared the ground for a postmodern generation's artis-tic and critical work to be declared illegal or to be perceived as such, making into brute fact the warning that copyright extensions of 1976 and later provide the means to use copyright for censorship (Patterson and Lindberg)—that is, to use copyright for suppressing texts troubling to the economic and propri-etary status quo. Those texts of the most apparent value, those which gather a following and thus come to the attention of copyright holders, would be most subject to litigation. If such litigation or the threat of it succeeds in suppress-ing GenX texts at home in a postmodern world, then we have acquiesced in a generation's being represented in the cultural canon only by its less appealing and less incisive texts. We risk losing the collage rant, one of GenX's most creative modes of civic and artistic literacy. The legally permissible cultural legacy we leave to our grandchildren and great-grandchildren will have been stripped by law or by intimidation of its best and brightest, at the least, of some of its most interesting. We have already set the climate of intimidation (Pat-terson and Lindberg's "*in terrorem*" effect") such that some of the most inno-vative work might never get beyond its creator's mind and certainly not be-yond his or her mailbox—in direct contradiction to the constitutional mandate for copyright.

Works Cited

Achtert, Walter S., and Joseph Gibaldi. *The MLA Style Manual*. New York: The Modern Language Association, 1985.

Acker, Kathy. *The Adult Life of Toulouse Lautrec by Henri Toulouse Lautrec*. 1975. In *Portrait of an Eye: Three Novels*. New York: Pantheon, 1992.

———. *Blood and Guts in High School*. New York: Grove, 1978.

———. "Dead Doll Humility." *Postmodern Culture*. http://jefferson.village.edu/pmc/.

———. *Don Quixote: Which Was a Dream*. New York: Grove, 1989.

———. *Empire of the Senseless*. New York: Grove, 1988.

———. *Great Expectations*. New York: Grove, 1989

———. *My Life My Death by Pier Paolo Pasolini*. 1984. In *Literal Madness: Three Novels*. New York: Grove, 1988.

———. *Pussy, King of the Pirates*. New York: Grove, 1996.

Adams, Thomas. "Trademarks." *English Today* 9 (1987): 34.

Adams, Peter Dow. *The HarperCollins Concise Handbook for Writers*. New York: HarperCollins, 1994.

Aim Your Dick. Berkeley: n.p., 1994.

Albee, Edward. Lecture at the University of California-Davis, May 27, 1996, reported by Deutsche Presse-Agentur.

Alford, William. *To Steal a Book Is an Elegant Offense: Intellectual Property Law in Chinese Civilization*. Stanford: Stanford University Press, 1995.

Aoki, Keith. "Adrift in the Intertext." *Chicago-Kent Law Review* (1993): 805–840.

Arieti, Silvano. *Creativity: The Magic Synthesis*. New York: Basic, 1976.

Aristotle. *Rhetoric*. Trans. W. Rhs. Roberts. Cambridge: Harvard/Loeb, 1964.

———. *The Poetics*. Trans. W. Hamilton Fyfe. *XXIII Aristotle*. Loeb Classical Library. Cambridge: Harvard University Press, 1932. 1–118.

Arnold, Matthew. "The Study of Poetry." *English Literature and Irish Politics,* vol. 9 of *The Complete Prose Works of Matthew Arnold*. Ed. R. H. Super. Ann Arbor: U. of Michigan, 1973.

Arnstein v. Porter. 154 F.2d 464. 2d Cir. 1946.

Ashton-Jones, Evelyn. "Asking the Right Questions: A Heuristic for Tutors." *The Writing Center Journal* 9.1 (1988): 29–36.

Atwood, F. G. "Manners and Customs of Ye Harvard Studente." Ed. Bernard Bailyn, Donald Fleming, Oscar Handlin, and Stephan Thernstrom. *Glimpses of the*

273

Harvard Past. Cambridge: Harvard UP, 1986. [originally published by J. R. Osgood (Boston) in 1877.)

Augustine. *On Christian Doctrine.* Trans. D. W. Robertson. New York: Bobbs-Merrill, 1974.

Bakhtin, M. M. *The Dialogic Imagination.* Trans. & ed. Michael Holquist and Caryl Emerson. Austin: University of Texas Press, 1981.

Ballard, Brigid, and John Clanchy. "Assessment by Misconception: Cultural Influences and Intellectual Traditions." *Assessing Second Language Writing in Academic Contexts.* Ed. Liz Hamp-Lyons. Norwood: Aablex, 1991. 19–35.

Baron, Dennis. "Word Law." *Verbatim* 16.1 (1989): 1–4.

———. *Guide to Home Language Repair.* Urbana: National Council of Teachers of English, 1994.

Barthes, Roland. "Day by Day with Roland Barthes" Ed. Marshall Blonsky. *On Signs.* Baltimore: Johns Hopkins University Press, 1985.

———. "The Death of the Author." *Image, Music, Text.* Trans. Stephen Heath. New York: Hill and Wang, 1977. 142–48

———. "From Work to Text." *Image/Music/Text.* Trans. Stephen Heath. New York: Farrar, Straus & Giroux, 1977.

Bartholomae, David. "The Study of Error." *College Composition and Communication* 31 (1980): 253–69.

Bartkowski, Frances. *Feminist Utopias.* Lincoln and London: University of Nebraska Press, 1989.

Baudrillard, Jean. La transparence du mal. Essai sur les phénomènes extrêmes. Paris: Galilée, 1990.

Bazerman, Charles. *Constructing Experience.* Carbondale: Southern Illinois UP, 1994.

———. *Shaping Written Knowledge: The Genre and Activity of the Experimental Article in Science.* Madison: U of Wisconsin P, 1988.

———. *The Informed Writer: Using Sources in the Disciplines.* 3rd ed. Boston: Houghton, 1989.

Beasley, Wm., and E. G. Pulleyblank. *Historians of China and Japan.* London: Oxford University Press, 1961.

Behm, Richard. "Ethical Issues in Peer Tutoring: A Defense of Collaborative Learning." *The Writing Center Journal* 10.1 (1990): 3–12.

Benhabib, Seyla. "On Hegel, Women and Irony." *Feminist Interpretations and Political Theory.* Ed. Mary Lyndon Shanley and Carole Pateman. University Park: Pennsylvania State University Press, 1991. 129–145.

Benoist, Jocelyn. "En guise d'introduction au texte de Fichte" *Qu'est-ce qu'un livre?* (Emmanuel Kant). Paris: Presses Universitaires de France, Coll. "Quadrige," 1995.

Berke, Jacqueline. *Twenty Questions for the Writer: A Rhetoric with Readings.* 3rd ed. New York: Harcourt, 1981.

Berkenkotter, Carol, and Thomas N. Huckin. *Genre Knowledge in Disciplinary Communication: Cognition/Culture/Power.* Hillsdale: Lawrence Erlbaum, 1995

———. "You Are What You Cite." *Professional Communication: The Social Perspective.* Eds. Nancy Roundy Blyer and Charlotte Thralls. Newbury Park: Sage, 1993. 109–27.

Berlin, James. "Literacy, Pedagogy, and English Studies: Postmodern Connections." *In Critical Literacy: Politics, Praxis, and the Postmodern.* Ed. Colin Lankshear and Peter L. McLaren. Albany: State U of New York. 247–269.

Berreby, David. "Student Withdraws in Plagiarism Uproar." *The National Law Journal* May 1983: 4.

Bhabha, Homi. "Of Mimicry and Man: The Ambivalence of Colonial Discourse," *October* 28. (1984): 125–133.

———. *The Location of Culture.* London and New York: Routledge, 1994.

The Bible. Revised Standard Edition. Cleveland: World Publishing, 1962.

Bills, Robert. "Plagiarism in Law School: Close Resemblance of the Worse Kind?" *Santa Clara Law Review* 31 (1990): 103–33.

Black's Law Dictionary. 6th ed. St. Paul: West, 1990.

Blackstone, Sir William. *Commentaries on the Laws of England.* London, 1765.

Blair, Hugh. Lectures on Rhetoric and Belles-Lettres. *The Rhetoric of Blair, Campbell, and Whately.* Ed. James L. Golden and Edward P. J. Corbett. New York: Holt, Rinehart, 1968.

Blau, Susan. "Issues in Tutoring Writing: Stories from Our Center." *The Writing Lab Newsletter* 19.2 (1992): 1–4.

Bloom, Harold. *The Anxiety of Influence.* NY: Oxford University Press, 1973.

The Bluebook: A Uniform System of Citation. 16th ed. Cambridge, Mass: The Harvard Law Review Assn., 1996.

Bollinger, Dwight. *Language: The Loaded Weapon.* London: Longman, 1980.

Booth, Mark. Letter to the author. November 15, 1992.

Borchard, William. *Trademark Basics: A Guide for Business.* New York: International Trademark Association, 1995.

Bouygues, Charles. "Yambo Ouologuem, où le silence des canons." *Canadian Journal of African Studies* 25 (1991): 1–11.

Bowers, Neal. "A Loss for Words: Plagiarism and Silence." *American Scholar* 63 (1994): 545–555.

Boyle, James. *Shamans, Software, & Spleen: Law and the Construction of the Information Society.* Cambridge: Harvard University Press, 1997.

———. "A Theory of Law and Information: Copyright, Spleens, Blackmail, and Insider Reading." *California Law Review* 80.6 (1992): 415–540.

———. "Alienated Information: The International Political Economy of Authorship." Conference on Cultural Agency/Cultural Authority: Politics and Poetics of Intellectual Property in the Post-Colonial Era. Bellagio, Italy, 8–12 March 1993.

Brautigan, Richard. *Please Plant this Book.* San Francisco: n.p., 1968.

Brodkey, Linda. "Modernism and the Scene(s) of Writing." *College English* 49 (1987): 396–418.

———. *Writing in Designated Areas Only.* Minneapolis: U Minnesota P, 1996.

Brooks, Jeff. "Minimalist Tutoring: Making the Student Do All the Work." *Writing Lab Newsletter* 15.6 (1991): 1–4.

Bruffee, Kenneth. "Collaborative learning and the Conversation of Mankind." *College English* 46 (1984): 645–52.

———. Writing and Reading as Collaborative and Social Acts. *The Writer's Mind: Writing as a Mode of Thinking.* Ed. Janice N. Hays et al. Urbana: NCTE, 1983. 159–169.

———. *Collaborative Learning: Higher Education, Interdependence, and the Authority of Knowledge.* Baltimore: Johns Hopkins UP, 1993.

———. Collaborative Learning: Some Practical Models. *College English* 34 (1973): 634–43.

Bruner, Jerome. *Toward a Theory of Instruction.* Cambridge: Belknap of Harvard University Press, 1966.

Brusaw, Charles T., Gerald J. Alred, and Walter E. Olin. *Handbook of Technical Writing.* New York: St. Martin's, 1976.

Buck v. Jewell-La Salle Realty Co. 283 U.S. 191. 1931.

Burke, Kenneth. *A Grammar of Motives.* 1945. Berkeley: U of California P, 1969.

——. *A Rhetoric of Motives.* 1950. Berkeley: U of California P, 1969.

——. *Attitudes toward History.* 1937. Berkeley: U of California P, 1984.

Buskirk, Martha. "Appropriation Under the Gun." *Art in America* June 1992: 37.

Butler, Melissa A. "Early Liberal Roots of Feminism: John Lock and the Attack on Patriarchy." *Feminist Interpretations and Political Theory.* Ed. Mary Lyndon Shanley and Carole Pateman. University Park: The Pennsylvania State UP, 1991: 74–94.

Carey, John. *The Intellectuals and the Masses: Pride and Prejudice among the Literary Intelligentsia, 1880–1939.* New York: St. Martin's, 1992.

Carino, Peter. "Early Writing Centers: Toward a History. *The Writing Center Journal* 15.2 (1995): 103–115.

Central Piedmont Community College. *Plagiarism: Statement Three.*

Chen Shou. *Sanguo zhi.* Beijing: Zhonghua shuju, 1959.

Cicero. *De Optimo Genere Oratorum.* Trans. H. M. Hubbell. Cambridge: Harvard UP/Loeb. 1993, 1949.

——. *de Oratore.* Cambridge: Harvard/Loeb, 1963.

——. *Topica.* Cambridge: Harvard/Loeb, 1963.

Clark, Irene Lurkis. "Collaboration and Ethics in Writing Center Pedagogy." *The Writing Center Journal* 9.1 (1988): 3–12.

"Maintaining Chaos in the Writing Center: A Critical Perspective on Writing Center Dogma." *The Writing Center Journal* 11.1 (1990): 81–95.

——. *Taking a Stand: A Guide to the Researched Paper with Readings.* New York: HarperCollins, 1992.

Clark, Irene L. and Dave Healy. "Are Writing Centers Ethical?" *WPA: Writing Program Administration* 20. 1/2 (1996): 81–95.

College Evils. Wrinkle. Vol. 11 (1893–94): 8–9. Michigan Historical Collections. Bentley Historical Library. University of Michigan.

Confucius. *Analects.* See also, D. C. Lau, Confucius: *The Analects.* Hong Kong: Chinese University Press, 1979.

Connors, Robert J. Overwork/Underpay: Labor and Status of Composition Teachers since 1880. *Rhetoric Review* 9 (1990): 108–26.

——. "The Abolition Debate in Composition: A Short History." *Composition in the Twenty-First Century: Crisis and Change.* Ed. Lynn Z. Bloom, Donald A. Daiker, and Edward M. White. Carbondale: Southern Illinois UP, 1996. 47–63.

Connors, Robert J., and Andrea A. Lunsford. "Frequency of Formal Errors in Current College Writing, or Ma and Pa Kettle Do Research." *College Composition and Communication* 39 (1988): 395–409.

Conrad, Joseph. *Heart of Darkness.* NY: Scribner's, 1901.

Cooley, Thomas. *The Norton Guide to Writing.* New York: Norton, 1992.

Coombe, Rosemary J. "Objects of Property and Subjects of Politics: Intellectual Property Law and Democratic Dialogue." *Texas Law Review.* 69 (1991): 1853–1880.

Cooper, Marilyn. "Really Useful Knowledge: A Cultural Studies Agenda for Writing Centers." *The Writing Center Journal* 14.2 (1994): 97–111.

Copeland, Rita. "The Fortunes of 'Non verbum pro verbo': or, why Jerome is not a Ciceronian." *The Medieval Translator. The Theory and Practice of Translation in the Middle Ages.* Ed. Roger Ellis. Cambridge: D. S. Brewer, 1989. 15–35.

Copyright Act of Feb. 3, 1831. Ch. 16, Sec. 2, 4 Stat. 436. 1831.

Copyright Act of 1870. Ch. 230, 16 Stat. 212. 1870.

Copyright Act of May 31, 1790. Ch. 15, 1 Stat. 124. 1790.

Copyright Act of 1909. Ch. 320, 35 Stat. 1075. Codified as amended at 17 US Code, Secs. 1–216. 1976.

Copyright Act of 1976, 17 US Code, Secs. 101–914. 1988.

Cozzens, Susan E. *Social Control and Multiple Discovery in Science: The Opiate Receptor Case.* Albany: State U of New York, 1988.

———. "What Do Citations Count? The Rhetoric-First Model." *Scientometrics* 15 (1988): 437–47.

Crews, Frederick, and Sandra Schor. *The Borzoi Handbook for Writers.* New York: Knopf, 1985.

———. *The Random House Handbook.* 4th ed. New York: Random, 1984.

Cronin, Blaise. *The Citation Process: The Roles and Significance of Citations in Scientific Communication.* London: Taylor Grahman, 1984.

Cross, Geoffrey. *Collaboration and Conflict.* Cresskill, N.J.: Hampton Press, 1994.

Crossan, John Dominic. *Who Killed Jesus?: Exposing the Roots of Anti-Semitism in the Gospel Story of the Death of Jesus.* San Francisco: HarperCollins, 1995.

Crowley, Carolyn Hughes. "Focus; College Cribbers . . . Ethics May Be In, but So Is Cheating." *The Washington Post* 6 January 1992: C5.

Crowley, Sharon. "A Personal Essay on Freshman English." *Pre/Text* 12 (1991): 156–76.

———. *The Methodical Memory: Invention in Current-Traditional Rhetoric.* Carbondale: Southern Illinois UP, 1990.

———. "Composition's Ethic of Service, the Universal Requirement, and the Discourse of Student Need." *JAC* 15 (1995): 227–40.

Day-Glo Corporation. *How to Use the Trademarks of the Day-Glo Color Corporation.* 1987.

de Certeau, Michele. *The Practice of Everyday Life.* Trans. Steven Rendall. Berkeley, Los Angeles, London: Berkeley University Press, 1984.

Deckert, Glenn D. "Perspectives on Plagiarism from ESL Students in Hong Kong." *Journal of Second Language Writing,* 2 (1993): 131–148 .

De Grazia, Margreta. "Sanctioning Voice: Quotation Marks, the Abolition of Torture, and the Fifth Amendment." *The Construction of Authorship: Textual Appropriation in Law and Literature.* Eds. Martha Woodmansee and Peter Jaszi. Durham and London: Duke UP, 1994.

Denton, George B. Letter to Fred Newton Scott. 3 March 1910. Fred Newton Scott Papers. Michigan Historical Collections. Bentley Historical Library. University of Michigan.

Derrida, Jacques. *Force de loi.* Paris: Galilée, 1994.

Dettmar, Kevin J. H. *The Illicit Joyce of Postmodernism: Reading Against the Grain.* Madison: U of Wisconsin P, 1996.

Dewey, John. *Experience and Nature.* Chicago: Open Court, 1925.

Diderot, Denis. *Encyclopédie ou dictionnaire raisonné des sciences, des arts et des métiers.* Genève: Pellet, 1777–79.

Dieckhaus v. Twentieth Century-Fox Film Corp., 54 F. Supp. 425. E.D. Mo. 1944.

Dihlmann, W. "Plagiarism: Copying for Advanced Students." *Radiologue* 31 (1991): 394–397.

Dillon, George L. "My Words of an Other." *College English* 50 (1988): 63–73.

Doi, Takeo. (Trans. John Bester.) *The Anatomy of Dependence.* Tokyo: Kodansha International. 1981.

Dornan, Edward A., and Charles W. Dawe. *The Brief English Handbook.* 2nd ed. Boston: Little, Brown 1987.

Drew, Elizabeth. *T. S. Eliot: The Design of His Poetry.* NY: Scribner's 1949.

Drum, Alice. "Responding to Plagiarism." *College Composition and Communication* 37 (1986): 241–43.

Du Bellay, Joachim. *Ladeffence et illustration de la langue francoyse.* Ed. Louis Terreaux. Paris: Bordas, 1972.

Ede, Lisa. "Writing as a Social Process: A Theoretical Foundation for Writing Centers?" *The Writing Center Journal* 9.2 (1989): 3–13.

Ede, Lisa, and Andrea Lunsford. *Singular Texts/Plural Authors: Perspectives on Collaborative Writing.* Carbondale: Southern Illinois UP, 1990.

Edelman, Bernard *La propriété littéraire et artistique.* Paris: Presses Universitaires de France, Coll. "Que sais-je?," 1989.

Edelman, Murray. *Constructing the Political Spectacle.* U Chicago P, 1988.

Editor and Publisher. New York: Editor and Publisher.

Edwards, Suzanne. "Tutoring Your Tutors: How to Structure a Tutor-Training Workshop." *Writing Lab Newsletter* 7.10 (1983): 7–9.

Eisenstein, Elizabeth. *The Printing Press as an Agent of Change.* 2 vols. Cambridge: Cambridge UP, 1979.

Eliot, T. S. "Philip Massinger." In *Essays on Elizabethan Drama.* New York: Harcourt, Brace, & World, 1932. 141–61.

———. *Selected Prose of T. S. Eliot.* Ed. Frank Kermode. New York: Harcourt Brace Jovanovich, 1975.

———. *Selected Poems.* New York: Harcourt, Brace & World, 1964.

———. *On Poetry and Poets.* New York: Farrar, Straus and Cudahy, 1957.

Emerson, Ralph Waldo. "Quotation and Originality." In *Letters and Social Aims,* The Centenary Edition of the Complete Works of Ralph Waldo Emerson, vol. 8. Boston: Houghton Mifflin, 1904.

Evarts, R. C. *Alice's Adventures in Cambridge.* Cambridge: The Harvard Lampoon, 1913.

Faigley, Lester. *Fragments of Rationality: Postmodernity and the Subject of Composition.* U Pittsburgh P, 1992.

Fan Zuyu. *Tangjan.* Shanghai: Shanghai tushuguan, 1980.

Fanon, Frantz. *Black Skin, White Masks.* Trans. C. L. Markmann. London: MacGibbon & Kee, 1986. Trans. of *Peau noire, masques blancs,* 1952.

———. *The Wretched of the Earth.* Trans. Constance Farrington. New York: Grove Press. 1963. Trans. of *Les Damnés de la terre,* 1961.

Feist Publications, Inc. v. Rural Tel. Serv. Co. 111 S. Ct. 1282. 1991.

Fichte, J.G. "Preuve de l'illégitimité de la reproduction des livres, un raisonnement et une parabole." Texte reproduit dans *Qu'est-ce qu'un livre?* (Emmanuel Kant). Paris: Presses Universitaires de France, Coll. "Quadrige," 1995.

Finn, Michael. "Beware of How You Color It." *Writer's Digest* June 1995: 57–60.

Flanagan, Anna. "Experts Agree Plagiarism Hard to Define, Hard to Stop." *The Council Chronicle* 3:3 (1994) National Council of Teachers of English 1, 6.

Flint, Anthony. "High Tech Blurs Boundaries of Plagiarism: Back on Campus," *The Boston Globe* 26 September 1993: National/Foreign 1.

Flower, Linda. "Cognition, Context, and Theory Building." *College Composition and Communication* 40 (1989): 282–311.

Flower, Linda and John Hayes. "A Cognitive Process Theory of Writing." *College Composition and Communication* 32 (1981): 365–387.

Forman, Janis. *New Visions of Collaborative Writing.* Portsmouth, NH.: Boynton/Cook Pub., 1992.

Foucault, Michel. "What Is an Author?" *The Order of Things.* New York: Vintage. 1970.

———. "What Is an Author? *Textual Strategies: Perspectives in Post-Structuralist Criticism.* Ed. Josue V. Harari. Ithaca: Cornell UP, 1979. 141–60.

———. "What Is an Author?" *Bulletin de la Société française de Philosophie* 63.3 (1969): 73–104. Rpt. *Language, Countermemory, Practice: Selected Essays and Interviews.* Ed. Donald F. Bouchard. Trans. Donald F. Bouchard and Sherry Simon. Ithaca: Cornell UP, 1977. 113–38.

———. "Qu'est-ce qu'un auteur?" in *Bulletin de la Société française de philosophie,* Vol. 63, No. 3, 1969, 73 to 104.

Frank, Jerome. "Mr. Justice Holmes and Non-Euclidean Legal Thinking." *Cornell Law Quarterly* 17 (1932): 568–603.

Freedman, Morris. "The Persistence of Plagiarism, the Riddle of Originality." *Virginia Quarterly Review* 70 (1994): 504–517.

Freedman, Sarah Warshauer. "Outside-In and Inside-Out: Peer Response Groups in Two Ninth-Grade Classes." *Research in the Teaching of English* 26 (1992): 71–107.

Friedman, Ellen G. "A Conversation with Kathy Acker." *Review of Contemporary Fiction* 9 (Fall 1989).

———. "Where Are the Missing Contents? (Post)Modernism, Gender, and the Canon." *PMLA* 108 (1993): 240–252.

Friedman, Monroe. "Commercial Influences in Popular Literature: An Empirical Study of Brand Name Usage in American and British Hit Plays in the Postwar Era. *Empirical Studies of the Arts* 4.1 (1986) 63–77.

———. "The Changing Language of a Consumer Society: Brand Name Usage in Popular American Novels in the Postwar Era." *Journal of Consumer Research* 11 (1985): 927–938.

Frisbie, Michael J., Douglas Chickering, Susan S. Frisbie, Arthur W. Hall, Jo Keroes, and Melanie Sperling. *The Active Writer.* New York: Macmillan, 1982.

Fruman, Norman. (1976) "Originality, Plagiarism, Forgery, and Romanticism." *Centrum* 4.1 (1976): 44–49.

———. Coleridge, The Damaged Archangel. New York, George Braziller, 1971.

Funk, Robert and Roy Hoover. "The Search for the Real Jesus: Darwin, Scopes and All That." *Five Gospels.* NY: Polebridge Press, 1993.

Furuya, Reiko. School of Glabal Business and Economics. Nagoya University of Foreign Studies. Nisshin, Japan. Personal interview (Dryden), 12 Feb. 1996.

Gage, John T. *The Shape of Reason: Argumentative Writing in College.* New York: Macmillan, 1987.

Genung, John Franklin. *The Working Principles of Rhetoric.* Boston: Ginn, 1900.

Gere, Ann Ruggles. "On Imitation." Paper given at the Conference on College Composition and Communication. Atlanta, March 1987.

————. *Writing Groups: History, Theory, and Implications.* Carbondale: Southern Illinois UP, 1987.

Gere, Anne Ruggles and Ralph S. Stevens. "The Language of Writing Groups: How Oral Response Shapes Revision." *The Acquisition of Written Language: Response and Revision.* Ed. S. W. Freedman. Norwood: Ablex, 1985. 85–105.

Gibson, William. *Virtual Light.* New York: Bantam, 1993.

Gifford, Don. *"Ulysses" Annotated.* Berkeley: University of California Press, 1988.

Gilbert, G. Nigel. "Referencing as Persuasion." *Social Studies of Science* 7 (1977): 113–22.

Gillam, Alice. "Writing Center Ecology: A Bakhtinian Perspective." *The Writing Center Journal.* 11.2 (1991): 3–11.

Gilyard, Keith. *Voices of the Self.* Detroit: Wayne State UP, 1996.

Giovannangeli, Daniel *Écriture et répétition,* Paris, Union Générale d'Éditions, 1979.

Gooch, G. P. *History and Historians in the Nineteenth Century.* London: Longmans, Green, 1913.

Goodstein, David. "Travails of Publishing." Rev. of *Stealing into Print: Fraud, Plagiarism and Misconduct in Scientific Publishing,* by Marcel C. LaFollette. *Science* 27 Nov. 1992: 1503–04.

Gracia, J. E. "Can There Be Texts Without Historical Authors?" in *American Philosophical Quarterly,* 31 (1994): 245 to 253.

Grafton, Anthony. *New Texts Ancient Worlds.* Cambridge, MA: Harvard/Belknap, 1996.

Greever, Garland and Easley S. Jones. *The Century Collegiate Handbook.* New York: Appleton, 1924.

Guinier, Lani. *The Tyranny of the Majority: Fundamental Fairness in Representative Democracy.* New York: Free Press, 1994.

Guth, Hans P. *The Writer's Agenda: The Wadsworth Writer's Guide and Handbook.* Belmont: Wadsworth, 1989.

Hacker, Diana. *A Writer's Reference.* 2nd ed. Boston: St. Martin's, 1992.

Hairston, Maxine. "The Winds of Change: Thomas Kuhn and the Revolution in the Teaching of Writing." *College Composition and Communication* 33 (1982): 76–88.

Hairston, Maxine et al. *The Scott, Foresman Handbook for Writers.* 3rd ed. New York: HarperCollins, 1993.

Hall, Donald, and Sven Birkerts. *Writing Well.* 7th ed. New York: HarperCollins, 1991.

Handelman, Susan. *The Slayers of Moses.* Albany: State U of New York Press, 1984.

Harkin, Patricia. "The Postdisciplinary Politics of Lore." *Contending with Words.* Eds. Patricia Harkin and John Schilb. New York: MLA, 1991. 124–38.

Harmon, William, and C. Hugh Holman. *A Handbook to Literature.* Seventh edition. Upper Saddle River: Prentice Hall, 1996.

Harris, Muriel. "Modeling: A Process Method of Teaching." *College English* 45 (1983): 74–84.

————. *Teaching One-to-One: The Writing Conference.* Urbana: NCTE, 1986.

Hartmann, Geoffry. "Coleridge, the Damaged Archangel." Rev. of *Coleridge, The Damaged Archangel,* by Norman Fruman. *New York Times Book Review* 12 Mar. 1976: 7, 32.

Haynes-Burton, Cynthia. "Intellectual (Proper)ty in Writing Centers: Retro Texts and Positive Plagiarism." *Writing Center Perspectives.* Ed. Bryon Stay, Christina Murphy and Eric H. Hobson. NWCA Press: Maryland, 1995.

Heffernan, James A. W., and John E. Lincoln. *Writing: A College Handbook.* 4th ed. New York: Norton, 1994.

Hegel, W. F. *Hegel's Philosophy of Right.* Trans. T. M. Knox. London: Oxford UP, 1952.

Hill, David J. *The Elements of Rhetoric and Composition.* New York: Sheldon, 1878.

Hobbes, Thomas. *Leviathan.* Ed. C. B. MacPherson. Harmondsworth, England: Penguin, 1951.

Hoffman v. LeTraunik. 209 F. 375. D.N.Y. 1913.

Hollander, John. *The Figure of Echo: A Mode of Allusion in Milton and After.* Berkeley: University of California Press, 1981.

Holt, Mara. "The Value of Written Peer Criticism." *College Composition and Communication* 43 (1992): 384–92.

Horowitz, Helen. *Campus Life: Undergraduate Cultures from the End of the Eighteenth Century to the Present.* Chicago: U of Chicago P, 1987.

Howard, Rebecca Moore. "A Plagiarism *Pentimento.*" *Journal of Teaching Writing* (Summer 1993).

————. "Plagiarisms, Authorships, and the Academic Death Penalty." *College English* 57 (1995): 788–806.

————. "The Gendered Plagiarist." Penn State Conference on Rhetoric and Composition, 15 July 1995. Eric document #ED 391 176.

Hughes, Justin. "The Philosophy of Intellectual Property." *The Georgetown Law Journal* 77 (1988): 287–366.

Hull, Glynda. "The Editing Process in Writing: A Performance Study of More Skilled and Less Skilled College Writers." *Research in the Teaching of English* 21 (1987): 8–29.

Hum, Sue. "On Assimilation and Accommodation Through Literacy: Disciplinary Discourse on the Value of Difference." Unpublished paper presented to the Texas Christian University Symposium on Composition and Rhetoric, Spring 1995. Cited with permission of the author.

Hyde, Douglas, ed. & trans. *The Love Songs of Connacht.* Shannon: Irish University Press, 1971.

International Trademark Association. *Trademarks: The Official Media Guide.* 1993.

Jameson, Frederic. *Postmodernism: or, The Cultural Logic of Late Capitalism.* Durham: Duke UP, 1991.

Jacobellis v. Ohio. 378 U.S. 184. 1964.

Jaszi, Peter. "On the Author Effect: Contemporary Copyright and Collective Creativity." *The Construction of Authorship: Textual Appropriation in Law and Literature.* Ed. Martha Woodmansee and Peter Jaszi. Durham, NC: Duke UP, 1994. 29–56.

————. "Toward a Theory of Copyright: The Metamorphoses of 'Authorship.'" *Duke Law Journal* (1991): 455–502.

Joyce, James. *A Portrait of the Artist as a Young Man.* 1916. New York: Viking, 1968.
———. *Finnegans Wake.* New York: Viking, 1939.
———. *Ulysses.* Ed. Hans Walter Gabler. New York: Random House, 1986.
Joyner, Michael. The Writing Center Conference and the Textuality of Power." *The Writing Center Journal* 12.1 (1991): 80–89.
K. W. (1972) "In Defence of Yambo Ouologuem." *West Africa* 2875, 21 July (1972): 939.
Kant, Emmanuel *Qu'est-ce qu'un livre?* Paris; Presses Universitaires de France, Coll. "Quadrige," 1995.
Keller, Helen. *The Story of My Life.* New York: Doubleday, 1903, 1954.
Kellogg, Brainerd. *Rhetoric.* New York: Effingham Maynard, 1889.
Kelman, Mark. *A Guide to Critical Legal Studies.* Cambridge: Harvard UP, 1987.
Kendrick, Walter. "The Other Side of Originality." Rev. of *Stolen Words: Forays into the Origins and Ravages of Plagiarism,* by Thomas Mallon. *New York Times Book Review* 29 Oct. 1989: 13–14.
Kennedy, Mary Lynch, and Hadley M. Smith. *Academic Writing: Working with Sources across the Curriculum.* Englewood Cliffs: Prentice-Hall, 1986.
Kiley, Mark. *Collosians as Pseudepigraphy.* Sheffield, England: JSOT Press, 1986.
Kinoshita, Yumiko. AV Center. Nagoya University of Foreign Studies. Nisshin, Japan. Personal interview (Dryden), 7 Feb. 1996.
Kitler, Friedrich A. *Discourse Networks: 1800/1900.* Trans. Michael Metteer. Stanford: Stanford UP, 1990.
Knoblauch, C. H. "Literacy and the Politics of Education." *The Right to Literacy.* Ed. Andrea Lunsford, Helene Moglen, and James Slevin. NY: Modern Language Association, 1990. 74–80.
Kolich, Augustus M. "Plagiarism: The Worm of Reason." *College English* 45 (February 1983): 141–48.
Koons v. Rogers, 506 U.S. 934; 113 S. Ct. 365. Cert. denied.
Koyen, Jeff. "Those Darn Zines." *FactSheet5* 57 (1995): 10.
Kroll, Barry M. "How College Freshmen View Plagiarism." *Written Communication* 5 (1988): 203–221.
———. "Why Is Plagiarism Wrong?" Paper given at the Conference on College Composition and Communication. Atlanta, March 1987.
Lachs, John "Fichte's Idealism" *American Philosophical Quarterly.* 9 (1972): 311 to 318.
———. "Is There an Absolute Self?" *The Philosophical Forum.* (1987–1988): 169 to 181.
LaFollette, Marcel. *Stealing into Print: Fraud, Plagiarism, and Misconduct in Scientific Publishing.* Berkeley: University of California Press, 1992.
Lannon, John M. *The Writing Process: A Concise Rhetoric.* 2nd ed. Boston: Little, 1986.
Larousse, Pierre. *Grand dictionnaire universel du XIXème siècle.* Paris: Administration du Grand dictionnaire universel, 1866–1870.
Latour, Bruno. *Science in Action: How to Follow Scientists and Engineers through Society.* Cambridge: Harvard UP, 1987.
Lauer, Janice M., Gene Montague, Andrea Lunsford, and Janet Emig. *Four Worlds of Writing.* New York: Harper and Row, 1981.
"Legal Practice." *The Second Draft* [The Institute of Legal Writing] 8.2 (1993): 7–8.

LeFevre, Karen Burke. *Invention as a Social Act.* Carbondale: Southern Illinois UP, 1987.

Le Guin, Ursula. *The Dispossessed: An Ambiguous Utopia.* New York: Harper Prism, 1974.

Leggett, Glenn C., David Mead, and Melinda G. Kramer. *Prentice Hall Handbook for Writers.* 11th ed. Englewood Cliffs: Prentice Hall, 1991.

Lester, James D. *Writing Research Papers: A Complete Guide.* 7th ed. New York: HarperCollins, 1993.

Levi-Strauss, Claude. *The Savage Mind.* Chicago: University of Chicago Press, 1966.

Li Tao. *Xu Zizhi tongjian changbian.* Beijing: Zhonghua shuju, 1957.

Lindey, Alexander. *Plagiarism and Originality.* New York: Harper, 1952.

Locke, John. *The Second Treatise of Government.* Ed. Thomas P. Peardon. Indianapolis: Bobbs-Merrill, 1952.

———. *Two Treatises of Government.* Ed. Peter Laslett. 2nd ed. Cambridge, England: Cambridge UP, 1967.

Logie, John. The Author('s) Proper(ty): Rhetoric, Literature, and Constructions of Authorship. Dissertation underway at Penn State University. Contact Logie at <antrobus@ripco.com>.

Lomer, Gerhard R., and Margaret Ashmun. *The Study and Practice of Writing English.* Boston: Houghton Mifflin, 1917.

Longinus, *On the Sublime.* Trans. W. Hamilton Fyfe. *XXIII Aristotle.* Loeb Classical Library. Cambridge: Harvard UP, 1932. 119–254.

Lotringer, Sylvère. "Devoured by Myths." In *Hannibal Lecter, My Father,* by Kathy Acker. New York: Semiotext(e), 1991.

Lu, Min-Zhan. "Professing Multiculturalism: the Politics of Style in the Contact Zone." *College Composition and Communication* 45:4 (1994): 442–58.

Lunsford, Andrea. "Collaboration, Control, and the Idea of a Writing Center." *The Writing Center Journal* 12.1 (1991): 3–10.

———. "Intellectual Property in an Age of Information: What Is at Stake for Composition Studies?" *Composition the the Twenty-First Century: Crisis and Change.* Ed. Lynn Z. Bloom, Donald A. Daiker, and Edward M. White. Carbondale: Southern Illinois UP, 1996. 261–272.

Lunsford, Andrea A., and Lisa Ede. "Collaborative Authorship and the Teaching of Writing." *The Construction of Authorship: Textual Appropriation in Law and Literature.* Ed. Martha Woodmansee and Peter Jaszi. Durham: Duke UP, 1994. 417–38.

———. *Singular Texts/Plural Authors: Perspectives on Collaborative Writing.* Carbondale: Southern Illinois UP, 1990.

Lunsford, Andrea, and Robert Connors. *The St. Martin's Handbook.* New York: St. Martin's, 1989.

Lunsford, Andrea, and Susan West. "Intellectual Property and Composition Studies." *College Composition and Communiations* 47 (1996): 383–411.

Lyotard, Jean-François *Dérive à partir de Marx et de Freud,* Paris: Galilée, 1994.

Mack, Burton. *The Lost Gospel: The Book of Q and Christian Origins.* NY: HarperCollins, 1993.

———. *Who Wrote the New Testament? The Making of Christian Myth.* NY: HarperCollins, 1995.

Maimon, Elaine P., Gerald L. Belcher, Gail W. Hearn, Barbara F. Nodine, and Finbarr
W. O'Connor. *Readings in the Arts and Sciences*. Boston: Little, Brown, 1984.
Mallon, Thomas. *Stolen Words: Forays into the Origins and Ravages of Plagiarism*.
New York: Ticknor & Fields, 1989.
Marius, Richard, and Harvey S. Wiener. *The McGraw-Hill College Handbook*. 3rd ed.
New York: McGraw-Hill, 1991.
Marr, John. "Present and Accounted For." *FactSheet5* 58 (1995): 8–9.
Marvin, Barbara. "Everything You Wanted to Know About Plagiarism But Were
Afraid to Ask." Unpublished research paper, The American University, 1994.
Mattel, Inc. Letter to *Hey There, Barbie Girl!* 7 April 1995.
Matthews, Peter. *Morphology*. 2nd ed. Cambridge: Cambridge UP, 1991.
Mawdsley, Ralph. "Plagiarism in Higher Education." *Journal of College and University Law* 12 (1986): 65–92.
———. *Legal Aspects of Plagiarism*. National Organization on Legal Problems, 1985.
McCracken, Ellen. "Metaplagiarism and the Critic's Role as Detective: Ricardo
Piglia's Reinvention of Roberto Arlt." *PMLA* 106 (1991): 1071–82.
McGill, Meredith. "The Matter of the Text: Commerce, Print Culture, and the Authority of the State in American Copyright Law." *American Literary History* 9.1
(1997): 21–59.
McCuen, Jo Ray, and Anthony C. Winkler. *Rewriting Writing: A Rhetoric*. New York:
Harcourt, 1987.
McLeod, Susan H. "Responding to Plagiarism: The Role of the WPA." *WPA: Writing
Program Administration* 15 (1992): 7–16.
Meinecke, Friedrich. "Values and Causalities in History," in Stern, Fritz, *The Varieties
of History* New York: Vintage Books, 1956.
Memering, Dean. The Prentice Hall Guide to Research Writing. 2nd ed. Englewood
Cliffs: Prentice Hall, 1989.
Merton, Robert K. *On the Shoulders of Giants*. New York: Harcourt, 1965.
Mervis, Jeffrey. "Don't Steal This Book." Rev. of *Stealing into Print: Fraud, Plagiarism, and Misconduct in Scientific Publishing*, by Marcel LaFollette. *Nature* 29
Oct. 1992: 787.
Meyer, Emily, and Louise Z. Smith. *The Practical Tutor* . New York: Oxford, 1987.
Miller, Christopher. *Blank Darkness: Africanist Discourse in French*. Chicago and
London: U of Chicago P, 1985.
Miller, Keith D. "Composing Martin Luther King, Jr." *PMLA* 105 (1990): 70–82.
———. "Martin Luther King, Jr., and the Black Folk Pulpit." *Journal of American
History* 78 (1991): 120–23.
———. "Martin Luther King, Jr., Borrows a Revolution: Argument, Audience, and Implications of a Secondhand Universe." *College English* 48 (1986): 249–65.
———. "Martin Luther King, Jr., and the Issue of Plagiarism." Conference on College Composition and Communication. Cincinnati, 19 March 1992.
———. "Redefining Plagiarism: Martin Luther King's Use of an Oral Tradition."
Chronicle of Higher Education 20 January 1993: A60.
———. Voice of Deliverance: *The Language of Martin Luther King, Jr. and Its
Sources*. New York: Free Press, 1992.
Miller, Keith D., and Elizabeth A. Vander Lei. "Collaboration, Collaborative Communities, and Black Folk Culture." *The Right to Literacy*. Ed. Andrea A.
Lunsford, Helene Moglen, and James Slevin. New York: MLA, 1990.

Miller, Susan. "The Death of the Teacher." *Composition Forum* 6.2 (1995): 42–52.
———. *Rescuing the Subject*. Carbondale: Southern Illinois UP, 1989.
———. *Textual Carnivals: The Politics of Composition*. Carbondale: Southern Illinois UP, 1991.
Miner, Earl. *Comparative Poetics: An Intercultural Essay on Theories of Literature*. Princeton: Princeton UP, 1990.
Moody, Patricia A. *Writing Today: A Rhetoric and Handbook*. Englewood Cliffs: Prentice-Hall, 1981.
Morrone, Michelle Henault. School of Global Business and Economics, Nagoya University of Foreign Studies. Nisshin, Japan. Personal interview (Dryden), 16 Feb. 1996.
———. 1 July 1996.
———. 5 Dec. 1996.
Mortier, Roland. Originalité. Une nouvelle esthétique au siècle des lumières. Geneva: Droz, 1982.
Morton v. Raphael. 79 N.E.2d 522. Ill. App. Ct. 1948.
Murphy, Richard. "Anorexia: The Cheating Disorder." *College English* 52 (1990): 898–903.
Murray, Donald M. *Write to Learn*. 3rd ed. Fort Worth: Holt, Rhinehart and Winston, 1990.
Naipaul, V. S. *The Mimic Men*. London: André Deutsch, 1967.
Neff, Julie. Learning Disabilities and the Writing Center. *Intersections: Theory-Practice in the Writing Center*. Eds. Joan Mullin and Ray Wallace. Urbana: NCTE, 1994. 81–95.
Nehamas, Alexander "What an Author Is" *Journal of Philosophy*, Vol. LXXXIII, No. 11, November 1986, 685 à 691.
Newcomer, Alphonso. *Elements of Rhetoric*. New York: Holt, 1898.
Nietzsche, Friedrich. "On the Problem of Translation." Trans. Peter Mallenhauer. From *Die Fröhliche Wissenschaft*. 1882. *Theories of Translation: An anthology of Essays from Dryden to Derrida*. Ed. R. Schulte and J. Biguenet. Chicago and London: U of Chicago P, 1992. 68–70.
Nodier, Charles. *Questions de littérature légale*. Paris: Crapelet, 1828.
Nord, James. Nanzan University. Nagoya, Japan. E-mail to the author (Dryden), 14 Feb. 1996.
Norris, Frank. Excerpt from *The Wave*. Reprinted in *The Origins of Literary Studies in America*. Ed. Gerald Graff and Michael Warner. New York: Routledge, 1989. 134.
North, Stephen M. "The Idea of a Writing Center." *College English* 46 (1984): 433–446.
Northwestern University. *Some Notes on Plagiarism and How to Avoid It*.
Nystrand, Martin, and Deborah Brandt. Response to Writing as a Context for Learning to Write. *Writing and Response: Theory, Practice, and Research*. Ed. Chris Anson. Urbana: NCTE, 1989. 209–30.
Nystrand, Martin, Stuart Greene, and Jeffrey Wiemelt. "Where Did Composition Studies Come From? An Intellectual History." *Written Communication* 10 267–333.
O'Keefe, Steve. "Shut Up and Write." *FactSheet5* 54 (1995): 115.
Oathout, John. *Trademarks: A Guide to the Selection, Administration and Protection of Trademarks in Modern Business Practice*. New York: Charles Scribner's Sons, 1981.
Olivier, Lawrence. *Michel Foucault. Penser au temps du nihilisme*. Montréal: Liber, 1995.

Ouologuem, Yambo. *Le Devoir de violence.* Paris: Seuil, 1968. Trans. as *Bound to Violence.* Trans. Ralph Manheim. New York, 1971.

The Oxford English Dictionary. 2nd ed. Oxford: Clarendon Press, 1989.

Packer, Nancy Huddleston, and John Timpane. *Writing Worth Reading: A Practical Guide and Handbook.* 2nd ed. New York: Bedford, 1989.

Papay-Carder, Debbie. "Plagiarism in Legal Scholarship." *Toledo Law Review* 15 (1983): 233–271.

Patterson, Lyman Ray. *Copyright in Historical Perspective.* Nashville: Vanderbilt, 1968.

Patterson, Lyman Ray, and Stanley W. Lindberg. *The Nature of Copyright: A Law of Users' Rights.* Athens: U of Georgia P, 1991.

Pattison, Robert. *On Literacy.* New York: Oxford UP, 1976.

Patton, Warren. *An Author's Guide to the Copyright Law.* Lexington: Lexington Books, 1980.

Pearsall, Thomas E., and Donald H. Cunningham. *The Fundamentals of Good Writing.* New York: Macmillan, 1988.

Pemberton, Michael. "Writing Center Ethics: Questioning Our Own Existence." *The Writing Lab Newsletter.* 19.5 (1995): 8–9.

———. "Writing Center Ethics: Teaching, Learning and Problem Solving." *The Writing Lab Newsletter* 19.8 (1995): 15–16.

———. "Writing Center Ethics: Ignorance and the Unethical Writing Center." *The Writing Lab Newsletter* 19.6 (1995): 13–14.

Perl, Sondra. "Understanding Composing." *College Composition and Communication* 31 (1980): 363–369.

Petronius. *Satyricon and the Fragments.* Harmondsworth: Penguin, 1969.

Piercy, Marge. *He, She and It.* New York: A. A. Knopf, 1991.

"Plagiarism in the Classroom: Readers Explain How They Define It and How They Deal With It." *The Council Chronicle* June 1994: 14–15.

Pope, Alexander. "The Dunciad." *Pope: Poetical Works.* Ed. Herbert Davis. London: Oxford UP, 1966. 470–619.

Pore, Jerod. "Notes from the Tropics." *FactSheet5* 57 (1995): 6–7.

Porter, James E. *Intertextuality and the Discourse Community. Composition in Four Keys.* Ed Mark Wiley, Barbara Gleason, and Louise Wetherbee Phelps. Mountain View: Mayfield, 1996.

Posner, Richard. "What Has Pragmatism to Offer Law?" *S. Cal. Law Review* 63 (1990): 1653–70.

Pratt, Mary Louise. "Arts of the Contact Zone." *Profession 91.* New York: MLA, 1991. 33–40.

Price, Derek de Solla. *Little Science, Big Science.* New York: Columbia UP, 1963.

"Property." *Black's Law Dictionary.* 6th ed. St. Paul: West, 1990.

Quackenbos, John Duncan. *Practical Rhetoric.* New York: American Book, 1896.

Quérard, Joseph-Marie. *Supercheries littéraires dévoilées.* Vol. 1. Paris: G.-P. Maisonneuve et Larose, 1964.

Randall, Marilyn. "Appropriate(d) Discourse: Plagiarism and Decolonization." *New Literary History* 22 (1991): 525–41.

Reinking, James A., and Andrew W. Hart. *Strategies for Successful Writing: A Rhetoric, Reader, and Handbook.* 2nd ed. Englewood Cliffs: Prentice Hall, 1989.

Ricks, Christopher. "The Moral Imbecility of a Would-Be Wunderkind." Rev. of *Coleridge, The Damaged Archangel,* by Norman Fruman. *Saturday Review* 15 Jan. 1972: 31–33, 49.

Robbins, Harold. *The Pirate.* 1974. New York: Pocket Books, 1975.

Rochelle, Larry. "The ABC's of Writing Centers." *The Writing Lab Newsletter* September 1981: 7–9.

Rogers v. Koons, 960 F.2d 301; 1992 U.S. App. p. 304.

Rohlen, Thomas P. *Japan's High Schools.* Berkeley and Los Angeles, CA: U of California P, 1983.

Ronsard, Pierre de. *Odes.* Ed. C. Guerin. Paris: Editions de Cèdre, 1952.

Rose, Mark. *Authors and Owners: The Invention of Copyright.* Cambridge: Harvard UP, 1993.

———. The Author as Proprietor: *Donaldson v. Becket* and the Genealogy of Modern Authorship. *Representations* 23 (Summer 1988): 51–85.

Rose, Mike. *Lives on the Boundary.* NY: Penguin, 1989.

Rose, Shirley K. "Citation Rituals in Academic Cultures." *Issues in Writing* 6 (1993): 24–37.

———. "What's Love Got to Do with It? Scholarly Citation Practices as Courtship Rituals." *Journal of Language and Learning Across the Disciplines* 1.3 (August 1996): 34–48.

Rose, Shirley K, William Reed, and Nancy Faye Johnson. "Community Discourse and Discourse Communities: A Grammar, a Rhetoric, and a Symbolic of Scholarly Citations." Unpublished manuscript.

Rousseau, Jean Jacques. *The Social Contract and Discourses.* Trans. G. D. H. Cole. New York: Dutton, 1950.

Roy, David. "How to Read the Chin Ping Mei." *How to Read the Chinese Novel.* Princeton: Ed. David Rolston. Princeton University Press, 1990.

Royster, Jacqueline Jones. "When the First Voice You Hear Is Not Your Own." *College Composition and Communication* 47 (1996): 29–40.

Rucker, Randy, R. U. Sirius, and Queen Mu. *Mondo 2000: A User's Guide to the New Edge.* New York: HarperCollins, 1992.

Rushkoff, Douglas, Ed. *The GenX Reader.* New York: Ballantine, 1994.

Russell, David R. "Romantics on Writing: Liberal Culture and the Abolition of Composition Courses." *Rhetoric Review* 6 (1988): 132–48.

Ryan, Leigh. *The Bedford Guide for Writing Tutors.* Boston: Bedford Books of St. Martin's Press, 1994.

Said, Edward. *Culture and Imperialism.* New York: Vintage Books, 1994.

———. *The World, the Text and the Critic.* Cambridge: Harvard UP, 1983.

Samuelson, Pamela. "The Copyright Grab." *Wired* 4.01 (Jan. 1996): 134+.

———. "Writing as a Technology." Confernce on Cultural Agency/Cultural Authority: Politics and Poetics of Intellectual Property in the Post-Colonial Era." Bellagio, Italy, 8–12 March 1993.

Schiffhorst, Gerald J., and John F. Schell. *The Short Handbook for Writers.* New York: McGraw-Hill, 1991.

Schlag, Pierre. "Normative and Nowhere to Go." *Stanford Law Review* 43 (1990): 167–91.

Scholes, Robert. *Protocols of Reading.* New Haven: Yale University Press, 1989.

288 Works Cited

Schwartz-Bart, André. "Letter to Paul Flamand." *Research in African Literatures* 4.1: 129.
Schwegler, Robert A. "Dichotomies: Composition vs. Rhetoric." "In New Rhetoric Courses in Writing Programs: A Report from a Conference for New England Writing Program Administrators." Ed. Linda Shamoon. *WPA: The Journal of the National Council of Writing Program Administrators.* 19.3 (1995): 12–15.
Scollon, Ron. "Plagiarism and Ideology: Identity in Intercultural Discourse." *Language in Society* 24 (1995): 1–28.
Scott, Fred Newton, and Joseph Villiers Denney. Composition-Rhetoric. Boston: Allyn and Bacon, 1897.
Sellin, Eric. "The Unknown Voice of Yambo Ouologuem." *Yale French Studies* 53 (1976): 137–62.
Seltzer, Leon E. *Exemptions and Fair Use in Copyright.* Cambridge, MA: Harvard U P, 1978.
Senghor, Léopold. *Liberté 1, Négritude et Humanisme.* Paris: Seuil, 1964.
Shakespeare, William. *A Midsummer Night's Dream.* Ed. R. A. Foakes. Cambridge, England: Cambridge UP, 1984.
Shamoon, Linda K., and Deborah H. Burns. "A Critique of Pure Tutoring." *The Writing Center Journal* 15.2 (1995): 134–51.
Sharples, Mike. *Computer-supported Collaborative Writing.* London: Springer-Verlag, 1993.
Shaughnessy, Mina P. *Errors and Expectations: A Guide for the Teacher of Basic Writing.* New York: Oxford UP, 1977.
Sheldon v. Metro-Goldwyn Pictures Corp. 81 F.2d 49. 2d Cir. *Cert. denied,* 298 U.S. 669, 1936.
Shelley, Mary. Author's Introduction. *Frankenstein.* By Shelley. New York: Bantam, 1981. xxi–xxviii.
Shields, Carol. *Small Ceremonies.* New York: Penguin Books, 1996.
Shilts, Randy. *And the Band Played On: Politics, People, and the AIDS Epidemic.* NY: Penguin, 1987.
Sima Guang. *Zizhi tongjian.* Beijing: Zhonghua shuju, 1956.
Singer, Joseph W. "The Player and the Cards: Nihilism and Legal Theory." *Yale Law Journal* 94 (1984) 1–70.
Sirico, Louis, J., Jr. "A Primer on Plagiarism." *Northern Kentucky Law Journal* 16 (1988): 501.
Skom, Edith. "Plagiarism: Quite a Rather Bad Little Crime." *American Association of Higher Education Bulletin* (October 1986): 3–7.
Slonczewski, Joan. A *Door into Ocean.* New York: Avon Books, 1986.
Small, Henry G. "Cited Documents as Concept Symbols." *Social Studies of Science* 8 (1978): 327–40.
Smith, Frank H. "Co-Education: A Story." *The Inlander* 5 (1894–95): 197–203. Michigan Historical Collections. Bentley Historical Library. University of Michigan.
Smitherman, Geneva. "'God Don't Never Change': Black English from a Black Perspective." *College English* 34 (1973): 828–33.
"Something *New* Out of Africa?" *Times Literary Supplement* 5 May 1972: 525.
Sommers, Nancy. "Revision Strategies of Student Writers and Experienced Adult Writers." *College Composition and Communication* 31 (1980): 378–388.

Sorkin, David. "Practicing Plagiarism." *Illinois Bar Journal* 81 (1993): 487–88.

Spear, Karen. *Sharing Writing: Peer Response Groups in English Class.* Portsmouth: Boynton/Cook: 1988.

Spenser, Edmund. *The Yale Edition of the Shorter Poems of Edmund Spenser.* Ed. William A. Oram. New Haven: Yale University Press, 1989.

St. Onge, K. R. *The Melancholy Anatomy of Plagiarism.* Lanham: University Press of America, 1988.

Stallybrass, Peter, and Allon White. *The Politics and Poetics of Transgression.* Ithaca: Cornell UP, 1986.

Stanley, Jo. *Bold in Her Breeches: Women Pirates Across the Ages.* London: Pandora, 1995.

Stewart, Donald C. "Collaborative Learning and Composition: Boon or Bane?" *Rhetoric Review.* 7 (1988): 58–83.

Stewart, Susan. *Crimes of Writing: Problems in the Containment of Representation.* New York: Oxford UP, 1991.

Stock, Brian. *The Printing Press As an Agent of Change.* Princeton: Princeton UP, 1986.

Storm, Beaver and Phlegm-Phlan. *Kablooie.* Merion Station, PA: n.p., 1994.

Stowe, David. "Just Do It." *Lingua Franca.* (November/December 1995): 32–42.

Strong, William. *The Copyright Book: A Practical Guide.* 4th ed. Cambridge: MIT P, 1993.

Sullivan, Paula. Letter to the Editor. *Council Chronicle* 3.5 (1994): 14.

Sullivan, Patrick. "Do You Object to Tutors Assisting Your Students with Their Writing?" *The WritingLab Newsletter* December 1985: 6–8.

———. "The Politics of the Drop-In Writing Center." *The Writing Lab Newsletter* May 1984: 1–2.

Swales, John. "Citation Analysis and Discourse Analysis." *Applied Linguistics* 7 (1986): 39–56.

Swearingen, C. Jan. "Ethos: Imitation, Impersonation, and Voice." *Ethos: New Essays in Rhetorical and Critical Theory.* Ed. James S. Baumlin and Tita French Baumlin. Dallas: Southern Methodist U P, 1994. 115–148.

Swift, Jonathan. "On Poetry: A Rhapsody." *The Complete Poems.* Ed. Pat Rogers. New Haven: Yale UP, 1983. 522–36.

Temple University. *University Statement on Academic Policies and Regulations.*

Terez, Angela. "Tricks of the Trade(marks)." *Writer's Digest* November 1994: 24–28.

The Citadel. *101 Course Information Sheet.*

Thomas, D. M. *The White Hotel.* Hammondsworth: Penguin, 1981.

Thompson, Thomas C. "'Yes, Sir!' 'No, Sir!' 'No Excuse, Sir!' Working with an Honor Code in a Military Setting." *Writing Lab Newsletter* 19.5 (1995): 13–14.

Thornton, Weldon. *Allusions in "Ulysses."* Chapel Hill: University of North Carolina Press, 1968.

Tibbetts, A. M., and Charlene Tibbetts. *Strategies of Rhetoric with Handbook.* 5th ed. Glenview: Scott, 1987.

Toffler, Alvin. *The Third Wave.* NY: Morrow, 1980.

Trimbur, John. "Composition Studies: Postmodern or Popular." *Into the Field: Sites of Composition Studies.* Ed. Anne Ruggles Gere. New York: MLA, 1993. 117–32.

———. "Peer Tutoring: A Contradiction in Terms." *The Writing Center Journal* 7.2 (1987): 21–28.

Trimmer, Joseph F., and James M. McCrimmon. *Writing with a Purpose*. 9th ed. Boston: Houghton, 1988.

Tuo Tuo. *Songshi* (Song History). Beijing: Zhonghua shuju, 1977.

Ujitani, Eiko. School of Foreign Languages, Department of British and American Studies, Nagoya University of Foreign Studies. Nisshin, Japan. Personal interview (Dryden), 15 Feb. 1996

United States v. Steele. 785 F.2d 743. 9th Cir. 1986.

University of Alabama-Birmingham. *Plagiarism Policy*. Birmingham: University of Alabama-Birmingham, n.d.

University of Illinois. *Statement on Plagiarism*. Champagne-Urbana: University of Alabama, n.d.

University of North Carolina-Chapel Hill. *The Source: The Resource Handbook for the University of North Carolina-Chapel Hill*. Chapel Hill: University of North Carolina, n.d.

———. *Staff Manual*. Chapel Hill: University of North Carolina, n.d.

———. *Guide to Freshman Composition*. Chapel Hill: University of North Carolina, n.d.

Vandendorpe, Christian "Le plagiat entre l'esthétique et le droit." In *Le plagiat* (sous la direction de Christian Vandendorpe). Ottawa: Les Presses de l'Université d'Ottawa, 1992. 7–15.

Twain, Mark [Samuel Langhorne Clemens]. *Adventures of Huckleberry Finn*. 1884. Harmondsworth: Penguin, 1966.

Veysey, Laurence R. *The Emergence of the American University*. Chicago: University of Chicago Press, 1965.

Vygotsky, Lev. *Mind in Society: The Development of Higher Psychological Processes*. Cambridge: Harvard UP, 1978.

Wagner, Richard. *The Authentic Librettos of the Wagner Operas*. NY: Crown, 1938.

Walker, Melissa. *Writing Research Papers: A Norton Guide*. 2nd ed. New York: Norton, 1987.

Wall, Wendy. *The Imprint of Gender: Authorship and Publication in the English Renaissance*.

Waring v. Dunlea. 26 F. Supp. 338. D.N.C. 1939.

Watkins, Mel. "Talk with Ouologuem." *New York Times Book Review* 7 Mar. 1971: 7, 34.

Watt, William. *An American Rhetoric*. 5th ed. New York: Holt, 1980.

Webb, R. K. Rev. of *Stolen Words: Forays into the Origins and Ravages of Plagiarism*, by Thomas Mallon. *Academe–Bulletin of the AAUP* 76.3 (1990): 70–71.

Webster's Third New International Dictionary of the English Language Unabridged. Springfield: G.&C. Merriam Co., 1961.

Webster's Third New International Dictionary of the English Language Unabridged. New York: Simon and Schuster, 1997.

Weiner, Bernard. *Achievement Motivation and Attribution Theory*.Morristown: General Learning Press, 1974.

Wells, Dorothy. "An Account of the Complex Causes of Unintentional Plagiarism in College Writing." *WPA: Writing Program Administration* 16 (1993): 59–71.

Wenyuange siku quanshu. Taibei: Taiwan shangwu yinshuguan, 1984.

West, Susan. "From Owning to Owning Up: Authorial Rights and Rhetorical Responsibilities." Unpub. Diss. Ohio State University, 1997. Contact West at <stwest@erinet.com>.

Wheelwright, John T. and Frederic J. Stimson. *Rollo's Journey to Cambridge Boston.* 1880. Reprinted in *The Harvard Book.* Cambridge: Harvard UP, 1959. 72.

Whelan Assocs., Inc. v. Jaslow Dental Lab., Inc. 797 F.2d 1222. 3d Cir. 1986.

Whitaker, Elaine E. "A Pedagogy to Address Plagiarism." *College Composition and Communication* 44 (1993): 509–513.

White, Howard D., and Katherine W. McCain. "Bibliometrics." *Annual Review of Information Science and Technology* 24 (1989): 119–86.

White, Merry. *The Japanese Educational Challenge: A Commitment to Children.* New York: The Free Press, 1987.

Wiksell, Wesley. "The Communications Program at Stephens College." *College English* 9 (1947): 143–45.

Wilcox, Delos F. "Dishonesty in College Work". *The Inlander* (University of Michigan) 3 (1892–93): 189–90.

Williams, Patricia. *The Alchemy of Race and Rights: Diary of a Law Professor.* Cambridge: Harvard UP, 1991.

Wimsatt, William. *The Verbal Icon: Studies in the Meaning of Poetry.* Lexington: University of Kentucky Press, 1954.

Winterowd. W. Ross. "A Grammar of Coherence. *College English* 31 (1970): 828–35.

Witte, Stephen P. "Topical Structure and Writing Quality: Some Possible Text-Based Explanations of Readers' Judgments of Student Writing." *Visible Language* 17 (1983): 177–205.

Wittenberg, Philip. *The Protection of Literary Property.* Boston: Writer, 1978.

Wolitz, Seth. "L'Art du plagiat, ou une brève défense de Ouologuem." *Research in African Literatures* 4.1 (1973): 130–34.

Womack, Craig. Personal Communication. April 1996.

Woodmansee, Martha. "The Genius and the Copyright: Economic and Legal Conditions of the Emergence of the Author." *Eighteenth Century Studies* 17 (1984) 425–63.

———. On the Author Effect: Recovering Collectivity. *The Construction of Authorship: Textual Appropriation in Law and Literature.* Ed. Martha Woodmansee and Peter Jaszi. Durham: Duke UP, 1994. 15–28.

———. *The Author, Art, and the Market: Rereading the History of Aesthetics.* New York: Columbia UP, 1994.

Woodmansee, Martha, and Peter Jaszi. "The Law of Texts: Copyright in the Academy." *College English* 57 (1995): 769–87.

———. "Introduction." *The Construction of Authorship: Textual Appropriation in Law and Literature,* Eds. Martha Woodmansee and Peter Jaszi. Durham and London: Duke UP, 1994.

———. *The Construction of Authorship: Textual Appropriation in Law and Literature.* Durham, NC: Duke University Press, 1994.

Wooley, Edwin C., and Franklin W. Scott. *College Handbook of Composition.* Boston: Heath, 1928.

Wordsworth, William. "Essay, Supplementary to the Preface." *The Prose Works of William Wordsworth.* Ed. W. J. B. Owen and Jane Worthington Smyser. Vol. 3. Oxford: Clarendon Press, 1974.

Writer's Digest. Cincinnati: F & W Publications.

Young, Edward. *Conjectures on Original Composition.* 1759. Leeds: Scolar P, 1966.

————. *Conjectures on Original Composition.* 1759. New York: Garland, 1970.

Zebroski, James. *Thinking Through Theory: Vygotskian Perspectives on the Teaching of Writing.* Portsmouth NH: Boynton Cook Heinemann, 1994, 72–118.

————. *Blue Collar Scholar: The Working Class Struggle for Composition and Rhetoric,* forthcoming.

Zhu Xi. *Yupi Zizhi tongjian gangmu.* Siku quanshu zhenben, series 6, Volumes 140–148.

Biographical Notes on Contributors

Lise Buranen is a Lecturer in the English Department at California State University, L. A., where she has taught composition, literature, and writing pedagogy for the past ten years and served as Chair of the Composition Committee for the past three years. She previously taught composition and ESL at two local community colleges. She has presented papers on plagiarism and part-time faculty issues at annual meetings of the Conference on College Composition and Communication.

Deborah H. Burns is Assistant Professor of English and Director of the Writing Center at Merrimack College. She has published articles on writing center theory and practice and has developed a Writing Fellows Program in which advanced undergraduates employ a social-rhetorical approach to discipline-specific tutoring. With six colleagues, she is developing *The Electronic Democracy Project,* a national e-mail writing project.

Shawn M. Clankie is a linguist, language teacher, and freelance writer. He holds a B.A. in French and M.A. in English as a Foreign Language from Southern Illinois University, and an M.Phil. in Linguistics from the University of Cambridge. He is currently a Ph.D. student in Linguistics at the University of Hawaii at Manoa.

Irene L. Clark directed the Writing Center at the University of Southern California for many years and is now codirector of USC's Expository Writing Program. Her publications include articles in *The Journal of Basic Writing, Teaching English in the Two Year College, College Composition and Communication, WPA: Writing Program Administration,* and *The Writing Center Journal.* She is the author of *Writing in the Center: Teaching in a Writing Center Setting* and several textbooks concerned with argumentation.

Kevin J. H. Dettmar is Associate Professor of English at Clemson University. He has written widely on topics in modernist and postmodern fiction; his books include *The Illicit Joyce of Postmodernism: Writing Against the Grain,* and, as editor and coeditor, *Rereading the New: A Backward Glance at Modernism* and *Marketing Modernisms: Canonization, Self-Promotion, and Rereading.*

L. M. Dryden taught English literature and composition for twenty years at the high-school and university levels in southern California. Since 1994, he has taught English as a foreign language at Nagoya University of Foreign Studies in Nisshin, Japan. He has done several presentations at Computer Using Educators (CUE) conferences in California and at an international conference of the Japan Association of Language Teaching (JALT), and he has published articles and software on using computers in the classroom.

Debora Halbert is Assistant Professor of Political Science at Otterbein College in Ohio. She has published several articles on intellectual property issues in *International Journal for the Semiotics of Law, The Information Society,* and *Technological Forecasting and Social Change.*

Carol Peterson Haviland is Associate Professor of English at California State University, San Bernardino, where she teaches undergraduate and graduate composition courses, directs the writing center, and codirects a faculty writing-across-the-curriculum seminar. She has presented papers at the Conference on College Composition and Communication and at writing center and WAC conferences for fifteen years. She is currently editing the forthcoming *Writing Centers and Collaboration: Interrogating Our Own Enactments* and has coauthored a number of other essays on writing centers and collaboration.

Rebecca Moore Howard is Associate Professor of English and Director of Compostion at Texas Christian University. Her articles have appeared in the *Journal of Teaching Writing, WPA: Writing Program Administration, JAC: A Journal of Compostion Theory, Computers and Compostion,* and *College English.* She is coauthor of *The Bedford Guide to Teaching Writing in the Disciplines* and the forthcoming *Roadmaps for College Writers,* and author of the forthcoming *Standing in the Shadow of Giants.*

Robert André LaFleur is Assistant Professor of History and East Asian Studies at Colby College in Waterville, Maine. His research interests lie in Chinese cultural and intellectual history. In addition to several articles on these subjects, he is currently finishing a book on Chinese historiography, entitled *A Rhetoric of Remonstrance: History and Commentary in Sima Guang's Zizhi tongjian.*

Gilbert Larochelle is professor of political philosophy at the University of Quebec in Canada. He has published *L'imaginaire technocratique* and

Philosophie de l'ideologie, Théorie de l'intersubjectivité, and *La commu-
nauté comme figure de l'État* and is coauthor with André Mineau of the forthcoming *The Ideological Use of Ethics.*

Terri LeClercq has taught writing and composition for many years, including fourteen years at the School of Law, University of Texas. She is the author of *Expert Legal Writing, Guide to Legal Writing Style, Ready Writing
Handbook* and numerous articles about writing theory and process. As chair-
man of a committee for the Institute of Legal Writing, she frequently responds
to questions concerning plagiarism.

David Leight is an instructor at Reading Area Community College in Reading, Pennsylvania. He is a Ph.D. candidate in Rhetoric and Communication
at Temple University in Philadelphia, where he is writing his dissertation on
how citations establish the authority of academic writers of composition theory articles.

Joan Livingston-Webber is Assistant Professor in the English Department
at Western Illinois University, where she teaches composition, rhetoric, and
linguistics and directs the writing center.

Joan Mullin established and directs the Writing Across the Curriculum Program and the Writing Center at the University of Toledo. She serves on various editorial boards and has published in *Composition Studies, American
Journal of Pharmaceutical Education, The Sociology Teacher,* and *The Writing Lab Newsletter.* Her edited collection, *Intersections: Theory-Practice in
the Writing Center* (with Ray Wallace), won the 1994 National Writing Center Association Award for Outstanding Scholarship. She is coauthor of the
forthcoming *ARTiculations.*

Marilyn Randall is Associate Professor and current Chair of Graduate Studies in the French Department at the University of Western Ontario in London,
Ontario, Canada, where she teaches primarily Québécois literature and culture. Her publications include *Le contexte littéraire: lecture pragmatique de
Hubert Aquin et Réjean Ducharme,* and, as coeditor, a critical edition of *Trou
de mémoire* by Hubert Aquin. She is currently working on a book-length
monograph on plagiarism.

Shirley K. Rose is Associate Professor of English and Director of Composition at Purdue University in West Lafayette, Indiana. She has published work
on pedadgogical and professional issues in *College English, College Composition and Communication, The Writing Instructor, Rhetoric Review,* and other
journals in compostion studies. Currently she is working on an analysis of the
citation histories of seven influential works in composition studies.

Alice M. Roy is Professor of English and Linguistics at California State University, Los Angeles, former Composition Coordinator, and currently director of the MA Option in Composition, Rhetoric, and Language. Her articles on language and literacy have appeared in *Text, Semiotica, College English, College Composition and Communication, WPA: Writing Program Administration, The Writing Instructor, Journal of Teaching Writing,* and others.

Linda K. Shamoon is Professor of English, Director of the College Writing Program, and Director of the Faculty Institute on Writing at the University of Rhode Island. She has published articles on writing across the curriculum, writing center theory, writing with computers, and the place of rhetoric in composition programs. In addition to developing a corps of undergraduate writing consultants at URI whose tutoring is guided by a social-rhetorical approach, she is collaborating with seven colleagues on a national e-mail writing project for undergraduates, *The Electronic Democracy Project.*

Sue Carter Simmons is Associate Professor of English at Bowling Green State University where she teaches historical rhetoric, writing, and writing pedagogy. She has published articles on the history of writing instruction at Harvard and Radcliffe as well as a first-year writing textbook, *Perspectives on Academic Writing.*

Candace Spigelman is Assistant Professor of English at Penn State University, Berks-Lehigh Valley College, where she teaches rhetoric and composition. She has presented papers and published articles on writing groups, intellectual property in the composition class, and literary non-fiction.

Laurie Stearns is a copyright lawyer with Oracle Corporation in California's Silicon Valley. Formerly a book editor at Random House and the Naval Institute Press, she received her J.D. from Boalt Hall School of Law at the University of California at Berkeley, and later was a judicial clerk to the Hon. Stanley Mosk of the Supreme Court of California.

C. Jan Swearingen recently served as Visiting Radford Chair of Rhetoric and Composition at Texas Christian University. Her book, *Rhetoric and Irony, Western Literacy and Western Lies,* shared the Journal of Advanced Composition's W. Ross Winterowd Award for the best book in Composition Theory published in 1991. Her teaching and research fields include feminist criticism and theory within rhetoric and composition, cross-cultural approaches to rhetoric and literacy, the rhetoric of religion, and the history of rhetoric. She is currently working on a book on multiculturalism in the ancient world. She serves on the Executive Council of the Conference on College Composition and Communication and the CCCC Committee on Language Policy. She has been reelected to the MLA Delegate Assembly as Representative of the Division on the History and Theory of Rhetoric and Composition, and was elected to serve on the Organizing Committee of MLA's Delegate Assembly. Professor Swearingen is President Elect and 1998 Program Chair for the Rhetoric Society of America.

Edward M. White is Professor of English at California State University, San Bernardino. His most recent books are *Developing Successful College Writing Programs; Inquiry: A Cross-Curricular Reader; Teaching and Assessing Writing*, 2nd ed.; and *Assigning, Responding, and Evaluating*, 3rd ed. He is also coeditor of *Composition in the Twenty-first Century* and *Writing Assessment: Politics, Policies, and Practices*.

Henry L. Wilson received his Ph.D. from the University of Tennessee, Knoxville. His dissertation investigated the relationship between plagiarism and collaborative writing. He is Associate Professor in the English Department at Bradley University in Peoria, Illinois, where he currently teaches a variety of writing and literature courses and serves as Coordinator of Composition.

James Thomas Zebroski is associate professor of writing at Syracuse University. He teaches undergraduate courses in writing and graduate courses in the theory and history of composition. He has written *Thinking Through Theory: Vygotskian Perspectives on the Teaching of Writing*. He has published extensively on the psychosocial theory of Lev Vygotsky and its implications for writing, and his work has appeared in *Cultural Studies and English Studies, Social Issues in the Teaching of English, Composition and Resistance, The Right to Literacy, Encountering Student Texts*, and various anthologies and periodicals.

Index